JOURNAL FOR THE STUDY OF THE OLD TESTAMENT
SUPPLEMENT SERIES
37

Editors
David J A Clines
Philip R Davies

Department of Biblical Studies
The University of Sheffield
Sheffield S10 2TN
England

Bernhard Word Anderson

UNDERSTANDING THE WORD

Essays in Honor of
Bernhard W. Anderson

Edited by
James T. Butler, Edgar W. Conrad
and
Ben C. Ollenburger

Journal for the Study of the Old Testament
Supplement Series 37

Published by
JSOT Press
Department of Biblical Studies
The University of Sheffield
Sheffield S10 2TN
England

Printed in Great Britain
by Redwood Burn Ltd.,
Trowbridge, Wiltshire.

British Library Cataloguing in Publication Data

Understanding the word : essays in honour of
    Bernhard W. Anderson.—(Journal for the
    study of the Old Testament supplement series,
    ISSN 0309-0789; 37)
    1. Bible—Commentaries
    I. Anderson, Bernhard W.   II. Butler, James T.
    III. Conrad, Edgar W.   IV. Ollenburger, Ben
    V. Series
    220.6   BS491.2

ISBN 0-905774-88-4

CONTENTS

PART III

The Word and the World

PART IV

Appropriating the Word

FOREWORD

The scholarly career of Professor Bernhard Word Anderson has spanned nearly fifty years since he first sat in the classroom of his revered teacher, Dr James Muilenburg, at Pacific School of Religion. Those fifty years have seen remarkable and sometimes bewildering developments in the field of biblical studies. Not only has Professor Anderson been at the forefront of several of those developments, especially in the 'rhetorical criticism' pioneered by his teacher, but he has also been perhaps the most articulate interpreter of those developments to a wider audience.

The audiences most immediately benefiting from Professor Anderson's interpretive abilities have been his students at Colgate University, the University of North Carolina, Colgate Rochester Divinity School, the Theological School of Drew University and Princeton Theological Seminary. His teaching has been marked by clarity, eloquence, and a passion for the truth. Those of us who have been his teaching assistants at Princeton have marveled at his ability to captivate a class of nearly two hundred students with his lucid expositions of Old Testament texts, and to bring his lectures to a crescendo just as the bell in Alexander Hall tolled the end of the hour. His lucidity as an interpreter of the Old Testament and his ability to mediate scholarship to wider audiences have marked his writing as well as his teaching.

With its initial publication in 1957, *Understanding the Old Testament*[1] became almost immediately the standard textbook in the field. In its third edition this work remains a standard text in universities and seminaries on several continents. Professor Anderson has also made a distinctive contribution to the field of Old Testament studies through his translation of Martin Noth's groundbreaking work, *A History of Pentateuchal Traditions*.[2] Anderson's translation of Noth's tortuous German attains such clarity that some students in Germany are reported to prefer it to the original. Professor Anderson's introductory essay to that volume is a landmark in the critical evaluation of Noth's work and the methodological foundation on which it is based. One might also point to Professor Anderson's essay, 'Politics and the Transcendent: Voegelin's Philosophical and Theological Exposition of the Old Testament in the Context of the Ancient Near East'.[3] This essay, a revision of one originally published in *The Political Science Reviewer* in 1971, evaluates the interpretation of Israel's religious history by the political philosopher and historian, Eric Voegelin, for a political science audience unfamiliar with Old Testament studies. It serves also as a masterful adumbration of Old Testament theology which all of us in the field would do well to read.

These and other of his publications exemplify Professor Anderson's ability to address a variety of audiences, and his willingness to undertake the effort of moving from technical, analytic treatments of the texts to a synthetic presentation. A part of his willingness to undertake such effort derives from Professor Anderson's commitment to the church and his conviction that critical biblical scholarship has an important contribution to make to the church's life. He came by his churchly interests honestly. In his early years Professor Anderson traveled with his father, a Methodist evangelist, and accompanied his meetings with inspired renditions of gospel songs on the piano. He himself has pastored churches and, as a theological educator, participated actively in the training of ministers. But his vision of the church has never been a narrow one. While Dean of the Theological School at Drew he marched with Rev. Martin Luther King, Jr, in Alabama. As Professor of Old Testament Theology at Princeton, he, a Methodist teaching at a Presbyterian seminary, worshipped with an Episcopal congregation and spoke at the ordination of Roman Catholic priests. Perhaps his closest personal friend was Will Herberg, the Jewish philosopher, whose essays Professor Anderson collected and introduced with an appreciative essay.[4] None of his students can have failed to recognize the profound influence that Jewish thinkers such as Herberg, Emil Fackenheim, Abraham Heschel and Franz Rosenzweig have exercised on his own understanding of the Old Testament.

Given his commitment to the church's faith and to critical scholarship, which he views as in no essential tension, it was perhaps predestined (a distinctively non-Methodist notion!) that Professor Anderson's greatest contributions would lie in the field of Old

Testament theology. His ability fruitfully and responsibly to transgress the narrow boundaries of technical textual scholarship has brought him into conversation with New Testament scholars, systematic theologians and church historians and has enabled him to appreciate and critically evaluate the intellectual contexts in which Old Testament theology and biblical theology have been conducted. It is this breadth of vision and the ability to handle the vocabularies of more than one discipline that are prerequisite to an appropriately theological understanding of the Old Testament. Professor Anderson's commitment to faith and scholarship, and his ability to mediate diverse concerns, are well attested in his presidential address to the Society of Biblical Literature, 'Tradition and Scripture in the Community of Faith'.[5]

It is the hope of the editors of this volume that these essays, whose authors represent a wide range of interests in theological scholarship, will bear similar testimony to Professor Anderson, and will testify as well to our appreciation of him and his work. While Professor Anderson has retired from teaching at Princeton Theological Seminary, and this volume celebrates the occasion of this retirement, it may properly be said that this *Festschrift* comes to him in mid-career. The writing projects underway and those planned for the future more befit a scholar just embarking on a career than one bringing his work to a conclusion. We eagerly await the fruit of these further labors and pause in the midst of them to honor a scholar who has contributed supremely to our understanding of the Old Testament, and indeed to what Christians confess to be the Word of God.

***

The editors wish to thank the former president of Princeton Theological Seminary, Dr James I. McCord, for his enthusiastic support of this project when it was in its initial stages. Furthermore, no volume honoring Professor Anderson would be complete without mention of Joyce, his wife. She has read everything he has written, and we may suspect that its clarity owes much to her wise counsel. She deserves our thanks as well for her advice in planning this volume.

NOTES

1. *Understanding the Old Testament* (Englewood Cliffs: Prentice-Hall, 1957). The third edition was published in 1975. This book is published in Britain under the title, *The Living World of the Old Testament* (London: Longmans, 1958). The third edition was published in 1978.

2. *A History of Pentateuchal Traditions* (Englewood Cliffs: Prentice-Hall, 1972). This work has recently been reprinted by Scholars Press. Noth's work was originally published as *Überlieferungsgeschichte des Pentateuch* (Stuttgart: Kohlhammer, 1948).

3. *Eric Voegelin's Search for Order in History* (ed. Stephen A. McKnight; Baton Rouge: Louisiana State University, 1978) 62-100.

4. *Faith Enacted as History, Essays in Biblical Theology* (ed. Bernhard W. Anderson; Philadelphia: Westminster, 1976) 9-28.

5. *JBL* 100 (1981) 5-21.

PART I

INTERPRETING THE WORD

1

IMAGINATION AS A MODE OF FIDELITY

Walter Brueggemann

Bernhard Anderson has recently published an important book on biblical interpretation, *The Living Word of the Bible*.[1] It is an important book, as is usual for him, carefully and precisely articulated. But predictably, because it is a popular book, it is largely a neglected book.

The following paper seeks to explore one theme from that book. The first chapter of Anderson's hermeneutical statement is entitled 'Word of Imagination'.[2] In that chapter Anderson identifies three fronts on which the question of biblical authority and interpretation is important:

1. In relation to literalists some of whom practice 'papal ecclesiasticism';
2. In relation to rigorously critical scholars who stress *the human character* of the text, with an acute historical sense;
3. In relaton to word-centered theologians who bracket out critical questions in relation to *theological authority*, a position not to be confused with literalism.

In relation to these various approaches, Anderson makes trenchant comments in two directions. First, he makes the point that good and faithful biblical interpretation must exercise *poetic sensitivity and artistic imagination* that lets us hear the live word of God in the text.[3] Second, he urges that we must find *scholarly methods and approaches* that serve and enhance such poetic and artistic imagination. Like many of us, Anderson is acutely aware that standard historical-critical methods are both important and problematic. They are important because they have liberated the scriptures from dogmatic tyrannies, by permitting the text to be seen 'in its own context' and not in the patterns of dogmatic perspective, so that all important claims are already preempted before meeting the text. But the limitations of historical-critical methods are increasingly apparent,[4] because such perspectives have not very well served the preaching task of the church. One has only to examine the arid and fragmenting offerings of the commentaries to draw such a conclusion, even when responsible methods are rigorously honored, or perhaps especially when such methods are used.

I

Anderson's urging then is this: 'The time has come for the kind of literary criticism that calls on our poetic and artistic imagination, without sacrificing the insights that historical criticism has provided'.[5] That is, Anderson's proposal is that new openness for live interpretation is to be found in new method. There is a great deal to be said for that. No doubt new (for scripture study) forms of literary criticism have provided new vitality and freedom in interpretation. But too much should not be claimed for this method either, because one can also find efforts at literary criticism that are practices of obfuscation that do not serve the live word well.

While attention should be given to the general methodological shift in the direction urged by Anderson,[6] he adds an important conclusion to his chapter on imagination. In it he makes a *theological* rather than a *methodological* statement. He links together *the practice of imagination* and *the work of the Holy Spirit*.[7] I take that to be a most important statement. Admittedly the liberating guidance of the Holy Spirit may use literary criticism, but obviously that work is not to be equated with or confined to this or any other method.

Thus Anderson's urging (with which I agree) is in two parts. It is *an urging about method*, that a new form of literary criticism gives us the best chance to discern the vitality, richness and power in the text. It is *a theological urging* that the interpreter must practice imagination that uses all methods available, but goes beyond all of them to encounter the theological claim of the text. The theological and methodological urgings are closely related to each other. But they are not to be equated. Nor is poetic freedom given by the spirit to be governed by any method. The relation of these two matters obviously will be settled in different ways by different interpreters, both in academic and ecclesiastical contexts.

Now the particular part of Anderson's provocative statement to be considered here is, *What role does imagination have in the articulation of Israel's faith?* While we would finally be concerned with our contemporary practice of imagination in the service of interpretation (as is Anderson), we may come at that contemporary question by asking how, in the process of scripture itself, imagination is understood, practiced and critiqued.[8] Perhaps there are clues in that ancient enterprise for our own practice of imagination.

At the outset we should seek to characterize—but not define—imagination. In this we may follow the characterization of two scholars. First, Ray Hart understands imagination as an activity:

> Wherever symbolic reference is cognitively rich, the imagination is actively at work; for imagination 'cracks' the focalized boundaries of the delineated object, gaining access to a field of actuality that was, from the perspective of the closed object in rational or sensuous apprehension, merely dormant, but now is through the active reflexivity of imagination, a vivacious stimulant to and limitant upon the will.[9] The activity of the imagination: the 'loosening' of the mnemonic 'given' so as to integrate its potency with expanding selfhood.[10] It 'loosens' or 'dissolves' the mnemonic given so that the potency of the past may fund, and be appropriated to the present.[11]

Hart uses language that is more dense than we need for our purpose. But his repeated statement will serve us well: it is a way 'to loosen the givens'.

Second, Tannehill characterizes the work of imagination in this way: 'Imaginative shock' is to challenge old structures of thought and suggest new visions.[12] Admittedly there are complicated socio-psychological aspects to such a phenomenon as well as suble literary factors. But it will suffice for us to speak of the generation of new images/metaphors which challenge, delegitimate, deconstruct old stable realities, and which anticipate and evoke the shape of new realities. While this no doubt requires artistic sensitivity, Anderson is surely correct that such an act is 'inspired', a gift of the Holy One as much as an achievement of skill. Or, said another way, such articulations are 'revelatory'.

II

So we consider the function of imagination within scripture as a way to find a clue for our own imaginative ways of interpreting the text. We begin with a consideration of two words that in various ways are rendered 'imagination'. The obvious beginning place is with *yṣr*, which five times is used as a noun for 'imagination'. But we begin with the verbal form which seems to have a curious connection to the noun.

1. There is no doubt that the term is related to the 'forming' which is done by a potter with clay. Thus it seems to refer to actual manual work (cf. e.g. Gen 2.8; Isa 41.25; 43.21; 44.10, 21; Jer 18.2-6; 19.1, 11; Pss 2.9; 95.5; 104.26).[13] Stuhlmueller concludes:[14] 'The word *yạsar* . . . stresses the idea of *careful workmanship*, like a potter at work, and possibly the notion of tender cultivation, like the concern of a farmer'.

2. But along with the material notion of 'careful workmanship', a different sense can be placed on it in some texts. In Isaiah 43.1, 7; 45.7, 18; and Amos 4.13 two factors are common. First it is Yahweh who does *yṣr*. Second in each case, the verb is parallel to *br'*. Now it is commonplace to say that only Yahweh can *br'*, for the term *br'* suggests some kind of active agent rather than physical material activity, much more sophisticated and not at all involved in actual fabrication. It seems to be an act of sheer holiness which evokes new reality. This word parallel suggests the *yṣr* cannot only be treated simply according to the metaphor of potter. On some occasions, it would seem to have a much more playful reference in parallel to *br'* which might better be taken as to 'foresee', 'to form in the mind or heart', i.e. to imagine. When the verb is parallel to *br'* it is fair to assume that it participates in something of the same understanding.[15]

3. This reading of the term would seem sustained by three other uses:

> Have you not heard that I determined (*'śh*) it long ago,
>> I *planned* (*yṣr*) it long ago,
>> what I now bring to pass (Isa 37.26; 2 Kgs 19.25).
> Behold I am shaping (*yṣr*) evil against you,
>> and devising (*ḥšb*) a plan (*ḥšb*) against you (Jer 18.11).
> I have spoken, I will bring it to pass,
>> I have purposed (*yṣr*), I will do it (*'śh*) (Isa 46.11).

In these three uses, it is clear that Yahweh, long before historical implementation, 'imagined, envisioned, conceived, determined, planned' what was to come. It is a constructive, creative act of freedom that 'forms' something over against what presently exists. That is, it is a way of speaking about a newness that will assault and shatter the givens of the visible world that have been presumed. The metaphor perhaps never breaks completely free of the linkage of clay and potter, but it is equally clear that now the 'forming' is not done at the potter's wheel, but in the heart or mind of the former. We have no better word for that than 'imagination'.

In the use of this word and related uses (especially *ḥšb*), we have the beginnings of a quite sophisticated psychology which Israel must articulate in its characteristically concrete modes. Anyone could see that potters 'form'. But it is equally clear that there is a forming that takes place prior to the work of hands with clay. That 'forming' may be said to take place in the 'mind' or 'heart'. What Israel discerns is that there is a forming which precedes at some distance the actual concrete fact. There is an anticipation or envisioning not immediate in the concrete physical act. And this previous act lives in some tension with what is visibly present. Thus the term 'forming' leads to 'forming' in the mind, hence imagination.

One other text is somewhat more enigmatic but makes the same point. In addressing those who have destroyed and plundered the city of Jerusalem, it is written:

> You did not look to him who did (*'śh*) it,
> > or have regard for him who planned (*yṣr*) it long ago (Isa 22.11).

That is, whoever destroys Jerusalem, mistakenly does not reckon with the fact that long ago, outside the current field of event, Yahweh has had other intentions for Jerusalem that cannot be violated or nullified. Clearly the word *yṣr* here cannot be taken concretely, but refers to the intentionality of Yahweh, or the resolve of Yahweh's heart.

This construal of the term is evident where the term occurs in parallel to *ḥšb* (Jer 18.11). And it is clear in the adverbial qualifiers (*mrḥq, qdm*) from long ago (cf. Isa 22.11; Isa 37.26; 2 Kgs 9.25) for these uses clearly place a distance between the time of imagining and the time of implementation. No such distance would be possible if the term referred only to manipulation of clay.

The metaphor still can be kept close to the work of the potter. On the one hand the potter must manipulate the clay as a physical act, as in Jeremiah 18 and 19. But obviously a good potter must be able to do more than manipulate clay. The potter must also be able to envision, to plan ahead, to foresee the shapes, to call into being in 'mind's eye'

what does not yet exist. That is, good potting requires *imagination* as
well as *physical skill*.

4. Now on that basis, we are prepared to consider the nominal
uses of our term. The most obvious uses are those in the beginning
and end of the flood story (Gen 6.5; 8.21). In these the 'imagination'
is understood to be evil, without qualification, and the flood does not
change that. It is worth noting that in 6.5, the term is used with *ḥšb*,
so that it is 'imagination of the thoughts of his heart', clearly a
reference to the creative activity of the human heart to plan or
envision or conceive that which is not yet visible in the historical
process. With these two texts, imagination is condemned. And
undoubtedly that reading of human capacity has exercised an
important influence on a negation of the aesthetic.

But we also note three other uses which are not so unambiguously
negative. In David's instruction to Solomon (according to the
Chronicler) it is said:

> Know the God of your father, and serve him with a whole heart
> and with a willing mind; for the LORD searches all hearts and
> understands every plan and thought (*yṣr mḥšbt*) (1 Chr 28.9).

Our term *yṣr* again occurs with *ḥšb*, suggesting that it refers to the
creative, constructive capacity of the human agent. And the reference
to whole heart and willing mind is an affirmation that the plans and
thoughts of the human person can be faithful and acceptable. Such
creative intentionality can be obedient.

And in David's great prayer after the generous offering for the
temple which David (and the Chronicler) regard as faithful and
generous, it is requested:

> Keep forever such purposes and thoughts (*yṣr mḥšbt*) in the hearts
> of thy people, and direct their hearts toward thee (1 Chr 29.18).

Again *yṣr* is linked to *ḥšb* and again it is treated as an arena for
faithfulness.

Finally, in Deuteronomy 31.21, Moses issues a warning about
covenant faithfulness as Israel is to enter the land. He says:

> For I know the purposes (*yṣr*) which they are already forming (*'śh*),
> before I have brought them into the land that I swore to give.

Here it is recognized that 'purposes' for the land may be wayward
and disobedient. Yet clearly the voice of Moses does not presume it is
necessarily so.

These five uses of the nomimal form indicate that in some cases, though not all, imagination is condemned. In three cases, it is risky and could be evil, but with a resolve to covenant obedience such thoughts can be faithful and obedient. Also, it is clear that in the three uses with *ḥšb* in Genesis 6.5, 1 Chronicles 28.8, and 29.18, the *yṣr* is a forming action which envisions and fashions or creates in the mind/heart something that is distinct from what is available in the 'real world' of visible experience. That is, it is an act that initiates an alternative, whether for good or ill.

III

The second word for imagination is *šrr*, which has a much more negative connotation. Indeed, except for a usage in Deuteronomy which concerns us, it might not be involved in our question. With but two exceptions its use is confined to the tradition of Jeremiah (3.17; 7.24; 9.12-13; 11.8; 13.10; 16.11-12; 18.12; 23.16-17). In each case Israel either *chooses* to live by the 'stubbornness of its own heart' (which either explicitly or implicitly is regarded as evil) or is *sentenced* to live by its own heart, that is, entirely by its own resources, having been abandoned by Yahweh.

In many of the uses, the negative alternative of one's own stubborn heart is contrasted with the positive alternative which could have been chosen, but has been rejected:

They abandoned torah (9.12; 16.11).
They abandoned Yahweh (16.11).
They did not listen (7.24; 9.12; 11.8; 13.10; 16.12; 23.16).
They despised the word of Yahweh (23.17).

These alternatives obviously are all in a very narrow range of covenant theology. And in each case, the negative imagination that is condemned is an assertion of *autonomy* which denies the covenant and the role of obedience (listening) and responsiveness to the claims of Yahweh.[16] Thus the 'imagination' that is condemned is a *disobedient imagination*. One particular usage is of interest in light of our analysis of *yṣr*. In 18.12, 'the stubbornness of heart' is in parallel to 'our plans' (*ḥšb*), which we have seen means 'foresight'. In v. 12, we have the parallel *ḥšb/šrr* in relation to *Israel's autonomy*, while in v. 11, there is the parallel *yṣr/ḥšb* in relation to *Yahweh's intent*. Thus our term (*šrr*) is drawn into the same world of language as *yṣr* and ḥšb. While Israel's own stubbornness is condemned, its practice of šrr fits our characterization as a 'challenge to old structures of thought'; only in this case the old structures are the torah stipulations. Thus the new alternative is an unacceptable statement of independence. And this is the imagination which is condemned in the Old Testament.

Beyond the scope of Jeremiah, one of the uses is in Psalm 81.12-13, a prophetic law-suit which contains language very much like that of Jeremiah. For the rejected alternative, in addition to 'not hearing', the text has lō' 'ābâ lî, which RSV renders tersely, 'would have none of me'. Here šrr is parallel with y'ṣ. 'They walk in their own counsel.'[17]

The final use we consider is in Deuteronomy 29.19. The text is a covenantal warning lest there be one,

> who, when he hears the words of this sworn covenant, blesses himself in his heart, saying, 'I shall be safe, though I walk in the stubbornness of my heart'.

Two observations can be made. First, the *hithpa'el* 'bless himself' is a striking articulation of *autonomy*. Such a one obviously has no need for the blessing of Yahweh. Second, the warning clearly indicates that faithful covenanting is possible, for v. 25 specifies that transgression as covenant violation. Thus in all these cases, Psalm 81.12-14 and Deuteronomy 29.19-19 as well as Jeremiah, the issue is an assertion of independence which does not refer life, thought, and action to the way of Yahweh. The terms thus are not used to preclude imagination, but to preclude imagination that is not shaped in covenantal ways.

Now in an analysis of these two words, it is clear that they function primarily in distinct pieces of literature, yṣr in the J narrative, the Chronicler and positively in Second Isaiah; šrr almost exclusively in Jeremiah. The single piece of literature using both is Deuteronomy, yṣr in 31.21 and šrr in 29.18-19. The convergence of the two uses requires that we look more closely at this material:

> One who, when he hears the words of this sworn covenant, blesses himself in his heart, saying, 'I shall be safe though I walk in the *stubbornness of my heart*' (29.19). For I know the purposes which they are *forming* before I have brought them into the land I swore to give (31.21).

The two uses come from different layers of the tradition. Noth may be followed in assigning our first usage (29.19) to the speeches of Deuteronomy, whereas 31.21 belongs to the introduction to the Song of Moses which bears the mark of the Deuteronomic historian.[18] The former is much more directly linked to the precise claims of covenant whereas the latter is more preoccupied with the dangers and temptations of the land. Because Deuteronomy usually is more positive about the prospect of obedience and the Deuteronomic historical more aware of the cost of disobedience, we might have expected that the more negative term *šrr* would be used in the latter. The fact that the terms are used inversely to what we might have expected reinforces the notion that the two awarenesses of the danger of imagination move in very much the same sphere of concern.[19]

Thus they share a common notion in the primal corpus and in the derivative corpus. Both passages partake of the same motifs which are crucial to the entire *Deuteronomic* corpus. Both of them are utterly committed to covenant and to the torah of covenant. Both of them have an eye over the Jordan into the land of promise and perceive the land as *a place of temptation to disobedient imagination*. And the ground for that danger is not difficult to discern. It is material independence,[20] which permits spiritual and cognitive autonomy, on which see Deuteronomy 8.17. The claims of torah are less compelling when they are not linked to issues of survival which make obedience more convincing. And the task of Deuteronomy is to make a case for obedience, including obedient imagination, in a situation suitable and tempting for *an autonomous imagination*.[21]

Our analysis thus far leads to two conclusions. First, imagination is understood as exceedingly dangerous and in some cases is utterly condemned. But it is also seen to be a capacity for obedience when the 'forming of an alternative future' is obedient to the claims of covenant. Second, while that agenda is found in many parts of the Old Testament, our analysis of two terms has led us especially to the tradition of Deuteronomy as a theological statement which is aware of the dangers but also is not completely closed to the possibilities of an obedient imagination.

IV

When we consider the tradition of Deuteronomy, we are astounded at what we find. We might expect to find a restrictive obedience that is devoid of and resistant to imagination. We might expect that from the warnings and awarenesses of 29.19 and 31.21. We might expect a narrow fundamentalism of the Mosaic tradition which functions like a frightened steward who buries the trust in order to protect it (cf. Matt 25.24-25), simply to keep it intact. One way for Israel to have maintained its tradition in the face of the affluence and temptations in the land would have been to guard and fix the shape of the tradition to be safe for all time. (In terms of methodological implications, one may observe that this is the tendency of some literalists on the one hand who want to arrive at an unchanging meaning. On the other hand, it is also the tendency of some forms of historical-critical study which want to identify and preserve forever 'the right meaning' of the text. In modern scientific form, the tendency of some unimaginative criticism is the same in its result as some literalism.)

But of course Deuteronomy does no such thing. Deuteronomy is fully aware of the danger of disobedient, i.e. autonomous, imagination. Nevertheless, it makes bold hermeneutical moves that go well beyond the old Mosaic tradition on which it is based and to which it appeals. The marvel of Deuteronomy is that while it warns against disobedient imagination, it is itself an act of radical obedient imagination. And that radicalness is measured by its own norms of covenant. Any imaginative act in statement consonant with covenant is permitted and even welcomed.

That extraordinary quality of Deuteronomy is evident on literary grounds:[22]

1. Deuteronomy is itself a 'copy' of the torah tradition (Deut 17-18). But it is surely no copy in any stenographic sense of anything we know from Moses, the book of Exodus, the Covenant Code or anything else.[23] Of course one may hypothesize that it is a 'copy' of something no longer extant. But it seems obviously the case that it is an inventive, imaginative act—a new statement 'formed' in the heart/mind of these teachers and preachers, a bold act which challenges old givens. The irony is that this very tradition warns against departing to the right or the left from these commandments (5.32; 17.11, 20; 28.14; Josh 1.7). And yet, at the very moment that it issues this solemn warning, it is indeed an imaginative restatement that exercises enormous freedom and authority to match. Specifically in 17.14-20, and precisely in vv. 18-20, which refers to a 'second' of the tradition, the very warning about *rigorous attentiveness to the commandment* is in the very act *a completely new articulation of commandment* that can have no precedent or rootage in any older teaching.

That particular act might be a case study for us in imaginative religious teaching and a clue about imaginative scholarship. This tradition which worries about autonomy in the land and the accompanying imagination, in the moment of that worry authorizes for Israel a new institution, monarchy, which in other traditions is a way of 'stubbornness of their own heart' but here is a way of not departing from the torah. And the reason this text is not disobedient imagination is that it enjoins obedience to the same God, the same perception of reality, the same social practice. That is, it is imagination faithful to and congruent with, but surely distinct from, old covenant commitments.

2. Von Rad has observed (and made a great deal of) the fact that Deuteronomy is not an address of Yahweh nor is it first of all the word of the Lord.[24] It is the word of Moses. And even if one were to reject critical theories for a later dating, we cannot on any grounds go behind the imaginative work of the person (or office) of Moses. Without being historically precise, von Rad has made a compelling case that this material is preaching or exposition, a literary residue from a regular and periodic *liturgic processing of the normative memory*. A liturgic processing means a combination of *fidelity* to the memory and *imagination* about an articulation that has force and relevance. The preaching of Deuteronomy is 'revelatory' precisely because it is the imaginative recovery of what lies at the root of the memory:

> If genuine revelation is the imaginative recovery of what lies at the root of memory, it is also an opening to what is present, yet still inchoate in one's heritage.[25]

This is, I submit, what the preaching of Deuteronomy is and does. It is the imaginative recovery of the root of memory. It opens what is inchoate in the heritage. And as a result it is revelatory: it is the disclosure of what had not been seen until now as a social possibility. But we note well that for all its freedom in discerning social possibility, the power and energy are in the memory and heritage which are clearly specified.

3. Polzin, with a rather heavy theoretical frame, has shown how the tradition out of Deuteronomy is constituted to encourage a dialogue. He labels the dialogue partners the voice of 'authoritarian dogmatism' and 'critical traditionalism'.[26] The argument Polzin mounts is persuasive, especially given the method he proposes from Voloshinov. Unfortunately, Polzin's method leads to a conclusion

about the book of Deuteronomy which I believe to be excessively pejorative. He concludes that the authority of the Mosaic voice is raised 'to a position almost indistinguishable from that of the voice of God'.[27] And the result is that the book of Deuteronomy (as distinct from the subsequent Deuteronomic history) is 'essentially mono-logic'.[28] Given Polzin's method, I think that conclusion follows.

But such a view seems overly committed to a particular method and fails to note the tendency of the entire corpus. This is a tradition intended to be *faithful* to the memory but also *imaginative* about the new circumstance. And therefore, both 'voices' (including the more 'authoritarian voice') are imaginative. That is, the 'old voice of Moses' is also a voice of enormous imagination, proposing the Israel a quite new discernment of the world.

4. The literary quality of Deuteronomy (and its spin-off traditions) shows the practice of imagination that breaks the givens for the sake of a freshly 'formed' future. But convenantal imagination in Deuteronomy is never contained as a *literary* fact. This covenantal imagination needs also to be understood on *sociological* grounds. And this dimension, it seems to me, is lacking in much current reflection on imagination. That is, imagination in this tradition concerns the shape of public, visible, institutional life. Imagination as a hermen-eutical practice is not simply a matter of subtlety and finesse with words. It is a use of words which function as inventive social facts. That is, it is imagination which concerns *social* possibility.

If imagination is here understood as 'forming' (*yṣr*) and 'planning' (*ḥšb*) for the land (as in Deut 31.21), then what is being *formed in the heart* of Israel and *planned for the land* is an alternative way of being in the land as an intentional social community.[29] It would have been the most unimaginative social act Israel could have committed to accept Canaan's gods and the oppressive social structures that accompany them. That would have been to retain and accept the old social givens already there. It is those that Deuteronomy condemns and prohibits and to which it offers a remarkable alternative.[30]

Israel's imagination is not primarily literary or aesthetic, though it utilizes those sensitivities. It is social and sociological. It thinks in terms of the reality of community and the ways that community can reorder its public existence in different and liberating ways. I have already suggested that literary critics and sociologists of ancient Israel might usefully make common cause and must not compartment-alize their methodologies.[31] Therefore, our assessment of imagination in Deuteronomy must attend not only to the ways in which the literature *says*, but also the ways in which the words *do*, as social intervention of a most powerful and abrasive kind.

So the thesis offered here is that Deuteronomy is an act of extraordinary social imagination, for which the genre of preached law is a serviceable literary form. Gottwald's particular hypothesis[32] concerning the character and function of early Israel is of course in dispute, though I find it most compelling, given the alternatives available to us. Without settling the question of whether Yahweh is a 'function' of a social experiment,[33] or even 'merely' a function of a social experiment, as Gottwald's critics accuse him of suggesting, we can allow that Gottwald's general hypothesis illuminates Deuteronomy at three important points:

a. Israel, especially in the perception of Deuteronomy, is a remarkable social experiment. This is evident not only in the 'sermons' of motivation but in the 'legislation' offered as well.
b. The Hexateuchal tradition forms a sturdy and energizing base for that social experiment. This, I suggest, is its function even if one does not follow in detail Gottwald's understanding of its origin.
c. More than any other part of that ideological base, Deuteronomy strikes one as 'originary' speech, i.e. speech which calls into being that which does not exist until the word is uttered (Rom 4.20).[34]

For now we can bracket out the many serious questions remaining in Gottwald's hypothesis. But we can suggest that Deuteronomy's preached law is indeed an imagining act of envisioning a social form that is not at hand in the circumstance of Canaan and that is not available in the 'old' Mosaic tradition. Deuteronomy exercises a 'forming (*yṣr*) function in 'planning/determining/proposing' a covenantal way to be in the land, a way not yet known, envisioned or evoked until Deuteronomy had its magisterial say.

V

We may consider three such acts of social imagination:

1. The law of release in 15.1-11 is a remarkable proposal. Obviously the notion of 'release and redemption' is not confined to Deuteronomy nor does it need to be demonstrated that the proposal was actually

practiced. It is enough to observe that the 'legislation' is a daring thought for a social order. To be able to anticipate 'there shall be no poor among you' (v. 4) in either the ancient or the modern world is almost as though one were to say, 'I have a dream'. Indeed, it would not take much to recast the entire piece into rhetoric like that of Martin Luther King, for it is all a dreaming vision of how social criticism can be made of a hierarchical community together with an alternative proposal. This paragraph then is indeed an imaginative act if we understand that to mean breaking old givens and proposing alternative forms of existence.[35]

2. The law on kingship (17.14-20) is equally extraordinary. We have already considered the strange way in which the 'copy' functions as an act of remarkable newness. Here we focus on the substantive act of imagination. This imaginative act proposes a third alternative to 'no king' (Judg 8.23) and 'a king like the other nations' (1 Sam 8.5, 20)—the two alternatives which dominate the discussion in 1 Samuel and which must have been the parameters of the debate.[36] But this unit takes a new way that is without precedent anywhere in the tradition. This statement takes the political institution which is at hand, but completely transforms it, robbing it of some of its most dangerous (and most attractive and seductive) features, and bringing it to a form acceptable in covenantal categories. The law is able to see that conventional kingship presumes to be a principle of order, but when there is a practice of silver and gold and horses and wives it acts in fact for disorder. This proposal then is that the kingship be organized to work in reality for the order it claims to sponsor.

3. The little law in 25.1-3 must have been an important break-through in the world of ancient Israel, for curbing violence in any society requires some remarkable freedom to break with harsh practices that command general assent. Taken by itself, this regulation does not seem less than barbaric. And yet, if society is organized to assault the guilty until vengeance is satisfied, then this impresses one as a first step in 'prison reform' and indeed in reform of all of society toward humaneness.

There can be no doubt that these three texts are all remarkably imaginative:

a.   15.1-11 a new characterization of the debt system,[37]
b.   17.14-20 a transformation of the institution of monarchy,
c.   25.1-3 a curb on authorized conventional violence.

The tradition is 'nervous' about purposes formed for the land (31.21). And yet these laws are precisely new purposes formed for the new life in the land. They are indeed acts of imagination and social construction. And one can believe that the impetus for this daring line of thought is the vision of humaneness grounded in the memory of the exodus, the reality of the covenant and finally in the sovereign will of Yahweh. But even given those groundings, this is nonetheless an act of creativity and daring. They are examples of liberated imagination in passionate service of Yahweh's sovereignty.[38]

One might wonder: How did this teaching strike its contemporaries? One can 'imagine' that from two sides it appears to be the 'imagination of an evil heart'. On the one hand, the old-line covenanters may have judged it to be accommodating the Canaanite practices of debt slaves and kingship, for it does take up these practices. And such an accommodation to existing practices was hardly envisioned in the initial movement of liberation. On the other hand, some may have waited eagerly to embrace Canaanite practices of wealth, power and security, and such proposals as these are terribly 'limiting'. Clearly Deuteronomy is at some pains to resist the charge of autonomous imagination by the firm insistence of not departing right or left from the parameters of covenant. From what we know of the tradition, this preached law does depart from the old tradition, does act in free ways in relation to the body of the torah. But what appears to make it acceptable and finally normative is that the *substance* as well as the *form* is rigorously referred to Yahweh and the tradition of Moses.

VI

Thus far we have considered the *practice of imagination* in Israel's articulation of sacred texts. We have tried to show that in the tradition of Deuteronomy (where we have been led by two word studies which overlap there), there is an awareness of the danger of imagination which is autonomous, and at the same time a vigorous practice of *emancipated imagination which is obedient*. That is how it is in the Bible itself. To take the texts most seriously is to see that they are indeed acts of imagination. It is to dishonor the texts, to flatten them either to agree with each other in conforming ways, or to reduce them to single, recoverable meanings.

With that discernment of the character of the text in view, we return to Anderson's suggestion for our own interpretive enterprise.

These conclusions, which I presume to be faithful to Anderson's intent and practice, may be drawn.

1. Faithful interpretation of scripture must be imaginative; that is, seeing the texts as powered by the revolutionary purpose of Yahweh, as evocative of new social possibility. Such a way of interpretation tries to take the text seriously according to its function in Israel, as it bears witness to this revolutionary God and as it serves as a vehicle for *this sovereignty* in terms of *social practice*.[39] To take the text as less or other than this is not faithful to the text's own intentionality.

Conversely, interpretation which is not attentive to this revolutionary urging is likely not to be faithful. On the one hand, interpretive postures which are 'literalist' tend to flatten the hopeful, evocative force of the text as a social function. That is, the text is taken only as descriptive and not as evocative or 'redescriptive'. But the same charge can be made concerning much historical-critical interpretation which tends to regard the text as flat and fixed, without attention to its evocative social function. Anderson's sense of the imaginative is surely correct in seeing that one-dimensional interpretation, either literalist or 'historical-critical' in that sense, is not faithful to the character and claim of the text. Either way is a means to deaden the dangerous evocation of the text.

2. Most scholarly attention is given to imaginative interpretation in terms of literary criticism which takes the text in and of itself as a single datum. This has much to commend it, and Anderson is much interested in this enterprise.[40]

3. Literary criticism which attends to the aesthetic dimension of the text must be related to *social criticism and social possibility*. That is, the word (text) is generative of an alternative world in which people live. Imaginative interpretation of the kind for which Anderson calls must be concerned with *sociological analysis*.[41] The text is never by itself, but is always related to a community in equilibrium or to the community in process of formation or transformation. Norman Gottwald has well articulated this in terms of the text as 'narrative objectification of the superstructure'.[42] However, Gottwald's tendency is to have the text *follow* the social reality. It may also be that the text *leads and evokes* social reality. In the texts cited from Deuteronomy, we dare think that the texts are anticipatory and summon Israel to a transformation of social power and social policy. And in any case for those who use the text in its canonical form, clearly the text leads social reality. If the initial preaching of Jesus in Luke 4.16-21 is

reminiscent of the law of release in one of its forms,[43] it is a clear example in which text *leads* social practice and social possibility. What Gottwald does not sufficiently allow for, I suggest, is that the text may stand at the *generative beginning* as well as the *ideological ending* of the process of social transformation.[44]

4. Because texts which are generative initiators do not get formed in a vacuum, literary criticism can also be usefully linked to what may be called *anticipatory psychology*. Israel may have had to work with quite elementary concepts for psychology.[45] Thus, it speaks of heart in a rather undifferentiated way. But the notion of 'forming in the heart' is not only bold and dangerous, but also a quite sophisticated psychological notion. It affirms that human thought is not bound by what is observable, but that the heart is capable of forming images of what could be that is not yet. The heart can make leaps in such images, even when it does not know how to get from here to there. That is, there is distance between *anticipated possibility* and *historical actuality*. And the human heart is understood to be the agent of that evoking at a distance. Indeed, the evidence is ample that God is one who images in his heart prior to his historical activity. And Israel recognizes that humankind has the same possibility. Like God, the human person is a generator of *images* that lead to *alternative acts* and *social possibilities*.

Of course Israel is aware of the danger of this capacity (Gen 6.5; 8.21). And Israel is aware that situations of prosperity and well-being may seduce Israel's heart into forming an autonomous notion of human well-being (Deut 8.17; 29.19; 31.21).

But the texts of Deuteronomy give one pause. What an incredibly generative act is imaging a social practice of release of slaves, a proposal that subverts economic vested interests. What an extraordinary invention to think about a new form of monarchy that is quite unlike every known model. And to think through the limitation of vengeance is based on the insight that new ways can be found to order social passion and social power. In a variety of small moves, we are offered proposals for a genuine social novum. We do not know from where it comes. Anderson inclines to see in this the work of the spirit, if I rightly understand his urging (cf. Matt 16.17 on such a transcendent source of disclosure). That is, one may conclude that 'flesh and blood' does not lead to such a profound proposal for the life of Israel. Or one may alternatively speak of poetic imagination, as Anderson also does. Either way, these texts are evidence of an originative generativity is what is given us in the text, to which we look for continued generativity.[46]

These two points, sociology of the new possibility and psychology of anticipation, need to be closely held together with literary ciriticism. Any one of these taken alone as a method is misleading. The text is a statement of a *generative heart* and reaches for a *social possibility*. But the sociological innovation by itself is flat, for unless there is aesthetic articulation with it, the new social possibility is readily oppressive. And an imaginative heart by itself is in a vacuum without text and without historical community, hardly an agent of power. Thus, we need methods of interpretation which take seriously the forming *heart*, the imaginative *text* and the emerging liberated *social possibility*.

5. But neither literary imagination, social generativity nor a psychology of anticipation give rise to the peculiar substance of social possibility sponsored by Deuteronomy. Finally, the interpreter is driven to *the theological question*. And when we ask how to understand the new vision of social power and social possibility offered here, Deuteronomy clearly intends a social inventiveness authorized by and obedient to the sovereign will of Yahweh. Thus, the ultimate measure of every imaginative thought, imaginative text and imaginative social possibility is how it corresponds to the character of God already disclosed in this tradition.

And we may understand that the laws on release, kingship and vengeance are evidences of Yahweh's rule made concrete; that is it is Yahweh who is the source of liberated Israel. Exegesis is thus translated and inadequate if it does not press this reference. All else may lead to autonomous imagination, not to bold obedience proposed in the text.

6. The interface of the claim of the text and the methods of interpretation required concerns the watershed of canon. The moment of canonization divides the dynamics of *how the text came to be* from the dynamics of *how the text causes to be*.[47] It is hardly disputed that in the text *coming to be*, the factors of liberated social possibility, anticipatory psychology, literary finesse and theological accountability have been operative. All of that is present in the formation of the text, and our methods reflect that. The kind of interpretation for which Anderson calls, I suggest, is a recognition that these same factors are operative in the text *causing to be* in the communities that claim these texts as normative and canonical. In that way, the imaginative power that *formed the text* may be continued to be *received from the*

text. But such a receiving from the text requires a mode different from the flat literalism of obscurantism or the flat historicism of rational positivism. The key to a legitimate receiving from the text is to recognize that the text belongs to its lord, or as Anderson says, 'God speaks to his people today through Scripture at the point of our imagination, that is, where the "inspired writing" meets the "inspired reader" and becomes the Word of God'.[48] Or perhaps as Ricouer says, the Poem belongs to the Poet, seen and heard, so the text continues to be a medium of *disclosure* that no method of interpretation is free to *close*.

Scholarship has focused almost exclusively on the text as the *receiving factor* at the end of the text-forming process. I suggest Anderson is calling for scholarship which views the text as the *generating factor* at the beginning of the community-forming process.

It is a delight to offer this piece in gratitude to Professor Anderson for his sensitivity to questions of method and for his unfailing attentiveness to the theological claims in the text. Hopefully, what is argued here is faithful to his lead, for so I understand and intend it.

NOTES

1. Bernhard W. Anderson, *The Living Word of the Bible* (Philadelphia: Westminster, 1979).

2. *Ibid.*, 13-35.

3. *Ibid.*, 29.

4. Those limitations are most formidably articulated by Brevard Childs, *Introduction to the Old Testament as Scripture* (Philadelphia: Fortress, 1979). See Anderson's assessment of Childs's word, 'Introduction to the Old Testament as Scripture', *TToday* 37 (1980) 100-108.

5. Anderson, *Living Word*, 29-30.

6. See Anderson's own important contributions in this regard, 'From Analysis to Synthesis: The Interpretation of Genesis 1–11,' *JBL* 97 (1978) 23-29, and 'Tradition and Scripture in the Community of Faith', *JBL* 100 (1981) 5-21. See the judicious programmatic statement of Robert Polzin, *Moses and the Deuteronomist* (New York: Seabury, 1980) 1-24.

7. Anderson, *Living Word*, 34-35.

8. Observe that Childs, 'Some Reflections on the Search for a Biblical Theology', *Horizons in Biblical Theology* 4 (1982) 1-12, has urged that any serious theological proposal must be articulated with reference both to the academy and the believing communities.

9. R.L. Hart, *Unfinished Man and the Imagination* (New York: Herder and Herder, 1968) 159.

10. *Ibid.*, 198.

11. *Ibid.*, 200; cf. p. 246.

12. R.C. Tannehill, *The Sword of his Mouth* (Philadelphia: Fortress, 1975) 54. See the use made of this construct by Micheal V. Fox, 'The Rhetoric of Ezekiel's Vision of the Valley of Dry Bones', *HUCA* 51 (1980) 1-15.

13. Cf. Carroll Stuhlmueller, *Creative Redemption in Deutero-Isaiah* (An Bib, 43; Rome: Biblical Institute, 1970), p. 115.

14. *Ibid.*, 215.

15. I suggest that scholars who slot *yṣr* simply as a metaphor for working with clay have failed to understand the elastic power of metaphor. Thus, the reference to potter may be the vehicle, but a more tensive meaning pushes the term toward a very different field in relation to *br'*. For a convenient summary of this characteristic of metaphor, see Phyllis Trible, *God and the Rhetoric of Sexuality* (Philadelphia: Fortress, 1978), chapter 2. As we shall seek to show, taking this metaphor in its flattest possibility no doubt contributes to our misunderstanding of imagination as a legitimate human activity in the Old Testament.

16. It is not accidental that 'not listen' is the key indictment, for 'listening is the antithesis of autonomy'. Paul Ricoeur, 'Naming God', *USQR* 34 (1979) 219, has a marvelous statement: 'Listening excludes founding oneself'. See also his comments on listening in *The Conflict of Interpretations* (Evanston: Northwestern University Press, 1974), 449-51.

17. Gerhard von Rad, *The Problem of the Hexateuch and Other Essays* (New York: McGraw Hill, 1966) 23-26, has of course linked this Psalm to the old credo. It becomes clear that in all of these texts dealing with the problem of an autonomy, they hold most closely to the credo-covenant claim of Yahweh's exclusive relation. The imagination that is condemned is understood to be antithetical to covenant and to the obedient hearing required by covenant.

18. Martin Noth, *The Deuteronomistic History* (JSOT Supp., 15; Sheffield: JSOT, 1981), 35.

19. Polzin, *Moses*, 69-72, finds little distinction here in the various elements of these two aspects of the literature.

20. Claus Westermann, *Elements of Old Testament Theology* (Atlanta: J. Knox, 1978) 106-108, discerns the dramatic moment in the present form of the text when *material independence* permits *spiritual and cognitive autonomy*:

> . . . they ate the produce of the land, unleavened cakes and parched grain. And the manna ceased on the morrow, when they ate of the produce of the land: and the people of Israel had manna no more, but ate of the fruit of the land of Canaan that year (Josh 5.11-12).

Westermann comments, 'The bread of blessing now takes the place of the bread of saving'.

21. Reference can usefully be made here to Lucy Bregman, 'Religious

Imagination: Polytheistic Psychology Confronts Calvin', *Soundings* 63 (1980) 36-60. Bregman analyzes Calvin's statements on imagination vis-à-vis those of James Hillman. It is clear that Calvin is not resistant to imagination as such, but to autonomous imagination which takes the self as the point of reference in place of God. Now we cannot move easily and directly from this analysis of Calvin to the tradition of Deuteronomy. But the positions are closely paralleled. Clearly what concerns the tradition of Deuteronomy is autonomy. In the land Israel may imagine itself self-made and therefore rely on the stubbornness of one's heart, without reference to God. Thus the *psycholgical* base of imagination is closely linked to *material* reality. Whem material life is precarious, psychological orientation may be more focused and yielding; when material life is sure, it may be more indulgent. It is that self-indulgence that Deuteronomy seeks to preclude. And the reason is that self-indulgent imagination is conformist to the ruling powers.

22. This openness of a certain kind characterizes the entire tradition of Deuteronomy, even into the Deuteronomic handling of Jeremiah. It is evident there as well that the second generation of preachers to the exile exercise great imagination in letting the tradition touch new historical reality. See E. Nicholson, *Preaching to the Exiles* (Oxford: Blackwell, 1970) for a balanced statement and Robert P. Carroll, *From Chaos to Covenant* (New York: Crossroad, 1981) for a more polemical treatment. The three texts especially identified by Hans Walter Wolff, 'Kergygma of the Deuteronomic Historical Work', in *The Vitality of Old Testament Traditions* (by Walter Brueggemann and Hans Walter Wolff; Atlanta: John Knox, 1975) 93-100, are Deut 4.29-31; 30.1-10; 1 Kgs 8.46-53. These three texts peculiarly give evidence of the free imagination of the tradition in meeting new challenges to the faith.

23. Of course I do not suggest that this remarkable quality is confined to the tradition of Deuteronomy, even though it is strikingly embodied there. Paul D. Hanson, 'The Theological Significance of Contradiction within the Book of the Covenant', *Canon and Authority* (ed. George W. Coats and Burke O. Long; Philadelphia: Fortress, 1977) 110-31, has explored the same dimension of the Book of the Covenant. He refers variously to 'a dynamic of creativity and liberating, sustaining dynamic' (124, 130), 'a creative, egalitarian and liberating dynamic' (129), 'a dynamic which is creative, liberating and life-giving' (130). But his final statement is theologically explicit: 'The ultimate referent is God who is confessed as creative, liberating, sustaining agent . . . ' (131). Walter Harrelson, 'Life, Faith and the Emergence of Tradition', *Tradition and Theology in the Old Testament* (ed. D.A. Knight; Philadelphia: Fortress, 1977) 11-30, argues that there is a clear core tradition to the Old Testament and that it has a revolutionary character. *Imagination*, I suggest in agreement with Hanson, is the way in which this core exercises its *revolutionary* quality.

24. Gerhard von Rad, *Studies in Deuteronomy* (SBT, 9; Chicago: Henry Regnery, 1953), chapters 1 and 2.
25. Carl Raschke and Donna Gregory, 'Revelation and the Archaeology of the Feminine', *The Archaeology of the Imagination* (ed. Charles E. Winquist; JAAR Thematic Studies, 48/2; Missoula: American Academy of Religion, 1981). L. Dornish, 'Symbolic Systems and the Interpretation of Scripture: An Introduction to the Work of Paul Ricoeur', *Semeia* 4 (1975) 6, characterizes Ricoeur's second hermeneutic as 'Restorative: moving toward a recollection of the original memory of the symbol'.
26. Polzin, *Moses*, 74.
27. *Ibid.*, 55.
28. *Ibid.*, 72.
29. With a rather odd expression, 'formed in the heart', the text combines in a fresh way two notions in a most sophisticated statement. 'Formed' refers to working with clay, but 'in the heart' is an imaginative forming that takes place apart from physical implementation. The metaphor thus maintains creative distance between the heart-constructing activity and the history-constructing in social practice.
30. Hanson, 'Theological Significance', 129-31, warns against treating any theological, social or ethical system as immutable. Henry Mottu, 'Jeremiah vs. Hananiah: Ideology and Truth in Old Testament Prophecy', *The Bible and Liberation* (Radical Religious Reader; Berkely: Community for Religious Research and Education, 1976) 58-67, in a more critical way, presents Hananiah as one who 'objectified and reified' a theological claim. The result is of course uncritical reactionary social practice and social policy. This lack of imagination leads to social control and oppression.
31. Walter Brueggemann, 'Israel's Social Criticism and Yahweh's Sexuality', *JAAR* 45 (Supp., 1977) 739-72, especially the concluding comments on 764-65.
32. Norman K. Gottwald, *The Tribes of Yahweh* (Maryknoll, N.Y.: Orbis, 1979).
33. *Ibid.*, 611-21.
34. On originary speech, see Raschke and Gregory, 'Revelation and the Archaeology', 90.
35. Michael V. Fox, 'The Rhetoric of Ezekiel's Vision', 7 and *passim*, has suggested that the vision of Ezek. 37.1-14 seeks to give hope by creating 'irrational explanation', by getting the community 'to expect the unexpected, to accept the plausibility of the absurd'. I suggest that the imaginative act of 'release' is as implausible and unexpected as is the rising of the bones. Hannah A. Arndt, *The Human Condition* (Chicago: University of Chicago, 1958) 236-43, argues that forgiveness (which is linked to the year of release) is finally more radical than are the miracles. In our context, social possibility, as practiced in Deuteronomy, is more dangerously imaginative than many 'religious' acts of hope. On the critical problems in social

imagination, see Paul Ricoeur, 'Imagination in Discourse and in Action', *The Human Being in Action, The Irreducible Element in Man II*, (Analecta Husserliana, 7; ed. Anna-Teresa Tymieniecka; Dordrecht and Boston: D. Reidel) 15-21.

36. See the careful summary of the debate in ancient Israel by Baruch Halpern, 'The Uneasy Compromise: Israel Between League and Monarchy', *Tradition in Transformation* (ed. B. Halpern and Jon D. Levenson; Winona Lake: Eisenbrauns, 1981) 59-96.

37. On the transformation of the debt system as a crucial theological act, see Fernando Belo, *A Materialist Reading of the Gospel of Mark* (Maryknoll: Orbis, 1981) 37-59.

38. These laws are examples of 'redescribing' the world, as Ricoeur puts it. But such redescription concerns not simply literary expression, but concrete social practice. The law in Deuteronomy is a forming in the heart of a new social world. On new possibility wrought by imagination, see Paul Ricoeur, 'Listening to the Parables of Jesus', *The Philosophy of Paul Ricoeur* (ed. C.E. Reagan and David Steward; Boston: Beacon, 1978) 245.

39. I have offered an example of this interface in interpretive process in 'Social Criticism and Social Vision in the Deuteronomic Formula of the Judges', *Die Botschaft and die Boten* (ed. Jörg Jeremias and Lothar Perlitt; Neukirchen-Vluyn: Neukirchener Verlag, 1981) 101-14.

40. See most recently Bernhard W. Anderson, 'The Problem and Promise of Commentary', *Int* 36 (1982) 341-55. On pp. 349-50, he writes concerning desirable method, that 'it has an open-ended dimension which appeals to the reader's imagination'. On p. 354, 'I would expect a good commentary to help me become more of a poet in my understanding of scriptural language and the Biblical story. It is difficult for the modern mind, with its prosaic, scientific bent, to enter into the poetic and mythopoeic language of Scripture.' A splendid example of the kind of interpretation offered by such literary methods is found in *Art and Meaning: Rhtoric in Biblical Literature* (ed. David J.A. Clines, David M. Gunn and Alan J. Hauser; JSOT Supp., 19; Sheffield: JSOT, 1982). It is clear that such critical attentiveness to imagination has nothing to do with the current fad of 'left brain/right brain' which tends to celebrtate undisciplined fantasy and free association of ideas. See Bregman, 'Religious Imagination', 37-41, for a critique of that 'ideological' fad.

41. For exploration of this factor with attention to method, see the collection of essays, *Anthropological Perspectives on Old Testament Prophecy* (Semeia 21, 1982), with particular reference to the articles of Long and Wilson. Note the comment of Long: 'Thus, anthropological study helps us compensate for distortions which arise from isolating religious ideology from other forms of social repression' (p. 50).

42. Gottwald, *The Tribes*, 100-14.

43. On the Lucan appeal to the Jubilee law, see the comments of James A.

Sanders, 'Isaiah in Luke', *Int* 36 (1982) 150-55, and especially footnote 13, on the dissertation of Sharon Ringe.

44. See my review of Gottwald's work, *The Tribes of Yahweh, JAAR* 48 (1980) 441-51.

45. See the summary of the data by Aubrey Johnson, *The Vitality of the Individual in the Thought of Ancient Israel* (Cardiff: University of Wales, 1949) 77-84. Johnson confines his discussion to the internal life of the individual and does not probe the social significance of the personal function or organ.

46. Note that in Ricoeur's comment cited in note 38, he still can do no better than to speak of *the heart* as the agent of new possibility.

47. The word 'cause' here is of course not used mechanically, but refers to the evocative, generative power of the text. I use it because it suggests a nice contrast to the word 'came'. With 'came to be', the text is the receiving factor at the end of the process. With 'cause to be', the text is the initiating factor at the beginning of the process. Paul Ricoeur, *The Conflict of Interpretation* (Evanston: Northwestern University, 1974) 319: 'Language is less spoken *by* men than spoken *to* men'.

48. Anderson, *Living Word*, 35.

2

BIBLICAL THEOLOGY: SITUATING THE DISCIPLINE

Ben C. Ollenburger

I

Some fourteen years ago Brevard Childs offered an analysis of the biblical theology movement in which he diagnosed the condition of biblical theology in America as critical.[1] Some thought at the time that this diagnosis meant that the patient would shortly die, but this expectation seems to reflect too pessimistic an understanding of 'crisis'. Jeffrey Stout defines an historical crisis as 'a relatively brief period preceded by malaise and followed by dramatic resolution of some sort'.[2] While it is a fairly simple matter to trace a period of malaise in biblical theology, or more properly, several such periods, it is not yet possible to point to a dramatic resolution. To be sure, Childs himself and others have offered proposals for such a resolution, but none of these has yet carried the day.[3] Biblical theology, I would suggest, is in a state neither of malaise nor of resolution, but of robust activity, to judge by the number of recent articles and books devoted to it. I do not propose in this essay to offer a dramatic resolution to the crisis of biblical theology, nor to offer anything like a comprehensive, critical review of current literature on the subject which is the fruit of this robust activity. Rather, this essay has the much more modest aim of making some general observations on the situation of biblical theology as a theological discipline.

To state my intention in just this way is already to make a controversial assumption: that biblical theology is a form of theological activity, or of theological inquiry. It is common today to emphasize the historical character of biblical theology and to point to strong continuities between this discipline and a history of religions approach to the biblical texts. Consequently, questions may be raised about the very integrity of biblical theology as a discipline. If biblical theologians do not study the texts with a set of methods peculiar to their discipline, in what does their disciplinary integrity consist? And if they employ the methods of historical research common to other students of antiquity, as well as focusing on the same subject matter,

is it not confusing to refer to them as theologians, rather than
historians, philologists, or what have you? Since these questions are
difficult to answer, and since they are posed with great frequency
(and have been for generations),[4] it has become controversial to
assume that biblical theology is indeed a theological discipline.

One could try to settle this controversy by appealing to semantic
considerations. 'Theology' is a noun and 'biblical' is an adjective
which modifies it, in the same way that 'theology' is often modified
by 'systematic' or 'practical'. A strong argument could be made that
those who first used the term meant 'biblical theology' to be an
analogue to the other branches of theology,[5] but semantic arguments
themselves are seldom convincing, or helpful. Rather, I want to
proceed historically. I suggest that in reflecting on the situation of
biblical theology as a theological discipline, and on why it has
become controversial to reflect on biblical theology in just that way,
we may gain clarity by thinking historically.

It is appropriate, I believe, that these historically oriented observations on biblical theology focus on the man credited with being the
'father' of this discipline, J.P. Gabler. It is appropriate not only
because this is as far back as we can get in the discipline, and because
we will soon celebrate its two-hundredth anniversary, but also
because Gabler enjoys a peculiar legacy. On the one hand, Gabler is
seen as having established within the field of theology a discipline
with its own integrity over against dogmatic theology. On the other
hand, Gabler is seen as having given biblical theology a purely
historical character, so that it enjoys a 'complete separation' from
dogmatics.[6] In situating the discipline of biblical theology today it
may be helpful for us to engage in a kind of 'historical-critical' study
of Gabler's proposals. In attending to the questions Gabler faced, as
well as to how he answered them and why, we may be assisted in
answering our own questions, or even in doing away with some
pseudo-questions—ones that we needn't be troubled about, but often
are.

This kind of historical approach to reflection on contemporary
problems has been used to good effect in other disciplines.[7] It is
seldom employed in biblical theology, perhaps because its history is
all too unfamiliar among those who see themselves as its practitioners.
An outstanding exception to this generalization is Professor Bernhard
W. Anderson, teacher, colleague and friend, whom this essay seeks to
honor.

II

This essay is concerned with the possibility of situating biblical theology in a theological context. The history of the discipline has moved in exactly the opposite direction. At the time of the Reformation there was a clear and consistent connection between scripture and theology.[8] The collapse of this connection was due in part to the consolidation of protestant theology in neo-scholastic orthodoxy, for which scripture could be ignored once the kernel of theological truth had been extracted. The place of scripture in this theology was reduced to that of providing the *dicta probantia*, on which the *loci* of dogmatic theology rested. There were two critical responses to this form of orthodoxy, both of which were aimed at reforming dogmatic theology. The first of these was pietism, which urged a more rigorous involvement with the text themselves. The second, a century later, was that of critics like Johann Salomo Semler, part of whose contribution was to draw a firm distinction between religion and theology, and to emphasize the former at the expense of the latter. Of these two, Semler's response has had the greater effect on the history of biblical theology.

Four years before Semler's death Johann Philipp Gabler gave as his inaugural address at the University of Altdorf, 'On the Proper Distinction between Biblical and Dogmatic Theology and the Specific Objectives of Each' (1787).[9] While Gabler drew in this address upon several of the distinctions already suggested by Semler, as well as upon the prior work of the hermeneuticians Ernesti and Morus, and of the Old Testament theologian, G.T. Zachariae,[10] the discipline of biblical theology has looked upon Gabler's 1787 *Antrittsrede* as its founding document. In this essay Gabler makes clear that his ultimate aim is to provide for the possibility of a Christian theology that (a) is suitable for its own time, and (b) rests upon an unchanging foundation of biblical truth. The assumptions behind this dual aim are (i) that theology will change from age to age, dependent in part on the philosophy of each particular age; (ii) that the legitimate purpose of theology is to assist the people in the practical exercise of religion; and (iii) that theology, in order to be true to its source, must rest upon the abiding truths of revelation which it is biblical theology's task to articulate.

The process of this articulation occurs in two stages, according to the *Antrittsrede*. First, biblical theology must attend to the individual documents of the Bible, placing them in their historical context and observing their forms of expression. Second, biblical theology must go on to compare the expressions of the individual documents with each other, in order to distinguish from the variety of expressions or assertions ('each single opinion') those which constitute 'universal ideas', 'which are appopriate to the Christian religion of all times'.[11] Later, Gabler designated these two movements as 'true' and 'pure' biblical theology. This distinction rests ultimately on the program for the interpretation of ancient myths developed first by C.G. Heyne and then elaborated by J.G. Eichhorn.[12] According to this program myths can be adequately interpreted only historically and critically, with a view toward establishing what is the essential (or natural) meaning of the myth, once its historical shell has been stripped away. This two-staged operation is then carried over by Gabler into the interpretation of the Bible and becomes the instrument for the production of a 'pure' biblical theology, which itself becomes the timeless, unchanging foundation for dogmatics.

We will look more closely at Gabler's approach below. It is appropriate now, however, to look at the reception of Gabler's proposals in the history of the discipline, particularly in light of the development of a fully historical approach to the study of religion. The principal element of Gabler's proposals which has endured is his emphasis on the (initially) historical character of biblical theology. This historical emphasis was worked out elaborately by two of Gabler's illustrious successors: his colleague G.L. Bauer and his student W.M.L. de Wette, and was developed into a History of Religions school by a circle of scholars at Göttingen centered around Albert Eichhorn.[13] This circle included among its members Gunkel, Bousset, Troeltsch and Wrede, who collectively set the course of biblical studies for the next century. Of this group perhaps Wilhelm Wrede best illustrates how a history of religions approach bears on the way biblical theology is conceived.

Wrede began his essay on 'The Task and Methods of "New Testament Theology"' by referring to Gabler's 'programmatic' *Antrittsrede*, and hoped to show what New Testament theology looks like along Gabler's lines.[14] Wrede believed that New Testament theology had consistently failed to become historical and was still bound by a system of *Lehrbegriffe* selected on dogmatic grounds. He saw the evidence of dogmatic influence in four failures of contemporary New Testament theology: (i) a failure to fully consider the particularity of individual authors; (ii) a failure to distinguish materials which are primarily theological (such as the writings of Paul) from those which are pristinely religious (such as the teachings of Jesus); (iii) a failure to distinguish historically the important from the trivial in the New Testament—a failure brought about by dependence on the canon and lack of attention to the *bewegtes Leben* of those who produced the texts; (iv) a failure to move through the theological layers of the New Testament to the religious vitality lying behind them.[15] Wrede contended, in sum, that New Testament theology was really the history of early Christianity's religion, a history made possible by the Enlightenment and one which, while sparing no dogma from analysis, can itself produce no theological doctrine. That is not to be considered a fault, according to Wrede, because

> How the systematic theologian gets on with its results and deals with them—that is his own affair. Like every real science, New Testament theology has its goal simply in itself, and is totally indifferent to all dogma and systematic theology.[16]

Wrede's nineteenth-century context is obvious in the way he formulates his attack on the then dominant paradigm of New Testament theology, but it is hard to overestimate the impact which Wrede's proposals have had on subsequent biblical theology.[17] For one thing, few today are writing biblical theologies according to an arrangement of doctrines. There is instead an increasing emphasis on the presence of an irreducible diversity in both Testaments, and a corresponding emphasis on the importance of a consideration of the category of experience in the study of biblical theology.[18] The appropriateness of the term 'theology', in speaking of the biblical documents, has been called into question in favor of 'religion'. Furthermore, there is an increasing resistance to the notion of a 'canon', to the parameters of which biblical theology should feel itself restricted, in some important sense.[19] Perhaps most importantly, the category of history has been almost universally accepted as that within which biblical theology works. This is the case with Schlatter, one of Wrede's interlocutors, and it remains the case with Pannenberg in his *Theology and the Philosophy of Science*.[20] These two differ from Wrede principally in investing history with a theological character that he would not have recognized.

There is a further legacy of Wrede to be mentioned. Wrede recognized it as an important consequence of his work, though he himself was unconcerned by it, that a historically conceived biblical theology presented critical problems for dogmatics or systematic theology. It has become immensely difficult, perhaps impossible, to move from historical conclusions to dogmatic or systematic propositions. Yet it is still frequently recognized as central to biblical theology to bridge in some way the chasm between historically contingent 'facts' and theological conclusions—Lessing's ugly ditch.[21] Biblical theology has thus largely accepted a history of religions paradigm for its work, yet persists in wanting to accomplish what Wrede acknowledged was impossible precisely according to this paradigm. A discipline for which the canon can play no constitutive role has become normative in a discipline which accepts the canon as in some sense decisive.[22].

III

Wrede understood his proposals to be, as we have seen, consistent with those of Gabler, who had never, in Wrede's view, carried out his promise to properly distinguish between biblical and dogmatic theology. Given the title of Gabler's *Antrittsrede*, it would seem that Wrede is simply carrying out his program by making biblical theology consistently historical. But, as Rudolf Smed has observed, the title of Gabler's address has been far more influential than its content.[23] What I wish to argue now is that Wrede, and biblical theology generally, has moved in a direction quite contrary to Gabler, and that Gabler's proposed method has no counterpart in the present.

It is interesting that both Gabler and Wrede were dissatisfied with certain uses of the term 'biblical theology' (or 'New Testament theology', in Wrede's case). Wrede thought that the term was inadequate for what New Testament theology should be about, namely describing the history of early Christianity. Gabler, on the other hand, thought the term was inadequate for what he himself called 'true biblical theology', by which he meant an exegesis of the individual biblical documents and a comparison of their various expressions. But, for Gabler, exegesis does not become theological until it is followed by explanation, or interpretation. Biblical theology, then, becomes theological only when it is accompanied by philosophical reflection on the subject matter of the texts, and it is only this kind of reflection, grounded in exegesis but supplemented by explanation, that warrants the term 'biblical theology', or what Gabler called 'pure biblical theology'.[24]

Corresponding to true and pure biblical theology are the operations of exegesis and explanation (*Auslegung* and *Erklärung*). Exegesis, Gabler explains, is concerned with both philology and history. It is an operation that does not leave the sphere of the texts themselves but seeks to explain the meaning of words and texts in their historical context. Here Gabler is following in the footsteps of J.A. Ernesti.[25] But Gabler goes on to say that biblical theology cannot remain with Ernesti, but must instead go on to explain what the text is about. It must engage in critical, philosophically informed reflection about the subject matter (*Sache*) of the text to determine what is of abiding importance and what is merely temporal. We have seen earlier that Gabler is here following the method of myth interpretation outlined by Heyne and J.G. Eichhorn, who wanted to separate what is true in myth from its historical *Einkleidung*.

The task of biblical theology is similar. It too must distinguish that which is universally true, the *notiones universae*,[26] from that which is merely temporal. The criterion upon which such judgments are based, says Gabler, is reason. Thus, biblical theologians, as opposed to mere exegetes, must be philosophically informed, and must employ their philosophy on the texts which it is their business to interpret. In this way dogmatic theology will be assured of a firm foundation, an unchanging foundation, for its work. It is not, however, that theologians merely take up where biblical theologians leave off. Rather, every theologian must proceed from grammatical interpretation if he or she wants to proceed assuredly.[27] Theology is not legitimate unless it begins with exegesis, and exegesis is not theological if it does not go on to philosophize, with a view to determining what is a-temporally true. According to Gabler, ' . . . the divine' is not to be sought 'in the particular, the specific, or the local aspects of Jesus' words and those of the apostles, but in the universal; and a dogmatics which rests only on the results of grammatical-historical exegesis will not satisfy a philosophizing theologian'.[28] Biblical theology is only achieved, then, when it is accompanied by a 'philosophical operation'. It is quite appropriate that Gabler called himself a 'Christian rationalist'.[29] (Klaus Leder prefers to call Gabler a 'late neologist',[30] to emphasize his opposition to mere rationalism, supernaturalism and idealism. For Gabler, God is an object, not merely a regulatory idea.)

It is interesting that Gabler was neither the only nor the first to use the term 'pure' to describe biblical theology, properly so called. One of the earliest uses of this term is in Immanuel Kant's *Der Streit der Fakultäten*, which was first written in 1793 and published in 1798.[31] Gabler seems to have adopted this terminology in 1802, and used it from that point forward, principally to sharpen and defend the points he made in his earlier *Antrittsrede*.[32] While the defense Gabler mounts is directly against Kant, and precisely against Kant's hermeneutics, it is impossible for me to say whether either of them used the term 'pure biblical theology' with reference to the other. Since, however, Gabler had obviously read Kant carefully, and since Gabler enjoyed a considerable reputation as a theologian, it is plausible to conjecture that this term was used polemically to focus the debate between them.

Kant speaks of 'pure (*reinen* [*purus*, *putus*]) biblical theology' in an ironical sense. More properly, he speaks of a pure biblical theologian as one who is 'not yet infected with the disreputable free spirit of reason and philosophy.'[33] This pure biblical theologian presupposes the factuality of revelation, and this presupposition is grounded immediately in a consciousness of the divinity of Scripture. A pure biblical theologian gives up any attempt to understand biblical theology or its tasks in relation to universal human reason[34] and thus possesses, even as a scholar, an 'immature faith'.[35] Kant did not contest that pure biblical theology is scholarly; he wanted merely to point out that this scholarship is done under the authority and legislative control of the *Volkskirche*, and that the pure biblical theologian is 'properly a scribe for the faith of the church'.[36]

It is clear that this understanding of pure biblical theology is the opposite of Gabler's, in which biblical theology is properly engaged in philosophical criticism. Kant's irony was not intended to oppose the discipline of biblical theology, but merely to show that this discipline is to be kept distinct from that of philosophical inquiry, as he says explicitly in the preface to his *Religion within the Limits of Reason Alone*, published first in 1793.[37] There he argues that biblical theology and philosophy are both legitimate components of the university faculty, but that each has its own sphere and that the one should not be allowed to legislate the proper activity of the other. In Gabler's conception of biblical theology the disciplines are susceptible of unification, and this, thought Kant, would destroy the freedom of each. If theology is to follow the operations of philosophy it will have to give up its positivist conception of revelation and abide instead by the dictates of reason. This would have disastrous consequences for the church, and hence the state. If, on the other hand, philosophy is made a joint heir to the results of historical investigation of Scripture, its freedom is sacrificed. Thus, biblical theologians are to be trained in their own discipline, with, perhaps, a lecture in philosophy at the conclusion of their course of study.[38] Kant did not want biblical theologians in the university to be ignorant of philosophy; he just wanted them to be theologians and not philosophers.

Kant thus granted that there are, and must be for practical or pragmatic reasons, Scripture scholars whose subject matter is derived from and whose loyalty is owed to ecclesiastical authority. But he insisted that Scripture *interpretation* was also legitimate, and that such interpretation (as opposed to mere scholarship) was under obligation not to ecclesiastical authority or tradition, but to 'the universal practical rules of a religion of pure reason'.[39] While Scripture scholarship, of the kind engaged in by 'pure' biblical theologians in Kant's sense, is merely doctrinal, Scriptural interpretation is authentic and universally valid, in that it recognizes its responsibility to interpret Scripture according to its moral sense in agreement with the Spirit of true religion. Scripture, in other words, must be subjected to 'the rules and incentives of pure moral faith'.[40] If the literal sense of Scripture will not bear this subjection, Kant counsels us to engage in the kind of 'willful misreading' which the moral sense may require.[41]

It is at this point that Gabler and Kant are in disagreement, that is, at the point of hermeneutics. Gabler was not disposed to disagree with Kant on the necessity of a practically motivated interpretation of Scripture, but he believed that this necessity was well served by a 'grammatical-historical' interpretation whose results were elaborated by philosophical criticism. Gabler accused Kant of allegorical interpretation because he dismissed the historical sense of Scripture in favor of the moral. Kant would have agreed that allegorical interpretation is not appropriate for ecclesiastical uses of Scripture, but would have insisted that these uses, and the purposes they serve, are not legislative for free, philosophical investigation. Gabler was not willing to grant this division of hermeneutical labor, but suggested another: that interpretation be divided between philological and philosophical operations. These operations are not to be carried out in different social locations, as Kant suggested, but in sequence. This sequence is executed by the biblical theologian and consists, as we have seen, in the determination of the text's historical sense, followed by the determination of its philosophical meaning according to the criterion of reason.

Both Kant and Gabler believed that history had its pragmatic justification in the interpretation of Scripture. Kant found this justification in the needs of the churches, needs not present in the university. Gabler found his justification for historical interpretation of Scripture in the need for a Christian dogmatics which had its departure in Scripture, and the only valid rule he recognized was that of historical (and *then*) critical interpretation. But ultimately, neither for Kant nor for Gabler was history important. In Kant's case this is clear, but it is not the usual interpretation of Gabler. It is essential to recognize, however, that for Gabler the reason biblical theology must always be grounded in historical investigation is that this kind of investigation, followed by critical evaluation, provides us with the only reliable criterion for determining what is historical, and hence dispensable. These two steps correspond, as we have seen, to *Auslegung* and *Erklärung*, and the criterion for the latter is reason. Reason is, to be sure, in no essential contradiction with revelation, and any reasonable Christian will hence be a Christian rationalist.[42] History is essential, in sum, because it alone provides the grounds for its own transcendence.

IV

It is clear, then, that Gabler has no methodological disciples in the discipline of biblical theology. With the collapse of rationalist epistemology, to which Gabler was in large measure tied, and to the collapse of which Kant himself in large measure contributed, the possibility of Gabler's program was foreclosed. Kant ascribed to the human subject a constitutive role in the construction of the world which is the object of knowledge. His particular method was attacked by the idealists who succeeded him, but this epistemological innovation was at the same time the necessary condition for the philosophical revolution they carried out.[43] The German *Aufklärung* was characterized from the beginning by an interest in the simple and the practical, and in religion this meant an interest in religion rather than theology, and in earlier rather than later stages of religious development. Semler and Gabler both, we have seen, were concerned to unburden religion from the accretions of theological complexity, and in this they shared in the *Aufklärung*'s ideal.[44] But Gabler was at odds with the primitivism that characterized the historical interests of romantic idealism, since it was important for him that later, Christian writers had evolved more closely to the truth than had their Jewish predecessors—even though it was an *Uroffenbarung* toward which they were evolving.[45]

In any event, the Kantian 'Copernican revolution' provided the possibility for a philosophy in which the human subject, or mind, is situated historically and is both the subject and the object of knowledge. History can then be seen as the relation of mind to itself and becomes the object of vigorous philosophical activity; for if history is in some sense the relation of mind to itself, then it is also, in some sense, revelatory of mind. And of course if the mind (or spirit) of which we are speaking is Absolute, then history is revelation. Given this philosophical armament, romantic interest in the particularity of historical events, especially orginal historical events, is no innocent preoccupation, but is rather the proper concern of both religion and philosophy, and hence of theology.

What all this means is that, among other things, Gabler's proposed method for biblical theology is obsolete. It is obsolete for two reasons. On the one hand, Gabler made it the crowning task of biblical theology to derive from the historical study of the Bible those expressions which are timeless and universal, and to expose all other expressions as merely historical. The concern of romantic idealism is, however, for the historical and the particular. The atemporal universals toward which Gabler strove would have to be considered at best merely abstract speculations, and at the worst, ideological distortions.

On the other hand, Gabler had described the study of Scripture which precedes philosophical analysis as 'grammatical-historical' interpretation. The assumptions behind the use of this term are that (i) historical, interpretive work can be purely descriptive; (ii) philosophically grounded criticism occurs in a second, distinct stage. Neither of these assumptions endured beyond Gabler. It is impossible here, for more than one reason, to go into the several theological, philosophical and more particularly hermeneutical developments in the early nineteenth century, but it suffices to say that already in the theologies of G.L. Bauer and W.M.L. de Wette it was recognized that historical and interpretive work itself is necessarily critical, if it is valid, and that the two stages of biblical theology proposed by Gabler must be collapsed into one: a historical-critical investigation of Scripture.[46] Biblical theology in the twentieth century, from Schlatter to Stuhlmacher, and from Vatke to von Rad, G.E. Wright and Gese, is largely the product of such a 'collapse', and to that extent departs from the program outlined by Gabler.[47]

It is easy to see that Wilhelm Wrede stands as an heir to developments in Germany reaching back to Gabler's day. But it is more difficult now to see Wrede as carrying out with greater clarity what Gabler had initiated a century earlier. Indeed, Gabler would have agreed with Wrede that there is little point, and much unclarity, in calling the history of early Christianity 'biblical theology'. Wrede was of this opinion because he supposed that there was nothing to biblical theology beyond historical study. Gabler, we may be assured, would have contested any such claim, had he been in a position to understand it, because his interest in history was ultimately governed by an overriding interest in biblical and then dogmatic theology, and finally in the life of the church.[48] Wrede's question is, 'What can theology contribute to history?'[49] Gabler would have answered, as did Wrede, 'Nothing!' But he would have wondered why Wrede had put it in this uninteresting way, rather than posing the more helpful question, 'What can history contribute to theology?'

V

It is appropriate now to draw some conclusions regarding Gabler's contribution to our present task of situating the discipline of biblical theology. I hope that what has been said thus far has made clear the limited degree to which Gabler can be understood as the 'father' of contemporary biblical theology.[50] That does not mean, however, that Gabler cannot be instructive for us, in both positive and negative ways. It is important, I remarked earlier, to understand the reasons behind Gabler's proposals for biblical theology, if only because this understanding may help us to avoid arguing about issues which arise as answers to Gabler's questions, but not to ours.

One such issue, very high on the list of problems in biblical theology, is the relation of biblical to dogmatic or systematic theology. I would not argue that the relation of biblical to dogmatic theology is not properly a problem about which contemporary biblical theology should be concerned. It is striking, however, to what degree the contemporary discussion of this issue is dominated by the way Gabler set it up.[51] It is still considered to be crucial to point to some way in which biblical theology can relate the results of its work to the needs of the sytematic theologian. This problem is then seen to consist in the relation of contingent, historical conclusions to universal and necessary propositions of faith, raising in turn the specter of Lessing's broad and ugly ditch.[52]

Such an understanding of the issue is evident, in a slightly nuanced form, in recent works which bear on biblical theology. Brevard Childs, for example, in his *Introduction to the Old Testament as Scripture*, believes that the 'canonical intentionality' behind a text places the meaning of the text at some remove from its historical particularity and thus provides a 'platform' from which theologically interested exegesis can be launched.[53] In Second Isaiah, for example, this canonical intentionality is apparent in the way that these chapters, and by implication the remaining chapters of Isaiah, have lost their historical context, 'giving the material an almost purely theological shape'.[54] It is this 'non-historical framework', in which the prophetic message is 'severed from its historical moorings', which renders the message 'accessible to all future generations'.[55] I am not concerned here to debate the merits of Childs's proposals regarding the literature itself, but want rather to point out how closely his theological concerns mirror those of Gabler. The prevailing assumption is that to be theologically useful in the present the texts, or their assertions, must be removed so far as possible from the particularities of their own history, no matter how important that history may be for arriving at conclusions about 'canonical intentionality'.

Similarly, Edward Farley and Peter Hodgson argue for the collapse of 'the house of authority', in part because

> since the content of Christian scripture is authoritative only insofar as it is universalizable, contents appropriate *only* to specific social, cultic, or ethical situations cannot be accorded redemptive significance ... The ecclesial community, moreover, is nonethnic, universal and culturally pluralistic, so that purely ethnic, provincial and culturally relative elements of scripture cannot be authoritative.[56]

What is interesting in these quotations is their claim that while some portion of Christian Scripture is authoritative, namely that portion that is 'universalizable', another portion is not authoritative, namely that portion which is culturally relative, or whose contents are appropriate just to certain specific situations.

Farley and Hodgson differ from Childs on a whole range of issues, but their understanding of what must be accomplished before Scripture is theologically useful is strikingly similar, and both of these positions bear striking resemblances to that of Gabler. In all three cases the historically particular, or culturally relative, is theologically inferior to the general, the non-historical, the universalizable. Furthermore, in the case of Childs and Farley–Hodgson this position is not supported with arguments, much less with evidence that might support these arguments. Rather, it is apparently assumed to be self-evident that historically particular literature which addresses historically particular concerns is somehow unable to function authoritatively or theologically, and is in some important way rendered inaccessible to those beyond the historically particular situation that produced it.

This assumption is understandable when it is made by Gabler. He was operating on an understanding of the relation of historical particularity to the universal propositions of dogmatic theology according to which there is no way to the latter by way of the former. But things have changed in two hundred years, in two ways that are relevant here. In the first place, theology is no longer conceived as consisting in the unfolding of universal and necessary propositions, whether of reason or of revelation. Nor, for that matter, has the understanding of the relation of contingency to necessity—an understanding which is essential to Lessing's problem and Gabler's method—gone unrevised.[57] Theologically normative descriptions do not *have* to be distinguished from historically contingent descriptions in such a way that a broad ugly ditch separates them. In the second place, it is far from self-evident that Scripture's authority, or its theological usefulness, should be seen primarily in terms of its capacity for translation (or interpretation)[58] into a dogmatic, generalized or universalized idiom. I am not arguing that there should be no concern for a possible relationship between biblical and dogmatic theology; rather, I am suggesting that this relationship be construed in such a way that Scripture retains its theological usefulness without sacrificing its historical particularity. There is actually a variety of senses in which Scripture is, *de facto*, authoritative in the church,[59] and the theologically interested questions posed to Scripture will be guided by the particular sense in which Scripture's authority is being invoked. More importantly, it could be argued, since the church is the locus of the truth of faith, or its probative context,[60] the fundamental sense in which Scripture functions theologically is, as Stanley Hauerwas has put it, in rendering a community.[61] Scripture is theologically useful in the first instance, that is, not bcause it is porous to universally normative explanations, but because precisely in conversation with the historical particularity of its stories and prophecies and proverbs the church is able to sustain its identity as a worshipping, working, protesting community.

Understood in this way, biblical theology would relate its work not in the first instance to the task of systematic elaboration, but to the concrete life of the church. The biblical theologian and the systematic theologian would be seen not as involved in a transaction in which the biblical theologian transfers the results of her careful historical scholarship to someone who can generalize and contemporize them.[62] Rather, they would be seen as participating in different (but complementary) activities, each of which corresponds to a different need in the life of the church.[63] Biblical theology could then be seen more as an activity (helping the church to engage in critical reflection on its praxis through a self-critical reading of its canonical texts) rather than as a genre of literature (consisting of those books that bear such titles as 'Theology of the Old [or New] Testament'). Krister Stendahl describes this activity as the 'Public Health Department of biblical studies'.[64]

What I have tried to make clear in this section is that contemporary reflection on the theological appropriation of Scripture is still very much under the influence of Gabler's understanding of how that appropriation should take place. I have also tried to point out that certain contemporary understandings of the problem inherent in relating biblical to systematic or dogmatic theology depend on assumptions which Gabler had no way around, but which are not binding upon us. It is a problem we can get around not by finding a solution, but by ceasing to regard it as a problem.

VI

Our discussion of Gabler, undertaken as an aid to a consideration of the situation of contemporary biblical theology, appears to have reached only negative conclusions regarding his work. This impression can be corrected first of all by pointing to Gabler's importance in establishing the integrity of biblical theology as a discipline. I would like now to conclude this essay by pointing to two ways in which the discipline of biblical theology can take its cues from Gabler.

1. First of all, Gabler, as a proper theologian of the *Aufklärung*, was concerned with the practical nature of religion, and hence with theology's task of bringing itself into relation with Christian praxis.[65] The concern for theology's practical consequences is stated explicitly in Gabler's *Antrittsrede* and dominated all of his own theological work. This is a concern which biblical theology would do well to emulate. Contemporary discussions of biblical theology tend to cluster around the question of method: What set of assumptions and what exegetical operations are necessary and sufficient for a specifically theological understanding of the biblical materials? How, for example, are the operations of biblical theology to be distinguished from those of history of religions?[66] While I do not mean to deny the fruitfulness of these discussions, it does seem to me that there are more fundamental questions to be answered, namely, questions regarding the community in the interest of which biblical theology goes about its work.[67]

Any disciplined form of inquiry directed to textual or historical (or any other) phenomena presupposes a community of interest whose methods and procedures rest upon commonly held assumptions that have endured over time (a tradition); and the phenomena to which inquiry is directed are chosen, or perhaps shaped, on the basis of their relevance to that community.[68] This is normally stated in the neutral sense that rootage in communities of interest—academic disciplines, for example—provides one with the necessary expertise to carry out such inquiry, but that explanation is not sufficiently comprehensive. It does not take into account that (i) such communities determine what is to be inquired after and how such inquiry will proceed; (ii) there is no extra-community foundation which provides the ultimate and objective justification for such 'what' and 'how'. Justifications for the 'what' and the 'how' are normally given in the form of a narrative delineating the history of the discipline which includes an exposition of its procedures.

My suggestion is that the church constitutes a legitimate community, in the sense just described, in the interests of which biblical theologians go about their work. This does not mean that biblical theologians can proceed in their work without attention to exegetical and historical procedures developed by the various disciplines on which they draw and in which they may work, or that biblical theologians should not be at the forefront of rigorous exegetical and historical exposition. It simply means that insofar as they are biblical theologians, rather than, say historians of religion, the texts which are the focus of their concern and the specific shape this concern takes are given in their repsonsibility to the life of the church.[69] What is the life of the church? Churches engage in systematic thought about God, in prayer, in celebration, fellowship and liturgy, in self-conscious reflection on their own character and form, in action, in conflict with each other, in conflict resolution, in reflection on their relation to the state, in reflection on public policy and on social problems, in mission, in counseling and in protest. In these and other aspects of its life the church does, as it turns out, make constant use of Scripture as that collection of texts by which it confesses itself to be guided. Biblical theology, I am suggesting, has its disciplinary integrity in its responsibility for guarding, enabling and critiquing the church's self-conscious reflection on its praxis.

2. Secondly, Gabler (again as a theologian of the *Aufklärung*) was concerned with the task biblical theologians have to be responsible interpreters of the texts. This meant for Gabler, and I suggest it means for us, that hermeneutics is an essential component of that activity which characterizes biblical theology. It was primarily the hermeneutical work of people like Ernesti that provided the background for Gabler's approach to biblical theology, and it was over questions of hermeneutics that Gabler engaged in heated debate with Kant. It seems to me once again that in its hermeneutical reflections biblical theology has its disciplinary integrity in the community of interest to which it is responsible. This means that biblical theologians will choose their interpretive approaches not arbitrarily, but pragmatically.

Contemporary hermeneutical discussions in biblical studies are burdened with the assumption that the task of interpretation is to recover *the meaning* of a text.[70] But the meaning of a classical text varies almost infinitely according to the questions put to it, and there is no general theory of meaning that would tell us which questions yield such a text's *real* meaning. As Jeffrey Stout has put it:

> We say that such texts possess inexhaustible meaning. I would rather say that they never manage to exhaust our interest. We happily let interpretation go on forever... For any text can be described in potentially infinite ways, and its relations to broader

levels of context are always changing as history lengthens. Let us then celebrate the diversity of interpretations as a sign that our texts are interesting in more ways than one. The only alternative would be to have texts that weren't.[71]

The question we address to a text (our methods) are determined by our interests, and these are given in the communities and traditions in which our work is rooted. This does not make our reading of texts arbitrary or subjective, merely pragmatic. To quote Jeffrey Stout once more:

> Given some set of interests and purposes, the assessment of interpretive categories and specific readings relative to that set is as objective as can be. This relativity would be cause for worry only if interests and purposes were themselves beyond the pale of rational appraisal and critical revision . . . Most readings, therefore, can and should be judged according to relatively determinate intersubjective criteria—criteria that follow straightforwardly from the collective adoption of interests and purposes of a certain kind.[72]

The hermeneutical task of biblical theologians is then twofold. First, they are called upon to be critically self-conscious about the interests and purposes their interpretations are to serve, i.e. those interests and purposes of the church engaged in critical reflection on its praxis. Secondly, they are called upon to appraise various readings or interpretations of the texts in the light of those interests and purposes.[73]

One final note: I suggested earlier that biblical theology ought to be considered more an activity (of the sort just described) than a literary genre. This should not, of course, be taken to mean that those efforts to write theologies of one or the other or both Testaments are useless or illegitimate theologically. It does mean, however, that a 'Biblical Theology' should not be regarded as a point of mediation between the particularities of the texts and the generalities of dogmatics. It should be regarded, rather, as an introduction which places the texts within an interpretive structure. Biblical Theologies do not mediate between texts and systematic reflection; they introduce us to the particularities of the texts in a way that aids our understanding. Biblical Theologies will continue to be theologically instructive insofar as they lead us into the texts, rather than away from the texts to some higher order of generality, and insofar as they do not confuse us with claims to have found *the meaning* or the geometric *Mitte* of one or both Testaments.[74] As Gabler said, any theologian of merit must begin with the texts themselves. A Biblical Theology cannot spare us that effort.

My suggestion, then, is that in these two areas—in the relation of biblical theology to churchly practice, and to hermeneutics—we may legitimately claim Gabler as our 'father'.[75] And in these areas he has been a wise father indeed, if one not sufficiently revered.

NOTES

1. *Biblical Theology in Crisis* (Philadelphia: Westminster, 1970).

2. *The Flight from Authority: Religion, Morality and the Quest for Autonomy* (Revisions, 1; Notre Dame: University of Notre Dame, 1981) x-xi. Stout draws this definition from Theodore K. Rabb, *The Struggle for Stability in Early Modern Europe* (New York: Oxford University, 1975).

3. Walter Brueggemann claims to see a resolution in the direction of various polar relations in the Old Testament Theologies of Westermann, Hanson and Terrien ('A Convergence in Recent Old Testament Theologies', *JSOT* 18 [1980] 2-18). See, however, the comments of Brevard Childs, in 'Some Reflections on the Search for a Biblical Theology', *Horizons in Biblical Theology* 4 (1982) 1-12, esp. p. 9.

4. See most recently the historical survey by Rudolf Smend, 'Theologie im Alten Testament', *Verifikationen. Festschrift für Gerhard Ebeling* (ed. E. Jüngel, J. Wallmann and W. Werbeck; Tübingen: J.C.B. Mohr [Paul Siebeck], 1982) pp. 11-26. An earlier assessment of the issues is provided by Justus Köberle, 'Heilsgeschichtliche und religionsgeschichtliche Betrachtungsweise des Alten Testaments', *NKZ* 17 (1906) 200-22. The later debate between Eissfeldt and Eichrodt is well known.

5. Even Wilhelm Wrede acknowledged this. See his 'The Task and Methods of "New Testament Theology"' in Robert Morgan, *The Nature of New Testament Theology* (SBT, 2/25; London: SCM, 1973) 115. Wrede goes on to comment, however, 'That can be set aside as irrelevant to us' (p. 115).

6. Representative are the comments of Claus Westermann, that Gabler insisted on the understanding of biblical theology as a purely 'historical science' ('The Interpretation of the Old Testament: A Historical Introduction', *Essays on Old Testament Hermeneutics* [ed. Claus Westermann; Richmond: John Knox, 1963] 41, note 2), and Robert C. Dentan, that dogmatic theology is distinguished from biblical theology, in part, by its uses of philosophy (*Preface to Old Testament Theology* [rev. edn; New York: Seabury, 1963] 22). Gabler was at pains to argue precisely against these two characterizations of biblical theology, as we shall see below.

7. See the above-mentioned book by Stout [note 2] and Richard Rorty, *Philosophy and the Mirror of Nature* (Princeton: Princeton University, 1979).

8. On the antecedent and early history of biblical theology see especially Gerhard Ebeling, 'The Meaning of "Biblical Theology"', *Word and Faith* (Philadelphia: Fortress, 1963) 79-97; Hans-Joachim Kraus, *Die Biblische Theologie: Ihre Geschichte und Problematik* (Neukirchen-Vluyn: Neukirchener Verlag, 1970); Walther Zimmerli, 'Biblische Theologie 1: Altes Testament', *TRE* 6 (1980) 426-55.

9. An English translation of the major portion of the address is given in John H. Sandys-Wunsch and Laurence Eldredge, 'J.P. Gabler and the Distinction between Biblical and Dogmatic Theology: Translation, Commentary, and Discussion of his Originality', *SJT* 33 (1980) 133-58. The full address is given in German by Otto Merk, *Biblische Theologie des Neuen Testaments in ihrer Anfangszeit* (Marburger Theologische Studien, 9; Marburg: N.G. Elwert, 1972) 273-84. References here are to the translation by Sandys-Wunsch and Eldredge. Merk also provides extensive quotations from Gabler's other works which were, unfortunately, unavailable to me.

10. Otto Merk points out that there were others upon whom Gabler drew (*Biblische Theologie*, 31).

11. Sandys-Wunsch and Eldredge, 'J.P. Gabler', 140-43.

12. The influence of Heyne and Eichhorn is discussed by Merk (*Biblische Theologie*, esp. pp. 45-81). See also Rudolf Smend, 'Johann Philipp Gablers Begründung der biblischen Theologie', *EvT* 22 (1962) pp. 345-57.

13. These developments are traced by Morgan, *New Testament Theology*, 2-12, and H.-J. Kraus, *Biblische Theologie*, 160-66.

14. Morgan, *New Testament Theology*, 68.

15. *Ibid.*, 73-84.

16. *Ibid.*, 69.

17. See, for example, James M. Robinson, 'The Future of New Testament Theology', *Hermeneutics and the Worldliness of Faith: A Festschrift in Memory of Carl Michalson* (ed. C. Courtney, O.M. Ivey and G.E. Michalson; *The Drew Gateway* 45 [1974-75]) 175-87. The importance of Wrede is particularly noted by Rudolf Bultmann in his *Theology of the New Testament* (2 vols.; New York: Scribner's 1951-55), II, 245-47.

18. See especially Gerhard Ebeling, 'Schrift und Erfahrung als Quelle theologischer Aussagen', *ZTK* 75 (1978) 99-116; 'Dogmatik und Exegese', *ZTK* 77 (1980) 269-86; Peter Stuhlmacher, 'Exegese und Erfahrung', *Verifikationen* [see note 4] 67-89; Christian Link, 'In welchem Sinne sind theologische Aussagen wahr?', *EvT* 42 (1982) 518-40.

19. James Barr has attacked the emphasis on canon, most recently in *Holy Scripture: Canon, Authority, Criticism* (Philadelphia: Westminster, 1983). His attack (directed primarily, it seems, at Childs) is hardly convincing, and seems strangely biblicistic: the people of the biblical period didn't assign theological importance to a canon so we shouldn't either. See also Edward Farley, *Ecclesial Reflection* (Philadelphia: Fortress, 1982). Since Farley's

definition of canon (e.g. p. 273) is not one held by any critical biblical theologian, his argument against the notion of canon loses much of its force. By saying that biblical theology should feel itself restricted in some important sense to the parameters of the canon, I mean only to claim that biblical theology has to do, analytically, with Scripture, the definition of which is a canon's function. What Farley proposes as the function of the Kerygma (his term for the reduction of Scripture; pp. 272-78) is precisely that described by Jonathan Z. Smith as the function, in various religions, of a canon. See below, note 22.

20. Wolfhart Pannenberg, *Theology and the Philosophy of Science* (Philadelphia: Westminster, 1976).

21. See, for example, Ulrich Luz, 'Erwägungen zur sachgemässen Interpretation neutestamentlicher Texte', *EvT* 42 (1982) 493-519.

22. Alfred Jepsen, for example, takes the canon as merely a 'historical phenomenon', and 'Old Testament science, consequently, has to do with the study of this part of the Christian canon' ('The Scientific Study of the Old Testament', *Old Testament Hermeneutics*, 250). History of religions cannot legitimately restrict itself to the canon, insofar as it wishes to study the history of Israel's religion. First, there are no historical warrants for such a limitation to a theologically governed selection. Second, such a limitation would provide an inaccurate portrayal of Israel's religion—namely, one which was illegitimately biased in favor of those groups who prevailed in the intra-Israelite religious debates. The canon is a legitimate object of history of religions research, of course, when that research is directed to something other than, in this instance, the history of Israel's religion in the biblical period. See Jonathan Z. Smith, 'Sacred Persistence: Toward a Redescription of Canon', *Imagining Religion: From Babylon to Jonestown* (Chicago: University of Chicago, 1982) 36-52: 'I have come to believe that a prime object of study for the historian of religion ought to be theological tradition, taking the term in its widest sense, in particular, those elements of the theological endeavor that are concerned with canon and its exegesis' (p. 43). Smith goes on to 'reflect . . . on the notion of canon as a way of exploring the proposition that sacrality persists insofar as there are communities which are persistent in applying their limited body of tradition; that sacred persistence . . . is primarily exegesis . . .' (p. 44). Biblical theologians, it sems to me, are interested in applying their (in historical terms) arbitrarily limited traditions exegetically in the interest of sacred persistence. They are, in Smith's terms, the objects of history of religions inquiry, not merely its practitioners.

23. Smend, 'Gablers Begründung', 345. Smend's comment is noted in Professor Anderson's presidential address to the SBL, 'Tradition and Scripture in the Community of Faith', *JBL* 100 (1981) 5-21. The reference is on p. 6.

24. Merk, *Biblische Theologie*, esp. pp. 69-81.

25. Gabler makes reference to Ernesti already in the *Antrittsrede*. Ernesti's

most influential work, *Institutio interpretis Novi Testamenti* (1809), was translated into English by Moses Stuart as *Elements of Interpretation* (Andover: Mark Newton, 1827). In fact, Ernesti may have anticipated Gabler's own distinction between biblical and dogmatic theology. See Pannenberg, *Theology and the Philosophy of Science*, 372-73.

26. Merk, *Biblische Theologie*, 96.

27. *Ibid.*, 95.

28. *Ibid.*, 96.

29. *Ibid.*, 105 note 11.

30. Klaus Leder, *Universität Altdorf: Zur Theologie der Aufklärung in Franken* (Nürnberg: Lorenz Spindler, 1965) 273.

31. The relevant portions of this document are reprinted with commentary in Karl-Heinz Crumbach, *Theologie in kritischer Öffentlichkeit: Die Frage Kants an das kirchliche Christentum* (Gesellschaft und Theologie, Systematische Beiträge, 21; München: C. Kaiser, 1977) 43-59.

32. Merk, *Biblische Theologie*, 97.

33. Crumbach, *Theologie*, 44. Karl Barth noted the importance of Kant's comments, perhaps, as Crumbach suggests, without appreciating the depth of Kant's irony (Crumbach, *Theologie*, 57-58; Barth, *Protestant Theology in the Nineteenth Century* [Valley Forge: Judson, 1973], 278-80).

34. Crumbach, *Theologie*, 46.

35. *Ibid.*, 52.

36. *Ibid.*, 63.

37. Immanuel Kant, *Religion within the Limits of Reason Alone* (New York: Harper & Brothers, 1960).

38. *Ibid.*, 9-10. Indeed, Kant proposed his own book as the most fitting such 'lecture'.

39. *Ibid.*, 100.

40. *Ibid.*, 103.

41. The term is that of Harold Bloom, though I do not presume that Bloom was influenced by Kant to use it (see Frank Lentricchia, *After the New Criticism* [Chicago: University of Chicago, 1980] 325).

42. Merk, *Biblische Theologie*, p. 105.

43. See, for example, Garbis Kortian, *Metacritique: The Philosophical Argument of Jürgen Habermas* (Cambridge: Cambridge University, 1980), and the Introduction to this work by Alan Montefiore and Charles Taylor.

44. The relations among Enlightenment, *Aufklärung* and romantic idealism are set out in exemplary fashion by Paul C. Hayner, *Reason and Existence: Schelling's Philosphy of History* (Leiden: E.J. Brill, 1967) 1-33.

45. Actually, the contrast between the two is not so great, since in both Gabler and romanticism Christ is seen as restoring something lost between religion's beginning and the first century of this era. Judaism does not fare well in either case.

46. On Bauer see especially Merk, *Biblische Theologie*. A superb treatment of de Wette and his intellectual milieu is offered by Rudolf Smend in several works: *Wilhelm Martin Leberecht de Wettes Arbeit am Alten und am Neuen Testament* (Basel: Helbing and Lichtenhahn, 1958); 'De Wette und das Verhältnis zwischen historischer Bibelkritik und philosophischem System im 19. Jahrhunder', *TZ* 14 (1958) 107-19; 'Universalismus und Partikularismus in der alttestamentlichen Theologie des 19. Jahrhunderts', *EvT* 22 (1962) 169-79. See also Klaus Reinhardt, *Der dogmatische Schriftgebrauch* (München: Ferdinand Schöningh, 1970) 55-63.

47. This is not to underestimate the considerable differences among those named, but to emphasize that for each of them a study of history itself assumes theological importance in a way that it could not for Eichhorn or Gabler. It should also be mentioned that this is not to be taken, necessarily, as a criticism.

48. Klaus Leder points out that Gabler saw his highest academic calling as the preparation of students for preaching (*Universität Altdorf*, 281-82). In the light of Gabler's insistence on the church's confessions as indispensable (*ibid.*, 273, 282), it is curious that Marten Woudstra chastizes him for being anti-confessional ('The Old Testament in Biblical Theology and Dogmatics', *Calvin Theological Journal* 18 [1983] 47-60, esp. pp. 50-52).

49. Morgan, *New Testament Theology*, 69. This is a paraphrase of Wrede, who asked, 'What can dogmatics offer' New Testament theology, since the latter is merely the history of early Christianity?

50. See Sandys-Wunsch and Eldredge, 'J.P. Gabler', 157-58.

51. This is not to say that Gabler was the only one to pose the question in this way, or that contemporary contributors to the discussion have necessarily read Gabler. It is only to say that Gabler's way of posing the question has its parallels in the present, even though the assumptions which provoked it have long since perished.

52. See above, note 21.

53. Childs, *Introduction*, 79, 83.

54. *Ibid.*, 326.

55. *Ibid.*, 337.

56. Edward Farley and Peter C. Hodgson, 'Scripture and Tradition', *Christian Theology: An Introduction to its Traditions and Tasks* (ed. Peter C. Hodgson and Robert H. King; Philadelphia: Fortress, 1982) 35-61. The quotations are from pp. 42 and 49. A fuller exposition of this approach is found in Farley's *Ecclesial Reflection*.

57. The most recent discussion is in Gordon E. Michalson, 'Theology, Historical Knowledge, and the Contingency–Necessity Distinction', *International Journal for Philosophy of Religion* 14 (1983) 87-98. The argument that there are, logically considered, only historically contingent propositions, not necessary ones, does not entail a judgment in favor of the unbridgeable chasm of Lessing. On the contrary, if there are no incorrigible propositions,

the fact that we are left with only corrigible ones is unproblematic. If there is no chasm, the lack of a bridge is not worrisome.

58. David Kelsey argues that such 'translation' is actually something else, namely, redescription (*The Uses of Scripture in Recent Theology* [Philadelphia: Fortress, 1975] 182-92). Recent semanticists argue that even 'translation' from one language to another is not translation, but interpretation (see Graham MacDonald and Philip Pettit, *Semantics and Social Science* [London: Routledge & Kegan Paul, 1981] 1-13). This does not contradict Kelsey's point, however.

59. This point is made well by Robert W. Jenson, 'On the Problem(s) of Scriptural Authority', *Int* 31 (1977) 237-50.

60. Cf. Christian Link, 'Theologische Aussagen' [above, note 18], 518-19; Christian Walther, 'Ein Plädoyer für die Vernunft des Glaubens', *Lutherische Monatshefte* 22/6 (1983) 246-48; Nicholas Lash, 'Ideology, Metaphor and Analogy', *The Philosophical Frontiers of Christian Theology: Essays Presented to D.M. MacKinnon* (ed. B. Hebblethwaite and S. Sutherland; Cambridge: Cambridge University, 1982) 68-94. The church is the probative context for the truth-claims of faith, because it is in the church's praxis that these truth-claims find what Lash calls their 'practical verification' (p. 87). This does not mean, for Lash or for me, that the truth-claims of faith are not exposed to various forms of citicism.

61. Stanley Hauerwas, 'The Moral Authority of Scripture: The Politics and Ethics of Remembering', *A Communty of Character: Toward a Constructive Christian Social Ethic* (Notre Dame: University of Notre Dame, 1981) 53-71, esp. p. 71.

62. Similarly Robert B. Laurin, 'Introduction', *Contemporary Old Testament Theologians* (ed. R.B. Laurin; Valley Forge: Judson, 1970) 19.

63. 'Hence theology as biblical theology is the question of the basis, as practical theology the question of the goal and as dogmatic theology the question of the content of the distinctive utterance of the church' (Karl Barth, *Church Dogmatics* 1/1 [2nd edn; Edinburgh: T. & T. Clark, 1975] 4-5). Barth speaks of this as the 'question of truth in its threefold form' which the church puts to itself in the form of a self-examination, falling 'into three circles which intersect in such a way that the centre of each is also within the circumference of the other two . . .'

64. 'Ancient Scripture in the Modern World', *Scripture in the Jewish and Christian Traditions: Authority, Interpretation, Relevance* (ed. F.E. Greenspahn; Nashville: Abingdon, 1982), esp. p. 205. Of course, there is no principled reason why biblical theologians should be interested *only* in the church's use of Scripture. Any actual theological, moral or religious use would be of potential interest, no matter where it took place. As it happens, these sorts of uses do take place most characteristically in the church. One could even say it is an essential part of what 'church' consists in.

65. See especially Klaus Scholder, 'Grundzüge der theologischen Aufklärung in Deutschland', *Geist und Geschichte der Reformation: Festgabe Hanns Rückert* (ed. H. Liebing and K. Scholder; Berlin: Walter de Gruyter, 1966) 460-86, esp. pp. 464-68.

66. Cf. Josef Pietron, *Geistige Schriftauslegung und biblische Predigt* (Düsseldorf: Patmos, 1979) 179-85. For Pannenberg, of course, no such question need arise, since history of religions study of biblical texts is an 'enquiry ... about the ability of the texts to show ... that the content of their religious message is the all-determining reality', by which he means God (*Theology and the Philosophy of Science*, 380).

67. These questions are fundamental however they are answered, because the answers will determine everything else. It is not sufficient to argue, as is sometimes done, that the literature—Scripture—itself demands a particular approach by virtue of its character. Its character will vary according to the historically particular community which is interested in it. One cannot argue against Wrede, for example, that the texts demand different questions from those he asked. We just say that the questions Wrede asked aren't the (only) ones that interest us. Hilary Putnam speaks in this connection of the 'interest-relativity of explanation' (*Meaning and the Moral Sciences* [London: Routledge & Kegan Paul, 1978] 41-45).

68. See, for example, Max Weber, *The Methodology of the Social Sciences* (ed. E.A. Shils and H.A. Finch; Glencoe: The Free Press, 1949) 80-81. Culture, according to Weber, is the conferral of significance upon otherwise meaningless constellations of reality, and hence the value-relatedness of a phenomenon, as determined by its empirically discernible significance within a culture, establishes it as a subject for research for social science. Not just culture but the social scientific community with its traditions confers such value-relatedness. See further Alisdair MacIntyre, 'Epistemological Crises, Dramatic Narrative and the Philosophy of Science', *The Monist* 60 (1977) 453-72; Nelson Goodman, *Ways of Worldmaking* (Indianapolis: Hackett, 1978).

69. Paul D. Hanson, 'The Responsibility of Biblical Theology to Communities of Faith', *TToday* 37 (1980) 39-50; Patrick Henry, 'The Plate Tectonics of New Testament Study,' *TToday* 37 (1980) 51-58; esp. pp. 57-58. In his contribution to the Michalson *Festschrift* Professor Anderson worries about the lack of a definition of 'church' in the proposals of Brevard Childs, especially since there is not just *one* church ('The New Crisis in Biblical Theology', *Hermeneutics and the Worldliness of Faith*, 159-64, esp. p. 168). But since the activity of a biblical theologian, as I am proposing, will vary according to differing understandings of the church and its mission, it would serve no purpose (even if it were possible) to set out in advance how 'church' must be defined. Certainly one of the crucial tasks of biblical theology is to bring to self-consciousness, and expose to critical readings of the texts, any community of faith's understanding of itself. One could argue that biblical

theology should not be defined in such parochial terms, but should rather serve a broader, public function. See Gordon Kaufman, *The Theological Imagination: Constructing the Concept of God* (Philadelphia: Westminster, 1981) 123-56. I share the desire to bring theology and Scripture to bear on the wider culture. It seems to me, however, that this is done more effectively (and more Christianly) by communities critically engaged with their traditions, than by attempts to work out a public apologetic for a theistic culture.

70.   Jeffrey Stout, 'What is the Meaning of a Text?', *New Literary History* 14 (1982-83) 1-12. I am very grateful to Professor Stout for making a copy of this article available to me.

71.   *Ibid.*, 8.

72.   *Ibid.*

73.   Nicholas Lash wonders whether, ' . . . if the tensions between practice and reflection are frequently destructive, rather than creative, this is partly because exegetes and historians have sometimes been invited to establish the grounds of belief, rather than critically to reflect on its past and present performance' ('Ideology, Metaphor and Analogy', 76).

74.   One might say that reading the texts is a far more important churchly activity than explaining them, or deriving propositions (or principles) from them. 'However important and even crucial it may be to formulate dogmatic and doctrinal clarifications which counter mistaken interpretations, it is the stories themselves which bear and retain the primary *and distinctive* level of meaning' (Frederick Crosson, 'Religion and Faith in St Augustine's *Confessions*', *Rationality and Religious Belief* [ed. C.F. Delaney; Notre Dame: University of Notre Dame, 1979] 166). See also Matthew Lamb, *Solidarity with Victims: Toward a Theology of Social Transformation* (New York: Crossroad, 1982) 103.

75.   Hans-Georg Gadamer has argued that hemeneutics and praxis are not to be distinguished: 'Hermeneutics and Social Science', *Cultural Hermeneutics* 2 (1974-75) 307-16; 'Hermeneutics as Practical Philosophy', *Reason in the Age of Science* (Cambridge, Mass.: MIT, 1981) 88-112. Note especially the comments of Richard J. Bernstein in his evaluation of Gadamer: 'If we follow out the logic of Gadamer's own line of thought . . . , then this demands that we turn our attention to the question of how can we nurture and foster the types of community required for the exercise of *phronesis* [practical wisdom]' ('From Hermeneutics to Praxis,' *Review of Metaphysics* 35 [1982] 823-45, quoting from pp. 840-41). This kind of nurturing, fostering and exercise I am proposing as central tasks for biblical theology.

3

THE SONG OF SONGS:
CRITICAL BIBLICAL SCHOLARSHIP
VIS-À-VIS EXEGETICAL TRADITIONS[1]

Roland E. Murphy, O.Carm.

By critical biblical scholarship is meant the use of historical-critical methodology in the analysis of the biblical text. This has been the dominant approach in the last two centuries, and seemingly has no apology to make. It has been enormously successful in illustrating such basic questions as vocabulary, historical background, the thought-world of the ancient Near East, literary criticism, etc. It has achieved what was simply impossible for previous generations. Hence it might appear that the history of exegesis must necessarily have little to offer to the professional exegete. His questions were not raised by his forebears. On the other hand, perhaps other questions deserve to be asked. In that case the history of exegesis presents us with a wide range of different questions and solutions that can stimulate modern exegesis. The colorful history of the interpretation of the Song of Solomon provides us with a test case in which we can contrast, weigh, and perhaps unite the contributions of past and present.

Recently a stout resistance has been mounted against the historical-critical approach to the Bible.[2] This has been done by scholars—not merely by those who fail to understand what it is they are rebelling against. The 'revolt' does not attack critical methodology on its own grounds in such a way as to accuse it of erroneous moves. Basically there is question of complaint rather than indictment. Moderns are seeking results that go beyond those available to the historical-critical approach. While the methodology has been productive of solid results, it is well for all to recognize its limitations.[3]

The first observation has an ironical edge. The very sense of the historicality which is at the heart of the approach makes one realize that it, too, is time-conditioned—as conditioned as the literature which it has studied and shown to be so deeply imbedded in the thought-world of antiquity. Historical-critical methodology is a creation of modern civilization, and it does not escape the limitations of its birth in a period that exalts historical positivism. There is no going back from this appreciation of our human historicality, but there is an uneasiness. How deeply are we immured in our own preferred methodology? Can we realize that it does not yield the ultimate in literary interpretation, that the questions it asks of the text are inevitably questions that arise from our own culture?

Second, the goal of critical scholarship remains an ideal that can be only approximated, never quite attained. This goal is the discovery of the original meaning of the text. The scholar aspires to neutrality and objectivity, but it is admittedly impossible to strip oneself of certain presuppositions.[4] The very approach to the text is dictated by twentieth-century concerns. As for the text, what does 'original meaning' mean when scholarship has demonstrated the ongoing process of tradition and reinterpretation within the text itself?[5] The issue has become terribly complicated: the 'original meaning' for what era, in what layer of tradition? Hypothesis builds upon hypothesis in the process of reaching into a text which turns out to have multiple meanings.

Third, there is the magnitude of the interpretive process in current biblical scholarship. It calls for skills in languages and linguistics, archaeology and geography, history and literary analysis, etc. How can all this be united and focussed in the interpretive process? Even if the burden is shared, the whole tends to make biblical interpretation a closed enterprise carried on by a caste. The Bible is removed from the people to academe, and only the 'expert' has the chance of being a correct interpreter. The result inevitably is that one is given the meaning of a text 'back then', with the attendant risk implicit in historical reconstruction.

Moreover, this leads to a study of a Bible that never existed. It is not the Bible as it was published, but as it is constructed, that frequently emerges from critical scholarship. There is no denying the gains that have been nade in our knowledge of the genesis of the Pentateuch from its various antecedent traditions. But too often one is left with only the pre-history of the text. This becomes the focus of intepretation, despite the recent emphasis on *Redaktionsgeschichte*.

It may seem unfair to point out limitations of critical methodology and not those of other approaches. But the weakness and mistakes of 'pre-critical' approaches, from Origen down to modern times, have been frequently exposed in the history of biblical interpretation. Presumably we have learned something from the shortcomings and erroneous directions of the past. The point here, however, is not a blithe return to the past but a critical assessment of the present situation, to discern possible moves that a modern interpreter can make in the light of the exegetical traditions of the past.

Despite the limitations which have just been described, biblical scholarship has achieved solid success in its analysis of the Song of Songs. There is today an almost unanimous consensus that the Song deals with sexual love between human beings. It is composed of love poems which can be compared with the love poetry of ancient Egypt and other cultures. They touch on the topoi common to all love settings: presence and absence, yearning, admiration, teasing, the subtleties of sexual relationship. It is of less importance that there remain several disputed questions: the precise literary genre of the work, the number of characters involved, the indebtedness of the imagery to previous cultic ritual, etc. The theological implications of the critical understanding of the Song are many and important for a community that honors the Bible.

Technical scholarship has been less successful with the question of the unity of the work as a canonical book. There is a theological issue here that is not easy to recover. What was the intention of the author(s) or editor(s) in putting the book forth, and what was the understanding of the community that received the book as canonical? We have no firm historical evidence to give answer to these questions. The oldest consistent Jewish tradition interpreted the book as dealing with the Lord and Israel; but it is also possible that the book was assembled by the sages who recognized in it an important testimony to the value of the relationship between man and woman (after all, the authorship of the book is attributed by the editor to Solomon the wise). Since we cannot point to any one factor as the cause of canonization, neither can we allege a dominant interpretation from the very beginning.

The understanding of the Song in the light of modern scholarship is clearly a gain, because past interpreters glossed over the human dimension in the Song. Now the community of faith can respond to a level of meaning that deals directly with human love, the mutual fidelity between love and beloved, and the strength of the love that unites them. It is no exaggeration to say that we owe this understanding of the Song to the efforts of critical scholarship.

It may appear hazardous, then, to expect that the history of exegesis will offer the modern reader another perspective equally important—all the more so in view of the characterization of this history as a 'sorrowful history', which has been likened to an 'armoire of oddities'.[6] These judgments are exaggerated. In principle, a fairly consistent picture emerges from the history of exegesis of the Song and thus it is a fitting choice for our purpose. This is not the place to try even to summarize the history of interpretation of the Song.[7] We can say that the traditional interpretation is very old, and it is basically the same for both the Jewish and Christian communities which accepted the work as canonical. Judaism understood the work to refer to the love relationship between the Lord and his people, Israel. Christianity recognized this, but extended this point of view into the New Testament perspective: the love relationship between God (Christ) and his people, the Church. Since the love relationship can be individualized, the Song was applied to God and the individual soul, and this gave rise to the development of the so-called mystical interpretation, beginning as far back as Origen. Deriving from this approach is the mariological interpretation which was given great impetus in the medieval period by Rupert of Deutz (d. 1129).[8] The point to be insisted upon is the basic unity of the interpretation throughout the history of Judaism and Christianity: the Song deals with the love of God for his people, and vice versa.

I deliberately avoid the term, 'allegorical', to denote the traditional view. The exegetical tradition of the past did make use of allegory as a means of explicating the text. But this methodological tool is not essential to the basic insight. In fact, it is really not a suitable means of interpreting the Song. We owe this recognition to critical scholarship, which has shown that the Song is not written as an allegory and therefore need not be interpreted as one. Allegories there may be in the Bible, but the Song is not one of them. This means that the meticulous correspondence between the terms in the Song and another reality is out of order.[9]

The allegorical method is not essential to the view that understands the Song in the light of the relationship between God and his people, any more than the story of the Prodigal Son needs to be interpreted allegorically in order to understand the Father's love for his children. One must distinguish between a literary work that is written as allegory (perhaps Eccl 12.4-5), and hence is to be so interpreted, and an allegorical reading of a work that was not written *as* allegory. The allegorical reading may well turn out to be an inadequate tool, but this does not militate against the basic interpretation which it tries to serve.

How can the traditional understanding of the Song be justified as an interpretation both reasonable and even convincing to the modern reader? Two points deserve consideration here.

1. The first is the fact that any text comes to have more meaning that the literal historical sense given to it by the author(s). This is true of all literary texts, and the Bible is no exception. The text comes to have a life of its own within the community that preserves it, and thus it acquires a surplus meaning. This is an inevitable hermeneutical process; as time passes, new horizons emerge. Both hermeneutical theory and the history of interpretation reckon responsibly with this fact. Hence one may not simply dismiss past exegetical traditions as 'precritical' and invalidated by the superiority of the historical-critical approach.[10] This does not mean that the vagaries in the history of the exegesis of the Song need be accepted. Rather, the basic insight that the Song also refers to God and people remains at the center of this issue.

2. The surplus meaning of the Song, or of any piece of literature, can be defended by modern hermeneutical theory, but this would require extensive development.[11] It is more interesting and important here to review the tools of critical historical scholarship which suggest the validity of a surplus meaning for the Song.

The first consideration is a biblical datum clearly recognized in current scholarship: the symbolism of sex in the Bible. The use of the sexual theme to describe the covenant love between the Lord and Israel is so very well known as to need no further comment (cf. Hos 1–3; Isa 62.5; etc.). It was used both negatively, to condemn Israel's infidelity, and positively, to remind her of her calling. The sexual experience was polyvalent for ancient Israel. It spoke of divine as well as human reality. This point is not meant to prove that the surplus meaning was intended by the original author(s) of the Song (else, how could it be surplus?). Rather, the subject itself, human love, had the intrinsic potential of expressing divine love.

Moreover, the Song itself seems to provide some support for this point of view. Canticles 8.6 speaks of the power of love. It is as strong as Death/Sheol, the personified enemy of human existence, according to the view of the psalmists (49.5-6; 89.49; etc.). Just as Death pursues every living being, so the lover pursues the beloved. Love is further characterized as *šalhebetyāh*; 'a flame of Yah' is its flame. The interpretation of this word is difficult. Some would consider it merely a superlative, a mighty flame, on the analogy of a giant tree being called 'cedars of God' (Ps 8.11).[12] But it is also possible that the function of *-yāh* (= Yahweh) is to indicate that human love is somehow related to divine love. It shares in the divine power and ardor. One may not be able to prove that this association was intended by the historical author. But the text remains open to this interpretation, and on the level of historical-critical methodology.

The title of this essay is not meant to suggest an adversary relationship. The modern interpreter cannot do without historical-critical methodology. Negatively, it serves to cut away what is arbitrary in the traditional interpretation, such as the use of inappropriate allegory. Positively, it lays down the lines along which the original meaning can be apprehended and extended into another level of meaning. This is not an either/or situation. Pride of place may be given to one meaning over the other. The literal historical meaning, where it can be reached, is normative and hence determinative in assessing the various levels of meaning in a literary work. The traditional understanding of the Song complements the literal historical sense by extending it along certain paths which, as we have seen, can themselves be illumined by means of modern scholarship.

NOTES

1. In honouring Professor Anderson, the present essay intends a modest contribution to the 'communal context' about which Professor Anderson has written in 'The Problem and Promise of Commentary', *Int* 36 (1982) 341-55. The first draft of this paper was presented at the 'History of Exegesis Consultation' at the annual meeting of the Society of Biblical Literature in San Francisco, December 19, 1981.

2. Among others one might mention W. Wink, *The Bible in Human Transformation* (Philadelphia: Fortress, 1973); P. Stuhlmacher, *Historical Criticism and Theological Interpretation of Scripture* (Philadelphia: Fortress, 1977). Concern has been expressed also by historians; cf. Wilfred Cantwell Smith, 'The Study of Religion and the Study of the Bible', *JAAR* 39 (1971) 131-40; David Steinmetz, 'The Superiority of Pre-Critical Exegesis', *Today* 37 (1980-81) 27-38. See also the balanced judgment of R.E. Brown, *The Critical Meaning of the Bible* (New York: Paulist, 1981), esp. pp. 23-44.

3. Cf. W. Vogels, 'Les limites de la méthode historico-critique', *Laval Philosophique et Théologique* 36 (1980) 173-94; see P. Stuhlmacher, *Historical*

Criticism, 62-63, on the 'functionalism' of historical criticism.

4. This very stance is questioned in modern hermeneutical theory; cf. S.M. Schneiders, 'Faith, Hermeneutics, and the Literal Sense of Scripture', *TS* 39 (1978) 719-36, esp pp. 730-35.

5. Cf. S. Brown, 'Exegesis and Imagination', *TS* 41 (1980) 745-51.

6. K. Budde uses the phrase, 'Leidensgeschichte', quoting S. Oettli, in 'Das Hohelied' in *Die Fünf Megillot* (KHCAT, 17; Freiburg: Mohr/Siebeck, 1898) xi. D. Lerch uses the word 'Raritätenkabinett' in 'Hoheslied', *RGG*[3], III (1959) col. 431.

7. There is an extensive summary in M. Pope, *Song of Songs* (AB, 7C; New York: Doubleday, 1977) 89-229. See also George L. Scheper, *The Spiritual Marriage: The Exegetic History and Literary Impact of the Song of Songs in the Middle Ages* (Princeton University dissertation, 1971); R.E. Murphy, 'Patristic and Medieval Exegesis—Help or Hindrance?', *CBQ* 43 (1981) 505-16.

8. A mariological understanding is found in isolated sources, such as Jerome and especially Ambrose, but it is Rupert who gave impetus to this interpretation. For the medieval period see F. Ohly, *Hohelied-Studien. Grundzüge einer Geschichte der Hohenliedauslegung des Abendlandes bis zum 1200* (Wiesbaden: Steiner, 1958); H. Riedlinger, *Die Makellosigkeit der Kirche in den lateinischen Hoheliedkommentaren des Mittelalters* (Münster: Aschendorf, 1958).

9. For details concerning such correspondence, see the commentary of A. Robert, *Le Cantique des Cantiques* (Paris: Gabalda, 1963).

10. Cf. David C, Steinmetz, 'John Calvin on Isaiah 6', *Int* 36 (1982) 156-70: 'The principal value of precritical exegesis is that it is not modern exegesis; it is alien, strange, sometimes even, from our perspective, comic and fantastical. Precisely because it is strange, it provides a constant stimulus to modern interpreters, offering exegetical suggestions they would never think of themselves or find in any recent book, forcing them again and again to a rereading and re-evaluation of the text. Interpreters who immerse themselves, however, not only in the text but in these alien approaches to he text may find in time that they have learned to see, with eyes not their own, sights they could scarcely have imagined and to hear, with ears not their own, voices too soft for their own ears to detect' (p. 170).

11. See, for example, P. Ricoeur, *Essays on Biblical Interpretation* (Philadelphia: Fortress, 1980), and the other literature cited in S. Schneiders (above, note 4).

12. Cf. D.W. Thomas, 'A Consideration of Some Unusual Ways of Expressing the Superlative', *VT* 3 (1953) 209-24, esp. 221.

Ochshorn 62-65, on the 'functionalism' of historical criticism.

4. This very stance is questioned in modern hermeneutical theory; cf.
S.M. Schneiders, 'Faith, Hermeneutics, and the Literal Sense of Scripture',
TS 39 (1978) 719-36; esp. pp. 20-3).

5. Cf. S. Brown, 'Exegesis and Imagination', *TS* 41 (1980) 485-51

6. K. Budde uses the phrase of Liedmagscherei, quoting D. Ochli, in
Das Hohelied in Dryander, *Megliko* (KHCAT, 17; Freiburg: Mohr/Siebeck
1898), xii; D. Lerch uses the word 'Raminakaburei' in *Hoheslied, RGG*
3rd (1959) col. 481.

7. There is an extensive bibliography in M. Pope, *Song of Songs* (AB, 7c;
New York: Doubleday, 1977) 89-229. See also George L. Scheper, *The
Spiritual Marriage: Ibn Ezra and the Canonical Dimension of the Song of
Songs in the Middle Ages* (Princeton University dissertation 1971); R.M.
Murphy, *Literature and Medieval Exegesis: Hope or Hindrance?*, *CBQ* 43
(1981) 505-16.

8. Allegorical understanding is found in isolated sources such as
Jerome and especially Ambrose, but it is Rupert who gave impetus to this
interpretation.... For the medieval period see F. Ohly, *Hohelied-Studien.
Grundzüge einer Geschichte der Hoheliedauslegung des Abendlandes bis um
1200* (Wiesbaden: Steiner, 1958); H. Riedlinger, *Die Makellosigkeit der
Kirche in den lateinischen Hoheliedkommentaren des Mittelalters* (Münster:
Aschendorf, 1958).

9. For details concerning such correspondence, see the commentary of J.
Robert, *Le Cantique des Cantiques* (Paris: Gabalda, 1963).

10. Cf. David C. Steinmetz, 'John Calvin on Isaiah 6', *Int* 36 (1982) 156-
70. The principal value of precritical exegesis is that it is not modern
exegesis, it is alien, strange, sometimes even, from our perspective, comic
and fantastical. Precisely because it is strange, it provides a constant
stimulus to modern interpreters, offering exegetical suggestions they would
never think of themselves or find in any recent book, forcing them again and
again to re-reading and re-evaluation of the text. Interpreters who immerse
themselves however not only in the text but in these often approaches to the
text may find in time that they have learned to see with eyes not their own,
sights they could scarcely have imagined and to hear, with ears not their
own, voices too soft for their own ears to detect (p. 170).

11. See for example, F. Rousseau, *Dialogue et fonctionnement d'habile
delphine-Proteast* 1980, and the other literature cited in §. Schneiders
(above, note 4)

12. Cf. D.W. Thomas, 'A Consideration of Some Unusual Ways of
Expressing the Superlative', *VT* 3 (1953) 209-24, esp. 221.

PART II

THE WORD AND ISRAEL'S SCRIPTURES

4

REUBEN AND JUDAH: DUPLICATES OR COMPLEMENTS?

Hugh C. White

Fifty years ago this year, Wilhelm Rudolph wrote a major challenge to the dominant view that the Joseph narrative was a conflation of two independent and parallel accounts stemming from the J and E Documents.[1] Gerhard von Rad, though retaining the theory of multiple sources, furthered this move toward perceiving the text as a unified work by his identification of the traditio-historical roots of the Joseph story as a whole in the wisdom tradition, and his emphasis upon the high literary quality of the final redaction.[2] But R.N. Whybray, in response, argued that these emphases were not consonant with the documentary hypothesis on two grounds. If *both* J and E versions reflected wisdom influence, as von Rad contended, the common source which must be hypothesized would have had to have originated before the early monarchy. But the absence of tribal traditions from this story causes von Rad to place the early stages of the story's composition after the beginning of the 'enlightenment' of the early monarchy. Thus, since the J writer would not have developed a new version of a recently written story, there does not appear to be a sufficient time span between the composition of the common source and the composition of the J document, which is generally dated in the Solomonic period.[3] A second difficulty arises from von Rad's view that the final work produced by the redactor is 'even richer' than were the earlier separate works.[4] That a 'novel of superlative merit could be the result of a *conflation* of *two* other novels', is difficult for Whybray to conceive.[5] He thus concludes that, 'If the Joseph story as we now have it is a literary masterpiece *in von Rad's sense*, it must be a complete literary unity both in conception and execution; if it is conflation of two sources, then von Rad's estimate of its high qualities *as a novel* must be largely illusory'.[6] He thus proposes that Rudolph's neglected critique be reexamined as a way out of this impasse.

Von Rad's traditio-historical views have subsequently been challenged[7] and partially modified.[8] The dissatisfaction with the documentary hypothesis on literary grounds continues, however, with both Donald Redford and Hans-Christoph Schmitt proposing variations on Rudolph's supplementary hypothesis,[9] and George Coats arguing more strongly for the literary unity of the central narrative by rejecting many of the arguments offered by source criticism for duplications and contradictions.[10] Subsequently, Horst Seebass surveyed the full range of this work and returned to the traditional hypothesis of independent sources largely on the grounds of a verse by verse refutation (relying often on ancient Near Eastern historical information) of the arguments presented by Coats and others for the unity of the narrative. He concedes in places, however, that Coats's arguments make source division only a 'possibility' and not a 'necessity'.[11]

This halting movement toward a more literary analysis of Hebrew narrative has been noted by the literary critic Robert Alter who is perplexed by the 'abundance of astute literary analysis' of the Greek and Latin classics, the criticism of which was also once dominated by various documentary hypotheses, but the dearth of such analyses in Biblical studies.[12] One of the narratives Alter has chosen for analysis is the Joseph story which he terms 'the preeminent instance of biblical narrative as a fictional experiment in knowledge'.[13] In his own close reading of chs. 42–43, as well as ch. 39, he deals with the text as a literary unity. The increasing tension in biblical scholarship between literary and historical criticism of the Joseph story can be seen in a recent article by Kenneth R. Melchin (in criticism of Coats) which attemps to practice literary, stylistic criticism upon the reconstructed J and E sources more carefully than has been done before.[14]

I would like to suggest that the reluctance in Old Testament studies to move toward a more literary mode of analysis is due to the uncertainty of the criteria by which one should analyze large units of text. This opens the possibility of excessive subjectivity and arbitrariness in interpretation. Though Redford is critical of the documentary hypothesis in his study of the Joseph story, he articulates a widespread view when he argues for the use of traditional literary-historical criteria for the identification of primary sources, because such an approach is 'empirical' and 'objective'.[15] It may be, however, that there are important dimensions of subjectivity involved in the literary-historical search for sources that are unacknowledged, and unreflected upon, which play a necessary role in the practice of source criticism itself. It will be the purpose of this article to examine the current state of research on the Joseph story to determine the extent to which subjective factors have played a role in this research and may account for the proliferation of its quite contradictory results. In conclusion a brief example will be given of how a more purely literary reading of one section of this narrative, ch. 37, might resolve some of the seemingly insoluble conflicts that have arisen in the research such as the question of whether the roles of Reuben and Judah here are duplicates (indicating a conflation of sources) or are complementary.

The most empirical dimension of this problem is probably found in what Redford terms the onomasticon. The incongruous or contradictory use of names of places and people can be a sign of a disturbance in the continuity of a text. One of the most widely regarded examples of such a contradictory occurrence of names in the Pentateuch is in the Joseph narrative where the text seems to portray Joseph as being both abducted from a pit and sold to Potiphar in Egypt by the Midanites, and purchased from the brothers and sold to Potiphar by Ishmaelites (Gen 37.27-28, 36; 39.1). So certain has this contradiction appeared that, as Redford says, 'Generations of Bible students have utilized this discrepancy as a show piece for demonstrating the validity of the Documentary Hypothesis'.[16] Redford, expressing a typical attitude, polemically refers to those who have opposed this viewpoint as 'conservatives' and 'harmonists' who attempt to circumvent the 'plain fact' that 'Ishmaelites and Midanites are distinguished in the mind of the writer'.[17]

One could safely say, then, that here we come as close to empirical evidence of redactional tampering with the text as can be found. It is such 'plain facts' that then require the pursuit of other evidence of duplications and editorial modifications which may be far less empirical. Redford himself acknowledges, particularly, that doublets— one of the primary forms of supporting evidence for multiple sources—are 'difficult to prove with certainty, since the arguments must be a priori'.[18] But without the support of doublets it is doubtful that a theory of multiple sources could be maintained even with the empirical evidence of names, beyond the argument for glosses and midrashic comments. Doublets provide the narrative substance of the plural sources. Contradictions such as that cited above would have to be explained some way other than as the consequences of the conflation of sources, if located in an absolutely seamless text. It is, however, precisely in the determination of doublets that a priori reasoning is the most often utilized, and that consensus has been so notoriously difficult to achieve.

The dilemma this presents to the interpreter of the Joseph story is a serious one. If contradictions in names such as the Midianite/ Ishmaelite discrepancy require, a priori, the development of theories of doublets, then the possibility of examining the text as a literary unity becomes also, a priori, illegitimate.

On the other hand, if one assumes, a priori, the unity of the text, this would present the danger of passing over or suppressing 'empirical' evidence of multiple authorship. The particular narrative under consideration constitutes an excellent example of this dilemma since it has been considered both as the most persuasive evidence for the theory of multiple authorship and praised as one of the most finely crafted narratives in the Biblical corpus. As Whybray noted fifteen years ago, these two views of the narrative are simply incompatible.

Since the 'empirical' keystone in the theory of multiple authors of the Joseph narrative is the Midianite/Ishmaelite contradiction, it would be advisable to examine carefully the nature of the evidence it presents in order to clarify this dilemma. The first significant point is that especially in recent years, this alleged contradiction has not been viewed as implying multiple authorship or even, for some, the literary disunity of the text. Redford himself attibutes this fissure not to the existence of separate original documents (J and E), but to a 'Judah version' of the story of the conspiracy which is an 'expansion of a preexistent version in which Reuben was the sole protagonist'.[19] The reference in v. 28a(a) is then seen as the original Reuben account of the theft of Joseph from the pit. The reference to the purchase of Joseph by the Ishmaelites would then be a later expansion intended to portray the execution of Judah's proposal to sell Joseph.

Schmitt similarly argues against the existence of separate narrative documents and in favor of a secondary expansion by a later editor. For him, however, the Judah level is primary, and the Reuben secondary. One of the chief arguments he makes for this sequence is that the reference to the Midianites' theft of Joseph in v. 29a(a) has the effect of removing the guilt for the sale of Joseph into slavery from the brothers where it would have fallen if Judah's plan had been enacted. Verse 28a(a) is not a continuation of the Reuben level then, since it constituted a redactor's response to the Judah speech. By having the Midianites steal Joseph before the brothers could sell him, the responsibility is ultimately given to God who is the 'lord of coincidences'.[20] This reinterpretation of the Judah level harmonizes it with what Schmitt regards as the overarching theological perspective of the final editor, and is thus evidence to him of the priority of the Judah level.

Coats, who argues generally for the literary unity of the basic Joseph narrative, deals with this apparent disruption only by means of the hypothesis of a textual gloss, although without any variant manuscript support. He acknowledges that the mention of the Midianites 'breaks the flow of the narrative and points to an element of disunity in the section'.[21] A possible reason for the addition of the Midianite reference would have been, as with Schmitt, to deflect direct responsibility from the brothers for the sale of a family member into slavery, since this was a capital crime in Israel.[22]

Contrary to Schmitt, however, Coats does not think that this suggests a more extensive secondary emendation which added the Reuben plan in 37.21,22. To argue that 37.28a(a) is a gloss, however, requires that 37.36a, which reports the sale of Joseph by the Midanites to Potiphar in Egypt (in contrast to 39.1), also be considered a gloss. He reasons that this is likely to have happened in connection with the insertion of the anomalous ch. 38 into the original narrative. At that time the redactor would have been, for a reason Coats does not explain, 'dependent upon the gloss' in 37.28a(a).[23]

Seebass rejects Coats's contention that v. 28a(a) is merely a gloss by questioning his assumption that Judah's plan for the sale of Joseph is a capital crime. He says that the brothers' mistake was in preempting the right of the supremely powerful father to decide about such matters.[24] If the Judah plan did not carry with it a death penalty, the motivation for the gloss is removed, and 28a(a) should then be considered as a continuation of the Reuben story.[25] To support this he contends that the scene which ended with Joseph in the pit (v. 24) requires a continuation. The boy could have escaped or been found and released to return to the father with another bad tale about his brothers. But Seebass does not think that the Judah speech in vv. 25-27 is that continuation. He asks, 'If Judah's measures should continue Reuben's, why it is not said that Reuben was absent when Joseph was sold?'[26] He thus prefers to see v. 28a(a) as a continuation of the Reuben story, parallel to the Ishmaelite sale which carries forward the Judah proposal.

This leads Seebass to support the traditional two-source theory of this narrative since he cannot accept either Redford's or Schmitt's opposing arguments for supplementary dependent levels. Both Redford and Schmitt draw a conclusion of dependency from evidence of similarity between the levels, and Seebass does not think this is an adequate basis.[27]

Two proposals have been offered for accepting the Midianite/Ishmaelite discrepancy as it stands, those of W. Rudolph and of H. Gunkel. Rudolph does not see the mention of the Midianite traders in v. 28a(a) as a sign of disunity. He simply accepts the Midianite theft as a surprising event that prevented the fulfillment of Judah's plan. He assumes that Reuben was present at the time the brothers planned the sale, but said nothing, planning to free Joseph from the pit before they could execute the plan. His astonishment in v. 29 was then due to the unanticipated intervention of the Midianites, rather than the unanticipated actions of his brothers.[28] This, however, still leaves the problem of the contradiction between 37.36 and 39.1. He resolves this by resorting to a gloss theory. He accepts v. 36a which tells of the Midianite sale of Joseph in Egypt, but rejects the reference to Potiphar as a harmonizing gloss made to strengthen the connection with 39.1 after the intrusion of ch. 38. The assumption beneath the reference to the Midanite sale in Egypt in v. 36a was not that the Midianites brought Joseph to Egypt, but rather that they sold him there through the intermediation of the Ishmaelites.[29]

Both Rudolph and Coats have been able to deal with this irregularity in the text only by means of physically *eliminating* the irregularity at one place or another *from* the text in spite of the absence of any textual variant support for so doing. Gunkel, however, sees it differently. What is for Redford (who rejects the theory of parallel source documents) a classic example of empirical evidence of an inescapable contradiction, is considered by Gunkel (who sees the story as a combination of J and E) as not at all contradictory at the final redactional level. He reasons that by the time of the redaction by R^JE, 'the Midianites were counted as a part of the Ishmaelites'. In this case the subject reference of the verb *wayyimšĕkû* was the brothers rather than the Midianites (Judg 8.24).[30] From this perspective, then, no contradiction exists for R^JE between 37.36 and 39.1. With its reference both to Potiphar (E) and the Ishmaelites (J), 39.1 is also the product of R^JE.[31]

This brief survey of the conclusions reached in major works of research regarding one of the most certain contradictions in the entire Pentateuch reveals a perplexing array of contrary and contradictory viewpoints. There is fundamental disagreement regarding everything from the facticity of the contradiction to the presence or absence of glosses. Every shade of opinion regarding the pre-history of the text seems to be present from no pre-history, to interdependent redactional levels, to dual contrary and contradictory sources, to dual sources harmonized successfully by a redactor, to theories of both disruptive and harmonizing glosses. The significant question here is why so many of the crucial differences seem undecidable on empirical grounds, such as whether Reuben was present and silent at the Judah speech or absent, or whether the author of the Judah speech would have included an explanation of Reuben's absence if the Judah scene were continuous with the preceding Reuben scene. An attempt will now be made to see more exactly the types of analytical and interpretive tasks within this methodology which seem to lead to such undecidable differences.

One of the areas where such differences seem to arise is in the critiques made of the existing narrative continuity and in reconstructing the logic of the separate narrative levels or sources. One reason for this may be that not once in any of these works is a general theory of narrative structure used to support the ad hoc judgments made about a possible narrative logic for this story in its present or earlier forms. Coats's very general outline of major narrative sequences is not applicable to the internal logic of individual scenes, though it is an admirable move in the right direction.[32]

The most obvious example of such an intuitive judgment is found in Redford's work where, writing more as a purely literary rather than as a historical critic, he asserts that, 'From the standpoint of the plot, the good brother who seeks to help his younger brother... constitutes a single role'. He accords this role a significant while ironic place in the narrative, but concludes that, 'To create a second role in which a second good 'brother' is trying to do exactly the same thing as the first, would be an incomprehensible weakening of this sub-plot'.[33] Thus he regards the Reuben speech and the Judah speech as duplications which would not be found in a work produced by a single author. He extends this theory of division by pointing to the repeated association in the text of Judah with the name Israel, and Reuben with the name Jacob, but it is clear that this grouping of names itself lacks significance unless supported by a convincing series of plot duplications and irregularities.[34]

But what theory of plot structure supports the idea that the good brother in a plot can only be a single role? Since Redford offers none, Coats, in opposition, can simply assert, 'The roles are not doublets . . . The two roles present different activity on the part of two distinct principles in the plot.' In Coats's view the two brothers 'add to the tension of the plot by their contrast'.[35] It is clear that the difference between Coats and Redford about this centrally important issue is undecidable on empirical grounds. Redford's intuitive reading of the plot leads him to emphasize the futile, ironic dimension of the good brother's attempts to save Joseph, when saving him completely would have prevented the fulfillment of the divine plan. To duplicate such an ironic role seems to Redford only to weaken the entire effect of this sub-plot. Coats, on the other hand, finds the contrast between the more idealistic Reuben and the practical, self-interested Judah to be significant and not repetitious. Here different intuitive readings are at work.

The same type of subjective impressions of narrative continuity are at the root of most of the other differences in the conclusions described above. On what basis is one to decide whether Rudolph is correct in assuming Reuben's presence during the Judah speech, and attributing his surprise in v. 29 to the unanticipated action of the Midianites, or whether Coats and Schmitt are right in supposing the absence of Reuben and seeing v. 28a(a) as an editor's gloss inspired by the desire to lift the responsibility of the sale of Joseph from the shoulders of the brothers? Seebass offers evidence against this latter interpretation from the history of religions but his evidence remains equivocal. Beyond this, what evidence can be brought forth to show, unequivocally, that Schmitt's opinion that the motivation of the author of v. 28a(a) was consistent with the theological perspective of the author of his Reuben level, rather than simply a gloss with no particular continuity, theologically or literarily, with the foregoing Reuben speech?

These judgments concerning the continuity of the text are largely governed by a priori assumptions regarding the structure and meaning of the narrative. Schmitt here offers as evidence for the continuity of v. 28a(a) with the Reuben level, its discontinuity with the Reuben proposal! This discontinuity makes it appear as a 'god-effected accident' and thus an expression of the theology of the last redactor who emphasized the divine control of the course of events.[36] Such *a priori* reasoning could find the same theological viewpoint behind the sudden unexplained appearance of the Ishmaelites, which suggests to Judah the possibility of Joseph's sale, in the other level of Schmitt's analysis.

Coats, in contrast, does not seek to link v. 24a(a) with the Reuben speech, because, in his view, the Reuben speech and the Judah speech are not discontinuous: 'There is no apparent reason that I can see that demands interpretation of this evidence [the Judah speech] as disruptive in the progress of the narration. It presupposes confinement in the pit, a part of Reuben's plan.'[37] Schmitt, whose perspective on the narrative structure is shaped throughout by the name groupings (Judah-Israel; Reuben-Jacob), does not raise the question of possible literary continuity between the two speeches. It is only in discussing the relation between passages within his delineated levels that evidence pertaining to continuity is presented, e.g. the theological continuity between the general perspective of the Reuben level, and v. 28a(a) mentioned above. Similarly, Seebass, though explicitly seeking to refute Coats's view of this passage, does not directly address the central point of Coats's argument, that the Judah proposal and its execution presuppose that Joseph is confined in the pit, although he attibutes v. 28a(b) (where Joseph is lifted out of the pit) to the same source as the Judah speech (J), and does not include in this source any previous references to Joseph being placed in the pit.[38]

Numerous other examples from the research on this single scene could be given which indicate the extent to which a priori assumptions regarding continuity and discontinuity govern the reconstruction of sources. The result of this has been that Old Testament scholars, in spite of their reliance upon the same basic objective literary and historical methods, have produced conclusions which exhaust almost every logical possibility within the terms in which the problems have been posed, regardless of how contradictory they may be. The text has been seen to present:

a. indisputable evidence of internal contradiction necessarily implying dual authors and sources (Seebass);

b. no inescapable contradictions but doublets which imply two independent sources (Gunkel);

c. contradictions and doublets which imply redactional levels but not two independent source documents (Schmitt, Redford);

d. contradictions due to glosses but no doublets, implying literary unity (Coats, Rudolph).

Within these groupings there is further disagreement between the proponents of the redactional-levels-theory pertaining to the priority and dependency of the Judah level upon the Reuben level (Redford and Schmitt), and between proponents of the gloss theory as to where the gloss is located and what constitutes a problematic contradiction (Coats and Rudolph). In light of the serious and undecidable nature of most of these differences, it is perhaps not surprising that the latest of these analysts (Seebass) has returned to the essential view espoused by Julius Wellhausen a hundred years ago regarding 37.28.[39]

The only reason which seems plausible for this lack of unanimity is that each analyst brings to the text a narrative theory which he assumes but does not explicitly state or defend. His assumptions then color whether he perceives, for example, Reuben and Judah as redundant duplications of a single role or as significant contrasting types. There do not seem to be any objective grounds upon which most of these questions can be decided, or else a greater degree of agreement among scholars who utilize essentially the same methods of interpretation would have been achieved during the last fifty years.

Where then should research go in order to escape this dilemma if not back to Wellhausen? I would suggest that the arduous and admirable attempt of biblical scholarship to evade the specter of subjectivity has not been completely successful. Traditio-historical and literary-historical reconstructions, lacking a more refined narrative theory, must rely upon purely individual literary intuition with regard to plot and character formation. But because little reflection has been given to narrative theory itself, intuitive judgments are given a free rein. The result is the source reconstructions have proliferated based on different a priori assumptions about narrative continuity.[40]

Within the numerous possibilities for analysis opened up by the previous work, there is one which, strangely, has not been explored previously. Coats has come closer to this remaining possibility than any other since Rudolph, but even he and Rudolph stopped short of its full realization. This is the possibility that Gunkel was correct about the absence of a necessary contradiction between the Ishmaelite/ Midianite references, and that Rudolph and Coats were correct in seeing this scene as lacking any genuine doublets. If these two views, which have been persuasively argued separately, are united, then the way is open for an analysis of the narrative as a unified literary work in the fullest sense.

One reason that this logical step may not have been taken is the danger of losing a critical perspective upon the text when it is understood to be a unity. In justifying his preference for the two-source theory, Seebass expressed this very pointedly when he wrote, 'The two-source theory has . . . the scientific advantage of not concealing the fragmentary nature of our knowledge about the old sources, and of bringing these, nevertheless, as accurately as possible into expression'.[41] The acceptance of fragmentariness is itself, however, an a priori assumption that must be justified with respect to each individual text, and is not an ipso facto guarantee of scientific detachment. When, after a century of assiduous scholarly labor upon passages such as 37.18-36, no real consensus has been reached about any of the signs of fragmentation, and so many of the points of difference seem undecidable on objective grounds, it seems that the usefulness of this idea as a governing assumption must be questioned. The vast discrepancies in the conclusions reached make it increasingly difficult to believe that the fragmentary hypothesis has been success-ful in preventing the extensive intrusion of the subjective intuition of the researchers into their work.[42] Coats's excellent study of the literary unity of the Joseph story has moved the discussion in the right direction, but is weakened by the lack of a theory capable of dealing with the complex detail of the plot.

In conclusion I would like to give, in briefest outline, a suggestive theory of narrative analysis, and an example of how it might lead to a new approach to the problems encountered in the criticism of Gen 37.12-35. To do this I will present some ideas from the work of the literary critic, Stanley Fish of Johns Hopkins University, who has struggled with problems in the field of literary criticism similar to those outlined above in biblical studies. This brief analysis should not, however, be taken as an authentic example of Fish's method. It owes only its most direct inspiration to his work. The analysis will also have no pretensions to definitiveness, or to providing the final solution to the problems described above. Its only goal will be to offer a suggestive hypothesis which might move the discussion of the Joseph story beyond the impasse to which it seems to have come.

Fish rejects the critical method which

> takes as its (self-restricted) area the physical dimensions of the artifact and within these dimensions . . . makes out beginnings, middles and ends, discovers frequency distributions, traces out

patterns of imagery, diagrams strata of complexity (vertical of course), all without ever taking into account the relationship (if any) between its data and their affective force.[43]

He turns aside, as well, from determining the meaning of a text in the usual sense, i.e. the informational content wherein 'components of an utterance are considered either in relation to each other or to a state of affairs in the outside world, or to a state of mind of the speaker-author'.[44] The fault of these approaches is that they attempt 'to consider the utterance apart from the consciousness receiving it . . .,' and to do so risks ' . . . missing a great deal of what is going on'.[45] Literature for Fish is 'a kinetic art' in spite of its apparently fixed outer form, because in the act of reading, 'it was moving (pages turning, lines receding into the past) and . . . we were moving with it . . .'[46] An analysis which pursues the ideal of objectivity by treating the literary work as a static object loses its objectivity by failing to deal with 'what is objectively true about the activity of reading'.[47]

How does one asses this? He proposes 'the rigorous and disinterested asking of the question, What does this word, phrase, sentence, paragraph, chapter novel, play, poem do?' followed by 'an *analysis of the developing responses of the reader in relation to the words as they succeed one another in time*' (his emphasis).[48] How does this approach avoid a solipsistic subjectivism? Chiefly through a self-critical examination of one's own responses to one's reading so as to weed out that which is personal and idiosyncratic, and an attempt to do everything possible to become a totally 'informed reader'.[49] This does not mean that a dimension of subjectivity will not remain, but in his view, given the options, 'I would rather have an acknowledged and controlled subjectivity than an objectivity which is finally an illusion'.[50]

In his analytical reading Fish has discovered two kinds of literary presentation which he describes as 'rhetorical' and 'dialectical'. The rhetorical aims at confirming and supporting the reader's way of thinking about the world. The dialectical, on the other hand, leads the reader subtly and non-didactically, into a scrutiny of everytthing he believes and lives by with the aim of transforming or converting him to a new understanding of life.[51] The rhetorical presentation is closed, the end corresponding to the beginning, whereas the dialectical approach is open. The openness is achieved in a most surprising way, that is by pointing 'away from itself to something its forms cannot capture'.[52] What is this transcendental goal? It is the transformation of the reader himself into the underlying reality, process, or value which has empowered the dialectic, whether it be pure reason the inner light, faith, or some idea of the Good. He calls this 'anti-art-for-art's-sake because it is concerned less with the making of better poems than with the making of better persons'.[53] Among the religious works in which he finds this dialectic at work are Milton's *Paradise Lost*,[54] and some of the works of Augustine, John Donne, and Bunyan.[55]

The following brief analysis of Genesis 37 will focus chiefly upon the narrator's perspective upon his characters, and the effect of this upon the reader. This will be seen primarily in the way in which the narrator motivates his characters' actions. Attention will also be given to the function of the direct discourse of the characters vis-à-vis that of the third person narrative framework in the movement of the plot. Objectivity is not the goal here, but a form of subjectivity which is responsive to the distinctive stylistic semantic system which generates the meaning of the narrative through its effects upon the emotions and intellect of the reader. It will be validated to the extent that it accounts coherently for the features of the text, and other critical readers confirm these modes of the text's interaction with them in the act of reading. A more extensive discussion by this writer of some of the theoretical issue involved in this approach can be found elsewhere.[56]

The narrator, in an unusually long introduction in 37.1-4 (direct discourse is not found until v. 5), establishes a triadic relation consisting of Joseph, Jacob, and the brothers (a collective entity), and defines that relationship with economy and poignancy. The sympathies of the reader are first drawn to the idyllic pastoral scene of the brothers together watching sheep, then disturbed and repelled by Joseph, at his age of seventeen, tattling on his brothers. Before Joseph falls into the position of the villain, however, our attitude is moderated when we are told of his father's preference for him above the others, the father thus being made largely responsible for his son's behavior. But before the father can be marked as the villain in our thinking, the father's action is also explained as being due to the fact that Joseph was a child of his old age. This at least softens the arbitrariness of Jacob's preferential treatment. And what did the other brothers think of this exclusive relation between their brother and their father? We are not told until the father expresses his prefernce in tangible form through the giving of a gift to Joseph—an unusual striped or sleeved robe (depending upon the translation of *passim*) which the favorite son will bear as an objective sign of his superior status. Thus we are told that 'the brothers *saw*' that the father 'loved' their brother more, and 'they hated him' (37.4). The reader is also not left to wonder how the hatred affected their behavior. This hatred had the outer effect of breaking the communication between him and the brothers. The narrator tells us that 'they could not speak *shalom* to him' (37.4), the speaking of *shalom* being a sign of mutual trust. With this the narrator points to the central problem with which the narrative will be occupied until it is initially resolved in 45.15b and finally resolved in 50.21, i.e. the problem of communication between Joseph and his rival brothers.

The narrator has now, in third person descriptive language, outlined for the reader a system of emotional forces in the family over which no one has control, along with its consequences. Jacob is hopelessly attached to this son of his old age, and this common human emotion inevitably intrudes into Joseph's relations with his brothers. When this state of affairs is flaunted openly before the face of his brothers, what one must assume to have previously been a latent hatred now becomes overt hatred expressed concretely in strained or broken communication. The sequence of this description is carefully designed to lead the reader from the initially placid, pastoral scene deeper and deeper into the tragic forces at work beneath the surfaces of the family life. The logic of this system implies a conflict between the brothers and Joseph, described as the absence of *shalom*, which suggests the real possibility that Joseph will be murdered by his brothers. The narrator has thus given the reader a description of a closed system of emotional forces which logically leads to conflict and death. But no unqualified villains are given as the focal point of negative feelings. Nevertheless, the logic of the passage leads one to understand most sympathetically the response of the brothers to this flagrant, inflammatory behavior by their father and brother.

We are next told that into this system a dream comes to Joseph which evoked in the brothers an intensification of their hatred of him. We are not told why the dream occurred, or who caused it. But a new element of mystery enters the narrative with this dream, opening up new possibilities. Dreams may reveal the future, and at this juncture in the narrative, when the narrator has led the reader to think that the future development of the plot will be determined by a closed system of emotional forces operating within the family, the mysterious occurrence of this dream may offer a different scenario for the future.

But in advance of finding out the content of the dream, we are told by the narrator that its chief significance is that it increased the hatred of the brothers for Joseph. This makes it clear that the dream is not to operate according to some occult process which is unrelated to the emotional system of the family. Its effect upon the future will be actualized through its effect upon the familial situation depicted in the previous verses.

Why will the dream have this effect? In part, we are told, because Joseph reported it to the brothers. The description of the act of reporting in the narrative framework alerts the reader to the significance of that action in itself, apart from the content of the dream. The narrator does not tell the reader the content of this dream in the narrative framework (as he does in 41.1-7). We learn of its content in the first instance of direct discourse in this story, as we hear Joseph reporting it to his brothers. Verse 5 thus introduces a new narrative element and conveys in an abstract way the mechanism by which this mysterious new factor will be brought into relation to the emotional system given in vv. 1-4. It is the *telling* of the dream by Joseph that links the dream to the previous system. The narrator then, after the dream report, explains that the brothers' hatred of Joseph increased 'because of his dreams, and *because of* his *words*' (37.8).

The linkage between this dream report and the tensions of the initial situation can be seen also in the position of this initial instance of reported direct discourse coming immediately after the narrator's remark that the brothers could no longer speak *shalom* to him. This dream report by Joseph to his brothers could not be construed as a gesture made toward the resumption of peaceful communication. Rather, the contrary is the case. Viewed from the perspective of the problems of the initial situation, it represents a translation of the meaning of the robe into the oblique, symbolic language of dreams. The telling of the dream then verbalizes these latent meanings so as to make them almost inescapable. The dream has merely to be interpreted by the brothers. The interpretation is vocalized by them in the form of rhetorical questions which carry a tone of shock, incredulity, and perhaps sarcasm: 'Will you indeed reign over us; or indeed rule over us?' (v. 8). In emotionally laden language utilizing repeated infinitive absolutes, the brothers in these incredulous rhetorical questions respond to what they perceive to be the implicit meaning beneath the symbolism of the dream, i.e. the arrogance of Joseph. There is a correspondence here between the coded language of the dream and the response of the brothers in the form of rhetorical questions. While the meaning of the dream report is clear to the brothers on the emotional level, the symbolic language of the dream retains a degree of ambiguity on the intellectual level. The form of the rhetorical question allows for this element of ambiguity while articulating the brother's emotional affront. This 'dialogue' between the language of dreams and rhetorical questions is one in which the meanings are deflected or displaced by both parties in different ways producing a multi-leveled, polysemic discourse.

A second dream follows which is significantly different from the first (and thus not a duplication) in that it sems to include his parents as well in this drama of submission. He told this dream not only to his brothers but also to his father. Jacob's response, as characterized by the narrator, is unexpected. He too voices incredulous rhetorical questions, but the narrator describes them in advance as a 'rebuke' (v. 10). His disclosure of the dream thus not only increased Joseph's alienation from his brothers; it has now angered Jacob, who obviously also interprets the dream in terms of the family situation. Through this rebuke the narrator shows Jacob as being aware of the problem of Joseph's arrogance now that it appears to have no limits. The second dream thus has the effect of momentarily aligning Jacob with the brothers against Joseph, an ominous development.

The scene is closed by the narrator with two phrases commenting on the brothers' final inner reaction, along with Jacob's. The brothers predictably 'envy' Joseph, but Jacob 'noted' (*šāmar*) this word (*haddābār*). Jacob's reaction is thus ambivalent. He responds to both levels of ambiguity in the dream. In his rebuke he responds overtly (for the benefit of the brothers?) to the level of familial emotions it signifies, but the narrator has him respond inwardly to the prognosticating feature of the dreams, i.e. the dream as an occult phenomenon signifying a hidden, providential force which determines the future. This is a word to the reader as well, that the dream's significance goes beyond the emotional encounter it has just precipitated. Thus at the conclusion of this scene the reader, if attempting to anticipate the future course of the narrative, would find two contradictory factors at work. On the one hand is the familial scene where fatherly favor and brotherly jealousy pose Joseph and his brothers in a potentially fatal conflict. On the other hand is the prognosticatory dream which contradicts the outcome seemingly dictated by the familial emotions. In the center of this conflict is the emotionally warped and semantically deflected discourse between Joseph and both his brothers and father. This discourse brings the occult dream into contact with the familial situation so as to inflame the jealous, brotherly emotions and weaken the father's support for him. The dream thus seems to be caught up within the emotional logic of the familial scene which will lead not to Joseph's triumph, but to his death. This has occurred because the reporting of the dream caused it to be incorporated into the fractured dialogical process at work in the family where it only intensified the crisis by bringing the latent emotions obliquely into expression.

When we are told next that Jacob will send Joseph to a distant place of pasturage, where the brothers have gone in the meantime, to get another 'report' (v. 14), the question 'Why?' presses upon the reader. All that the narrator has told us of the brothers thus far is their increasing hatred of Joseph, and the lack of *shalom* in their discourse. Now, after a scene in which he has provoked even his doting father into anger, he is sent alone into the hands of his brothers in a distant place to engage once again in the same type of activity that is at the root of their hatred. This action by Jacob is thus overladen with ambiguity.

With his departure from his father, the sympathies of the reader begin to focus upon Joseph for the first time. He is being sent, defenseless, into the camp of his virtual enemies. This transfer of sympathies is aided by the inclusion of this strange scene (which has always puzzled commentators) of Joseph wandering in the field at Shechem unable to find his brothers (vv. 15-17). He, strangely, does not seek someone to ask of their whereabouts. Rather, an unnamed man, with whom the reader may identify, 'finds' him in his wandering and asks him, 'What are you seeking?' Why did Joseph not seek the man to ask *him* about his brothers? Why did he not return home to report that he couldn't find his brothers? Joseph appears suspended here between two worlds. Behind him is his angry father, and before him is his hate-filled brothers. So Joseph 'wanders' in the fields appearing lost and helpless; the reader sees him through the eyes of the unnamed man, in all his vulnerability.

The narrator now shifts our attention away from Joseph to the camp of the brothers to hear their reaction when he first appears on the horizon. They spot him across the pasture some time before he arrives, doubtless aided in their identification by his unusual robe. Now, for the first time, when the brothers are far from home and Joseph is approaching at a distance, we are privileged to hear the direct, and unrestrained expression of the brothers' feelings about Joseph. The narrator summarizes for us the essence of this conversation before relating it in direct discourse: he tells us with brutal directness that they 'conspired against him to kill him' (v. 18). This has the effect upon the reader of bringing to a close the logic generated by the depiction of the emotional system of the family. It also dispels any remaining sympathy for the brothers.

The discourse of the conspirators which now follows is not so predictable. Again without singling out particular voices, the narrator tells us what they said 'to one another'. No individual responsibility can thus be assigned for originating this conspiracy. They speak again in discourse determined by the dream, and distored by emotion: 'Behold the dream-lord has come. Now come, let us kill him, and throw him into one of the cisterns, and we will say an evil beast has eaten him; then we will see what will become of his dreams' (vv. 19, 20). As the dream previously evoked incredulous questions from the brothers, now it evokes sarcasm. The language of the conspiracy is still entirely determined by the images of the dream. It is his transcendent dream-identity which distorts their language into sarcasm and evokes from them the ultimate limit-breaking transgression of murder. The dream, now that it has entered the world of familial discourse, is about to be consumed by that discourse. Murder will be simply a means of mocking the dream, an extension of sarcasm into action. Joseph's end will be the pit, not the stars.

The crucial question, of course, is whether the solidarity of the brothers will hold in the face of this brutal murder of the 'dream-lord'. The ambiguity of this dream is keenly sensed by the brothers; the dream is both a mysterious prognostication and an example of unbridled arrogance. It is this ambiguity that underlies the sarcasm. Can such an ambiguous object evoke the absolute act of murder? Is Joseph altogether responsible for this dream? There must be, as well, some kind of hierarchy among the brothers, in which one, the eldest, would bear the responsibility for such an act more directly than the others, though the narrator does not allude to this.

At this crucial juncture, the narrator reports that 'Reuben heard, and delivered him from their hand' (v. 21). We must assume then, that one brother, Reuben, was not a part of the conspiracy, and when he 'heard' he acted to halt the murder. Why did he act? We are not told. Perhaps the writer assumes that we know that Reuben is the eldest brother. Or perhaps there is a rhetorical link between the idiom used by Reuben here for murder, 'Let us not smite his soul', and the rhetoric of the conspiracy, directed so explicitly toward killing Joseph's dream. This counter move comes now as a dialogical response, however—a hearing followed by an opposing utterance. The dialogization of the dream, which initially crystallized the hostility against Joseph and inspired the resolve to kill him, now brings forth a voice on his behalf. Reuben continues with a second more physical enjoinder against murder, 'Do not shed blood'. This often cited duplication serves as a rhetorical contrast to the intial, more abstract enjoinder, and as a grounding for the 'realistic' alternative proposal which follows: 'Throw him into this cistern which is in the pasture. Do not put a hand on him...' The statement concludes with the narrator moving back into third person discourse to end the sentence with an explanation to the reader: '... in order to deliver him from their hand, to return him to his father'. The concluding phrase joins with the introductory phrase, 'And Reuben said to them', to enclose Reuben's proposal with its grounding and provide its interpretation.

We now see the solidarity of the brothers decisively fragmented. They were halted in the midst of a murderous attack by one of their own number. For the first time there is an individual, independent voice among the brothers, while Joseph waits in the pit. As Seebass has indicated (see above), the story cannot end here since Joseph may survive somehow to return with this piece of news for Jacob. And how are the brothers themselves to assess Reuben's intentions?

The reader finally finds in Reuben a hero with whom he can identify. The ambiguity of the early scene now has resolved itself into good and evil poles. Joseph, interestingly, is at neither. He is the person in the middle; the passive, non-resisting victim. What will happen to the family when Joseph returns with his 'bad report' this time? What will be the fate of Reuben if he is successful? Reuben's intervention is thus a decisive turning point in the plot since it disrupts the logical movement of the the emotional system given by the narrator at the outset and by so doing serves indirectly the counter program of the prognosticating dimension of the dream. One brother does not share in the sarcasm and cannot kill the 'dream-lord'.

Now the narrator tells us that the brothers go apart to eat, a sardonic observation which also conveys a certain inconclusiveness. Have they given up their intention to kill him, and are they content to leave him in the pit? Do they intend to return and kill him without the knowledge of Reuben (an alternative which Reuben later assumes they chose, 42.22)?

At this critical moment, the narrator (as a *deus ex machina*) brings on stage an Ishmaelite caravan heading toward Egypt, and a new single voice is suddenly raised among the brothers, articulating a new proposal. Judah, seeing the opportunitiy presented by this caravan, offers the proposal to sell Joseph as a slave to the Ishmaelites. This proposal contains the elements of an ingenious compromise. On the one side is the powerful urge to kill Joseph, with the attendant problems of blood guilt (and the implicit danger of discovery inherent in Reuben's lack of support). On the other side is Reuben's proposal which implicitly leaves open the possibility of Joseph's escape (or his deliverance by Reuben). To sell him into slavery has the virtue of both proposals (ridding themselves of Joseph), with neither of the disadvantages (blood guilt, or the possibility of his escape and return).

Judah couches his proposal in terms of a new system of motivation when he asks (clearly assuming the continuation of the brothers' intent to kill): 'What does it profit if we kill our brother and conceal his blood?' This cleverly sets in motion the motivation of material gain as a counter pole to the motive of jealous vengeance. Through a simple transaction they may exchange Joseph for silver, thereby ridding themselves of Joseph permanently (as in death, they think), while not acquiring blood guilt. Can Judah be termed a 'good brother' for this proposal, a duplicate of Reuben? His motivation seems to be primarily self-serving within the set of options given by these circumstances. His argument is primarily that of enlightened self-interest which has only the secondary effect of saving Joseph's life. This is not the 'stuff' of heroism. We are led away from the clear differentiation of good and evil which occurred in the Reuben scene, back toward gray ambiguities.

But it is precisely this ambiguity that enables Judah's proposal to be consonant with the prognosticating dimension of the dream. On the one hand, by replacing Joseph with money, a certain closure is achieved with respect to the primary emotional system of the family, while on the other, his sale to the Ishmaelites/Midanites leaves his future relatively open with no complicating problems from the past. It also leaves the brothers with no righteous heroes (Reuben ending up the pathetic failed hero, rending his clothes), but also with no blood guilt. With the help of the narrator's *deus ex machina*, bringing the Ishmaelites by at the precise moment of crisis, Judah's proposal, as a brilliant compromise, represents the triumph of the dialogical process over the deterministic emotions of the familial system. Through a combination of discourse and circumstance, the logic of that initial system has been brought to speech and deflected from its morbid goal, and Joseph has been left in a state of relative openness to the future. Reuben's words were needed not only to halt the murder, but also to establish one extreme pole in the dialogical process which makes Judah's proposal appear as a reasonable compromise. Through Reuben's words, Joseph is alive but waiting in the pit with knowledge that would be disastrous to the brothers if related to Jacob. But with Joseph in the pit, emotions have been vented, and there is the opportunity for reason to be heard.

Reuben's return to the cistern, and his shock over the disappearance of Joseph (he rends his garments) reawaken in the reader the idealistic emotions he once shared with Reuben. But with the surrender of Reuben to the emotions of self-pitying bathos ('The lad is not, and I, where shall I go?'), idealism dies, and the reader knows that Reuben has been silenced. There remains only the deception of Jacob through the presentation of misleading evidence (rather than an outright lie). The narrator then reports in direct discourse Jacob's response to this deception, and his sorrowful laments over the conclusion he draws from it, that Joseph is dead. The narrator in a final comment tells how 'all' Jacob's sons and 'all' his daughters sought unsuccessfully to comfort him. The eloquent intensity of his grief which firmly (and bitterly?) closed itself against attempts by his children to comfort him ('I shall go down to Sheol to my son, mourning') is a sign the narrator gives us the cleavage which now exists in the family at the deepest level. Why does he reject the efforts of his children? Is his absolute grief another sign of his attachment to Joseph, or does he suspect the brothers? In either event Joseph's absence is now a more serious problem for his brothers' than his presence had been. Jacob's grief was a problem the brothers cover-up scheme did not anticipate, and it is a problem whose only solution is now in Egypt (v. 36).

The narrative which began with the breaking of peaceful, trusting communication between Joseph and his brothers now depicts a deep and apparently permanent verbal estrangement between Jacob and his other children. The removal of the envied Joseph, rather than bringing the brothers into intimacy with their father, has apparently made such intimacy forever impossible, as Jacob prefers communion with Joseph even in death to the solace of his other living children.

The analysis must end here before closure has been achieved. The narrator tells us that the object of Jacob's grief is now in Egypt, a slave in the household of an officer of the king (v. 36). The juxtaposition of Joseph's good fortune and Jacob's infinite grief here at the end of this scene portends much for the future.

Though the narrative process has not reached its culmination, something of the dialectical process Fish described is already in evidence. Both the deterministic system of familial emotions and the occult, prognosticatory dreams with their contradictory ends have been drawn into the familial discourse and the process of their dialogization has begun. The brothers have been both incited to murder by the discourse about the dream and also deflected from it by the discursive process. The meaning of the narrative has thus far been in the dialogical process in which the brothers have been provoked to articulate their latent feelings and deal with the full consequences of their hatred. Jacob as well has been confronted with the outer results of his own partiality. The crisis with which the last scene ends is also one which cannot be resolved apart from a dialectical process which will effect a transformation, if not in the character of the personages, at least in their communicative relations. A comprehensive analysis of the entire narrative would reveal that it is in the achievement of open trusting communication between these rival brothers that the dialectic of the narrative and the ideology of the narrator reach their goal, if not their end. The climactic event of this dialogical process is the transmission of the promise, for the first time, from one brother to another (50.24), an event which signals at least the momentary transcending of the problem of rivalry and the possibility of a new open history beyond such determinations.

NOTES

1. 'Die Josefsgeschichte', in P. Volz and W. Rudolph, *Der Elohist als*

Erzähler: ein Irrweg der Pentateuchkritik?' (Giessen: Alfred Töpelmann, 1933) 143-83.

2. Gerhard von Rad, 'Josephsgeschichte und "altere Chokma"' in *Gesammelte Studien zum Alten Testament* (München: Kaiser, 1961) 272-80.

3. h.N. Whybray, 'The Joseph Story and Pentateuchal Criticism', *VT* 18 (1968) 526.

4. *Genesis: A Commentary* (OTL Philadelphia: Westminster, 1961) 343.

5. Whybray, 'The Joseph Story', 525.

6. *Ibid.*

7. Donald B. Redford, *A Study of the Biblical Story of Joseph* (VTS, 20; Leiden: E.J. Brill, 1970) 104, 105; J.L. Crenshaw, 'Method in Determining Wisdom Influence upon "Historical" Literature', *JBL* 88 (1969) 129-37.

8. George W. Coats, 'The Joseph Story and Ancient Wisdom: A Reappraisal', *CBQ* 35 (1973) pp. 285-97.

9. Redford, *Biblical Story of Joseph*; Hans-Christoph Schmitt, *Die nichtpriesterliche Josephgeschichte: Ein Beitrag zur neuesten Pentateuchkritik* (BZAW, 154; Berlin: Walter de Gruyter, 1980).

10. George W. Coats, *From Canaan to Egypt: Structural and Theological Context for the Joseph Story* (CBQM5, 4; Washington, D.C.: The Catholic Biblical Association, 1976).

11. Horst Seebass, *Geschichtliche Zeit und theonome Tradition in der Joseph-Erzählung* (Gutersloh: Gerd Mohn, 1978) 76.

12. Robert Alter, *The Art of Biblical Narrative* (New York: Basic Books, 1981) 12.

13. *Ibid.*, 159.

14. Kenneth R. Melchin, 'Literary Sources in the Joseph Story', *Science et Esprit* 31 (1979) 93-101.

15. Redford, *Biblical Story of Joseph*, 10.

16. *Ibid.*, 145.

17. *Ibid.*, 145 n. 2.

18. *Ibid.*, 138.

19. *Ibid.*, 141.

20. Schmitt, *Die nichtpriesterliche Josephsgeschichte*, 29.

21. Coats, *From Canaan to Egypt*, 17.

22. *Ibid.*, 17.

23. *Ibid.*, 61.

24. Seebass, *Geschichtliche Zeit*, 74.

25. *Ibid.*

26. *Ibid.*

27. *Ibid.*, 91.

28. Rudolph, 'Die Josefsgeschichte', 153, 154.

29. *Ibid.*, 154.

30. Hermann Gunkel, *Genesis* (6th edn; Göttingen: Vandenhoeck und Ruprecht, 1964) 409.

31. *Ibid.*, 420. Redford's argument that this reference in Judg 8.24 is an 'identifying gloss which would hardly have been necessary had the two words been commonly accepted terms for the same ethnic group' is somewhat peculiar in light of the obvious function of the comment (*Biblical Story of Joseph*, 145 n. 2). It is not to identify the Midianites, but to explain why the Israelite army was able to respond to Gideon's command to turn over the earrings which they had taken as spoil after conquering the Midianites. The explanatory comment, that 'they had gold earrings because they were Ishmaelites', clearly presupposes that the author himself assumed the identity of the two groups and was assuming that his readers would, with his reminder, share his assumptions. Schmitt's argument, that the identification of these tribes in 37.28 would have required an explanatory gloss similar to that found in Judg 8.24, thus does not reflect an accurate reading of that verse (*Die nichtpriesterliche Josephgeschichte*, 29). This phrase is not meant to explain that the Ishmaelites were Midanites, but to inform the reader about a custom of the Midianites. To satisfy a reader such as Schmitt, this phrase would have had to continue on to say, 'and the Ishmaelites are the same as Midianites'. The fact that such an additional explanation was not needed shows the extent to which the writer could presuppose that his readers would naturally make this connection, and identify these two groups.

32. Coats, *From Canaan to Egypt*, 30.

33. Redford, *Biblial Story of Joseph*, 132, 133.

34. *Ibid.*, 135.

35. Coats, *From Canaan to Egypt*, 69.

36. Schmitt, *Die nichtpriesterliche Josephgeschichte*, 27.

37. Coats, *From Canaan to Egypt*, 35.

38. Seebass, *Geschichtliche Zeit*, 74.

39. Julius Wellhausen, *Die Composition des Hexateuchs und der historischen Bücher der Alten Testaments* (4th edn; Berlin: Walter de Gruyter, 1963) 53.

40. See Hans W. Frei, *The Eclipse of Biblical Narrative: A Study in Eighteenth and Nineteenth Century Hermeneutics* (New Haven: Yale University, 1974) 138, 150.

41. Seebass, *Geschichtliche Zeit*, 93.

42. For a discussion of subjectivism at the macroscopic level of Old Testament critical theory see Robert M. Polzin, *Biblical Structuralism: Method and Subjectivity in the Study of Ancient Texts* (Philadelphia: Fortress, 1977) 126-202.

43. Stanley E. Fish, 'Literature in the Reader', *Reader Response Criticism: From Formalism to Post-Structuralism* (Baltimore: John Hopkins University, 1980) 83.

44. *Ibid.*, 75.

45. *Ibid.*, 80.

46. *Ibid.*, 83.

47. *Ibid.*
48. *Ibid.*, 73.
49. *Ibid.*, 87.
50. *Ibid.*
51. Stanley E. Fish, *Self-Consuming Artifacts: The Experience of Seventeenth-Century Literature* (Berkeley: University of California, 1972) 1, 2.
52. *Ibid.*, 4.
53. *Ibid.*
54. Stanley E. Fish, *Surprised by Sin: The Reader in Paradise Lost* (Berkeley: University of California, 1971).
55. Fish, *Self-Consuming Artifacts*.
56. Hugh C. White, 'A Theory of the Surface Structure of the Biblical Narrative', *USQR* 34 (1979) 159-74.

5

THE COMMUNITY AS KING IN SECOND ISAIAH

Edgar W. Conrad

Introduction

It has frequently been noted that Second Isaiah democratizes royal traditions, that is, he transfers to the people traditions associated with the king. H. Wildberger has argued, for example, that the election tradition in Second Isaiah is to be traced to traditions associated with the election of the Davidic king.[1] O. Eissfeldt and others have also noted that in Isaiah 55.3-5, Second Isaiah is transferring traditions concerning the everlasting covenant from the Davidic king to the people.[2]

In this essay, which I dedicate to my teacher and friend Bernhard W. Anderson with whom I have shared many treasured hours of discussion on Second Isaiah, I would like to argue that five 'fear not' oracles in Second Isaiah (41.8-13; 41.14-16; 43.1b-4; 43.5-7 and 43.2b-5) offer further evidence of the democratization of royal traditions. It is my contention that these five texts represent a genre which I have termed the War Oracle. It is spoken by the deity to a king in the face of military attack. In the oracle the deity promises that he will fight for the king and that the king need not be engaged in the battle. Second Isaiah uses the War Oracle to comfort or assure the exilic community, not only in the context of the rise of Cyrus to power (ch. 41) but also in the context of the war which Yahweh had formerly fought against his people (chs. 43 and 44).

'Fear not' and the Oracle of Salvation

These five 'fear not' texts in Second Isaiah have usually been understood as representing the Oracle of Salvation, a thesis first propounded by Joachim Begrich.[3] Earlier scholars had noted that some of the individual psalms of lament ended in praise (e.g. Ps 22). They reasoned that there must have been a priestly oracle given in answer to the lament and petition of the individual which changed the lament of the supplicant to praise.[4] While these Oracles of Salvation do not occur in the Psalter, Bergrich argued that Second

Isaiah imitated this originally priestly form of speech in his prophetic announcement of salvation to the exilic community.

I have argued in another place[5] that Begrich's criteria for identifying the 'fear not' oracles in Second Isaiah as Oracles of Salvation are questionable for three reasons:

1. He fails to consider those places in the Psalter in which Oracles of Salvation do not contain the phrase 'fear not' (Pss 12.5; 21.8-12; 60.6-8 = 108.7-9; 75.2ff.; 81.6-16; 91.14-16; 95.8-11).[6]

2. He fails to consider those texts outside Second Isaiah which contain the phrase 'fear not' but which are clearly not answers to lament.[7]

3. He unwittingly calls his thesis into question in a later study written in 1938 in which he demonstrates that the pervasiveness of the language of lament in Second Isaiah extends beyond those pericopes containing the phrase, *'l tyr'*.[8]

It is my contention, then, that these five texts are not Oracles of Salvation. They follow the stereotypical structure of the War Oracle used to address a king who is threatened by a military threat to his kingship.[9]

War Oracles Addressed to Kings

To prove the point that Second Isaiah uses the War Oracle to address the community as king, it will be necessary to examine War Oracles outside Second Isaiah where kings under military threat are assured with a 'fear not' oracle. The first passage to be considered is Isaiah 7. In this passage, Ahaz, king of Judah, is threatened by a military alliance between Syria and the northern state of Israel. While Ahaz is in the Fuller's field apparently inspecting the water supply as part of the preparations for defense, Isaiah is instructed by Yahweh to speak a War Oracle to him. The structure of the war Oracle (7.4-9) can be outlined as follows:

(a)	Directive	Take heed, be quiet,
(b)	Assurance	do not fear (*'l tyr'*) and do not let your heart be faint (*wlbbk 'l yrk*)
(c)	Object of Fear	because of these two smoldering stumps of firebrands, at the fierce anger of Rezin and Syria and the son of Remaliah . . .

(d) Basis of Assurance thus says the Lord God:
It shall not stand.
and it shall not come to pass.
For (*ky*) the head of Syria is Damascus,
and the head of Damascus is Rezin.

(e) Orders If you do not believe,
surely you shall not be established.

As many commentators have noted, this text has undoubtedly been expanded in transmission. Yet it still contains the basic stereotypical structure of the War Oracle: the Assurance with *'l tyr'*, and Object of Fear with causative *mn*, a Basis of Assurance stating the reason not to be afraid usually introduced with *ky* and Orders formulated in the second person. In this particular example there is also a Directive in the imperative.

It is important to observe in this oracle that the king is instructed not to be actively engaged in defense against the enemy. He is directed to be quiet and is given orders to trust in the deity. A key feature of War Oracles addressed to kings is that the king need not be actively engaged in battle against the enemy.

When Sennacherib attacked Jerusalem during the reign of Hezekiah, Isaiah delivered a War Oracle on behalf of Yahweh to the Judean king (Isa 37.6).[10]

The structure of this oracle can be outlined as follows:

(a) Assurance Do not be afraid (*'l tyr'*)
(b) Object of Fear because of the words that you have heard with which the servants of the king of Assyria have reviled me.
(c) Basis of Assurance Behold I (*hnny*) will put a spirit in him, so that he shall hear a rumor, and return to his land;
(d) Promise and I will make him fall by the sword in his own land.

This oracle is quite similar in structure to the oracle Isaiah spoke to Ahaz. There is an Assurance with *'l tyr'*, an Object of Fear with causative *mn* and a Basis of Assurance stating the reason why the king should not fear. Unlike the oracle addressed to Ahaz, however, it does not have Orders addressing the king in the second person; instead it has a promise in the first person in which the deity indicates what he will do to defend the king. As we will see below this variation in the structure of the War Oracle, which may contain either Orders or a Promise, is also reflected in the War Oracles in Second Isaiah.

The intent of this oracle addressed to Hezekiah is like that of the oracle addressed to Ahaz. The king is not to be afraid of the military threat nor is the king to be actively involved in the battle with the enemy. The deity will defeat the enemy for the king.

A number of extra-biblical texts containing the phrase 'fear not' or 'do not fear' should also be understood as War Oracles.[11] They are structurally similar to the oracles Isaiah spoke to Ahaz and Hezekiah, and they also assure the king that he need not fight against the enemy because the deity will fight for him.

The first text to be considered is an oracle spoken by Be'elshamayn to Zakir, king of Hamat and Lu'ath. The text dates from the beginning of the eighth century,[12] i.e. the century when Ahaz and Hezekiah were kings of Judah. The occasion for the oracle is an alliance of kings threatening Zakir similar to the alliance that threatened Ahaz.

> Barhadad, the son of Hazael, king of Aram, united [seven of] a group of ten kings against me: Barhadad and his army; Bargush and his army; the king of Cilicia and his army; the king of 'Umq and his army; the king of Gurgum and his army; the king of Sam'al and his army; the king of Milidh and his army. [All these kings whom Barhadad united against me] were seven kings and their armies. All these kings laid siege to Hatarikka. They made a wall higher than the wall of Haratikka. They made a moat deeper than its moat.

In response to this military threat Zakir brings the matter before Be'elshamayn who speaks a War Oracle to him through seers and diviners. The structure of the oracle can be outlined as follows:

(a)	Assurance	Do not fear,
(b)	Basis of Assurance	for I made you king,
(c)	Promise	and I shall stand by you and deliver you from all [these kings who] set up a siege against you. [Be'elshamayn] said to me: [*I shall destroy*] all these kings who set up ...

The structure of this oracle is quite similar to that of the oracle Isaiah spoke to Ahaz. There is no Object of Fear, but this is often missing in War Oracles and, as we will see, is missing in the War Oracles in Second Isaiah. The Basis of Assurance here states that the king should not fear because the deity made him king. This is reminiscent of royal ideology in the Old Testament expressed by the deity's promise to continue the elected Davidic monarchy (e.g. 2 Sam 7.11b-

16 and Ps 89). The oracle also promises that it is the deity who will fight for the king.

Another text that is important for our consideration is 'An Oracular Dream Concerning Ashurbanipal' dated about the middle of the seventh century.[13] It does not contain the full text of a War Oracle but is important because of the ideology associated with the deity who fights for the king. The text opens with Ashurbanipal saying that Ishtar had heard his 'anxious sighs' and had said 'fear not'—which gave him confidence. That the goddess is comforting Ashurbanipal with the assuring 'fear not' in the context of a military threat is evident from what follows. The text describes a seer's vision of Ishtar in full battle regalia:

> Ishtar who dwells in Arbela came in. Right and left quivers were hanging from her. Se held the bow in her hand (and) a sharp sword was drawn to do battle.

In the vision a conversation ensues between Ashurbanipal and Ishtar in which Ishtar tells Ashurbanipal that he need not fight; she will fight for him. She says to Ashurbanipal,

> You will stay here, where the dwelling of Nabu is. Eat food, drink wine, supply music, praise my divinity, while I go and do that work in order that you attain your heart's desire. Your face (need) not become pale, nor your feet become exhausted, nor your strength come to nought in the onslaught of battle.

This text, then, while containing only the Assurance, 'fear not', makes it clear that when the king is assured with a War Oracle, he need not become actively engaged in fighting; the deity will fight for him.

While there are other Assyrian containing the phrase, 'fear not', in a War Oracle,[14] one other text can help demonstrate our thesis.[15] In this text the goddess Ninlil comforts Ashurbanipal. The structure of the text is as follows:

(a)	Assurance	Fear not,
(b)	Address	O Ashurbanipal!
(c)	Basis of Assurance	Now as I have spoken, it will come to pass: I shall grant (it) to you.
(d)	Orders	Over the people of the four languages (and) over *the armament* of the princes you will exercise sovereignty.

This particular text contains Orders rather than a Promise. The occasion for the oracle is again the threat of a military alliance: '[The kings] of the countries confer together (saying), "Come (let us rise against Ashurbanipal . . ."'' The text also makes clear that when fighting is to be done it is the deity who will fight for the king:

> I shall arise, break the thorns, open up widely
> my way through the *briers*. With *blood* shall I turn the land
> into a rain shower, (fill it with) lamentation and wailing.

This analysis of War Oracles addressed to kings indicates that the phrase 'fear not' is a key element in a genre which prophets, seers and diviners use to speak to a king on behalf of the deity. The occasion for the oracle is a military threat to the kingship. While the genre is somewhat flexible and displays the peculiarities of individual 'authors' there is a general recurring pattern. The Assurance, 'fear not', is followed by a Basis of Assurance stating the reason not to fear. The oracle is concluded with either Orders giving the recipient of the oracle instructions on what he is to do or with a Promise in which the deity promises that he/she will fight for the king. In these oracles the king need not fear because he will not be actively engaged in the war against the enemy; the deity will fight for him.

War Oracles in Second Isaiah

A general observation about the structure and setting of the War Oracles in Second Isaiah will provide a helpful introduction to the discussion of his use of this genre. The two War Oracles in 41.8ff. are introduced by *w'th*, 'but you', the oracles in 43.1ff. and the oracle in 44.1ff. are introduced by *w'th*, 'but now'. These introductory phrases are important clues not only to the particular form of the War Oracle but also to the *Sitz im Text* of the oracles. The War Oracles in Second Isaiah are not only to be understood in terms of their *Sitz im Leben* as oracles addressed to a king faced with a military threat to his kingship, but also in terms of their setting in the context of Second Isaiah's poetry. The two oracles in 4.8ff. introduced by 'but you' are formed with Orders. The orders given to Jacob/Israel contrast with the actions of the nations (41.5-7) who are afraid of the military threat posed by the new conqueror Cyrus whom Yahweh has 'stirred up' to fight his battles for him (41.1-4). The oracles in 43.1ff. and 44.1ff. introduced by 'but now' are formed with a promise. The promise given to Jacob/Israel that Yahweh will rescue his 'offspring' (*zr'*) is a reversal of Yahweh's former military defeat of his chosen people (42.25 and 43.28).

That Second Isaiah is following the conventional form of the War Oracle is evident from the following structural outlines of the oracles.[16]

Isa 41.8-13

(a) Address   But you, Israel, my servant,
                             Jacob, whom I have chosen,
                             the offspring of Abraham, my friend . . .

(b) Assurance   fear not (*'l tyr'*) // be not dismayed (*'l tšt'*)

(c) Basis of Assurance for (*ky*) I am with you // for (*ky*) I am your God.
                             I have strengthened you, I have helped you;
                             I have upheld you with my victorious right hand.

(d) Orders   Behold, all who are incensed against you
                             shall be put to shame and confounded;
                           those who strive against you
                             shall be as nothing and shall perish.
                           You shall seek those who contend with you,
                             but you shall not find them;
                           those who war against you
                             shall be as nothing at all.

(e) Basis of Assurance For (*ky*) I, the LORD your God,
                             hold your right hand;
                           it is I who say to you, 'Fear not,
                           I have helped you'.

Isa 41.14-16

(a) Assurance   Fear not (*'l tyr'*),

(b) Address   you worm Jacob,
                           you men of Israel!

(c) Basis of Assurance I have helped you, says the LORD;
                           your Redeemer is the Holy One of Israel.
                         Behold (*hnh*), I made you a threshing sledge,
                           new, sharp, and having teeth;

(d) Orders   you shall thresh mountains and crush them,
                           and you shall make the hills like chaff;
                         you shall winnow them and the wind
                           shall carry them away,
                           and the tempest shall scatter them.
                        And you shall rejoice in the LORD;
                         in the Holy One of Israel you shall glory.

Isa 43.1b-4

(a)	Assurance	Fear not (*'l tyr'*),
(b)	Basis of Assurance	for (*ky*) I have redeemed you;
		I have called you by name, you are mine.
		When (*ky*) you pass through the waters
		I will be with you . . .
		when (*ky*) you walk through fire you shall not
		be burned . . .
		For (*ky*) I am the LORD your God
		the Holy One of Israel, your Saviour.
		I gave Egypt as your ransom.
		Ethiopia and Seba in exchange for you . . .
(c)	Promise	I will give men in return for you,
		peoples in exchange for your life.

Isa 43.5-7

(a)	Assurance	Fear not (*'l tyr'*),
(b)	Basis of Assurance	for (*ky*) I am with you;
(c)	Promise	I will bring your offspring from the east,
		and from the west, I will gather you;
		I will say to the north, Give up,
		and to the south, Do not withhold . . .

Isa 44.2b-5

(a)	Assurance	Fear not (*'l tyr'*),
(b)	Address	O Jacob my servant,
		Jeshurun whom I have chosen.
(c)	Promise	For (*ky*) I will pour water on the thirsty land
		and streams on the dry ground;
		I will pour my Spirit upon your descendants
		and my blessing on your offspring.

The structure of these 'fear not' oracles in Second Isaiah indicates that the prophet is following the genre of the War Oracles addressed to kings which we analyzed in the preceding section. The Assurance, *'l tyr'*, is followed by a Basis of Assurance giving the reason why the recipient of the oracle should not fear. In Second Isaiah the Basis of Assurance is introduced by *ky* in all but one instance (41.14-16).[17] This element is unusually long in 43.1b-4 where four lines introduced by *ky* offer support for the Assurance not to fear. The Basis of Assurance is missing in 44.1-5 although there *ky* introduces the

Promise and the Promise doubles as a Basis of Assurance. The fact that it is missing in 44.1-5 can perhaps be explained by the fact that this is the last War Oracle to appear in the text and follows the oracle in 43.1b-4 where this element has been greatly expanded. The oracles conclude either with Orders addressed to Jacob/Israel in the second person concerning the actions of the community, or with a Promise in which Yahweh describes his actions in the first person. In Second Isaiah's use of the War Oracle the Basis of Assurance is always stated in the perfect tense and the Orders and the Promise are always stated in the imperfect tense. The Basis of Assurance appeals to something Yahweh has done in the past as the basis for the future Orders given to Jacob/Israel or for Yahweh's Promise about the future.

In the introduction to this section of the paper we noted that the use of the War Oracle makes sense in its *Sitz im Text*. We will now need to say more about the *Sitze im Text* of the oracles to clarify the orders given to Jacob/Israel and the promises Yahweh makes to the community and to understand in what sense Yahweh is addressing the community as king.

Chapter 41 opens with a trial scene against the nations (vv. 1-4). This unit functions to demonstrate that it is Yahweh who is the power behind Cyrus, the new conqueror. After the trial scene the nations are described (41.5-7) as building gods as a way of finding safety and power to defend themselves against this conqueror. The word that the nations use to comfort one another, 'take courage' (*ḥzq*), is a word commonly used to encourage a warrior before battle (cf. Josh 1.6, 7, 9). The War Oracles that follow in 41.8ff. with the opening, 'but you', offer comfort to Jacob/Israel from a god who does not need to be made from wood and stone and from the god who unlike the gods of the other nations is the power behind Cyrus. Jacob/Israel need not fear because Yahweh is fighting for Jacob/Israel through Cyrus. Cyrus is not an enemy. Therefore in the first War Oracle Yahweh orders Jacob/Israel to look for those who 'contend with you' and for those who 'war against you'. When Jacob/Israel carries out those orders, however, the enemies will be found to be nothing at all.

The orders in the second oracle (41.14-16) are that Jacob/Israel, whom Yahweh made a 'threshing sledge', is to 'thresh' (*dwš*), 'crush' (*dqq*), 'make like chaff' (*kmṣ śym*) and 'winnow' (*zrh*), 'mountains' (*hrym*) and 'hills' (*gbʿwt*). This language has not always been easily understood; however, its occurrence in the War Oracle helps clarify its meaning. The verbs concerning threshing, crushing, making like chaff, and winnowing are sometimes used to speak of the defeat of the enemy and in that sense are military idioms suggested by the War Oracle.[18] However, Israel is not to crush the enemy because Israel is not fighting enemies. Israel is rather to destroy mountains and hills. I would suggest that this language makes sense when it is read in conjunction with the prologue (40.1-11). In the prologue it is suggested that Israel's warfare (*ṣb'h*, v. 2) is ended and that a highway is to be made in the desert for the victory march of Yahweh. Every valley will be lifted up and every hill and mountain made low (40.3-5). Further, the community (here addressed as Zion/Jerusalem) is to be a 'herald of good tidings' (*mbśrt*) announcing Yahweh's victory (40.9). When Zion/Jerusalem is given that task of being a herald of good tidings in 40.9, she is assured with 'fear not', the first time this important element of the War Oracle occurs in the book. In this context, then, the destroying of mountains and hills in the orders in 41.14-16 begins to make sense. Yahweh is ordering Jacob/Israel as the herald of good tidings. Yahweh has made Jacob/Israel a threshing sledge, to destroy the mountains and hills to make a highway for the victory march of Yahweh to Jerusalem. I would suggest further that mountains and hills should be understood figuratively to refer to the obstacles that will be met on the journey to Jerusalem. The word 'mountain' is used in this figurative sense, for example, in Zech 4.7 to refer to the obstacles facing Zerubbabel who has the responsibility of completing the building of the temple.[19] Before Zerubbabel the mountain of obstacles will become a plain. Likewise before Jacob/Israel the mountain of obstacles will be easily overcome for Yahweh has made them a threshing sledge. The order given to Jacob/Israel to overcome the obstacles facing them in the desert in their victory trek with Yahweh is picked up in the unit (40.17-20) following the War Oracles where Yahweh promises to make that barren wilderness a fertile place.

The War Oracles in 41.8ff. then order Jacob/Israel to look for enemies, which will be found to be non-existent, and to destroy the obstacles to be met as Jacob/Israel heralds Yahweh's victory. Even this last task will be an easy one, however, for Yahweh will make fertile the barren desert.

In the introduction to this section we noted that the War Oracles 43.1ff. and 44.1ff. promise Jacob/Israel that Yahweh will rescue the 'offspring' (*zr'*) of the community, although his former actions led to the defeat of the people in battle (42.25 and 43.28). While space does not permit us here to develop the point, I would suggest that the promise of the restoration of the offspring of Jacob/Israel should be understood on the basis of Second Isaiah's understanding of the patriarchal promise in which Yahweh had promised Abraham that he would have abundant offspring. In Second Isaiah the community is understood as 'the offspring of Abraham' (41.8; cf. 51.1-2). Furthermore, the Pentateuch in its present form also uses the War Oracle to promise the patriarchs offspring (cf. Gen 15.1 and 26.24).[20]

Conclusion

The thesis that Second Isaiah uses a royal form, the War Oracle, to address the community adds support to those who see a democratization in his thought. Wildberger has argued that the election tradition in Second Isaiah is to be traced to a royal setting. In the War Oracles Jacob/Israel is identified as the chosen servant of Yahweh (41.8 and 44.2). The fact that Second Isaiah uses a royal form to address the chosen community is further evidence that Second Isaiah is applying royal traditions to the community.

The War Oracles also are related to Isaiah 55.3-5 in a significant way. There it is suggested that when Yahweh made an everlasting covenant with David, he made him a witness to the nations. Now that vocation is to be assumed by the community. Significantly, the vocation of the royal community as witnesses of Yahweh is linked with the two War Oracles in 43.1-7 and 44.1-5. Following each of these War Oracles which promise the rescue of the offspring of Jacob/Israel are trial scenes (43.8-13 and 44.6-8). In both trial scenes the community is to be Yahweh's witnesses (43.10; 44.8) to the nations who are on trial.

In Second Isaiah, then, the community is the king, and it is Yahweh who will fight for his people. This insight into the theology of Second Isaiah has important implications for those who attribute authority to the Bible in a contemporary setting. Victory is not given to the king; it is given to the people. Peace is not achieved in the panic efforts of the nations to build implements of power (44.5-7) but in God who ultimately gives the victory.

NOTES

1. See, for example, 'Die Neuinterpretation des Erwählungsglaubens

Israels in der Krise der Exilzeit', *Wort-Gebot-Glaube: Beiträge zur Theologie des Alten Testament: Festschrift für W. Eichrodt* (ed. Joachim Stoebe; ATANT, 59; Zürich: Zwingli, 1970) 318ff.

2. O. Eissfeldt, 'The Promises of Grace to David in Isaiah 55.1-5', *Israel's Prophetic Heritage: Essays in Honor of James Muilenburg* (ed. B.W. Anderson and W. Harrelson; New York: Harper and Brothers, 1962), 196-207. See also C. Westermann, *Isaiah 40-66: A Commentary* (OTL; Westminster, 1969), 283.

3. 'Das priesterliche Heilsorakel', *ZAW* 52 (1934) 81-92. Reprinted in *Gesammelte Studien zum Alten Testament* (TBÜ, 21; München: Chr. Kaiser, 1964) 217-31.

4. The first scholar to propound this thesis was F. Küchler, 'Das priesterliche Orakel in Israel und Juda', *Abhandlungen zur semitischen Religionskunde und Sprachwissenschaft, Wolf Wilhelm Grafen von Baudissin* (ed. W. Frakenberg and F. Küchler; Giessen: Töpelmann, 1918) 285-301.

5. E. Conrad, 'Second Isaiah and the Priestly Oracle of Salvation', *ZAW* 93 (1981) 234-46.

6. Küchler understands these as Oracles of Salvation ('Das priesterliche Orakel', 298-99.

7. The only text in the Old Testament that can be construed this way is 2 Chr 20.1-17. This is a significant text for A. Schoors who sees it as further evidence for Begrich's thesis that the 'fear not' texts in Second Isaiah should be understood as Oracles of Salvation. See his *I am God you Saviour: A Form-Critical Study of the Main Genres in Is. XL-LV* (SVT, 24; Leiden: E.J. Brill, 1973) 34. See also E. von Waldow, 'Anlass und Hintergrund der Verkündigung des Deuterojesaja' (Dissertation of Rheinische Friedrich Wilhelms Universität, 1953) 80ff.

8. J. Begrich, *Studien zu Deuterojesaja* (TBÜ, 20; München: Kaiser, 1963) 14ff.

9. These texts are also related to 'fear not' passages in the Deuteronomic History and in Genesis. For a discussion of those texts see my 'The "Fear Not" Texts in Second Isaiah', *VT* 34 (1984) 129-52. This essay moves slightly beyond that article in that it sees all the 'fear not' texts in Second Isaiah as War Oracles. I am currently writing a monograph on 'fear not' texts in the Old Testament tentatively titled, *Fear Not Warrior: A Study of 'al tira' Pericopes in the Old Testament* (to be published in Brown Judaic Studies; Chico: Scholars Press). In that study I make the point that the War Oracle addressed to kings has been used in a quite distinctive way in the Deuteronomic History.

10. This text is also found in 2 Kings 19.6.

11. P. Harner in an article ('The Salvation Oracle in Second Isaiah', *JBL* 88 [1969] 418-34) understood these Mesopotamian texts as Oracles of Salvation. However, he recognized the military significance of these oracles (p. 422).

12. Here I am dependent on the translation of F. Rosenthal, *ANET*, 655-56.

13. Here following the translation of R. Pfeiffer in *ANET*, 451.

14. See, e.g., the oracles addressed to Esarhaddon in *ANET*, 449-50 and p. 605.

15. Here following the translation of F. Rosenthal, *ANET*, 450-51.

16. For sake of brevity the full text of the oracle is not always given. I have changed RSV translation by consistently translating the perfect verbs in the past tense and the imperfect verbs in the future tense.

17. The particle, *hnh*, is used in Isa 41.14-16. Compare Isa 37.6.

18. See, e.g., Isa 17.13 and 29.5. See also C. Westermann, *Isaiah 40–66*, 76-77.

19. See P.R. Ackroyd, *Exile and Restoration* (London: SCM, 1968) 173, who understands 'mountain' in Zech. 4.7 in this way.

20. See my dissertation, 'Patriarchal traditions in Second Isaiah' (Princeton Theological Seminary, 1974).

6

LOT: A FOIL IN THE ABRAHAM SAGA

George W. Coats

Who was Lot? In Genesis 11.31, the priestly source leaves no doubt about an answer to the question. Lot was a son of Haran; together with Terah (Lot's grandfather), Abram, and Sarai, Lot left Ur of the Chaldeans and settled in a city named Haran. Genesis 11.27 and 31 show that according to the genealogical tradition of the priestly source, Haran and Abram were brothers, the sons of Terah. Lot was, then, the nephew of Abram. In Genesis 12.5, P makes the same point: 'Abram took Sarai, his wife, and Lot, the son of his brother . . .' If the question called for nothing more than a historical, genealogical answer, it would deserve little more than a moment's attention among more important issues of early Israelite history.

Yet, historical and genealogical answers do not in themselves provide an adequate perspective for meeting the challenge of the question. In the narrative traditions of Genesis, who was Lot? How does the literature depict him? What role does he play for the larger narrative context? These question are relevant for an adequate evaluation of the priestly narratives. In Genesis 19.29, for example, P ties Lot to tradition about a survival of the cataclysmic destruction of the cities in the valley. Where does P derive that connection? The question is even more pressng for an evaluation of the Yahwistic narrative. Is Lot simply Abram's nephew? Is Lot ever Abram's nephew? Or does the text preserve an independent tradition about Lot? And if so, what is the character of that tradition?

Martin Noth summarizes previous efforts to establish a history of tradition about Lot.

> The uncle-nephew relationship hardly represents an original element in a folk narrative, since it is not in itself an essential kinship relation . . . The core of the narrative of Genesis 19.30-38 was attached originally to the figure of Lot. According to the narrative, Lot, who lived as a hermit in that cave with his daughters, came to be the ancestor of the inhabitants of the mountain country above Zoar, on the basis of assumptions unknown to us.[1]

Noth concludes that the local tradition about Lot in a cave near Zoar became a part of the tradition about Haran and thus about Abram when the tradition made its way to Hebron-Mamre.

John van Seters objects to this reconstruction of a Lot tradition-history. The first point in his evaluation is an argument that the theme about heavenly visitors to Lot or to Abram is not in itself the subject of an independent tradition. The content of a Lot tradition, if there is one, cannot find its roots in a scene describing a heavenly visitation. This point seems to me quite convincing. Certainly in the Lot scene in Genesis 19, the visitors function as a part of the narrator's technique for depicting a quite different point. Van Seters concludes: 'This complete freedom in the author's use of the heavenly visitation theme points to the fact that there was no strong and fixed tradition about such a theme'.[2]

But the traditio-historical reconstruction focuses on Lot's connection with the cave in Zoar, not so much on the theme of heavenly visitors. Van Seters argues that this scene cannot be taken as an independent, etiological tradition. Rather, it must be seen as a natural part of the larger Lot narrative. 'There are no reasons for regarding the Zoar motif as a tradition or source independent from the *rest* of the main Lot story.'[3] It would not be possible, then, to reconstruct a distinct tradition about Lot on the basis of the cave scene alone. Van Seters draws the same conclusion for the narrative motif about Lot's wife and a pillar of salt. And concerning the daughters of Lot, he observes that 'the unit of vv 30-38 has few other marks (in addition to the apparent etiological dimension) basic to oral storytelling. It only functions as a concluding scene of a much longer literary unit . . . '[4] Van Seters's final argument about Lot sets the stage for the guiding question in this essay: 'Nowhere prior to P is Lot regarded as Abraham's nephew . . . This calls into question Noth's whole elaborate tradition-history of the Lot tradition, in which he sees Haran as a primary figure behind much of the Lot tradition.'[5]

This conclusion seems to me to be correct. But it leaves several critical questions unanswered. (1) What, then, is the functional value of the Lot figure in the tradition about Abram/Abraham? (2) Is there any evidence of a Lot tradition that might have been independent of Abram? Or is the Lot tradition essentially dependent on the Abram/Abrahm saga? (3) Does the Lot figure appear in consistent ways when the Yahwistic narrative is compared to the priestly source? Is this image confirmed by any earlier, pre-Yahwistic levels of tradition?

(4) Does the Lot tradition contribute a distinctive theological point to the Yahwistic saga? Or is the Lot tradition a tool for the Yahwist's larger theological program? What is the point of view that might characterize the (hypothetical) tradition behind the Yahwist? Does the priestly narrative simply duplicate that pattern? Or is there a distinctive priestly edition of the Lot tradition?

I

Lot appears in Genesis 11.27, 31; 12.4, 5; 13; 14.12, 16; and in ch. 19. Outside of Genesis, Lot is a part of only three Old Testament texts: Deuteronomy 2.9, 19 and Psalm 83.9. In these three texts no distinctive evidence for defining the role of Lot in the Abram tradition or an independent Lot tradition appears. In all three cases the texts refer to the sons of Lot. The two allusions in Deuteronomy are harmonious with the Genesis tradition since the sons of Lot appear there as the Moabites and the Ammonites, clearly assuming the tradition in Genesis 19.30-38. The Psalm text apparently assumes that the Assyrians derive from Lot, although no further evidence facilitates reconstruction of a tradition history along those lines. In addition to these few Old Testament texts, the New Testament refers to Lot in Luke 17.28-29, 32, and in 2 Peter 2.7-8. These texts tie Lot explicitly to the Sodom–Gomorrah tradition as a survivor of the catastrophe. The point of investigation for this essay, then, is limited to the Yahwistic and priestly narratives of Genesis. The genealogy in Genesis 11 and the allusion to Lot in Genesis 12.5 belong to P. These texts note nothing more about Lot than his genealogical position. Fundamental to these priestly texts, however, is Lot's relationship to Abram. The same point is made by the Yahwist in 12.4. It is not important here that Lot should be identified as Abram's nephew. But it is esential that Lot appear in relation to Abram. 'Abram went, just as the Lord told him. And Lot went with him.' The key to a definition of the Lot tradition thus lies in Genesis 13, 14, and 19.[6]

A. *Genesis*

The first reference to Lot, 13.1, functions simply as an item of information in the itinerary that reports Abram's move from Egypt to the Negeb. The only consequence of this redactional item from the Yahwist is to emphasize that dominant part of the tradition that places Lot with Abram: 'Lot went with him (Abram)'. The pericope in ch. 13 that sets the pattern of relationship between Abram and Lot for the Yahwist appears in vv. 2-13. This unit opens with expositiory information about both Abram and Lot. Verses 2-4 define Abram's wealth, not only in terms of siver and gold, but also in terms of cattle (*bammiqneh*). And then, with a itinerary formula, it reports Abram's travel. Verse 5 contrasts this statement about Abram's position with similar information about Lot. The first point of identificaton is again Lot's association with Abram (*haholēk 'et-'abrām*). 'Lot, who went with Abram, . . . had flocks, herds, and tents.' Even though Lot does not appear here as Abram's nephew, his association with Abram is nonetheless clear. Lot acompanied Abram on his journey. But the weight of this exposition rests on the notation that Lot was also a vey wealthy man. The item clearly intends the contrast since the opening word for v. 5 connects the Lot information with the preceding description of Abram. 'Lot, who went with Abram, *also* had flocks, herds, and tents' (*we gam le lot . . . hāyâ ṣō'n ûbāqār we 'ōhālîm*).[7]

Verses 6-7 develop this contrast as a point of tension in the narrative. Strife (*rîb*) broke out between the herdsmen of Lot and the herdsmen of Abram because the land could not support the cattle of both parties. This kind of information casts the principals in the narration as participants in a conflict that might well serve as the subject for an extensive narrative tradition.[8] How can the strife between the two kinsmen be resolved? Yet, insofar as this particular pericope is concerned, the tension does not develop into a narrative unit, building suspense until a final point of resolution breaks the tension. Perhaps a tale about Abram and Lot lies behind the notation. But in the received text, this tradition does not appear as a tale.[9] To the contrary, the narration jumps across another item of expository information in v. 7b to an Abram spech that resolves the tension. 'Let there be no strife (*me rîbâ*) between me and you, between my herdsmen and your herdsmen, for we are kinsmen' (v. 8). The speech continues in v. 9 with the method of resolution. Lot could choose the land most suited for his needs, and Abram would take the parts that would be left over. The unit is simply a report of an event. The key term here, however, is the verb, 'to separate' (*hippāred nā'*). The land will not support Lot and Abram together. These brothers must live apart.

At this particular point the audience might assume a value-neutral report about a decision by Abram and Lot that leads to a simple separation between the two wealthy families. There is no tale about strife between Abram and Lot. There is only a report that strife occurred between the herdsmen and the parties developed a plan to resolve the problem. Indeed, vv. 10-12 simply state what the parties did in carrying out the plan. Lot chose the Jordan valley and Abram dwelt in Canaan. But the report cannot emerge in clear lines with an assumption that its content is value-neutral. If the report belongs to the Yahwist, then the audience has a right to expect the Yahwist to do something explicitly with the notation in v. 11b. 'Each man separated (*wayyippārᵉdû*) from his brother.' Genesis 12.3 makes the Yahwist's program clear: Those who bless Abram will receive Yahweh's blessing, but those who hold Abram in contempt Yahweh will curse. Could we not expect a simple report by the Yahwist that Lot chose land away from the land of Abram as a resolution of the strife betwen them to be loaded with the freight of that opening Yahwistic exposition? To separate from Abram is to separate from the Lord's blessing, indeed, to invite the Lord's curse.[10]

The pericope makes this point clear and thus demonstrates that it is not a value-neutral report. Verse 10 describes the land of Lot's choice as the valley of the Jordan, with plenty of water. But a parenthetical remark places that land in the context of the catastrophe at Sodom and Gomorrah. Verse 12b then defines Lot's place of dwelling as the cities of the valley. Why would a family with so much cattle that the pressure of their presence in the open field conflicted with the herds of Abram move to the city? Has Lot lost the signs of his wealth? But that is not the only problem. Verse 12b reports that Lot's city was Sodom. And the gloss in v. 13 reveals the intention of the pericope. Lot's city friends were wicked, indeed, sinners against the Lord. This point contrasts sharply with the expository information in v. 4: 'There Abram called on the name of the Lord'. Abram and Lot are opposites.

If this pericope is not properly a tale with its own point of tension and a narrative resolution of the tension, if it is simply a report of a tradition about Abram and Lot that emphasizes the contrast between righteous Abram and his opposite, what kind of narrative function does it carry in just this position in the Genesis narration? The expository nature of the pericope is manifest. Abram was rich, but so was Lot. There was strife, and the strife led to separation of the parties. Abram settled in a place where he could call on the name of the Lord. Lot settled in a place of wicked sinners against the Lord. This report functions generally as exposition.[11] It uncovers information about the narrative principals necessary for telling the story. Indeed, it establishes a fundamental contrast that will be a substantial part of the story. As exposition it sets up the following story about Abram and Lot, or perhaps better, a story about faithful Abram highlighted by Lot, a contrasting foppish foil.

This exposition is expanded in vv. 14-18 by reference to God's promise to Abram that he and his descendants would possess a great land and that indeed he would be father of great descendants. This promise theme unifies much of the patriarchal narratives. Yet, at just this point it is curiously unrelated to the essential content of the the exposition, a contrast between Abram and Lot rooted in strife. With the exception of the bridge in v. 14, the pericope shows no contact with Lot tradition or any other expression of strife in the Abram/ Abraham saga. It does not therefore expose essential Abram/Abraham tradition for the following narratives but rather stands as extraneous tradition, imposed on the patriarchal story.[12] Insofar as the Lot tradition is concerned, the promise theme offers no essential element and no effective point of unity that might tie the Lot narrative to the traditions about Abram.

B.   *Genesis 14*

Genesis 14 appears to be a special source in the Abram/Abraham saga, not primarily the product of either the Yahwist or the priestly narrative.[13] 'The events are not told with the usual vividness but are reported like a chronicle. Almost every sentence is full of antiquarian information, and nowhere in the partriarchal stories do we find such a mass of historical and geographical detail.'[14] If, however, the pericope in ch. 14 derives from a special source, a historical chronicle that documents the movement of ancient peoples and their leaders, it has been adapted (by the Yahwist) to fit into the Abram saga. And the adaptation occurs by reference to Lot. The simple battle itinerary breaks in v. 8 with a report that five kings joined battle against a marauding coalition of four kings. The five-king coalition included the king of Sodom. The result of the battle combined a defeat of the five-king coalition with a sack of Sodom and Gomorrah. The special emphasis on Sodom and Gomorrah breaks the simple report about the battle and sets the stage for v. 12: 'They took Lot and his possessions, the son of the brother of Abram'. This verse captures a remarkable irony about Lot. The nephew of Abram, the man with so many herds that he could not fit into the same region with Abram, is now a city dweller and liable for the same fate as all the rest of the inhabitants of Sodom. And Lot's possessions, once the cause for strife with Abram, now constitute only part of the spoil taken from the city.

This battle chronicle has been expanded, however, not only by the brief allusion to Lot in v. 2, but also by the more lengthy report in vv. 13-16.[15] Lot chose his land and separated from Abram in order to live there. Then, not by virtue of his own act but only by virtue of being a city dweller, he was taken as spoil by a foreign king. He could not then effect his own escape. He had no control over his own destiny. Verses 13-16 report to the contrary that Abram took his 'trained men' ($h^a n\hat{i}k\bar{a}yw$ $y^e l\hat{i}d\hat{e}$ $b\hat{e}t\hat{o}$) in pursuit of the raiding party. As a result he rescued all the spoil taken in the raid. And that rescue included 'Lot, his kinsman and his possessions, and also the women and the people'. Lot, the one who chose the good land and lived apart from Abram, could not effect his own fate. Rather, he and his possessions were rescued by Abram. The narrative thus highlights Abram's role as hero.[16] But it also sets the contrast to Abram with the passive role of Lot. Lot suffers defeat at the hands of the foreign kings, not so much because of his sin or the sin of the wicked Sodomites, but because his defeat serves simply to establish Abram's heroic stature. Lot, the passive foil, is the rescued, the one who enables the heroic stature of Abram to emerge. It is not quite accurate to label Lot here as an anti-hero. He does not demonstrate heroic qualities by his opposite deeds, although his move away from Abram to the wicked citizens of Sodom might suggest at least a foppish character. But the point is that Lot is not, at least in this text, an independent character which might draw heroic or anti-heroic tradition. He is simply a passive foil in the literary depiction of heoric Abram.

C. *Genesis 19*

1. Verse 1 defines two of the principals for the following story as two messengers who came to Sodom in the evening. This definition apparently assumes the context where, in 18.1-15, three men visited Abram. The weight of that pericope rests on the annunciation of pregnancy and the coming birth of a son to Abraham and Sarah. And, of course, the word play in v. 12 shows a connection between Isaac and Sarah's laugh, *wattiṣḥaq*. John van Seters is certainly correct in arguing that no genre of narrative about special visitors, no tradition history about heavenly heralds can be reconstructed here.[17]

The visitors constitute narrative principals for this particular tradition, not a tradition in themselves. It may be that Abraham's gracious reception of these visitors stands as a contrast to Lot's reception in ch. 19. That contrast will be considered below. But at this point, the only observation necessary is that this Yahwistic narrative sets the stage for the Lot episode in ch. 19.

2. The two messengers of v. 1 appear to be identical to the three men of 18.2. The pericope in 18.16-23 recounts the events in the tradition that constitute the link. 18.16 shows the men in question to be underway to Sodom. The two speeches, vv. 17-19 and 20-21, constitute soliloquies of the Lord, the first anticipating an announcement to Abraham of the coming destruction of Sodom, the second a resolution to investigate Sodom and Gomorrah in order to determine the gravity of their sin. Verse 22 reports that two of the men proceeded toward Sodom while Abraham stood before the Lord.[18] The dialogue in vv. 23-33 then contains Abraham's negotiation with Yahweh for delivery of Sodom from the announced destruction. This text has nothing to contribute to the history of a Lot tradition. It does not mark ch. 19 as an Abraham tradition. Rather, its one intention is to emphasize the wickedness of Sodom. Abraham bargains with God for the sake of Sodom by asking a key question, 'Will you destroy the righteous with the wicked?' Then in successive stages Abraham sets the number of righteous necessary for saving Sodom from its doom at fifty, forty-five, forty, thirty, twenty, and finally ten. The point here, however, is not so much that ten righteous could save a city full of wicked people. If that were the case, we would be forced to ask about five or even one righteous person whose merit might save the city. And we would need to explore the character of righteousness that could counter so much evil. It is not even that Lot, a citizen of Sodom, is righteous enough to save the city, or even to save himself.[19] The point is that not even ten righteous people could be found in Sodom.[20] It was the classic example of a wicked city. And that demonstration of its wickedness sets the stage for the narrative in ch. 19.

3. The Yahwistic narrative, 19.1-28, sets out a tradition about Lot that is quite independent of the Abraham saga. The priestly note in v. 29 shows a tendency in the tradition to draw the Lot material into the larger umbrella of the Abraham saga: 'When God destroyed the cities of the valley, God remembered Abraham and sent Lot from the midst of the overthrow . . . ' But no sign of that traditional connection

appears in the Yahwistic elements of vv. 1-28. To be sure, vv. 27-28 refer to Abrahm. But the reference alludes to the dialogue in 18.22-33. At best it incorporates Abraham into the tradition as a kind of affirmation that the event occurred. No intrinsic relationship between Abraham and Lot, however, appears here. Since the Lot tradition to this point has shown a tendency to depict Lot as a passive foil to the active, heroic character of Abraham, it may be that this pericope, at its earliest levels free of allusions to Lot's relationship with Abrahm, can reveal a distinctive, if not the primary, character of the Lot tradition. If the periocope does contain evidence of essential Lot tradition, then a pressing question would probe why the Lot narrative so easily cast Lot as a passive foil to Abraham. Is there anything in the tradition that facilitates the literary function of the Lot figure in the Abraham saga?[21]

The pericope begins with an exposition in v. 1a that does not necessarily presuppose the context. The context presupposes this narrative. It shows who the 'two messengers' coming to Sodom are. Indeed, 18.22 sets Abraham's visitors on the road to Sodom. But the exposition in v. 1a does not demand that context. It simply defines the participants in the story. 'Two messengers came to Sodom in the evening, while Lot was sitting at the gate of Sodom.'

The element of crisis that gives character to a plot opens in vv. 1b-2 with an account of Lot's polite introduction of himself to the visitors, then with a dialogue and comment that bring the visitors as guests into Lot's house. Verse 3 shows the successful completion of the invitation: The visitors entered Lot's house and ate his food. The crisis comes in vv. 4-9. The citizens of Sodom press Lot to surrender the visitors for public sexual abuse (so, v. 5). Lot responds to the threat as a host should. In defense of his guests, he presents himself to the crowd, closing the door of his house on his guests and thus separating them from the crowd's pressure. His task as host is to protect his guests. That protection is, however, less than heroic. In exchange for the safety of his guests, he offers the crowd his two virgin daughters for their pleasure.[22] The scene is duplicated exactly in Judges 19, although obviously a different tradition is involved.[23] A Levite visited Gibeah with his concubine, received an invitation to spend that night in the house of an old man, and found himself confronted by the men of the city. These men demanded that the host surrender his guest for their sexual abuse, just as the citizens of Sodom had done. And the old man's response duplicates Lot's response. He offers his virgin daughter and the Levite's concubine for the sexual pleasure of the crowd in exchange for the safety of his male guest. When the crowd presses, the Levite himself pushes the concubine out of the house to her death by the abuse of the crowd. Hardly heroic, the Levite protects himself by sacrificing his own concubine. It is perhaps telling that the host, who offered both his own virgin daughter and the guest's concubine, does not execute the act that secures the safety of the guest. The guest saves himself by sacrificing his concubine. So, in neither case can the act of the host be defined as heroic or even effectively protective for the guest.

Yet, at least at this point in the narrative, Lot takes action. His action may be unheroic. It may be unsuccessful. It may even make the audience of the story relieved not to be among the daughters of Lot. But at least he does not appear to be passive, just as the host in Judges 19 also does not appear to be passive. The active role of both hosts, however, fails. The citizens refuse the offer. The old man of Gibeah does nothing. His guest must save himself by submitting his concubine to the crowd. Lot also does nothing. The citizens of Sodom press hard against him, threatening his very safety (v. 9). And he can do nothing to prevent them from fulfilling the violent threat. The structure of the story reaches a marked peripeteia at just this point. The crisis can build no furher. Yet, the story teller paints a picture of a Lot who cannot act. He is passive. In the face of this hopeless plight, Lot is saved from the abusive crowd by his guests (vv. 10-11). Just as in ch. 14 Lot cannot effect his own fate but must be saved by Abram, so here Lot must be saved by the very guests he himself sought to protect.[24]

The tale about violated hospitality comes to an end in v. 11. The guests are safe. The host in his pitiful effort to protect his guests has been saved. The hostile citizens, struck by blindness, fight their way to frustration in a feeble effort to find the door of the house. Verses 12-28 represent, then, an extension of the basic story. Here the guests in Lot's house are clearly representatives of the Lord (v. 13). Their task is to announce destruction of a city known by reputation as an evil place (13.12), proven in a divine probe to contain not even ten righteous people (18.22-33), and now demonstrated by the citizens' vile abuse of hospitality to be a dangerous and violent locale.

But the first concern of the messengers is for the safety of Lot and his family. The messengers seek again to save Lot from the coming disaster. And in their quest Lot's passive role, indeed his position in the tradition as a foppish fool, comes to the fore. At the instrucion of the visitors, Lot calls his sons-in-law together in preparation for leaving the city. Thus, again Lot appears to be taking active leadership in saving his family as well as himself from the destruction. But the sons-in-law respond to his action by considering him a laughing stock, a fool. The key word describing that position in v. 14, *kimṣaḥēq*, is a participle from the same verbal root used in the puns on the name of Isaac.[25] In 21.9 the participle describes Ishmael's behavior. In this text, the verb, loaded with negative content, facilitates Sarah's paranoia that Ishmael would replace Isaac as the son of the promise. Perhaps in the Lot tradition the participle paints Lot as one who plays, one who laughs, one who does not take the world seriously. What better definition could one imagine for a passive fop, a foil who highlights the character of an alter ego?

But in just this particular collocation, the participle with *kaf* suggests that the sons-in-law see Lot as the play itself, the laugh, the one who in himself is the object of ridicule. Whether the text warrants so strong a translation as 'like a fool' or something a little softer, such as 'like a joker' or 'like a fop', the point is that the sons-in-law did not take him seriously. Lot, the passive object of a strange fate, here is defined as a jester, a fool, someone to be ignored. Lot separated from Abraham is a figure unable to control essential points in the development of the plot even though he affects those points by a negative contrast. Lot separated from Abraham is a figure who misses the blessing of God.

The foolishness of that character emerges in greater relief when the visitors urge Lot and his family to leave the city. Their speech, vv. 15-17, reflects the urgency of the occasion. Lot must flee to the hills immediately, before the holocaust strikes. But Lot could not bring himself to leave. Once again, the messengers take the initiative to save him. Verse 16 reports that they took him and his family by the hand and led them to safety outside the city. Passive Lot remains passive, unable to leave the city under the urgency of the messengers, unable even to save his own life and the life of his family. It is no surprise that the sons-in-law could not take him seriously. Again, the messengers urge Lot to flee. But again, he hesitates, this time responding with an argument, 'I am not able to flee to the hills, lest evil catch me and I die'. Instead he pleads for permission to go to another city. At a moment of great urgency, with an invitiation to flee and thus to save his own life and the life of his family, he stops to

debate. To be sure, this stage in the narration sets up an etiological
element for Zoar.[26] But even if local tradition has been imported
here, it adds to the picture of Lot as passive fool, indecisive, unable to
effect his own fate.

Verses 24-28 contain concluding elements, rounding off the
narrative with an obvious final thrust, vv. 24-25, but also with an
etiological element that anticipates the following pericope and a
notation that Abraham saw the signs of the tragedy. Significantly, the
tradition remebers a connection between Lot and Abraham. But here
the connection is peripheral, obviously not an essential part of the
narration. The more important element here is v. 26, the report that
Lot's wife looked behind her in explicit disobedience to the command
of the visitors in v. 17. John van Seters denies independent etiological
status to this brief note, although typically an etiological element has
been detected here.[27] Without debating the traditio-historical dimension of this text, we can at least observe that the notice performs a
narrative function for the larger context. It eliminates Lot's wife from
the picture, leaving the sole survivors of this tragedy as Lot and his
daughters (see the discussion of 19.30-38 below).[28]

This story, complex in its constructon and subtle in the development
of collateral themes, is perhaps a pivotal tale in a larger saga about
Lot and his family, the refugees from a cataclysmic tragedy. Certainly,
the cluster of tradition around the tale, including not only 18.1-15
and 16-33, but also 19.30-38, would argue for such a complex
tradition. In this case Lot would parallel Noah as the survivor of a
cosmic disaster, perhaps world-wide disaster (so, compare the connection between Lot and Noah in Luke 17.28-29 and 32 or 2 Peter 2.5
and 7-8). Moreover, the comparison between Lot and Noah recalls
the traditional positon of Noah as a righteous hero, one that might be
remembered simply as a folk hero (so, cf. Ezek 14.20). Lot might be
implicitly the righteous citizen of Sodom, the only one who, with his
family, can be saved from divine destruction. The pericope in 18.22-
33 may imply that Abraham negotiates for mercy on Sodom, not
simply for the sake of the righteous, but specifically for the sake of
Lot. Yet, the tradition does not paint Lot as the fortunate recipient of
God's mercy because he was a kinsman of Abraham. But for the
earliest levels of the tradition that connection is not essential. In fact,
the tradition does not explain why Lot was chosen to escape the
catastrophe. The concern of the tradition does not fall on reasons for
God's mercy. It falls on Lot's penchant, despite God's mercy, to

fumble. Lot does not resist the mercy offered him. He simply fails to act on the gift. Lot is by tradition the passive fool, a survivior of the catastrophe at Sodom despite his foolish reluctance to leave. For the Yahwist that character results from Lot's decision to separate from Abraham. Apart from Abraham, Lot has no blessing. He has no intimacy with people or place that might give his character positive form.

4. The brief tale in 19.30-38 enlarges this picture of Lot, the passive fool. Verse 30 sets the exposition for the tale. Lot left his new city to dwell in the hills with his two daughters. The allusion to fear in v. 30a seems clearly to connect this tale with the tradition of a catalysmic, if not a cosmic destruction. Verse 30b then places Lot with his two daughters in a cave. In the speech of the first born, vv. 31-33, the crisis of the tale emerges. There are no males 'on earth' available to provide children for Lot's two daughters other than the old father. The plight suggests that Lot and his two daughters are the only survivors of a world-wide catastrophe, the only source for repopulating the world. The Lot tradition would thus parallel the Noah tradition.[29] To be sure, the girl's cry might be understood simply as hyperbolic. But in the context of 19.1-29, the narrative setting providing a reason for Lot and his daughters to be stranded in a cave, the cry should be taken seriously. The expression, 'no man in the land' (*'iš 'ēn bā'āreṣ*), might be understood as a report of a local, not a world-wide disaster. Yet the point would remain the same. Whether world-wide or local, the destruction of Sodom was cosmic. And its total devastation left no man (in the region?) to impregnate the daughters.

In order to meet this fundamental crisis, the daughters lay a plan. They will make the father drunk and then, while he is in a stupor, they will use him for achieving a pregnancy. So they carried out their plan. First the older, then the younger manipulated the old father into intercourse. Lot, the passive fool, becomes the father of two sons, indeed, of two nations without taking the initiative. In fact, vv. 33b and 35b report that Lot was in such a great stupor that he did not even know that he had been used.

The character of this tradition must be explored one step further. The sons of the two sisters become the fathers of the Moabites and the Ammonites. The etiological element, *'ad hayyôm*, in vv. 37 and 38 makes this point unmistakable. Yet, why would etiological tradition, if it were Moabite or Ammonite in origin or even sympathy, report the origin of its own people in an incestuous relationship, indeed, in a relationship that remembered the father as a passive drunkard, unaware that he had been used for fathering two sons? This tale does not appear to me to have been originally Moabite or Ammonite.[30] I cannot see convincing evidnce that it sought to explain the local significance of the cave near Zoar. Rather, this Lot narrative about a foolish, passive man who escaped the cosmic destruction of Sodom through no effort of his own and then became the father of the Moabites and Ammonites, through no effort of his own, confirms the image of Lot as a passive foil. In this case he appears opposite the initiative of heroic mothers, rather than the heroic Abraham. But the image is the same. Lot had children, indeed, posterity large enough to become two nations. But Lot was in fact a passive foil. As father of two nations, this foil would appear, at least on the surface, to share a blessing from God with heroic Abraham. Yet, how could that posterity mark a blessing comparable to the blesing of Abraham? Lot had no contribution to make to such a blessing; indeed, he did not even know that he was the father. Even apart from active involvement of Abraham, Lot is the opposite of Abraham. He is the father of two great nations. But he enjoys none of the fruits of that fact. He is not even the principal hero of the act that repopulates the world. By virtue of their heroic courage to take matters into their own hands, the sisters win that heroic position. And Lot is simply the foil for their heroic deeds.

II

On the basis of this exegesis of the Lot narratives, some conclusions about the Lot tradition are in order. (1) What is the functional value of the Lot figure in the Abram/Abraham tradition? Lot appears in the later stages of the tradition as Abraham's nephew. But that familial relationship is not essential to the shape of the Lot tradition, indeed, to the content of the earlier stages in the tradition. In the earlier stages of the Abraham saga, however, some kind of relationship between the two is crucial. And that relationship is a literary device. Lot appears consistently as a passive foil, not to highlight Lot's own sin by separating himself from Abraham, but rather by contrast to highlight Abraham's stature as the father of the nation. Even that part of the Lot tradition that remembers him as father of two great nations does so in a negative light. The negative element does not come from a judgment against incest. In any case the judgment would have been against the two daughters, a point confirmed by the parallel in the Noah tradition (cf. Gen 9.20-27, especially vv. 24-27). At this early stage of tradition, with no reference to Lot's relationship with Abraham, Lot is a passive, foolish figure. In the context of the Abraham tradition, this traditional fool functions well. Lot, the passive father who did not even know that he was a father, contrasts with Abraham, the faithful father whose fatherhood brings blessing and intimacy to all the people of the world. The contrast develops between Abraham the righteous and Lot a foil to that righteousness, a fool in contrast to Abraham's blessedness.

(2) Is there any evidence of a Lot tradition that might have been independent of the Abram/Abraham tradition? Even in the earliest narrative source, Lot appears simply as a foil to Abraham. But especially in ch. 19, Abraham retreats from center stage and plays no essential part in the story. It is possible that an independent Lot tradition connected Lot to the Moabites or the Ammonites (so, cf. Deut 2.9, 19 and Ps 83.9). Or perhaps that independent tradition connected Lot with a specific locale, a cave near Zoar. Yet, the etiological interests that associate Lot's sons with Moab and Ammon seem extraneous to the development of the Lot narrative and thus not the focal point of an independent tradition.[31] Moreover, the cave scene seems to be dependent on the Sodom tradition and not the subject of an independent tradition. Certainly, the account of Lot's wife turning to a pillar of salt reveals dependence, if not on the Sodom tradition, at least on the tradition about incest between Lot and his daughters who are alone, unencumbered by a wife/mother. The evidence is different, however, when one considers the connection between Lot and the tradition about Sodom. Ties between Abraham and Sodom appear to be redactional, not essential at least at the earliest stages of the Abraham tradition. But if the exegesis of ch. 19 is sound, Lot's role in the Sodom narrative is not only essential but indeed the focus of a Sodom tradition.[32] Could we not hypothesize, then, that a Lot–Sodom saga featured a passive foil to the heroic daughters and that that saga has now been adapted by the Yahwist so that Lot can function as a foil for his central figure, father Abraham?

(3) Does the Lot figure appear in consistent ways when the Yahwistic narrative is compared with the priestly narrative? Does that figure gain strength and consistent shape when the earliest levels of the tradition and perhaps even a hypothetical pre-Yahwistic figure are considered? Priestly allusions to Lot are fragmentary. In 11.27 and 31, a priestly genealogy and itinerary simply note that Lot was related to Abram. In v. 27 the relationship is incidental. In v. 31 the relationship appears in conjunction with a report that Abram and Lot both accompanied Terah from Ur to Haran. The most telling reference to Lot in P is the note in 19.29 that God saved Lot from the destruction at Sodom for the sake of Abraham. Thus, the priestly tradition places Lot in relationship to Abraham, subordinated to Abraham, but not sharply enough defined to suggest a passive foil. Perhaps the more important point about P is the association of Lot with Sodom. In the Yahwistic narrative Lot is the passive foil to a dominant, active Abraham and thus, by contrast, functions to highlight Abraham. But in addition to the literary function, Lot shows what the impact of the Yahwist's theological conception about Abraham might be. Lot chooses to separate himself from Abraham and thus from the blessing of God. And his image as passive foil, or better, as passive, foppish fool, demonstrates the folly any person must own in losing access to that blessing. Loss of intimacy with Abraham is loss of intimacy with Abraham's God, with God's land, with Abraham's family, even with one's own family, and finally with oneself.

A reconstruction of early, pre-Yahwistic tradition about Lot supports this evaluation of the Yahwist's picture. If the hypothesis is sound that Lot was tied originally to tradition about Sodom, the survivor of a cosmic disaster, and if even there he was a passive foil, first to the heavenly visitors and then to his own daughters, if indeed even there he was a passive fool unable to speak to his sons-in-law without projecting an image of a fool, then the construct given Lot by the Yahwist would be consistent with the earliest forms of the Lot tradition. The Yahwist would have used a traditional figure, a passive and foppish fool, as a foil for Abraham in a way that is consistent with the earliest levels of the tradition.[33]

(4) The Lot tradition is clearly a tool for the Yahwist to give contours to his distinctive theology. God's blessing comes to the world through Abraham. But to separate oneself from that blessing, as the result of strife or as the result of an effort to end strife, reduces

one to a passive fool, unable to participate in shaping one's own destiny. If the reconstrucion of a Lot tradition that might have existed prior to the Yahwist version is sound, then that tradition would have had the seeds of the passive, foolish anthropology of J already in it. Even apart from Abraham, Lot was a passive figure, perhaps available to J from tradition as an obvious foil for his narration in much the same way that Noah was available from tradition as a righteous hero (cf. Ezek 14.20). But could that tradition about Lot have had a distinctive theological point of view? Apart from the program of the Yahwist, the tradition does not judge Lot negatively for being passive. It suggests to the contrary that God blesses even passive, foppish, foolish people with his long-suffering and patience. If a fool like Lot can escape tragedy as the result of God's patience and mercy, perhaps fools in later generations can too. Being apart from Abraham makes life negative, foolish. That is the point of view of the Yahwist. But Lot nevertheless lives. And indeed, he becomes the father of two nations, a sign that despite his foolish, passive wandering, he does not live entirely outside of God's blessing. That is the contribution of the Lot tradition to the Yahwist.

NOTES

1. Martin Noth, *A History of Pentateuchal Traditions* (tr. Bernhard W. Anderson; Englewood Cliffs: Prentice-Hall, 1972), 152-53. See also A. Lods, 'La caverne de Lot', *RHR* 95 (1927) 204-19.

2. John van Seters, *Abraham in History and Tradition* (New Haven: Yale University, 1975) 212.

3. *Ibid.*, 218. Italics mine.

4. *Ibid.*, 220.

5. *Ibid.*, 226. Contrast R. Kilian, 'Zur Überlieferungsgeschichte Lots', *BZ* 14 (1970) 23-37.

6. Gerhard von Rad, *Genesis, a Commentary* (OTL; Philadelphia: Westminster, 1972) 225.

7. *Ibid.*, 172. See also Claus Westermann, 'Arten der Erzählung in der Genesis', in *Forschung am Alten Testament* (TBÜ, 24; München: Chr. Kaiser, 1964) 65. Westermann observes: 'In eine negative Beleuchtung tritt das Geschehen dann in der Komposition, die in der Linie der Familiengeschichte Lots stillschweigend einen Kontrast zur Linie der Familie Abrahams andeutet'.

8. R. Kilian, *Die vorpriesterlichen Abrahamsüberlieferungen* (BBB, 24; Bonn: Paul Hanstein, 1966) 18-19.

9. Van Seters, *Abraham*, 222-23.

10. George W. Coats, 'The Curse in God's Blessing: Gen 12.1-4a in the Structure and Theology of the Yahwist', *Die Botschaft und die Boten* (ed. J. Jeremias and L. Perlitt; Neukirchen-Vluyn: Neukirchener Verlag, 1981) 39-40. See also 'Strife without Reconciliation: A Narrative Theme in the Jacob Traditions', *Werden und Wirken des Alten Testaments* (ed. R. Albertz, H.P. Müller, H.W. Wolff and W. Zimmerli; Neukirchen-Vluyn: Neukirchener Verlag, 1980) 82-106.

11. Kilian, *Abrahamsüberlieferungen*, 161. One must consider a hypothetical Lot saga which might lie behind this Lot narrative, now simply a complement to the Abraham saga.

12. Claus Westermann, *Genesis* (*BKAT* 1/2; Neukirchen-Vluyn: Neukirchener Verlag, 1978) 210-12; *The Promises to the Fathers* (Philadelphia: Fortress, 1976) 2-30. Westermann raises a key question for traditio-historical inquiry into the Abraham–Lot material. In what manner is the promise theme ever rooted essentially in a narrative about the patriarchs? If the promise theme is secondary, what is primary for these narratives?

13. Von Rad, *Genesis*, 170.

14. *Ibid.*, 170.

15. The source identity of this pericope is unclear. The chronicle must be a special source, not the creation of J or P. But the expansion may well be the work of the Yahwist. At least it harmonizes the chronicle with the larger J context about Lot and Sodom.

16. J.A. Emerton, 'The Riddle of Genesis XIV', *VT* 21 (1971) 403-39.

17. Van Seters, *Abraham*, 209-12.

18. One should observe the *Tiqqune Sopherim* here. The tradition had originally reported that Yahweh stood before Abraham.

19. Cf. von Rad, *Genesis*, 214.

20. Contrast van Seters, *Abraham*, 214. Von Rad, *Genesis*, 213, observes: '"Righteous action" is always defined by a communal relationship . . . Does Yahweh's "righteousness" with regard to Sodom not consist precisely in the fact that he will forgive the city for the sake of these innocent ones?' One might raise a question here about the heroic dimension of Abraham. Intercession can be characteristic of heroic tradition, thus placing this text more firmly within the Abraham tradition than the position developed here has allowed. See George W. Coats, 'The King's Loyal Opposition: Obedience and Authority in Exodus 32–34', *Canon and Authority: Essays in Old Testament Religion and Theology* (ed. George W. Coats and Burke O. Long; Philadelphia: Fortress, 1977) 91-109. Yet, in just this text, Abraham does not appear to present himself in defense of Sodom. The dialogue does not represent the people of Sodom as in any manner the people of Abraham. Rather, it seems to be a scholastic exercise, an artificial construct that shows something about Sodom, not something about Abraham. Abraham does not place himself between Sodom and God. He argues a point to an incomplete stage, proving only that Sodom does not have even ten righteous people.

21. A methodological problem appears just at this point. It is not adequate to conclude, just because this form is different from the other narrative units about Lot, that it must contain the primary shape or the earliest content of the tradition. I might just as well conclude that at a later stage in the tradition history the essential relationship with Abraham was dropped. The investigation must ask, then, whether anything in this unique form of the Lot tradition accounts for the loss of reference to relationship with Abraham. Or does the tradition reveal fundamental elements that can be understood apart from Abraham, indeed, elements that might account for a secondary association with Abraham?

22. Von Rad, *Genesis*, 218.

23. Von Rad, *Genesis*, 218, raises a question about the relationship between these two: 'One might ask even so whether the striking similarity of our narrative in this respect to that of the "infamy of Gibeah" does not point to a relationship, perhaps even a distant dependence of the one saga on the other (Judg 19)'.

24. Von Rad (*Genesis*, 219) describes the collapse of his 'heroic gesture' as 'a bit comical'.

25. Coats, 'The Curse', 37-39.

26. Hermann Gunkel, *Genesis* (HKAT 1/1; Göttingen: Vandenhoeck und Ruprecht, 1910) 211.

27. Van Seters, *Abraham*, 218-19. Gunkel, *Genesis* 206, suggests that the notice comes too late in the story and is thus secondary. See also p. 214. Von Rad, *Genesis*, 221.

28. Von Rad (*Genesis*, 223) relates this section to the narrator who skillfully joins a Lot saga and an Abraham saga.

29. Lods, 'La caverne', 204-19. See also Gunkel, *Genesis*, 218-19; Westermann, *Genesi*, 366.

30. Contrast von Rad, *Genesis*, 224. Gunkel, *Genesis*, 218, recognizes that in an original Moabite or Ammonite tale, the goal would not have been to make sport of a foolish ancestor, but to elevate the stature of the mothers. Westermann, *Genesis*, 65, highlights a positive dimension of this item, dependent as it is on the Sodom narrative. The negative dimension comes only in the context of the Abraham narrative.

31. See Burke O. Long, *The Problem of Etiological Narrative in the Old Testament* (BZAW, 108; Berlin: Töpelmann, 1968) 51-53. Long observes: 'Yet one cannot overlook the fact that the etymologies are not the final item in the unit. The laconic concluding formula ('He is the father of... to this day') appearing in both v. 37 and v. 38 prohibit (*sic*) understanding the function of the whole solely in terms of etymology ... Thus at best, one can say that the etymological interests helped shape the narrative... But the etymology is subordinate to the wider interest expressed sharply by the "extension formulae."'

32. Van Seters (*Abraham*, 209-26) discusses the Lot material and the

Sodom material together. But he draws no conclusions about an original attachment of Lot to the Sodom tradition.

33. Alfred Jepsen, 'Zur Überlieferungsgeschichte der Vätergestalten', *Wissenschaftliche Zeitschrift der Karl Marx Universität Leipzig* 3 (1953-54) 276. Jepsen defines Lot by observing 'dass er in der Abrahamerzählung eine ähnliche Stellung einnimmt wie Laban in der Jakob- und Ismael in der Isaakgeschichte, das heisst, die Stellung des Rivalen'. My impression is, however, that Lot is not so much a rival, a competitor, as he is a negative complement. He casts opposite images to contrast with Abraham, not as Laban contrasts with Jacob, an opposite, perhaps even an enemy who stands as a peer of Jacob, but rather as a foolish, impotent fop.

7

THEOLOGICAL AND REDACTIONAL PROBLEMS IN NUMBERS 20.2-13

Katharine Doob Sakenfeld

Over the past several years I have had several occasions to give continuing education lectures or seminars on Pentateuchal materials. Consistently and persistently the audiences, whether lay or theologically trained, have asked, 'Why didn't Moses get to enter the promised land?' Until this question received some attention, it was difficult to move on to other aspects of the figure of Moses. This oft-repeated experience provoked my interest in Numbers 20.[1]

The first and most obvious observation from reading the chapter is that the deaths of Miriam and Aaron are recorded here, and that whatever Moses did wrong involved Aaron as well. Perhaps it is not remarkable that none of the inquiries from my general audiences raised this larger issue or even found it very interesting—since neither of these figures has played a very large role in the Christian lore with which they were familiar. But surely the juxtaposition of the three characters provides a clue and raises issues which are critical to understanding the chapter.

Yet the relation between Aaron, Moses, and Miriam is only the tip of the iceberg here. The chapter confronts us with geographical and chronological problems, especially in v. 1; and the redactional question of the relation of vv. 2-13 (water from the rock and the judgment upon Moses and Aaron) and vv. 22-29 (death of Aaron and installation of Eleazar) to a number of other pericopae[2] has its own impact upon our understanding of the 'sin of Moses' recounted here. It is the thesis of this essay that the relationship between Moses and Aaron is a focal concern of Numbers 20.2-13 and that a number of the theological and redactional problems associated with the passage can at least be comprehended, if not solved, by keeping this focal concern at the forefront.

Issues in the Text

We may begin with a brief overview of the interlocking problems of vv. 2-13. Attempts to solve any one have usually involved ignoring some of the others; we hope to conclude with a more comprehensive interpretation.

The problems may be categorized under three headings: source/ redaction questions, the sin of the two leaders, and the relationship between Moses and Aaron.

(1) *Source/redaction issues.* The classic source analyses of the nineteenth century were in general agreement, and their consensus persists in the modern commentaries of Noth[3] and others. To J or to the Old Epic (OE) tradition are attibuted v. 3a ('And the people contended [*rîb*] with Moses and said') and v. 5 ('And why have you made us come up out of Egypt to die in this evil place? It is no place for grain or figs or vines or pomegranates, and there is no water to drink'). Then there seems clearly to be OE material (or tradition, or memory) incorporated into vv. 8-11, but the attempt to sort the material into separate strands meanders into a quagmire. Many who subscribe to an independent P source and an R[JEP] redactor simply allude to extensive recasting. The chief problem is that 'the rod' of v. 8, not there identified, seems in v. 9 to be Aaron's budding rod of Numbers 17 (the rod 'from before the LORD'), while in v. 11a the rod is identified as Moses' rod ('his', with Moses as subject antecedent), thus recalling explicitly the OE tradition of Exodus 17.5 in which Moses is commanded to strike the rock with 'the rod with which [he] struck the Nile', taking us in turn back to the plague narrative of Exodus 7.14-25. Aaron, we may note, has no place in the Exodus 17 narrative of water from the rock; but in Exodus 7 the identity of the rod and relationship between Moses and Aaron exhibits an ambiguity in some respects parallel to that in Numbers 20. The differences in vocabulary for rock (Num 20 *sela'*, Exod 17 *ṣûr*) and in vocabulary for cattle (Num 20 *b^e'îr*, Exod 17 *migneh*), suggest further that different tellings of the story are before us. Yet the motif of striking the rock clearly joins the two stories at some level.

(2) *The sin of the leaders.* God declares that Moses and Aaron did not believe in (*h'myn*) the Lord; they did not sanctify (*hqdyš*) the Lord before the people (v. 12). While the declaration of unfaith is clear enough, the specific content of the wrongdoing is another matter. God commands that address be made to the rock. No use for the staff is given. One of the two leaders (presumably Moses) speaks to the people (not to the rock) and then Moses strikes the rock. The sin may lie in failure to follow instructions as given, with the focus on striking the rock.[4] Or, the sin may lie in the words spoken, which

Psalm 106 describe as 'speaking rashly' (*yĕbaṭṭē'*). The words could be taken as part of the disobedience because they are addressed to the rebels, not to the rock; or the content of the words could for some reason be regarded as inappropriate. We will see that the obscurity and/or seeming insignificance of the sin committed has led some scholars to rather elaborate reconstructions of earlier stages of the text and to the assumption that the original wrongdoing has been 'toned down' in the course of transmission of the narrative. The deeper question, I would suggest, is why this event is asked to bear all this weight of sin and judgment. On the face of it, the golden calf incident (for example) or even the challenge of Aaron to Moses' authority (Num 12) would seem more likely loci for the judgment on Aaron. And certainly Moses is recorded to have complained to God or castigated the people in other stories (e.g. Num 11, Exod 32 [breaking the tablets]). So why this occasion, this story, as the basis for both leaders' death outside the land of promise?

(3) *The relationship between Moses and Aaron.* Here we may simply trace the sequence through the text in anticipation of our subsequent analysis. Verse 2 joins Moses and Aaron as recipients of the complaint. Verse 3a (probably older tradition) narrows the address to Moses, but the 'you brought in' (*hăbē'tem*) of v. 4 is second masculine *plural*. The 'you brought us up' of v. 5 (probably old tradition) is likewise plural as pointed in MT (*he'ĕlîtunû*). (Though it could be pointed as singular, there is no LXX or versional support for such a change.) In v. 6 Moses and Aaron are conjoined again, but in v. 7 the Lord addresses Moses only. The content of the quotation is mixed, however: 'take the rod' is singular imperative, while 'speak to the rock' is second masculine plural, following immediately on the specific inclusion 'you and Aaron your brother'. The remaining two verbs of v. 8 are singular in MT but plural in the LXX. In v. 9 Moses is the sole actor, but in 10a Moses and Aaron are again subjects. In 10b we read, 'and he said to them'. The speaker is taken to be Moses on account of his independent status in other verses and because of the tradition of Psalm 106, but the text does not actually specify the speaker. The words spoken contain a first common plural reference (*nôṣî'*). Moses alone acts in the striking of the rock (v. 11). Finally, the words of judgment in v. 12 are addressed in plural verbs explicitly to Moses and Aaron by name.

The picture appears haphazard, but on closer examination parts of the tradition most closely reminiscent of Exodus 17 seem to be just those parts in which a special focus on Moses persists (v. 3a, the people's *rîb*; v. 9, the taking of the rod: and v. 11, the striking of the rock). Elsewhere throughout the section (except in God's address to Moses alone, v. 7), the picture includes Aaron—especially if we follow the LXX plurals in v. 8 and recognize the ambiguity of speaker and joint emphasis in content of the quotation in 10b. Whether Aaron is original to this narrative or not, is debated; how well he is integrated into the text and why he is included will need to be discussed below.

Review of Previous Studies*

The interlocking of the three problem areas just described is apparent, and various studies of the pericope have balanced them differently. The major source-critically focused investigation of the passage, which was done by Cornill in 1891,[5] laid out the difficulties of analysis discussed above. Cornill's final reconstrucion, however, exhibits the 'cut and paste' approach, as he reconstructs a hypothetical 'Ur-J' text by weaving phrases from Numbers 20.1aβ and 5 into Exodus 17.1-2, 7 to produce three non-overlapping versions of the story. His J material reports and etymologizes only on the complaint (with no divine response), while his E material (Exod 17.3-6) contains both a complaint and also God's response. Cornill's reconstruction of the P account of Numbers 20 is fairly straightforward up through Yahweh's command in v. 8; only the rod is omitted as misplaced. But after v. 8 (apparently following an earlier suggestion of Nöldeke) he introduces the second part of the leader's words of v. 10b as words of rebellion spoken by Moses and Aaron *to Yahweh* and in dispute of Yahweh's command. Verse 10b itself is then to be understood as *words of Yahweh addressed to Moses and Aaron* ('you rebels', with appropriate changes in suffixes). The command of 8a about the rod is then resumed (as Yahweh's Plan B) and vv. 9, 10a, 11 recount the giving of water. The use of the staff is Yahweh's response to the lack of confidence of Moses and Aaron in the power of the spoken word. The reactor R[P] modified the text in order to suppress Moses' sin. Cornill's proposal is intriguing, but at least two problems must be noted. First, the text itself gives us no evidence for a prior stage in which the speakers and audience were so different. Second, Cornill's interest is more in reconstructing orderly sources than in explaining why we have received such a comparatively 'garbled' (by hs standards) text. No serious attention is given to any reason for alleged modification of P by R^P (why should the sin be so much obscured?). And the appearance of Aaron receives no comment.

Recently the passage has been treated from a traditio-historical perspective by F. Kohata,[6] whose approach concentrates on stages in the development of the P tradition. Despite its differing presuppositions, the analysis may be classified with Cornill's because of Kohata's proposing of very specific reconstructions of earlier written stages of the text. Rather than supposing that R^P has woven the text together (Cornill) or that an unidentified later redactor has inserted material from Exodus 17 to exonerate Moses (and Aaron) and castigate the people,[7] Kohata identifies three layers within the P tradition itself. Beginning with P's concern for command and execution, he notes that the phrase *ka'ăšer ṣiwwāhû* (v. 9) comes in the middle of Moses' action, and suggests that the phrase indicates the breaking point between obedient execution of the divine command and other action not related to the command. Moses' angry speech to the people constitutes his sin; the goal of the earliest author is to suggest that it is the word of God, not human zeal, which binds God and the people together. Kohata's second stage features reworking of vv. 8 (God's command) and 12 (the declaration of judgment). Here, he suggests, the tradent's theological intention is to strengthen the original theme of the effective power of the word of God. This is accomplished first by revising the command to Moses. The first level is reconstructed to include a command to 'strike' (*nkh* hi.) the rock; this verb is now in level two changed to 'to speak' (*dbr* pi.)—in the plural because Aaron has meanwhile been brought into the story. Thus Moses is to serve as a sort of 'relay station' (p. 18) for God's word, and Moses' role as mediator is heightened. This word substitution, however, puts Moses' sin in a graver light; for he is no longer supposed to strike the rock, and the words which he speaks in v. 10 cannot be regarded as extra, but only as in further disregard of God's command. This reviser wants to emphasize the necessity for complete obedience. While Kohata finds that he cannot reconstruct in detail the changes to v. 12, he assumes that the verbs *h'myn* and *hqdyš* are introduced in his stage two. Kohata's third stage author is responsible, finally, for adding the noun *qāhāl* in its three occurrences (vv. 4, 6, 12). The use of *qāhāl* is taken to show that the people value themselves highly, and thus the purpose of the addition is to show that the people—despite their own view—really stand far from

Yahweh because they have objected to the leadership pf Moses and
Aaron. Thus the theophany comes only to Moses and Aaron.

The tradition, Kohata concludes, was originally a wilderness
tradition unrelated to Moses' death; the connection to Moses' death
was made in level one. Aaron was added either in or prior to level
two; for Kohata 'levels' are to be labeled only when theologically
significant, and he does not attach more than casual importance to
the appearance of Aaron here. Psalm 106.32ff. is to be related to level
one because the psalm does not refer to Aaron.

Several questions must be raised concerning Kohata's analysis.
The proposal of an original *wĕhikkîtā* and substitution of *wĕdibbartem*
for it in level two does resolve some tensions in the text. But it leaves
the sin of Moses in level one even more obscure. The theme of God's
power may well be important here, but the emphasis on 'word' seems
ad hoc, as does the suppostion that all occurrences of *qāhāl* are
tertiary.[8] Kohata provides no indication of any setting or audience
which would provoke the tradents' concern for making the changes
he has identified.

Other treatments of the passage may receive briefer notice. George
Coats[9] emphasizes that even the earliest P version of the text has
incorporated Meribah into the murmuring tradition (cf. vv. 3a, 13),
and thus that the text of vv. 2-13 must be regarded as all from P. The
narrative outline then is basically like its Old Epic counterpart of
Exodus 17. The addition of Aaron to a story earlier about Moses
alone is of no special significance, in Coats's view, except that at that
level of tradition the story can be reused to explain why both great
leaders do not enter the promised land. Against most interpreters
Coats argues that even in Numbers 20 the fate of Moses is to be
attributed to the people's sin rather than to Moses' own, for it was
their rebelion which provoked Moses to speak 'rashly' (Ps. 106.32).

I am doubtful about Coats's attempt to see an exoneration of
Moses in Numbers 20.2-13 since it seems to fly in the face of v. 12
(and the related traditions of Num 20.24; 27; Deut 32) which place
the blame squarely and frankly on Moses and Aaron. It is more likely
in my view that Ps. 106.32-33 represents an attempt to harmonize
this Numbers type of tradition with the 'on your account' type of
tradition of Deuteronomy 1.37 (*biglalᵉkem*) and 3.26 (*lĕmaʿanᵉkem*).[10]

M. Margalith focuses his attention just on the matter of Moses'
and Aaron's sin.[11] Like Coats, he adheres to the unity of the passage.
But he goes further to suggest that Numbers 20 is independent of

Exodus 17 and furthermore that Numbers 20 contains no contradictions or obscurities. The sin of Moses and Aaron is identified as the
words of v. 10b, in accordance with Ps. 106. While Margalith's view
of the passage as a basic unity is not impossible, and his identification
of the sin is congruent with my own conclusions, I find that he has
oversimplified the problems of the passage.

Eugene Arden, like Margalith, focuses on the sin and also concludes
that it lies in Moses' words.[12] He points out that we have here no
expression of God's being angry at the people and concludes that
Moses' anger is 'blasphemous' because it presumes to state that God
is angry too. Arden's interpretation is based on the assumption that
the 'we' of v. 10b refers to Moses and God, rather than Moses and
Aaron, but this seemingly improbable supposition is not argued. The
essay is written as if Aaron were not part of the story. On the other
hand, Arden's suggestion that Moses' words in v. 10b 'destroy the
hallowed moment which God had so clearly intended' bears further
consideration.

Finally, we must mention the important essay of Norbert Lohfink[13]
who is unique in asking after the role of the passage in the P work (P^g
for him) as a whole. Lohfink proposes that we view the entire P
narrative as one great pre-history ('*Urgeschichte*') with three typological instances of sin developed at critical points. The first of these
is the sin of all humanity in violent action against one another (the
flood narrative). The second is the sin of the elect people of Israel and
its political leaders in speaking ill of the promised land, God's gift
(Num 13–14, with the key phrase *dibbat hā'āreṣ*, ' an evil report
about the land', in 13.32). And finally, the sin of Moses and Aaron
symbolizes the sin of Israel's religious leaders—their lack of trust in
the power of God (Num 20.12 with the key phrase *lō' he'ĕmantem bî*,
'you did not trust in me', as illustrated by the words spoken in
v. 10b). The purpose of the Numbers 20 story, in Lohfink's view, is
thus not primarily to explain why Moses and Aaron did not get into
the land. Rather, the focus is on the danger which threatens the
spiritual leadership of Israel in exile, the danger of failing to trust in
and proclaim the wonder-working power of God through which even
the seemingly impossible (return to the land) can be made possible.

Lohfink's provocative analysis provides an excellent springboard
for our own analysis of the passage, but two of his points will require
further attention toward the conclusion of this essay. First, the key
words which he selects from Numbers 13–14 and Numbers 20 do not

seem to be properly parallel. 'Slandering the land' is a quite specific act, compared to 'not trusting in Yahweh'. In fact the identical constuction, *lō' ya'ămînû bî*, appears in God's speech concerning the people's sin in Numbers 14.11 (a verse, to be sure, which Lohfink would exclude from his analysis as not pertinent to P^g). Second, Lohfink gives no attention to the location of the Numbers 20 story either within the larger P^g narrative or within the received form of the Pentateuch. We may add that he notes the tension over the role of Aaron but sees it only as a clue to identifying the sin with the words spoken (by one but on behalf of both) rather that with the rock struck (by Moses only).

The Relation between Moses and Aaron

Earlier in this essay we outlined the tensions in the present text which seem to be occasioned by the inclusion of Aaron alongside Moses in vv. 2-13. An inconsistent pattern of singular and plural verbs, both in the divine command and in the leader's response, is apparent. The verb of v. 10b, 'and he spoke', lacks a clear antecedent; and except for the sporadic plural forms it appears that Aaron could fairly easily be omitted from the narrative. Thus many scholars have posited a form of this P tradition in which Aaron was not represented.[14] If such an earlier form of the tradition is regarded as pre-literary, with Aaron being added in P's original composition, then the grammatical confusion characteristic of these verses requires some explanation. A review of other murmuring texts in which Aaron appears alongside Moses indicates that, however loosely Aaron may be fitted into the text, their grammar is fairly smooth by comparison to Numbers 20.

In Numbers 13–14, for example, there is no reason to suppose that Aaron's role is literarily secondary, other than his infrequent and non-essential role. Here indeed he appears to be just the 'alter ego' of Moses.[15] Aaron is referred to in 13.26 and 14.2, 5, 26 as recipient with Moses of the spies' report, of the people's complaint and of a P section of the Lord's word of judgment on the people. Of course this section needs to be viewed in connection with Numbers 20. It is important that in chs. 13–14 Aaron like Moses be excluded by role from the rebellion of the people. Otherwise attention to some particular sin of Aaron's in ch. 20 would appear superfluous.

Aaron is also relatively smoothly integrated into Exodus 16, the pre-Sinai material concerning manna and quail. The extent of P material here has long been disputed,[16] but Aaron appears only in agreed-upon P sections. The narrative opens with murmuring against Moses and Aaron (v. 2)—a phrase identical (except for stem of *lwn*) to Numbers 14.2 (but note that the verb of Num 20.2 is different, *qhl*). Moses and Aaron answer the people in v. 6 (although in v. 8 Moses speaks on behalf of both of them), and in v. 9 Moses instructs Aaron to speak to the people. After Aaron does Moses' bidding in v. 10, Aaron disappears from the narrative until v. 33, when once again he follows instructions given him by Moses. The formulae of vv. 2 and 6 are 'alter ego' material: Aaron is present but with no distinctive role. Verses 9-10 and 33-34 are different, however, for in each instance Aaron's assignment involves specific action on his own, each one related to cultic concerns: in the first instance the Glory of Yahweh appears; in the second, manna is placed in a jar 'before the testimony'. While Moses' initiative in these matters is suggestive for an understanding of P's view of the relationship between the leaders, our point here is simply that the key verses present no special grammatical or logical difficulties.

Despite the relative smoothness of these comparable texts, I suggest that on the whole the grammatical and logical problems of Numbers 20 can be accounted for without resorting to a hypothesis of late literary supplementing. The argument proceeds along four lines.

(1) *Concerning God's address to Moses alone.* The address of God to Moses alone, even though Aaron is specifically present, can be found elsewhere in P tradition.[17] While the P material does present God as speaking to both Moses and Aaron,[18] some of these formulaic passages, especially in legislative material, may represent sporadic additions of the name Aaron over the centuries of text transmission. On the whole, however, P reserves divine speech for Moses alone. There are some examples, even in narrative material, where God addresses Moses but Aaron is not even brought into the picture.[19] Furthermore, God frequently gives Moses information pertinent to Aaron or commands to relay to Aaron.[20] By contrast, divine address directly to Aaron alone is extremely rare.[21]

This special role of Moses as recipient of God's word is consistent with the expression of the relationship between the two leaders in Exodus 4.15-16, however old the tradition of this notice may be. Noth views these verses as a supplement to the OE in literary transmission. A comparable P statement appears in Exodus 6.28–7.2. Although the focus in 6.28ff. is on speaking to the Pharaoh rather than to the Israelite people, the P theme of Moses standing between Aaron and God is even more explicit than in 4.15-16.[22] This theme of Moses' role as communicator is highlighted once again in the incorporation of Aaron into the story of Miriam's challenge to Moses' authority in Numbers 12.[23]

In sum, P's strong penchant for directing God's words to Moses alone provides sufficient ground to account for this alleged unevenness in the text of Numbers 20.2-13. In this regard our passage simply reflects an older general tradition (cf. Exod 4.15-16) of Moses' special role in comparison to Aaron which P has highlighted in his own narrative presentation. There is no need to resort to a hypothesis by which P's written narrative omitted the figure of Aaron.

(2) *The form* wĕdibbartem *in v. 8*. The most conspicuously difficult inconsistency of singular and plural usage in Numbers 20 pericope is the form *wĕdibbartem* in the string of singular verb commands to Moses within God's address to him. Two factors render this exceptional plural understandable. First, it follows immediately on the phrase 'you and Aaron your brother', so that the joint character of the entire action is in the forefront and a plural subject has just been stated. Second, the verb itself is critical to the narrative, as the key to what goes wrong for Moses and Aaron seems to be in the speaking (v. 10b) which subsequently takes place (see below, regarding the sin of Moses and Aaron). The plural verb form thus emphasizes Aaron's participation in the event.

(3) *The indefinite subject of v. 10b*. The problem of the unidentified speaker in v. 10b is not unique to this passage. In some cases (e.g. Exod 24.1; Exod 7.20—see below), an unspecified subject is of course taken to be evidence of source weaving; in others (e.g. Num 27.23), the story as a whole makes probable who the speaker is. But generally, Hebrew seems to have allowed for more stylistic vagueness than English in the matter of antecedent subjects; modification of a written text is not necessarily to be assumed.

Furthermore, Aaron is in other places as well not so perfectly integrated into the narrative as we might expect; as we have already seen, he seems to appear, to drop out, and to reappear in Exodus 16 and Numbers 14, texts in which the presence of Aaron in P's first written form is widely accepted. If we assume that Moses is the speaker here (as is generally agreed), the plural verb for speaking (*wĕdibbartem*) in v. 9 (God's command) and the first common plural verb (*nôsî'*) in the words to the people make clear that Aaron's formal silence does not eliminate his presence from the writer's purview. The writer simply regards one as speaking for both and in fact may highlight this reality by not specifying a subject (cf. Exod 16.6, 8, where both Moses and Aaron speak, then Moses alone).

(4) *Water and rods.* Apparent tensions concerning the role of Aaron in the text may have been increased by the specific subject matter—the problem of water, and its association with rods elsewhere—coupled with the parallel but mixed traditions of rods belonging to Moses and to Aaron. Noth solves this problem by allowing 'a later hand'[24] to add four phrases under the influence of Exodus 17: 'take the rod' (8a), 'and you shall bring forth water from them form the rock' (8b), the taking of the rod (9), and the striking of the rock (11a); thus Noth's original P version contained nothing about the rod at all. But at least two difficulties attend Noth's solution. First, the word for rock in the excised sections remains consistently *sela'* as in P's vv. 8, 10b, while the word in Exodus 17 is always *ṣûr*. Furthermore, the rod which Moses takes in v. 9 is described as *millipnê Yhwh*, a phrase which is widely agreed to refer to the rod of Aaron placed 'before the testimony' in resolution of the challenges to Aaron's authority in Numbers 17 (cf. 17.25 = Eng. v. 10).

I would not disagree that influences from the Exodus 17 story of water from the rock are present, but I would locate them more in the warp and woof of the complex tradition motif of a water/rock story plus the traditions about special rods, rather than in a separable redactional layer. If there has been an addition to the basic P text, it is probably found only in v. 11a (see below).

In Numbers 20 the ownership of the rod in v. 8 is unspecified, the rod of v. 9 would seem to be Aaron's, but the rod of v. 11 is specified as Moses'. The attribution of the rod to Moses in v. 11 could refer just to the fact that Moses was holding the rod; but Hebrew could quite easily have made this point by using the definite article and omitting the possessive suffix (as MT does in v. 9, and as in fact the LXX does in both phrases). Thus v. 11 is best understood as mentioning the rod *belonging* to Moses. So the MT appears to contain reminiscences both of Aaron's rod and of Moses' rod. As we trace these rods backwards through the narratives, the picture becomes even more complex.

In Exodus 17, of course, Moses' own rod is clearly in view and its use is commanded by God. Exodus 17 has its own problems; here our interest is restricted to the rod used to strike the rock (*nkh ṣwr* hi.), the rod described as 'with which you struck the Nile' (*'ăšer hikkîtā bô 'et-hay'ōr*, v. 5). This phrase in turn sends us back to Exodus 7.14ff.

In Exodus 7 we find that the story begins with the clear command of God to Moses that Moses announce to Pharaoh that he (*Moses*) will strike the Nile with 'the rod that is in my hand' (v. 17), the rod identified by God as the one 'which was turned into a serpent' (v. 15). Since God's address is to Moses, we take this rod to be Moses' rod of 4.3, not Aaron's of 7.8 which also became a serpent. Abruptly in v. 19 God tells Moses to tell *Aaron* to 'take his rod and stretch out his hand . . .' There follows the notice that '*Moses and Aaron* did as the Lord commanded' (v. 20a), and then we read that '*he* lifted his rod and struck the Nile'. From a classic source-critical perspective it seems clear that the command to Aaron and the statement of God's command being followed by Moses and Aaron belong to P, while the part about the rod of Moses belongs to the OE (presumably J here). The 'he' of v. 20 is identified as Moses because of the verb 'to strike' (*nkh* hi.) which is not included in Aaron's instruction but alludes to Moses' instructions in v. 17, and also because of the specific allusion to this tradition in Exodus 17. The important point, however, is that *in the final form of the Exodus 7 text the actor is left vague and the participation of both men with their rods is in view.*

Aaron's rod comes into play again in 8.12-13 (= Eng. 8.16-17, gnats), where Aaron is told (again through Moses) to 'strike' (*nkh* hi.) the dust. Moses uses his rod again in 9.23 (hail), but God's command of v. 22 refers only to Moses' hand and the LXX reads hand, not rod, in v. 23. The identical pattern with LXX variant occurs again in 10.12-13 (locusts). Finally in Exodus 14.16 Yahweh commands Moses to 'lift his rod and stretch out his hand over the sea', but the execution statement (v. 21) refers only to Moses' hand.

Not surprisingly, source analysis generally identifies all the references to Moses' rod as OE, the three bits of Aaron material as P. Outside of the long narrative about the rod of Aaron in Numbers 17 (P), the only other reference to either rod in the Pentateuch is in Exodus 17.9, the story of the battle against Amalek which immediately follows the water story, usually attributed to OE, where Moses holds 'the rod of God' in his hand as he holds up his hands. Furthermore there are no allusions to either Moses' or Aaron's rod outside the Pentateuch.

Thus it seems plausible to propose that the rod material of Numbers 20 should be neither completely excised as a late supplement (Noth), nor regarded as an inadequately covered remnant of an older version of the story (Kohata). Rather the rod may be seen as a clue to the relationship between Moses and Aaron and to the meaning of the passage. The rods of both leaders in the larger tradition have two functions: First, they are a symbol of true authority in the community—for Moses in Exodus 4.1-5 (OE), for Aaron in Numbers 17 (P). Second, they are wonder-working rods, which by their results confirm God's power and God's designation of the leaders' position. Especially in Egypt, both Moses' and Aaron's rods bring signs and wonders.

We will suggest below that v. 11a comes into the text through a scribe who did not catch P's theological intent. This leaves only the rod of Aaron in P's own composition. But even with the elimination to any explicit reference to Moses' (own) rod (since no other clear example of Moses' rod anywhere can be attributed to P), the balance of relationshp betwen Moses and Aaron is highlighted here at the close of the wilderness era: Aaron's rod held by Moses suggests that both have authority, both can act to bring about God's blessing on the people. At the same time, Moses' special relationship to God, even compared to Aaron's, is kept in view, as the reader recalls that Moses was in charge of the event of the budding rod in which Aaron's authority was proclaimed; Moses, who now 'takes' the rod, had himself placed the rod 'before the testimony'.

Once v. 11a comes into the text, if it was not there originally, this balance of relationship between the two leaders is accented still further. Just as in Exodus 7 the act of one (Moses) in striking the Nile water is understood explicitly as an act of obedience by both, so now in our received text of Numbers 20 the act of one (again Moses) is explicitly regarded as an act of *dis*obedience by both. There is balance between the two, and yet the asymmetry in which Moses stands between Aaron and God is also carried forward in the asymmetry by which Moses is the formal actor in the sin in which both men participate.

Although Aaron is introduced in various ways in both P and OE materials, such a concern for assessing the balance of relationship betwen the two ancestral leaders seems reasonable to attribute to the P tradition. The controversy over a Mushite priestly line[25] may have fallen into the background; but if Moses is to be presented as mediator *par excellence*, then it is important to clarify Aaron's place vis-à-vis Moses. The complex text of Numbers 20 presents Aaron as 'equal yet subordinate', or 'subordinate yet equal', a tension which summarizes the larger picture of the P tradition. The use of the rod motif in vv. 8-9 points to this theme; and the presence (possibly the addition) of the third rod reference in v. 11a reinforces it. On the 'subordination' side, we see that Aaron is subordinate to Moses in the matter of receiving the word of divine address (which we have seen comes only to Moses even though Aaron is obviously present at the theophany and is included in the content of the message). Relative rank may be further indicated in the tradition by their order of subsequent death, although P may here be dealing with an ancient 'given' of the tradition.

On the other hand, the two are 'equal' in their participation in the sin which leads to their judgment. Despite the fact that the text does not specify that Aaron 'did' any particular act, except helping to gather the people, v. 12 makes clear that the two are held fully and equally accountable for whatever took place. This emphasis on equality or balance is carried forward in the subsequent P passages concerning their deaths. The rationale for Aaron's death in 20.24 uses the plural verb *mĕrîtem*.[26] Likewise Numbers 27.13-14 relates Moses' death to Aaron's explicitly, again uses the plural *mĕrîtem*, and adds a form of the root *qdš*[27] from 20.12. And finally, in Deuteronomy 32.50-51 we find again specific comparative allusion to Aaron and again the plural verbs, *lō' qiddaštem, mĕ'altem bî*.

In connection with the death notices of Numbers 20 and 27 we find one additional indication of the pattern of balance between Moses and Aaron, namely the patterns of installation of their successors. The priest Eleazar's position is established by Moses, who is instructed to move the priestly garb from Aaron to his son (20.26, 28). Moses' successor Joshua in turn is commissioned before Eleazar and must hearken to Eleazar's use of the Urim (27.19, 21, 23). Neither line continues on its own, apart from the other.

We conclude that Aaron was part of the basic P version of Numbers 20.2-13. The unevenness of the text can be accounted for and in fact can serve to highlight, in this last event of their joint careers, the relationship of 'equal yet subordinate' between the two great leaders as it was established early in Exodus and as it appears in the larger P tradition. The only part of the key section in vv. 6-12 which might still be regarded as a later supplement with the Exodus

17 story in mind is v. 11a, which adds something concerning Moses, not Aaron. The status of this verse has obvious implications for the interpretation of the leaders' wrongdoing, and these will be taken up in the final section of this paper.

The Sin of Moses and Aaron

We turn at length to the question which provoked our larger investigation. If we look at the narrative as a whole, we can see that the first two actions of Moses and Aaron (taking the rod and assembling the congregation) correspond to the first two items in God's commands.[28] But then one leader speaks to the people and Moses strikes the rock, neither act specifically according with the command, yet neither openly contradicting it. The ironic summation of the sin in 20.24 and 27.14, *mĕrîtem ('ēt) pî*, suggests that divergence from God's command is especially in view, but what or which divergence is not specified. As the review of literature amply shows, scholars have been tempted toward all sorts of imaginative reconstructions in the face of the frustrating reticence of the text. Conceivably there has been an irrecoverable ancient haplography; but suggestions in the literature are quite *ad hoc*. It might even be suggested that there is no wrongdoing inherent in vv. 9-11, that only the assertion of sin in v. 12 forces us to find some wrong in the text. But the author of v. 12 (which I would regard as original to the basic pericope) must have thought the point could be seen, however it may appear to us. Assuming that the text itself is sound, we may review the options.

The efforts to identify the sin purely as speaking rashly, or purely as striking the rock when not commanded to do so, seem to me to state the options too narrowly for the extant form of the text. The judgment of v. 12 does not provide vocabulary specific enough to highlight either one of these options. Nor do the allusions to the sin in the death narratives (Num 27; Deut 32) provide any greater specificity, with their vocabulary of *mrh 't py, qdš* (from v. 12), or *m'l* (similar to *l' 'mn* of v. 12). Psalm 106, to be sure, represents our one biblical-period clue to ancient Israel's view of the matter, but even its statement is not explicit in identifying Moses' speaking as sin.[29]

Is there then something wrong—beyond sheer disobedience by omission of speaking to the rock—in the words spoken or the deed done? We consider first the words spoken. I remain unconvinced by Arden's suggestion that the participle *hammōrîm* is a totally inappropriate word for the people in this situation. Clearly they have complained against their leaders and said they wished they had already died at God's hand (vv. 2-3). If the Meribah etymology of v. 13 is original in P, not added by an independent later hand,[30] then contention against the Lord is explicitly stated by the P tradition. It is true that in the text there is no word of condemnation or judgment on the people by God; in this regard alone can the use of *hammōrîm* be questioned.

The 'we' of *nôṣî'* (v. 10b) I take to refer to Moses and Aaron, not to Moses and God (*contra* Arden), since I view Aaron (whom Arden completely ignores) as integral to the original composition of the passage. Thus the speaker of v. 10b is not overtly attributing any attitude or motive to God. Kohata suggest that this first common plural verb form arrogates to Moses and Aaron the divine power to bring forth water. But against this interpretation, God's own statement seems to prepare the way for this word when the Lord says to Moses, 'you shall bring forth *hôṣē'tā*, pl. in LXX) water for them from the rock'.

We are pressed then to consider the scene as a whole and the tone of the question addressed to the people in v. 10b. The *he*-interrogative can be used in three different ways,[31] each of which is conceivable here, given our scanty context, and each of which would give a different nuance. First, the sentnce may be construed simply as an open-ended question to the rebels: 'Shall we (or shall we not) bring forth water?' In this tone the question would expect that the people must beg Moses and Aaron to give the water ('Yes, please do'), despite God's command to Moses and Aaron to produce water for the people. Second, the *he*-interrogative can be used when the tone of the question expects a negative answer (so English: 'Can we bring forth water?'). With such a nuance either the people are being invited to disbelieve in the power of God given to Moses and Aaron, or there is a suggestion of Moses' and Aaron's own disbelief that water will come forth. Or third, the question could be merely a rhetorical form to express an indignant refusal to produce the water. (English: 'Shall we indeed?! / Why should we . . . ?') The emphatic position of 'from this rock' at the beginning of the question can be taken in support of the second option. But on any of these three interpretations the question itself can be understood to take away from the holiness of God and of the occasion itself (regardless of the epithet used to address the congregation). Thus the unfaithful content of the question itself would lead to the judgment of God.

A consideration next of Moses' striking the rock returns us to the possibility suggested above that v. 11a may not have been original to the P narrative of this event. Surely v. 11a is the most reminiscent of Exodus 17 of any part of this text; it uses the verb *nkh* (hi., strike), and is the clearest reference in the pericope (MT version) to Moses' rod. We have seen already that the previous rod references are Aaron's or ambiguous, and that the rod has been a basis for source division in a variety of pericopae. I would suggest that P may have composed the story without 11a (cf. also Ps 106 and its focus on Moses' *words*). Thus in P the words of Moses to the people, with all the nuances described above, were follwed directly by the appearance of water, the assuaging of thirst, and then the judgment of God upon the leaders.

Note that God's judgment does not say that the two will not personally enter the land; rather the emphasis is that they will not '*lead* (*tābî'û*, hi.) this congregation' into the land.[32] By their 'rash words' Moses and Aaron have not served as instruments of God's blessing; they have instead implied doubt of God's plan to help the people, perhaps doubted their role as instruments, or even have wanted to withhold from the people the goodness God has promised to give. Such leadership must be replaced. But the water comes forth from the rock anyway. Just as God throughout the wilderness murmurings supplied every need, whether or not the complaint was justified and regardless of the merit of the recipients, so here human failing of the leadership does not prevent the gracious springing forth of water. Blessing and judgment are conjoined.[33]

Verse 11a is then to be regarded as the addition of some later scribe (probably not a formal 'redactor' of large blocks), who knew the Exodus 17 story, saw the rod reference in vv. 8-9, and wondered too prosaically why the water appeared. The word *pa'ămāyim* suports this view, as it can mean not the traditional 'twice' but 'a second time'—alluding to Exodus 17 (cf. Nah 1.9). For later readers this explanatory addition about striking the rock simply reinforced the theme of wrongdoing, since no command to strike the rock had been given. To the extent that the addition suggested a lack of faith in the power of God to work by word alone (Kohata), it reinforced the wrongness of the words in v. 10b.

Thus we come at length to the conclusion that Arden and Lohfink (although they come to the text from very different directions, with different methodologies and reasoning, and with many arguments to which the present essay takes exception) are perhaps closest to the heart of the matter in their conclusions, since they focus on the spoiling of the sacred moment. Even as in Numbers 14 God's forgiveness of the community transcends judgment in the change of generations,[34] so here, as the people are once again poised to enter the land, the giving of water despite the leaders' action highlights God's power and gracious willingness to bring good out of evil, to be sanctified (v. 13) even when the leaders fail in this responsibility.

We referred earlier to Lohfink's focus on the words *lō' he'ĕmantem* as the third of the 'original sin' sequence of P, and we suggested that the phrase was not properly parallel to his identification of *dibbat hā'āreṣ* as the sin in Numbers 13–14. From our analysis and from Lohfink's own development of the theme, the question put to the people should more properly constitute the parallel sin because it gives (as he interprets the question) the concrete evidence of the leaders' lack of trust in the power of God. Since we have shown that the question may be multivalent, however, we conclude by suggesting that the message for the exiles in the Numbers 20 narrative should be broadened beyond what Lohfink has suggested. Not only are the leaders urged to trust in the power of God to do the impossible, and so to inspire rather than discourage their flock in exile; they are also warned not to set themselves over against the people in harsh judgment, not to stand in the way of God's mercy. It is almost as if to say that judgment will come upon any leaders who view as unredeemable or unworthy the exiles for whom God wills to care, to do a 'new thing', to open 'springs of water in the desert' as the highway through the wilderness unfolds.

Conclusion

We have seen that Moses and Aaron belong together in the priestly telling of the Numbers 20 narative. While it is quite possible that such a story of failure of leadership was once told about Moses alone, we have no pre-P literary deposit which lifts up that theme. Nor is Aaron a post-P insertion into the narrative. In this concluding episode of the wilderness era, P presents Aaron as 'equal yet subordinate' to Moses, just as the relationship between the two is pictured in their encounter with the Pharaoh in the early chapters of Exodus. Once this emphasis is recognized, the need for dissection and reconstruction of the pericope is greatly reduced. The joining of the two figures and the placing of this story at the very end of the wilderness era highlights P's balance between Moses and Aaron in a way that could never be achieved by attaching such radical consequences to differing individual or earlier failures of each leader alone.

The consequence of the leaders' failure is that they 'shall not bring this assembly into the land' (20.12). While the narratives concerning the deaths of Moses and Aaron relate their deaths outside the land to this event, it is important to notice that ch. 20 is interested more in faithful leadership for the community than in any personal privilege to enter the land. To be sure, it is judgment on their disobedience that they will be unable to see their task through to its conclusion. But the question which is answered in Numbers 20 is not exactly that of my audience, 'Why didn't Moses go into the land?' Rather, the question answered is, 'Why didn't Moses and Aaron lead the people into the land?'

Whatever our modern opinions about the gravity of some specific action, P understood what transpired as disbelief and as failure to sanctify God before the people. For God's chosen leadership, no sin could be more serious than that which by lack of trust impedes God's mercy to the community. The tragic and painful warning which P offers to Israel's leadership in the crisis of the exile echoes down through the ages and stands as reminder even to us today. For the sake of the people, God needs faithful leadership. Because God cares for the people, unfaithful leadership, especially any leadership which disdains or disparages the flock, will not finally endure.

NOTES

1. The present essay is offered in honor of my friend and colleague Bernhard Word Anderson, in special appreciation of his abiding interest in the ways in which scripture is heard in the church.

2. Viz. Num 27.12-23 (anticipated death of Moses and commissioning of Joshua), Deut 32.48-52 (command to Moses to go to view the land and die), Deut 34.1-8, 9 (death of Moses plus reprise of Joshua's 'installation'), and of course Exod 17.1-7 (water from the rock, before Sinai).

3. Martin Noth, *Numbers* (OTL; Philadelphia: Westminster, 1968) 143-47.

4. This traditional explanation is advocated, e.g., by George Coats, 'Legendary Motifs in the Moses Death Reports', *CBQ* 39 (1977) 39.

5. C.H. Cornill, 'Beiträge zur Pentateuchkritik', *ZAW* 11 (1891) 20-33.

6. Fujiko Kohata, 'Die priesterschriftliche Überlieferungsgeschichte von Numeri XX 1-13', *Annual of the Japanese Biblical Institute* 3 (1977) 1-34.

7. Wilhelm Rudolph, *Der 'Elohist' von Exodus bis Josua* (BZAW, 68; Berlin: Topelmann, 1938) 84ff.

8. Jacob Milgrom has shown that in preexilic usage *qāhāl* and the related verb have to do with the concept of an assembly in general, while in later texts there emerges a technical use equivalent to the older *'ēdâ* (as the nation, adult males, or tribal leaders) ('Priestly Terminology and the Political Structure of Pre-Monarchic Israel', *JQR* 69 [1978] 5-81). Thus the word *qāhāl* can be seen as typical P usage for the people. The only peculiarity is the people's reference to themselves in the third person as the *qhl yhwh* in their complaint in v. 4.

9. George Coats, *Rebellion in the Wilderness* (Nashville: Abingdon, 1968) 71-82.

10. The absence of Aaron from Ps 106 suggests to some scholars its basis in a tradition about Moses' sin in which Aaron was not included. Again it would seem that the inclusion of Aaron in Num 20 deserves more attention than it has usually received. In my own view of the matter, the psalmist's point precludes the mention of Aaron because he combines the content of Num 20 with the vicarious interpretation of Deuteronomy.

11. 'The Transgression of Moses and Aaron—Num 21.1-13', *Proceedings of the Fifth World Congress of Jewish Studies* (ed. Pinches Peli; Jerusalem: Hacohen, 1969) 21-26 (Hebrew; English summary).

12. 'How Moses Failed God', *JBL* 76 (1957) 50-52.

13. 'Die Ürsunde in der priesterlichen Geschichtserzählung', *Die Zeit Jesu* (ed. G. Bornkamm and K. Rahner; Freiburg: Herder, 1969) 38-57.

14. One might put forward two other hypotheses to account for the unevenness: a redactor tryiung to improve Aaron's image (a) could have tried to *reduce* his role in the story, or (b) inspired by the Exod 17 parallel account, could have heightened the apparent emphasis on Moses alone. Option (a) is not unthinkable; there is some evidence for this kind of activity in the case of the golden calf narrative (Exod 32), where even differences between the MT and LXX may reflect this concern. On the whole, however, the literary picture, especially in v. 8 ('you and Aaron your brother'), suggests adding rather than subtracting. Option (b) may contain some truth, as we will suggest subsequently, although the motive does not appear to be the exoneration of Aaron. It should be noted that the singular forms in the passage as a whole are more widespread than the verses usually taken to be reminiscent of Exod 17.

15. The expression comes from F.M. Cross's description of Aaron's relationship to Moses in P generally (*Canaanite Myth and Hebrew Epic* [Cambridge, Mass.: Harvard University, 1973] 206).

16. For a convenient catalog of major opinions, see Brevard Childs, *Exodus* (OTL; Philadelphia: Westminster, 1974) 275. Noth follows the weight of opinion in assigning all except vv. 4-5, 28-30 to P. Verses 13b-15, 21, and 27-31 are the ones most often suggested to be non-priestly.

17. E.g. Exod 16.11; by implication in Exod 16.23, 24; Num 17.8-9 (= Eng. 16.43-44; very similar to ch. 20, at the tent of meeting, with the Glory of the Lord appearing).

18. Exod 7.8; 9.8; 12.1; 12.43; Lev 11.1; 13.1; 14.33; 15.1; Num 2.2; 14.26; 16.20; 19.1.

19. E.g. Exod 11.9; 14.1, 15, 26. Of course the legislative materials are replete with divine address to Moses and no reference to Aaron.

20. Conspicuously, in the case of Aaron's death (20.23). But also in other instances, e.g. Exod 7.19; Num 6.22; 8.1; Lev 17.1-2.

21. Only in Lev. 10.8 (a prohibition of drinking wine when entering the tent of meeting) and Num 18.1, 8, 20 (concerning duties of Aaronic priests and Levites).

22. One notes, incidentally, in Exod 4.17 the sudden command concerning Moses' rod, with its verbal affinities to Num 20.

23. In Num 12.1 we find Aaron introduced in a way which produces grammatical rarity: a third feminine singular verb followed by subject Miriam and then 'and Aaron'—suggesting supplementation at the literary level. (GKC, §146f, suggests, however, that gender agreement may be simply with the nearest subject. Examples are too infrequent to establish a clear pattern. Most commentators agree that Aaron is secondary, regardless of the grammatical issue.) Since the chapter is generally regarded as OE in its basic form, literary supplementing is no direct clue to dating the inclusion of Aaron. The chapter is certainly complex: Aaron's role in the face of Miriam's leprosy is confusing and debated; an old poem in vv. 6-8 asserts the supremacy of Moses. F.M. Cross connects the dispute to an early pro-Mushite priesthood group, and this is possible (*Canaanite Myth*, 203-205). The heart of the issue, however, seems to be the poem about Moses' unique place before God, which is focused on prophecy and revelation rather than on priestly affairs. If the introduction of Aaron were placed in the context of prophetic challenge to priestly leadership, then the issue of this text would seem to me to have a better setting. However ancient the poem, it presents Moses as the source of torah *par excellence*. Aaron—and the priesthood—must be subject to the torah of Moses. In this respect the message could even be significant for the era of Ezra much later. Cf. Noth's discussion in *A History of Pentateuchal Traditions* (trans. B.W. Anderson; Englewood Cliffs: Prentice-Hall, 1972), 127. He suggests the tradition is 'scholarly' and 'rather late'.

24. Noth, *Numbers*, 144. Elsewhere he identifies this hand as R^P (*Pentateuchal Traditions*, 15).

25. See Cross, *Canaanite Myth*, 194-215.

26. How this verb *mrh* enters the tradition remains a puzzle, since it is not found in 20.12-13 and is not related to the Meribah etymology. Probably it is an ironic twist on the use of the participle *hammōrim* which 'Moses' uses to address the people in v. 10b.

27. The MT form is actually identical (infinitive construction plus object) to the form of 20.12. But a syntactical problem arises, since such a form after *mrh* would be expected to state what they *did* do, rather than what they failed to do. The LXX and Syriac use of the negative shows that the meaning was clear in the tradition.

28. The verb *ṣiwwāhû* does not come at the end of the obedience section, *contra* Kohata, who supposed the substitution of *qāhāl* for *'ēdâ* in v. 10a and thus suggested lack of precise correspondence. See above.

29. Saying only, 'it went badly for Moses on their account'. See above, n. 10, for my explanation of the absence of Aaron from this Psalm text.

30. That is, if we assume either that P used the OE Meribah tradition (Coats) or that the Priestly writer himself incorporated OE as he wrote (Cross).

31. GKC, §150d.

32. See above for the pattern of relation between the two new leaders. The MT allusions to the sin in the death narratives in 20.24, Deut 32.52 use the qal of *bô'* with no object (Sam V of 20.24 read hi. + his people). Kohata observed this difference which led to his view that the *bô'* (hi.) + obj. *qāhāl* in 20.12 was secondary. I would suggest just the opposite direction of change; if in fact the difference is significant, the sin-rationale verses in the death narratives can be regarded as secondary and can be associated with a period when the question of the leaders' personal entrance into the land had taken precedence over the more immediate concern for faithful leadership.

33. One might regard v. 11b as secondary also and suppose that P's version had no water, only judgment. Such an approach would highlight the need for new leadership; but the consistency of divine provision for material needs throughout the tradition suggests that 11b be retained as integral to P's narrative.

34. See the present writer's essay, 'The Problem of Divine Forgiveness in Numbers 14', *CBQ* 37 (1975) 317-30.

* Regrettably I have been unable to incorporate the recent work of Jacob Milgrom, 'Magic, Monotheism, and the Sin of Moses', *The Quest for the Kingdom of God*, ed. H.B. Huffmon, F.A. Spina, and A.R.W. Green, (Winona Lake, Ind.: Eisenbrauns, 1983), which appeared after the present essay went to press.

8

AMOS 6.1-7

J.J.M. Roberts

Amos 6.1-7 presents the interpreter with a number of significant textual, literary, form critical, and historical problems despite the fact that there is fairly general agreement on the extent of the oracle.[1] The solution to many of these problems, as I hope to show in this paper, hinges on the conrrect analysis of the structure of the *hôy* oracle and a better appreciation of the historical setting for Amos's work.

Amos 6.1-7 is one of two oracles in the book of Amos introduced by the textually certain exclamation *hôy*. In addition to the other certain *hôy* oracle found in 5.18-20, a number of scholars also reconstruct *hôy* oracles in 5.7[2] and 6.13.[3] Their suggested reconstructions have merit, but since these last two *hôy* oracles are reconstructed, they may only be used with extreme caution in discussing the structure of the *hôy* oracle. The *hôy* oracles have traditionally been known as woe oracles, but in an earlier article I argued that this was a misnomer.[4] I will not repeat the whole argument here, but it will be necessary to go over the main points, since the true structure of the *hôy* oracles is widely misunderstood, and that misunderstanding has skewed the interpretation of this text. This study is intended to correct that misunderstanding and bring new clarity to the reading of Amos 6.1-7. With those intentions it is offered as a tribute to my colleague and friend, Bernhard W. Anderson, a scholar who has a long and distinguished career of bringing new clarity to the reading of the biblical text.

> Hey! You who are at ease in Zion,
> Who are secure in Mount Samaria,
> Mark the foremost of the nations,
> And go to them, O house of Israel:
> Pass over to Kullane and see,
> Go from there to Hamath the Great,
> Then go down to Gath of the Philistines.
> Are [you] better than these kingdoms?
> Is your border greater than their border?
> You who thrust away the evil day,

And bring near the reign of violence;
Who lie upon beds of ivory,
And sprawl upon their couches;
Who eat rams from the flock,
And calves taken from the stall;
Who improvise to the sound of the harp,
And like David invent for themselves musical instuments;
Who drink from the wine bowls,
And anoint themselves with the choicest oils,
But are not made sick over the ruin of Joseph;
Therefore they shall soon go into exile at the head of the column,
And the banquet of the sprawlers will cease.
Says Yahweh, the God of Hosts.

(1) 'Hey!' The particle *hôy* has traditionally been lumped together with the related *'ôy* and translated as 'woe to'. But while this is appropriate for *'ôy*, which is normally constructed with the preposition *l*, it is inappropriate for *hôy*, which is construed without the preposition.[5] *Hôy* is simply an exlamation used to get the attention of the hearers, and as such it is often used to introduce direct address, so that its characterization as a vocative particle is not inappropriate.[6] In and of itself *hôy* has no overtones of weal or woe; it can be used to introduce a positive message (Isa 55.1) as well as a negative message.[7] Any negative overtones the particle may acquire derives from the particular speech context in which it is used, not from the inherent meaning or syntactical function of the particle itself.

'You who'—The adjective and participle following *hôy* are clearly vocatives as the imperatives and second person pronominal suffix in v. 2 and the second person verb form in v. 3 demonstrate.[8] The article may be used with them precisely to mark them as vocatives. The vocative address is clearly continued through v. 3 and probably through v. 6, since the third person pronominal suffixes and verb forms may be explained as a syntactically conditioned feature in relative clauses following an opening vocative, but this feature ultimately causes the speaker to slip into the third person. The announcement of judgment in v. 7 is formulated in the third person, the directness of the original vocative address having been lost in the series of syntactically conditioned third person forms in vv. 4–6.

'Zion' is not expected in this verse, since Amos's message was primarily directed against the northern kingdom, Israel, and this has led a number of scholars to emend the text. Rudolph is certainly correct in rejecting both *ad hoc* metaphorical interpretations of the word and the arbitrary deletion of the first stich of v. 1a, but his own emendation is not very convincing.[9] Without more compelling reasons any emendation is venturesome. Given the reference to David in v. 5, it is possible that the reading Zion is original and that Amos himself drew Judah into his critique of Israel in this passage. The view that Amos rigorously restricted his message to Israel according to the terms of his commission in 7.15 can be maintained only if one consistently denies to Amos such passages as 1.2, 2.4-5, and 9.11, as well as the passage under discussion. How such an address to the leaders of Zion alongside the leaders of Samaria would make sense will become clearer when the historical context of the oracle is discussed.

ngby r'šyt hgwym—This expression has always been a crux to interpreters. The traditional rendering, represented by the RSV's, 'the notable men of the first of the nations', suffers under several difficulties. Poetically the line so rendered is parallel to 6.1ab, thus making a tri-stich, but this leaves 6.1d, 'to whom the house of Israel come', without any parallel line. Neither its logical connection nor its syntactical tie to the preceding stich is very smooth. Thus it is not surprising that scholars who accept the traditional reading of 6.1c, often emend 6.1d, sometimes drastically,[10] or even delete it entirely.[11] Moreover, the traditional rendering provides no lead-in to the following verse, and the resulting abruptness is partly responsible for Wolff's deletion of 6.2 as a secondary Judean addition.[12] These difficulties largely disappear without the need for radical emendation or major surgery when *ngby* and *wb'w* are read as second masculine plural imperatives, a matter of simple repointing and, in the case of *ngby*, of the slight correction of *waw* for *yodh*. Ehrlich saw this long ago, though he failed to note the versional evidence for this corrected reading.[13] The LXX reading *apetrugēsan arxas ethnōn*, 'They gathered the first fruits of the nations', which may be an inner Greek correction for *apetrupēsan* . . . , 'They pierced . . . ', clearly presupposes a consonantal text *ngbw*, though the LXX translator read it and the following *wb'w* as qal perfects. Because he misread them as perfects, he was forced to construe *byt yśr'l*, which he correctly recognized as a vocative, with the following imperatives of 2a, but that, of course, overloads 2a and cannot be correct. When the verbs are read as imperatives, everything falls into place. The prophet commands his audience to mark or note the most prominent nations and go to them for instruction, and this is elaborated in the following verse where three such nations are singled out for specific mention.

(2) Why are these three particular cities singled out? What do Kullane,[14] Hamath, and Gath have in common? As Rudolph correctly notes,[15] our knowledge of the eighth century is too fragmentary to be overly dogmatic about Amos's precise historical allusion, but within the limits of our actual knowledge of this period the only occasion when precisely these three cities fit into a common sequence of events is immediately before and during the Assyrian campaign against the Azariah-led, anti-Assyrian coalition of northern Phoenician cities and north Syrian states that ended in the Assyrian capture of Kullani(a) in 738 BC.[16] In the course of Azariah's expansion into the Philistine territory he destroyed the walls of Gath (2 Chr 26.6), but the destruction of the other two territories must be primarily attibuted to the Assyrians. The nineteen districts of Hamath, including the northern Phoenician coastal cities and the region of Hatarikka, which had been taken away from Hamath and had joined Azariah's coalition, were turned into the two Assyrian provinces of Simirra and Hatarikka as a result of the coalition's defeat.[17] Hamath itself appears to have remained loyal to Assyria,[18] and it was neither destroyed nor turned into a province, but the loss of its nineteen western and northern districts radically reduced Hamath's importance. It could no longer be legitimately called Hamath the Great. Kullani(a), the capital of Unqi, which had apparently participated in the same anti-Assyrian coalition,[19] fell to the Assyrians in 738 BC. Tutamu, the ruler of Unqi, was taken into exile along with his high officials, and Unqi was turned into an Assyrian province.[20]

If the destruction of Gath, the reduction of Hamath the Great, and the fall of Kullani(a) can all be tied in with Azariah's growing power and his futile attempt to halt further Assyrian expansion in the west, can the date of these events be squared with the attibution of Amos 6.2 to the prophet Amos? His ministry is normally dated much earlier than 738 BC. Robert B. Coote, however, argues from this oracle and other observations that Amos's ministry actually fell during the reign of Jeroboam II's successors.[21] He makes a number of good observations, but in my opinion he goes too far in denying that Amos's ministry overlapped with the reign of Jeroboam II at all. I cannot accept his theory about the composition of the book, and thus I am unwilling to dismiss either 1.1 or 7.10-17 as historically without value. Whoever supplied the dating formula thought Amos's ministry began in the reign of Jeroboam II, and the same may be said for the individual(s), not necessarily the same, who formulated and preserved the account of Amos's encounter with Amaziah. There is not sufficient internal evidence in the book of Amos to prove these tradents wrong, but neither is there evidence sufficient to rule out the possibility that Amos's ministry extended as late as 738 BC, or even a few years later. Amos 1.1 places Amos's ministry during the reigns of Jeroboam II of Israel and Uzziah/Azariah of Judah, but according to 2 Kings 15.8, 13, 17, 23, 27, Azariah's reign extended beyond that of Jeroboam II and overlapped with the later reigns of Zechariah, Shallum, Menahem, Pekahiah, and the first two years of Pekah.[22] The fact that the date formula does not mention any Israelite kings later than Jeroboam II is no proof that Amos's ministry was restricted to the early part of Azariah's reign. The similar date formula in Hosea 1.1 places Hosea's ministry in the reigns of Azariah, Jotham, Ahaz, and Hezekiah of Judah, but of the contemporary northern kings it lists only Jeroboam II. For some reason the tradent who supplied the date formula did not think any of the northern kings after Jeroboam II worth mentioning, though Hosea's ministry obviously extended through the reigns of Zechariah, Shallum, Menahem, Pekahiah, Pekah, and Hoshea if it lasted into the reign of Hezekiah. If the same bias against the late northern kings were held by the tradent who supplied the date formula to Amos, the reference to Jeroboam II cannot be taken as a *terminus ad quem*. It merely indicates when his prophetic ministry began. The same may be said for the earlier notice in Amos 1.1b. 'Two years before the earthquake' is probably intended to date the beginning of Amos's prophetic activity. It is hardly legitimate to derive from this notice that his whole ministry lasted less than a year or, as one noted scholar has argued, consisted in a single short sermon.

Verse 2b brings out the point of this visit to these famous and once powerful cities. Israel and Judah are neither better nor larger than these notable states once were, hence if these states could be destroyed, reduced, or robbed of their independence, so can Israel and Judah. There is no rational basis for the false sense of security that still pervaded the ruling classes in the two states.[23]

(3) Verse 3 resumes the characterization of those addressed that was begun in 1a. Amos castigates them as, 'You who put off the day of disaster', and 'who bring near the reign of violence'. The precise meaning of *šbt ḥms* is disputed,[24] but it probably refers to the ruling

class's oppression of the poor. Such a characterization of the nobility would fit the situation in both Israel and Judah after the Assyrian victory over the coalition in 738 BC. Tyre, Damascus, and Samaria apparently took advantage of Azariah's defeat to free themselves from Judean domination, and Menahem, at least, saw Tiglath-pileser as a helpful ally to confirm his control over the northern throne (2 Kgs 15.19). The price, however, was a very heavy tribute that Menahem could raise only by onerous extractions (2 Kgs 15.20), and one may be sure that the wealthy who had to pay the 50 shekels of silver passed the costs on to their less fortunate countrymen who were dependent on them. Thus one could well speak of the 'ruin' of Joseph (Amos 6.6).

The situation does not seem to have been much better in Judah, however. With the loss of control over Israel, the Arameans, and the Philistines that resulted from Azariah's defeat, Judah's control of the trade routes disappeared, and with it the basis for much of Judah's prosperity during the earlier years of Azariah's reign. Apparently Judah made no attempt to recoup her loses, but shifted to an isolationist, defensive posture.

(4-6) Neither the ruling class of Israel nor that of Judah allowed this economic disaster to change their life style, however. They continued to live in luxury as though nothing had changed. Isaiah characterized the arrogance of the northern leaders during this period when he quoted them as saying, 'The bricks have fallen, but we will build with hewn stones; the sycamores have been cut down, but we will replace them with cedars' (Isa 9.9),[25] and his portrayals of the Judean leaders in his early oracles, some of which probably date to approximately this same period, reflect the same attitudes and behavior scored by Amos.[26] The state of the nation, the suffering of the lower classes, and the impending collapse of the whole society caused them no concern.

(6c) The failure of Samaria's ruling class to be sickened by the hurt of their own people was obviously grounds for condemnation, but why should the rulers of Zion be charged for ignoring the plight of Joseph? Yet, if Zion is original in v. 1, Amos's charge would seem to be addressed to the ruling class of both states. To understand Amos's outlook one must pay more attention than scholars usually do to the evidence from this period for the prophetic ideal of a single Davidic state. This is clearly evidenced in Isaiah's promise of a light to the northern territories (8.23-9.6), in his promises to Ahaz and threats against Ephraim at the time of the Syro-Epraimite war,[27] and in his vision of a new, glorified Zion.[28] It is reflected in Amos's vision of Yahweh roaring from Zion (1.2) and in his vision of the restoration of the fallen booth of David (9.11-12), and the underlying ideology of the Davidic empire is probably also presupposed in his oracles against the surrounding nations (1.3–2.5). It is likely that the period of Judean expansion under Azariah had revived this vision of the old Davidic empire. If this is so, Amos may have regarded the post-Kullani(a) decision of the Judean leaders to draw back from involvement with the now pro-Assyrian Samaria under Menahem as a lack of concern for an important part of God's people. Such isolationism was doomed to fail. A resurgent Damascus stepped into the power vacuum left by the retreating Judah and soon dominated the foreign policy of the northern kingdom. By a cruel twist of fate, isolationist Judah was then faced with an anti-Assyrian Israel backed by the power of Damascus and her Phoenician and Philistine allies. Judah's refusal to concern herself with the situation in the north after the defeat at Kullani(a) led to a new situation in which the north could not be ignored, and the nobility, who paid no more attention to Isaiah than they had to Amos, shifted their policy from isolationism to Assyrian vassalage.

(7) Verse 7 introduces the punishment. The announcement of punishment or judgment is a very common element in the *hôy* oracles, though there is no single method of introducing it,[29] and I would argue that it is a constituent part of the full form of such oracles. *Hôy* oracles without an announcement of judgment are secondary, clipped forms.[30]

The judgment announced is full of poetic justice. Amos makes a nice play on the root *r'š*. He had urged the nobles to consider the foremost (*r'šyt*) nations and he had characterized the nobles as those who anointed themselves with the best (*r'šyt*) oils. Now he says that because of their unconcerned self-indulgence these nobles, who were satisfied only with the best for themselves, would go into exile at the head (*r'š*) of the column. They would share the same fate as the nobility of the foremost of the nations. Just as Tutamu and his high officials were the first to go into exile from Kullani(a), so they would be the first to go into exile from Israel and Judah. In that way Yahweh would bring their thoughtless, profligate feasting to an end.[31]

Verse 8b, the phrase translated, 'Says Yahweh, the God of Hosts', but which is actually a nominal phrase, 'Oracle of Yahweh, the God of Hosts', is lacking in the LXX, and is curiously redundant in its present position after the oath formula in v. 8a. If the line is original at all, it has probably been transposed from the end of v. 7. Restored to that position, it reinforces the closure of the oracle in 6.1-7 and marks it as the word of Yahweh.

NOTES

1. Artur Weiser is one of the few commentators to define the extent of the oracle as anything other than 6.1-7, and his analysis of the oracle (6.1, 13, 2-3, 14) is too arbitrary to be taken seriously (*Das Buch der zwölf Kleinen Propheten I* [ATD 24; Göttingen: Vandenhoeck & Ruprecht, 1963] 175). Several scholars do take the second line of v. 8, 'Thus says Yahweh, the God of Hosts', as the misplaced conclusion of the oracle, but this is not a major problem whatever one's decision on the matter.

2. James L. Mays, *Amos: A Commentary* (OTL; Philadelphia: Westminster, 1969) 90; Wilhelm Rudolph, *Joel–Amos–Obadja–Jona* (KAT 13/2; Gütersloh: Gerd Mohn, 1971) 194; Hans Walter Wolff, *Dodekapropheton 2: Joel und Amos* (BKAT 14/2; Neukirchen-Vluyn: Neukirchener Verlag, 1969) 268.

3. Rudolph, *Joel–Amos–Obadja–Jona*, 225; cf. Wolff, *Dodekapropheton 2*, 332.

4. 'Form, Syntax, and Redaction in Isaiah 1.2-20', *The Princeton Seminary Bulletin*, NS 3/3 (1982) 293-306.

5. *Ibid.*, 297-98. Cf. also Gunther Wanke, "אוי und "הוי", *ZAW* 78 (1966) 215-18; Richard J. Clifford, 'The Use of *Hôy* in the Prophets', *CBQ* 28 (1966) 458-64; Waldemar Janzen, *Mourning Cry and Woe Oracle* (BZAW 125; Berlin & New York: de Gruyter, 1972); and Delbert R. Hillers, '*Hôy* and *Hôy*-Oracles: A Neglected Syntactic Aspect', *The Word of the Lord shall Go Forth: Essays in Honor of David Noel Freedman in Celebration of his sixtieth Birthday* (ed. Carol L. Meyers and M. O'Connor; Winona Lake: Eisenbrauns, 1983) 185-88.

6. Janzen, *Mourning Cry*, 13.

7. Clifford artificially separated three different uses of the particle: 1. to describe actual funeral laments, 2. a cry to get attention, and 3. a use limited to the prophets where the word introduces announcements of doom ('The Use of *Hôy*', 458). The second usage he described as a 'curious use of *hôy* as a cry to get attention'. According to Clifford, 'It apparently is related to the prophetic and funerary *hôy* only by sound. These four examples may be a further indication of the divorce of the word from its funeral origin' (463). Against his view Janzen correctly points out that the use of *hôy* as an exclamation is not a different and special kind of *hôy* (*Mourning Cry*, 20). Actually all three uses are syntactically identical. Even in the funeral context the particle is used as an exclamation to get the attention of the dead person,

who is typically addressed in the second person in the funeral lament.

8. Wolff regards v. 2 as a secondary insertion, and he corrects the verb form in v. 3 to third person largely under the mistaken notion that the *Anredestil* is not found in the context of the 'old Woe-oracles', though to his embarrassment he must admit that the *Anredestil* is found in 5.18b (*Dodekapropheton 2*, 316). In fact, the *Anredestil* or vocative address is found in every possible occurrence of the *hôy* oracle in Amos: 1. in 5.7ff. note the second person pronominal suffix and second person verb forms in 5.11, 2. in 5.18 the second person follows directly after the initial vocative address; and 3. in 6.13ff. the second person pronominal suffix is found in v. 14. Wolff has simply erred in following Gerstenberger's analysis of the *hôy* oracles (*Dodekapropheton 2*, 298-99), in which the syntactically conditioned use of the third person following a vocative was misunderstood as impersonal, wisdom-style speech (E. Gerstenberger, 'The Woe-Oracles of the Prophets', *JBL* 81 [1962] 249-63; Roberts, 'Form, Syntax, Redaction', 299-301). Given the fact that *hôy* never occurs in a wisdom book, it is more than a little curious that Gerstenberger's analysis of the *hôy*-oracle as a genre derived from wisdom won so much acceptance.

9. Rudolph, *Joel-Amos-Obadja-Jona*, 215.

10. See the discussion of various emendations in Rudolph, *Joel–Amos–Obadja–Jona*, 216.

11. Wolff, *Dodekapropheton 2*, 315-16.

12. *Ibid.*, 317-18

13. Arnold B. Ehrlich, *Randglossen zur hebräischen Bibel* (Leipzig: J.C. Hinrichs, 1912), 5, 243-44.

14. As is generally recognized today, the MT's Kalneh is to be identified with the city Kullani(a) or Kinalua, the capital of the north Syrian Unqi (J.D. Hawkins, *RLA* 5, 597-98; 6, 305-306).

15. Rudolph, *Joel–Amos–Obadja–Jona*, 219.

16. The best reconstruction of this war and its historical background remains that of Hayim Tadmor, 'Azriyau of Yaudi', *Scripta Hierosolymitana* 8 (1961) 232-71. One should also compare Manfred Weippert's, 'Menahem von Israel und seine Zeitgenossen in einer Steleninschrift des assyrischen Königs Tiglathpileser III. aus dem Iran', *ZDPV* 89 (1973) 26-53; Karlheinz Kessler's, 'Die Anzahl der assyrischen Provinzen des Jahres 738 v. Chr. in Nordsyrien', *WO* 8 (1975-76) 49-63; and R. Borger and H. Tadmor, 'Zwei Beiträge zur alttestamentlichen Wissenschaft aufgrund der Inschriften Tiglathpilesers III', *ZAW* 94 (1982) 244-51. Nadav Na'aman has demonstrated that the cuneiform text K 6205, published by G. Smith in III *R* 9, 2, does not belong to the Tiglath-pileser corpus, hence there is no clear reference to Azariah of Judah in Tiglath-pileser's inscriptions ('Sennacherib's "Letter to God" on his Campaign to Judah', *BASOR* 214 [1974] 25-39), but contrary to Na'aman (pp. 38-39), that is not sufficient reason to disassociate the Azariah mentioned in Tiglath-pileser's text (III *R* 9, 3) from the biblical Azariah. To

judge from the biblical record he was the dominant ruler in southern Syria at this time, there is no other more likely candidate, and Assyria's failure to attack Judah in 738 BC may be explained in a variety of ways. Assyria may have had to consolidate her gains in the north before pressing farther south. At any rate Assyria does not seem to have penetrated beyond the northern end of the Lebanon and Anti-Lebanon ranges until the later Philistine campaign of 734 BC (Kessler, 'Die Anzahl', 62-63). One should note that Kessler was aware that K 6205 could not be ascribed to Tiglath-pileser when he accepted Tadmor and Weippert's identification of Tiglath-pileser's Azariah as the biblical Azariah/Uzziah of Judah (p. 53, nn. 19-20).

17. Kessler, 'Die Anzahl', 58-59.

18. Tadmor, 'Azriyau', 268.

19. Kessler, 'Die Anzahl', 52.

20. Paul Rost, *Die Keilschrifttexte Tiglath-Pilesers III*, 1 (Leipzig: Eduard Pfeiffer, 1893) 16-19: lines 92-101; H.W.F. Saggs, 'The Nimrud Letters, 1952—Part II', *Iraq* 17 (1955) 1343, ND. 2696.

21. *Amos Among the Prophets: Composition and Theology* (Philadelphia: Fortress, 1981) 21-22.

22. The chronology for this period is a mess, but Tadmor calculates the end of Azariah's reign to the late spring of 733 BC ('Azriyau', 265).

23. The text of v. 2b requires two slight corrections. Either the pronoun *'tm* has fallen out by homoeoteleuton between *htwbym* and *mn*, or it is simply omitted because it is clear from the context (cf. Josh 24.22; Ruth 4.11), and *gbwlm mgblkm* should be corrected to *gblkm mgbwlm*. The reason for the transposition of the suffixes could be an attempt to save Jewish honor from an invidious comparison with the Gentiles (so Rudolph, *Joel–Amos–Obadja–Jona*, 216), but it could also be the result of a simple misunderstanding caused by the ellipsis of the preceding *'tm*.

24. The rendering adopted in my translation identifies *šbt* as the infinitive construct from *yšb*. Ehrlich suggested another rather attractive possibility. He understood the word in the sense of Exod 21.19 and paraphrased the meaning of the phrase as 'while you bring within your reach a life of idleness secured through the exercise of violence' (*Randglossen*, 244). Rudolph derives the word from *šbt* and translates the phrase *šbt hms* as 'ein gewaltsames Ende' (*Joel–Amos–Obadja–Jona*, 215-16), but this forces him to see v. 3b as already alluding to the coming punishment and therefore as parallel to v. 7, while vv. 4-6 correspond to vv. 1-3a (p. 218). That seems unlikely to me, though the presence of allusions to judgment, particularly with double entendres, are found in similar contexts before the formal announcement of judgment in the *hôy* oracles of Isaiah. See 5.8 and 5.11 for examples.

25. This quotation occurs in the context of an oracle clearly directed against the northern kingdom (Isa 9.7-8), and the following verse (9.10), which mentions the hostility of Aram and the Philistines against Israel,

suggests that the boasting took place before Menahem's dynasty was replaced by the pro-Aramean Pekah. The continuation of the passage with its reference to sectional strife in Israel culminating in Israel's attack on Judah at the time of the Syro-Ephraimite war (9.18-20) suggests that the judgments described are indeed sequential and thus justify taking 9.9 as a rather specific description of the situation in Israel following Menahem's submission to Tiglath-pileser III. One must stress that the profligate partying and luxurious unconcern of the upper class that Amos attacks in Amos 6.1-6 does not presuppose an earlier period of unthreatened prosperity. Isaiah also spoke of the drunkards of Ephraim, bloated with rich food and overcome by wine (28.1-4; see the JPS translation), and his oracle could hardly date from any earlier than the last few years of Azariah, probably not prior to 738 BC.

26. Cf. Isa 3.13-15, 16-4.1, 5.1-7; 5.8-24; 10.1-4. Note especially his attack on those who spend their time at lavish banquets characterized by an abundance of alcoholic beverages and musical entertainment, but who have no eye for what God is doing in history (5.11-13).

27. See my study, 'Isaiah and His Children', to appear in the Iwry Festschrift, *Biblical and Related Studies Presented to Samuel Iwry*, ed. by Ann Kort and Scott Morschauser.

28. For the present see Henri Cazelles, 'Qui aurait visé, à l'origine, Isaïe II 2-5?', *VT* 30 (1980) 409-20.

29. For other *hôy* oracles that introduce the judgment with *lkn* see Isa 5.13, 24. Many other patterns are also used (Isa 1.5-7; 5.9; 33.1; Hab 2.7, 10-11, 13, 16; etc.).

30. Roberts, 'Form, Syntax, Redaction', 300.

31. The meaning of the term translated in the text as 'banquet' (*mrzḥ*) has been clarified to some extent by the occurrence of its Ugaritic cognate in the Ugaritic texts. It apparently can refer to a ritual banquet or to the cultic association that sponsored such banquets. Whether these banquets had a funerary character is still debated, but that they were often characterized by an overindulgence in wine is clear enough. The most thorough treatment of all of the evidence for the *mrzḥ*, including the biblical, rabbinic, Ugaritic, Phoenician, Aramaic, and Nabataean texts as well as the Greek and Semitic texts from Palmyra, remains the unpublished Johns Hopkins dissertation of David Bryan, 'Texts Relating to the Marzeah', completed during the early 1970s. Other discussions include Marvin H. Pope, 'A Divine Banquet at Ugarit', *The Use of the Old Testament in the New and Other Essays: Studies in Honor of William Franklin Stinespring* (ed. James M. Efird; Durham: Duke University, 1972) 170-203; Bezalel Porten, *Archives from Elephantine: The Life of an Ancient Jewish Military Colony* (Berkeley and Los Angeles: University of California, 1968) 179-86; Patrick D. Miller, 'The *MRZḤ* Text', *The Claremont Ras Shamra Tablets* (ed. L.R. Fisher; An Or, 48; Rome: Pontifical Biblical Institute, 1971) 37-49; K.J. Cathcart and W.G.E.

Watson, 'Weathering a Wake: A Cure for a Carousal. A revised translation of Ugaritica V text 1', *Proceedings of the Irish Biblical Association* 4 (1980) 35-58; B. Margalit, 'The Ugaritic Feast of the Drunken Gods: Another Look at RS 24.258 (KTU 1.114)', *Maarav* 2/1 (1979-80) 65-120, especially p. 101 and the literature cited in n. 101; and M. Dietrich and O. Loretz, 'Neue Studien zu den Ritualtexten aus Ugarit (I)', *Ugarit-Forschungen* 13 (1981) 88-98, especially p. 95.

9

RAHAB AND THE CONQUEST

Murray L. Newman

The story of Rahab the harlot in Joshua 2 cannot be said to occupy a particularly prominent place in the Bible. Apart from the Book of Joshua, Rahab is mentioned in no other book of Hebrew Scriptures. In the New Testament there are only three references to her, none of which seems to stand forth as especially significant: she is an example of faith in Hebrews 11.31; she is one who is justified by her works in James 2.25; and in Matthew 1.5 she is cited as an ancestor of Jesus. This suggests at best a role in a passing episode in the history of the people of God.

However, a more careful examination of her story in the context of sociological concerns of contemporary biblical scholarship may reveal it to be more valuable than is generally assumed, at least in illuminating the early history of Israel.

I

The story of Rahab in ch. 2 of the book of Joshua follows the address by Joshua to his people in Transjordan in ch. 1, and begins the account of the actual invasion itself. It depicts a harlot in the city of Jericho who gives protection from its king to two spies sent by Joshua to scout the land. The central figures are introduced in the first verse and a half: the nameless spies, Rahab, and the nameless Canaanite king. In brief, the narrative can be summarized as follows: After leaving their camp in Shittim with their instructions from Joshua, the two spies cross the Jordan, enter Jericho and find lodging in the house of a harlot named Rahab. When the king of the city learns of their presence, he demands that Rahab deliver them over. After hiding the two men, she insists that they have already left and tricks royal messengers into a fruitless pursuit toward the Jordan. Then she returns to the spies and gives voice to her belief that Yahweh had acted in the event of the exodus for the freedom of his people and will surely give them the land of Canaan. Since she has saved them from the king, she requests that the invaders save her and her clan when

they conquer the city. The two spies solemnly agree and slip out
through the window. After they have formulated their own version of
their oath to Rahab, they make their escape and report back to
Joshua. The story is completed in Joshua 6.17, 22-23, 25. When
Jericho is taken, Joshua is true to the commitment and spares Rahab
from the destruction of Yahweh War. The story concludes with the
comment on Rahab: 'And she dwelt in Israel to this day, because she
hid the messengers whom Joshua sent to spy out Jericho' (v. 25).

II

Literary critics of the Old Testament have long been in agreement
that Joshua 2 is composed of early material and a few Deuteronomic
additions. Most scholars find evidence of D in vv. 10-11, and some do
also in vv. 9b, 14b and 24.[1] This Deuteronomic material, of course, is
recognized to be part of the Deuteronomic framework in Joshua, chs.
1–12. Traditional literary criticism has found J and E strands in the
chapter.[2] The separate statements in vv. 4 and 6 that Rahab hid the
men can be interpreted as pointing to two sources. But even more
significant in this regard is the evidence in vv. 12-21.[3] In the present
arrangement of the material, after Rahab has acknowledged her
belief that Yahweh's power, demonstrated in past history, will ensure
the conquest of the land by the Israelites (vv. 9-11), she proposes an
agreement with the two men (vv. 12-13). Since she has dealt graciously
with them, by saving them from the king of Jericho, they should deal
graciously with her and her family when the invaders take the city.
After the men agree, Rahab lowers them by a rope through a window
and gives them parting advice concerning the best way of escaping
their pursuers (vv. 14-16). But suddenly in v. 17 the conversation is
resumed, presumably with the men standing outside speaking up to
Rahab in the window above. In this conversation it is the men, not
Rahab, who take the initiative. They produce a scarlet cord and
instruct Rahab to tie it in her window as a sign for the invaders when
they conquer Jericho (vv. 18-19). If Rahab and her family remain in
the house during the conquest of the city, they will be spared. After
she has agreed not to reveal their business, the men depart and she
binds the scarlet cord in her window (vv. 20-21).

It is possible to argue for the unity of the material on the basis that
Hebraic narratives do not follow the same logical laws of historical
sequence as do ours.[4] Consequently, the narrator may have thought

of the final conversation as having occurred shortly before or during the descent of the spies through the window. It is more probable, however, that we are dealing with two separate traditions,[5] or perhaps better (as this study will suggest presently) two distinct stages in the oral development of one tradition.[6] In one (12ab^a, 13-16) Rahab takes the lead in the conversation. In the other (12b^b, 17-21) the spies dominate in the dialogue.

Although the existence of doublets in the chapter is clear, it is doubtful that there is any J material in it, even if one is open to the possibility that J can be found beyond the Pentateuch. Verses 17-21, which some assign to J, reflect none of the concerns of terminology that are distinctly the Jahwist's. Moreover, the J account of the conquest, if it is preserved at all, is more likely to be found in Judges 1.1–2.5.[7] The northern orientation and origin of the entire Rahab story would seem clear. It is the northern hero Joshua of Ephraim who commissions the spies and to whom they report when they have accomplished their assignment. And the city of Jericho, where the incident occurs, is in the territory later controlled by the northern tribe of Benjamin, very near the border of Ephraim. This would seem to point to circles similar to those that produced the Elohist source, if not E itself.[8]

III

Beyond the identification of the literary source lie questions concerning the purpose of this chapter in its present context, its earlier oral form and significance, and its historical value.[9] Recent sociological studies of the Old Testatment can perhaps contribute to dealing with these questions. Although it has triggered many interesting and controversial works since its publication in 1962,[10] the seminal monograph by George Mendenhall, 'The Hebrew Conquest of Palestine',[11] remains basic in this regard. Key to a sociological approach to the conquest is an understanding of Late Bronze Age Canaanite society as 'feudalistic'. Like the term 'amphictyony', the word 'feudal' comes from another age and another culture than fourteenth/thirteenth-century Canaan. Is it, therefore, appropriate to use such an analogy?

The Tell el-Amarna letters provide the primary extra-biblical evidence for such a social analysis.[12] Most of the nearly 400 Amarna tablets represent the diplomatic correspondence between the Egyptian courts of Amenophis III (1403–1364) and Amenophis IV/Akhenaton

(1364–1347) and a number of foreign rulers associated with the empire in various ways. The majority of the letters are from vassal kings in Syria and Palestine to their Egyptian suzerains. Among the vassals writing to the Egyptian court appear such personages as Labayu of Shechem, Abdi-Heba of Jerusalem, Shuwardata of the Hebron region, Milkilu of Gerzer, Biridiya of Megiddo, and Abdi-Tirshi of Hazor. Although coming from the fourteenth century, it is reasonable to assume, that used with discretion, *mutatis mutandi*, they provide information concerning the Canaanite society into which Joshua and his people entered in the thirteenth century. One important difference is that weakening Egyptian control of its empire in the fourteenth century was even weaker during the second half of the thirteenth century. This may be the reason for the lack of any reference to an Egyptian presence in the book of Joshua, although we know from other sources that there was Egyptian influence in the Maritime Plain and the Esdraelon Valley well into the twelfth century.[13]

A brief survey of a few Akkadian terms appearing in the Letters may be helpful in considering the appropriateness of the expression 'feudalistic' for Canaanite society.[14] The word *ḥazzanu*, usually rendered 'prince', refers to a vassal king of a city state.[15] If he paid the required tribute to the Egyptian court, the Canaanite king apparently could rule from his fortress city and control the surrounding countryside with its villages in any despotic way he chose. He was aided by his military forces, including chariotry, his civil servants, and his priestly hierarchy. His was a society characterized by political centralizatin and rigid stratification.

The technical term for 'aristocratic charioteer' in Akkadian, *maryannu*,[16] does not appear in the Amarna texts themselves, no doubt fortuitously. However, the phenomenon is clearly there, for frequent reference is made to warriors (*ṣabu*) and chariots (*narkabtu*), or horses (*sisu*) and chariots (*narkabtu*). It is reasonable to assume, therefore, that there was a military elite in Canaanite society skilled in the use of chariots, elsewhere called *maryannu*. This elite would have been crucial for the king to maintain himself in power and to effect his will in his domain.

These two phenomena, therefore, the *ḥazzanu* and the *maryannu*, suggest the presence of a royal establishment in Cannan. Other terms point to the other main segment of Canaanite society.

The word *ḥupšu* refers to the peasant farmer in the Canaanite populace.[17] The *ḥupšu* worked the land owned by the king or his aristocratic supporters. He was not a slave (although slaves too were part of the society), and could own livestock, tools, even his own house in a village inhabited by his own kind. But he did not own the land he worked; that belonged to the king or the king's nobility. Gottwald[18] points out that the society in the north Syrian town of Alalakh had a ratio of approximately five peasant farmers to one of all other social elements, and one can probably assume a somewhat similar ratio in Canaan to the south, although the proportion of shepherds may have been somewhat larger in its rugged hills. For use of the royal land, the *ḥupšu* paid taxes. The taxes would, first of all, have been in kind. But also there was a tax of labor—forced labor, the corvée system of the ancient world. Biridiya, the king of Megiddo, for example, refers to his use of this kind of labor at Shunem in the Esdraelon Valley.[19] The system of royal land ownership and taxes in kind and in labor would have kept this large sector of the Canaanite population in an onerous situation of subservience.

Another important and very active component of the second segment of the Canaanite society were the *ḥabiru*.[20] This is a name of people which appears in texts throughout the Near East during most of the second millennium BC, and it figures prominently in the Amarna texts. There is general agreement that the term is not racial or ethnic but social. It refers to groups of people who stand outside the established social order; people who are propertyless, rootless, with no legal status. They are not necessarily foreign intruders, as many scholars formerly believed. More frequently they are people who, for whatever reason, have withdrawn from the established social order (or have never been part of it) and stand over against it, as was the case with David and his group of social misfits who withdrew from Israelite society under King Saul (1 Sam 22.1-2). Although elsewhere they function in other ways, in the Amarna texts the *ḥabiru* are primarily involved in military activity. At times, they seem to be acting alone against a particular Canaanite king; at other times they join one or more kings against a rival. The presence of the *ḥabiru* indicates that there were unruly, distuptive elements operating in Canaan, which contributed to destabilizing the social order.

This concise sketch of Canaanite society, making use of a few key words, is merely suggestive. Certainly the society was much more complex and nuanced than we have indicated, with more components. But in broad outline, it may be accepted as accurate, certainly as far as its two main segments are concerned. The term 'dimorphic' has been used to characterize this society.[21] One is the city-state morpheme, the royal segment; the other the village-pastoral or farmer-shepherd morpheme, the people's segment. One can conclude, therefore, if not pressed too far, that the term 'feudalistic' is not inappropriate to characterize Canaanite society in the fourteenth–thirteenth centuries.

Mendenhall stresses the vast chasm which existed between the two segments, the kingship undergirded by the Canaanite religion, on the one hand, and, on the other, the masses who 'were suffering under the burden of subjection to a monopoly of power which they had no part in creating, and from which they received virtually nothing but tax collectors'.[22] He suggests that the appearance in Canaan in the latter half of the thirteenth century of the small Israelite community that had experienced the events of the exodus from Egypt and the covenant at Sinai polarized the existing population throughout the land. Some joined the invaders: others resisted. In the latter category would have fallen primarily the Canaanite kings and their supporters. In the former would have been the 'Hebrews', the term which Mendenhall uses in this connection for all those groups who in some sense rejected or stood outside the existing political and social order.[23] He makes the important point that the tradition of Yahweh's deliverance of some Hebrews from Egyptian bondage must have had a strong appeal to the peasants in Palestine suffering in Canaanite political bondage.

> Entire groups having a clan or 'tribal' organization joined the newly-formed community, identified themselves with the oppressed in Egypt, received deliverance from bondage, and the original historical events with which all groups identified themselves took precedence over and eventually excluded the detailed historical traditions of particular groups who had joined later.[24]

And he contends that in one sense there was really no conquest of Canaan at all, certainly no radical displacement of population, no genocide, no large scale driving out of people. The only ones who were completely dispossessed were the royal administrators, which was of course necessary. Basically, then, he contends, what was involved was a 'peasant's revolt against the network of interlocking Canaanite city states',[25] ignited by the penetration of the land by a small group of seventy or so families,[26] with a radically new and appealing religious faith.

IV

Mendenhall does not deal with Joshua 2 in his article,[27] but if there is validity to his position, it would seem to contribute to the interpretation of the chapter. There are three groups in the story. First are the *two unnamed spies*. They have been sent by Joshua and therefore represent the invading group who have a tradition of a God who freed a group of 'Hebrews' from bondage in Egypt and entered into covenant with them. This God, Yahweh, had led them to victory over Canaanite kings to the east of the Jordan and now is prepared to establish them in the land to the west of the Jordan. Then there is the unnamed and very nervous *king of Jericho* with his men. He evidently does not feel that his crown is too secure. When he learns of the presence of the spies in his city, he immediately sends to Rahab's house to capture them. But the king's men are duped into a wild goose chase by the clever harlot. Finally, there is *Rahab*. She and her clan quite clearly are not a part of the royal establishment. On the contrary, they belong to the 'peasant' class; they are those who stand over against the royal political system. Indeed, Rahab's activity is such that she could well be termed a '*Ḥabiru*' or 'Hebrew', in the sense that she rejects the existing political and social order, albeit surreptitiously. Moreover, she responds to the ideology of the invaders, in the sense that she acknowledges Yahweh's power to act in history. There is of course no indication that she and her family become full members of the covenant community, but they are spared the fate of the royal house and remain in the ruins of Jericho under the permanent protection of the Israelites.

Mendenhall's work would seem to supply a possible reason why the Rahab tradtion has been used in the present account of the conquest. The story is really not needed to make the conquest narrative intelligible.[28] It could be omitted without marring the picture of the conquest. Indeed, in the present arrangement of the traditions the visit of the spies seems to accomplish nothing as far as the fall of Jericho is concerned. The city apparently falls because of the cultic processional around it and not because of the activity of the spies. However, one purpose of this anti-monarchical Rahab story in its present position could be to provide an illustration of the two general kinds of response on the part of the inhabitants of the land when Joshua led his people into Canaan; it was typological in intent.[29] One group, symbolized by the king of Jericho, resisted and was destroyed. The other group, symbolized by Rahab, welcomed the invaders and was spared. In placing the story here the composer of the pre-Deuteronomic account of the conquest,[30] followed by the Deuteronomic editor, was presenting in a broad way the actual historical situation at the time of the Joshua invasion.[31]

V

If this was a reason for the use of the Rahab tradition in the early literary account of the conquest in Joshua 1–12, the further question arises as to the purpose of the story in its oral stage before being incorporated into the larger literary complex. Some have sought to explain it purely as an etiological legend created to explain the presence of a Rahab clan living in the ruins of Jericho.[32] That the tradition in its present form has an etiological interest seems clear from its conclusion in 6.25. But that the story was *created* for this purpose is another matter, and seems unlikely.[33] One striking fact that might contribute to an understanding of the original purpose of the story is that through its entirety Rahab the Canaanite harlot[34] dominates most of the action and is placed in a favorable, even heroic, light. This is unusual in the Old Testament, which tends to look with little favor on Canaanites, harlots, or any combination of the two. Moreover, for the most part the two Hebrew spies are depicted as extremely cautious, if not even a little cowardly, in comparison with the brave and resourceful harlot. One might conjecture, therefore, that in its earliest oral form this story did not come from the Israelites, but was told by the Rahab clan which was still dwelling in the ruins of Jericho, or at least in the neighborhood. If this was the case, a primary purpose of the account would have been to ensure the status and safety of the clan from overzealous Yahweh worshippers. That this was a danger in the period of the tribal confederation and early monarchy is evident from the story of Saul's slaughter of the Gibeonites in 2 Samuel 21. Thus Joshua 2 might originally have been a type of 'security clearance' legend. It was told by the Rahab clan as a reminder to the Israelites of their debt to this particular group of non-royal Canaanites.

If this was the significance and the *Sitz im Leben* of the original story, its earliest elements are to be discerned in the non-Deuteronomic portions of vv. 1-16 and 22-24 where Rahab plays the leading role.[35] When the legend was appropriated by the Israelites for use as part of their conquest story, vv. 17-21 would have been combined with it. The purpose of these verses, of course, was to place the spies in a somewhat more forceful and favorable light.[36]

VI

To be sure, the old story would have been useful as a 'security clearance' narrative only if it were true and generally known to be true by the Israelites. This would mean that the story of Rahab in Joshua 2 (along with the account of the fall of Jericho in ch. 6) preserves the memory of an authentic historical event in the life of early Israel.[37]

And it is possible to view the taking of Jericho as a not unimportant part of the over-all conquest under Joshua, reflected in chs. 1–12. A succinct reconstruction of the general course of this history might be stated in this way.[38] It was the Rachel group (the nuclear root of the tribes called Joseph–Manasseh/Ephraim, and Benjamin in various historical periods) which made a decisive penetration into the land of Canaan across the Jordan river in the latter part of the thirteenth century. This group was under the leadership of Joshua of Ephraim. His theophorous name, meaning 'Yahweh is salvation', is the first certain proper name in the Old Testament with 'Yahweh' as one element.[39] His name argues strongly for his origin in Mosaic circles where Yahweh of the Exodus and Sinai was first worshipped.[40] The Rachel group under Joshua crossed the Jordan and engaged in guerilla warfare out of Gilgal over a period of years (5?, 10?, 15?). The enemy in this warfare was clearly the Canaanite royal establishment, since every battle in Joshua 2–11 involves Canaanite kings. After the taking of Jericho (chs. 2–6), this Joshua-led group moved up into the hill country around Bethel and Ai (chs. 7–9), eventually fought kings in the southern part of the land (ch. 10), and finally engaged royal enemies in the far north in the area of Hazor (ch. 11). Although more than 'social revolution' was certainly involved,[41] it seems clear that there were many groups already in the land who responded favorably to the invaders with their radically new religion, and in one way or the other made common cause with them (chs. 2, 9, 24). The final rseult of this 'guerilla warfare', 'social revolution', 'missionary activity' ('Choose you this day whom you will serve', Josh 24.15)[42] was the establishment of a Yahweh confederation in the hill country, comprising 10, perhaps 12 tribes,[43] most of whom were already in the land when the Rachel group entered.

Jericho was the first city taken by the invaders and it was a key conquest. The excavations at Old Testament Jericho, *tel es-sultan*, by Kathleen Kenyon[44] have made it clear that Jericho could not have been more than a small village in the time of Joshua. Large Canaanite cities with high walls had indeed existed on the site, but long before Joshua. The fall of the last sizeable city took place in the first half of the sixteenth century and therefore more than three hundred years before the thirteenth-century date frequently assigned to Joshua. If one is inclined to accept the Old Testament text in Joshua 6 as preserving an authentic historical memory involving Joshua and the Rachel group (which the archaeological evidence does not preclude), Jericho at best would have been a small settlement with jerry-built walls ruled by a petty king.[45] Nevertheless, with its fine spring, Jericho guarded key passes up into the hill country, and control of it was necessary if the group was to carry on guerilla activity in the hill country out of a base in the vicinity. Moreover, it was taken by the group which was bringing into Canaan for the first time traditions concerning Yahweh, the Exodus and the Covenant. In addition, it was the *first* city to be taken by this group after crossing the Jordan. It may have been preceded by victories in Transjordan, and was followed by a series of conquests of key cities in the hill country. But Jericho was the *first* city to be taken by this group of Yahweh worshippers in that land which was to become the center of Israelite life. As the first, it had singularly symbolic significance.

This is apparently the reasons for the stongly cultic character of Joshua 6. When the first city was taken, it meant that Yahweh had given the invaders a surety for the whole land. So the conquest of Jericho was remembered, retold and reenacted in the worship of subsequent generations of Israelites. As Gerhard von Rad,[46] H.-J. Kraus[47] and others have conjectured, a conquest festival seems to have emerged which had as its central theme the affirmation: 'He brought us into this place and gave us this land'. In connection with this festival and under its influence the various layers of tradition discernible in Joshua 6 evolved.

Although the later layers of tradition in Joshua 6 are clearly cultic character and would have been influenced by the conquest ceremony in its various stages, the contours of an original conquest may be discerned in its earliest layer: vv. 1-3a, 5a^{a}b, 10, 12a, 14a^a, 16b, 20b^b, 21.[48] Joshua and a group of 'men of war' (v. 3a) lead in the attack.

They silently (v. 10) surround (vv. 3, 14a^a, *sābab* in Hebrew can mean 'surround' or 'encircle' in addition to 'march around') the city under the cover of darkness and attack at dawn (v. 12a). The attack comes with an order from Joshua (v. 10), the blowing of the 'ram's horn' (v. 5) and a 'mighty shout' from the people who are following (vv. 10, 16b). A weak section of the city's defenses is breached, probably revealed to the spies by the anti-monarchical Rahab family who had previously sheltered them (ch. 2).[49] The invaders pour through the breach 'one after the other' (*'iš negdô*, vv. 5, 20b^b) to capture the city. The conquest is carried out with a sense of the guiding presence of Yahweh, who is giving them the land (vv. 2, 16b). This is a Yahweh War, so Jericho with its petty king is put to the ban (v. 21). Although probably added to the tradition at a later stage in its development, vv. 17, 22, 23, 25 can be accepted as historically realiable in stating that the Rahab clan was spared. They lived to tell their story.[50]

VII

To summarize our conclusions on Joshua 2:

1. The story was originally told by the Rahab clan and served as a 'security clearance' legend. It was effective because it was based on historical fact. It told of Rahab's aid to the invaders in the time of Joshua. She hid the two spies from the king of Jericho, and apparently also helped with the subsequent conquest of the city.

2. At a later stage the Israelites appropriated the story, and the spies were given somewhat more prominence with the addition of vv. 17-21.

3. When the story became a part of the pre-Deuteronomic account of the conquest by all Israel (E), it served a typological function. It illustrated the two kinds of people in the land when Joshua invaded and their varying responses. Thus it served as a prelude to the subsequent wars against the Canaanite royalty.

5. Ultimately, of course, the Deuteronomic editor incorporated the entire conquest narrative, including the Rahab story, into the larger corpus, the Former Prophets, where it remains to this day.

* * *

I am honored to submit this article as a tribute to my esteemed friend and mentor, Bernhard W. Anderson.

NOTES

1. Some representative views: S.R. Driver, *An Introduction to the Literature of the Old Testament* (new rev. edn; New York: Charles Scribner's Sons, 1913) 105, regards only vv. 10-11 as Deuteronomic, as do W.O.E. Oesterley and T.H. Robinson, *An Introduction to the Books of the Old Testament* (New York: Meridian Books, reprinted 1958) 69. Robert Pfeiffer, *Introduction to the Old Testament* (New York and London: Harper & Brothers, 1941) holds vv. 9-11 as D (p. 305), but views the rest of the chapter as Deuteronomic with an E substratum (p. 302). Martin Noth, *Das Buch Josua* (HAT 7; 2nd rev. edn; Tübingen: J.C.B. Mohr, 1953) 24, 26, 29-31, assigns vv. 9b, 10b, 11b, 14b, 17b to D. John Bright, *The Book of Joshua* (IB 2; New York and Nashville: Abingdon-Cokesbury, 1953), 543, finds D in vv. 10-11 and possibly 9b and 24b. Ernst Sellin and Georg Fohrer, *Introduction to the Old Testament* (New York and Nashville: Abingdon, 1968), 213, attribute vv. 10-11 to D. And G.M. Tucker, 'The Rahab Saga (Joshua 2): Some Form-Critical and Tradition-Historical Observations', *The Use of the Old Testament in the New and Other Essays* (Durham, N.C.: Duke University, 1972), 66, assigns vv. 9b, 10b, 11b, 24b to D.

2. Driver (*Introduction*, 105) assigns vv. 1-9, 12-24 to JE without further refinement, as do Sellin and Fohrer (*Introduction*, 201). Bright (*Book of Joshua*, 54) takes a similar position, designating vv. 1-9a, 12-24a as JE. Oesterley and Robinson (*Introduction*, 69), while assigning vv. 1-9 to JE, specifically attribute vv. 12-16, 22-24 to E and vv. 17-21 to J. Pfeiffer (*Introduction*, 302), however, denies that there is any J in the chapter, claiming that there is only an E stratum in vv. 1-9, 12-23. But he does acknowledge that 'two narrative strands are interwoven in these verses'. Arthur Weiser, *The Old Testament: Its Formation and Development* (New York: Association, 1961), 144, thinks that E forms the basis of the whole section of Joshua, chs. 1–12 (in a D framework), which would include ch. 2, of course. On the other hand, Noth (*Das Buch Josua*, 24, 26, 29-31), takes the position that there is only one early tradition in the chapter, which he finds in vv. 1-9a, 10a, 11a, 12-14a, 15-17a, 18-24. It is a literary unity and not to be identified with either J or E. Noth's position has been very influential. See, for example, the discussion by G.E. Wright in Robert G. Boling and G. Ernest Wright, *Joshua: A New Translation with Notes and Commentary* (AB 6; Garden City: Doubleday, 1982), 55-72. Those (like the present writer) who continue to see the completion of the early Pentateuchal strands in Joshua (and Judges 1.1–2.5) are probably in the minority in contemporary scholarship.

3. See especially Hans Wilhelm Hetzberg, *Die Bücher Josua, Richter, Ruth* (ATD; Göttingen: Vandenhoeck & Ruprecht, 1954), 20-21.

4. So Noth, *Das Buch Josua*, 31.

5. Hertzberg's position, *Die Bücher Josua, Richter, Ruth*, 20-21.

6. In agreement with Tucker, 'Observations', 75-76.

7. A position taken by a number of scholars since Eduard Meyer, 'Kritik der Berichte über die Eroberung Palästinas', *ZAW* 1 (1881) 117-46. More recently: Norman K. Gottwald, *The Tribes of Yahweh: A Sociology of the Religion of Liberated Israel, 1250-1050* (Maryknoll: Orbis, 1979), 163-65. I have developed this thesis in an unpublished article: 'Is Judges 1.1–2.5 the Conclusion of the Jahwist Epic?'

8. With Weiser (*The Old Testament*, 144-45), Gottwald (*Tribes of Yahweh*, 177-79), Sellin and Fohrer (*Introduction*, 202), Otto Eissfeldt, *The Old Testament: An Introduction* (New York: Harper and Row, 1965), 243, and others I view Jos 1–12 as largely E in a Deuteronomic framework.

9. Tucker's discussion ('Observations') on these questions is penetrating, although this study does not arrive at all the same conclusions.

10. Above all, Gottwald's *Tribes of Yahweh*.

11. *BA* 25 (1962), 66-87.

12. The basic collection of the tablets is found in J.A. Knudtzon, *Die El-Amarna Tafeln* (2 vols.; Leipzig: J.C. Hinrichs, 1907/15, reprinted 1964), supplemented by A.F. Rainey, *El Amarna Tablets* (2nd rev. edn; Neukirchen-Vluyn: Neukirchener Verlag, 1978).

13. For example, a statue of Ramses III (1183–1152) has been found at Beth-shan in the upper Jordan valley. A. Rowe, *The Topography and History of Bethshan* (Philadelphia: University Museum, 1930), 38.

14. The letters are written in Akkadian, the *lingua franca* of the period. Three of the four key terms we examine here are found in the Amarna letters (see the glossary prepared by Erich Ebeling in Knudtson, vol. 2), but their full significance comes from their appearance in other north Syrian writings as well, especially those from Ugarit and Alalakh. See Gottwald's discussion, *Tribes of Yahweh*, 389-409.

15. The Akkadian word for 'king', *šarru*, is reserved for the Egyptian pharaoh.

16. See Gottwald, *Tribes of Yahweh*, 756 n. 296, for a bibliography and brief discussion.

17. Again see Gottwald's discussion, *ibid.*, 481-83, which has guided my own treatment of this word.

18. *Ibid.*, 482.

19. EA, 365.

20. Also termed *'apiru*. See Gottwald's analysis and his extensive biblio-graphical references, *Tribes of Yahweh*, 398-409.

21. *Ibid.*, 464-73.

22. Mendenhall, 'Hebrew Conquest', 74.

23. *Ibid.*, 71-73. Linguistically related to *ḥabiru*.

24. *Ibid.* 74.

25. *Ibid.*, 73.

26. *Ibid.*, 79.

27. Gottwald, *Tribes of Yahweh*, 556-58, does have a suggestive analysis.

28. As has been frequently noted, e.g., Tucker, 'Observations', 69, 71-72.

29. The narrator clearly has his eye not only on Jericho, but on 'the land' or 'all the land': vv. 1, 2, 3, 9(2), 14, 18, 24. Boling, *Joshua*, 145, correctly comments on the expression 'the whole land' in v. 3: 'Far more was at stake then the great Jordan valley oasis alone'.

30. Which I believe is E. By this time it had become the story of the conquest by all Israel.

31. If it was not a perfect story for E's purposes, it was what was available for inclusion at this point.

32. So Noth, *Das Buch Josua*, 22-23, 29-31.

33. See especially B.S. Childs, 'A Study of the Formula, "Until this Day"', *JBL* 82 (1963), 279-92, and also B.O. Long, *The Problem of Etiological Narrative in the Old Testament* (BZAW 108; Berlin: Töpelmann, 1968).

34. I find no evidence of cultic prostitution in the narrative, and am in agreement with J. Alberto Soggin (*Joshua: A Commentary* [OTL; London: SCM, 1972] 39) on this point. As John L McKenzie observes: 'The scouts who entered Jericho took lodging in a house of prostitution; the inn and the brothel have been found in one establishment often in the history of mankind' (*The World of the Judges* [Englewood Cliffs: Prentice-Hall, 1966], 48).

35. I assume an authentic historical memory at the core of Rahab's confession behind the present Deuteronomic text.

36. One element in these verses, however, that apparently derived from the original situation is the scarlet cord in the window (v. 18). It probably is to be connected with the means by which Rahab subsequently helped the invaders in the conquest of the city, perhaps 'the agreed signal for the attack on the city' (Soggin, *Joshua*, 42), or more probably, as we suggest below, a means of identifying a weak point in the city's defenses (cf. John Gray, *Joshua, Judges and Ruth* [NCB; London: Oliphant's, 1967], 53). Tucker refers broadly to Rahab's 'treason' ('Observations', 78).

37. Along with the reference to the conquest of Jericho in Jos 24.11.

38. Generally following my reconstruction in *The People of the Covenant: A Study of Israel from Moses to the Monarchy* (New York and Nashville: Abingdon, 1962), 103-107.

39. Martin Noth, *Die israelitischen Personennamen in Rahmen der gemein-semitischen Namengebung* (*BWANT* 3/10; Stuttgart: W. Kohlhammer, 1928), 107.

40. To say nothing of the various early and late traditions that associate him with Moses.

41. In the final analysis that is what Gottwald reduces the conquest to in his *Tribes of Yahweh*.

42. By which I mean the offering of the Yahwistic faith to non-Yahwists. See my *People of the Covenant*, 108-10.

43. Although I would not press the analogy with the Greek amphictyonies as far today as I did in my *People of the Covenant* in 1962, or use the term as frequently, Noth's thesis that the system of twelve tribes originated in this historical period, *Das System der zwölf Stämme Israels* (Stuttgart: W. Kohlhammer, 1930), still commends itself as more plausible than any alternative that has been proposed since, including Gottwald's conjecture that it emerged in the time of David (*Tribes of Yahweh*, 358-75).

44. *Digging Up Jericho* (London: Ernest Benn, 1957), 256-65.

45. Roland de Vaux has a convincing discussion on this point, *The Early History of Israel* (Philadelphia: Westminster, 1978), 610-12. Note also Boling's comment, *Joshua*, 212: 'On the mound itself the scant evidence points to something which might at most have been the unfortified hangout of a local strongman'.

46. 'The Form-critical Problem of the Hexateuch', *The Problem of the Hexateuch and other essays* (New York: McGraw-Hill, 1966), 41-48.

47. *Worship in Israel* (Oxford: Blackwell, 1966), 152-65.

48. This is my own analysis. Although I have made use of the studies of various scholars in working out this analysis, my conclusions do not correspond in all detail with those of any of them. For that matter, I have found no two scholars that are in complete agreement with one another. For varying points of view on Jos 6, besides Noth (*Das Buch Josua*, 40-43), Gray (*Joshua, Judges and Ruth*, 75-80), Hertzberg (*Die Bücher Josua, Richter, Ruth*, 38-45), and the other standard commentaries, see particularly J. Dus, 'Die Analyse zweier Ladeerzählungen des Josuabuches (Jos. 3-4 und 6)', *ZAW* 72 (1960) 107-34; J. Maier, *Das altisraelitische Ladeheiligtum* (*BZAW* 93; Berlin: de Gruyter, 1965) 18-32; and Soggin, *Joshua*, 81-88 with his further bibliography on pp. 80-81. The next stage in its development I would see in vv. 3b, 5a^b, 6a, 7, 11, 12b, 14a^{bb}, 15a, and 20b, which would reflect an early form of the cult drama, based, of course, on the authentic memory preserved in the first stage. A more elaborate form of the ceremony is reflected in an even later stage: vv. 4, 6b, 8-9, 15b, 16a, 20a.

49. Soggin (*Joshua*, 83-84) suggests that chs. 2 and 6 are parallel traditions behind which lies an historical 'incident' involving the taking of a Canaanite settlement at Jericho by incoming Israelites, in which Rahab had a role. To him 'the version of events given in ch. 2 seems older, and more historically probable, than that attested by ch. 6, which is simply a liturgical and cultic transfiguration of the events, retold as history at a later period'. We are suggesting, however, that they preserve the memory of two episodes of the same event.

50. F.-M. Abel, 'Les stratagèmes du livre de Josué', *RB* 56 (1945), 321-29, believes that Rahab, as well as other Canaanites, were treated like proselytes.

PART III

THE WORD AND THE WORLD

10

CONFLICT IN ANCIENT ISRAEL AND ITS RESOLUTION[1]

Paul D. Hanson

1. *The Relation of Scripture to the Contemporary Problem of Conflict*

Commonly in our society Scripture is used as a source of quick and sure answers to problems which have resisted other avenues of resolution. The problems of Middle Eastern conflicts, Central American revolutions, the threat of nuclear war, as well as problems of a more personal nature, are solved with a biblical citation, such as that drawn from the Johannine Gospel: 'Peace I leave with you; my peace I give to you; not as the world gives do I give to you. Let not your hearts be troubled, neither let them be afraid' (John 14.27). While no Christian would dispute the profound bearing of such a citation on the problem of conflict, there is reason to be alarmed at the increasingly popular practice of eliciting a 'biblical' answer to a problem by application of one 'proof-text', rather than by studying the problem carefully and critically in the light of the entire testimony of Scripture. The result of the former practice is to mute the autonomy of the scriptural witness, with the results that the authority of Scripture is discredited and the potential constructive impact of biblical faith on contemporary life is blunted. For few thoughtful persons can take seriously the claim that a proposed solution to a given problem should be accepted on the basis of a verse quoted in utter disregard of its original historical context or relation to other biblical texts. They will simply observe that most problems are more complex than to be amenable to such a mechanical process of problem-solving. Not a few people will also raise the question of the bearing of other verses on the question of conflict which seems to state a contrary message, such as the saying of Jesus found in the Synoptic Gospels, 'Do not think that I have come to bring peace on the earth; I have not come to bring peace, but a sword' (Matt 10.34 and parallels).

Christians should be the first to admit that the task of understanding the meaning of Scripture as it relates to contemporary problems is often a very difficult and demanding one. Those who claim to present the message of Scripture by demanding uncritical assent to a particular political position all too frequently direct masses of people away from the stringent righteousness and profound compassion which unfolds in the Bible. A disturbing example of this is found currently in several Central and South American countries, where a number of well-organized missionary societies are presenting an interpretation of the Bible which is having the effect of strengthening the hand of oppressive regimes by claiming that the Christian's duty is to obey political authorities in all matters. Though a passage like Romans 13.1-7 can be used to defend this position, the central biblical confession of the God who takes the side of those struggling to be freed from the bonds of oppression must also be drawn into the question of the relation between the governing authorities and their subjects. What happens to the credibility of a church which actually strengthens the chains of exploitation and bondage placed by unjust leaders on their citizens? What remains of the influence of missionaries who allow themselves to be drawn, whether by inaction or conscious collaboration, into the designs of dictators and military juntas to crush every attempt of the poor to break out of their misery and to assert their basic human rights? Is this kind of peacekeeping not similar to that condemned by Jeremiah? 'They have healed the wound of my people lightly, saying, "Peace, peace", when there is no peace' (Jer 6.14 and 8.11).

We face a task which is difficult and urgent, if we are going to offer an alternative to highly organized and well-financed crusades which make exclusive claims to the truth even as they wed the biblical message to oppressive economic and political systems. From the side of biblical studies, the hour calls for the courage and the energy to reenvision the divine order which unfolds among the faithful through the history of God's relation to God's people and which does not diverge from the goal of the universal wedding of peace and justice. This can be done only if the need to prove personal, national, or denominational positions as correct yields to the willingness to be called into question both by Scripture's word and by the interpretive word arising from those who struggle today against injustice and oppression.

Clearly our contribution to a task as broad as this can be no more than a brief moment in a vast process. But when addressed to fellow believers, perhaps the only justification necessary is to indicate that it is offered in the spirit of seeking to interpret aright the source which has more to teach us about conflict and its resolution than any other. Moreover, if our fear is justified that the tragedy of civil injustice is being abetted through the false application of the Bible to situations of internecine conflict in many countries, we as members of communities holding to the authority of Scripture, while at the same time understanding the implications of that authority in vastly different terms, are conscience-bound to give clear expression to our biblically informed convictions.

2. *Conflict and Ultimate Reality in the Ancient World*

The Bible took shape in a world within which conflict was not only ubiquitous, but was regarded as a central religious category. In ancient Mesopotamia and Syro-Palestine, it was out of conflict between the gods that the universe came into being. On its most basic discernible level, reality was characterized by conflict, manifested by the struggle between fertility and sterility, life and death, spring rains and the killing drought of summer. The most important myth in this part of the world was the conflict myth, in which the conflicts discerned at the center of life were traced to ultimate reality, the realm of the gods. For the gods themselves were believed to be locked regularly in savage, deadly conflict.[2]

3. *The Source of Conflict according to Early Hebrew Belief*

The ubiquity of conflict in life was acknowledged by the early Hebrews, but in the sagas with which they described the origins of the world, the roots of conflict and evil in ultimate reality underwent a radical challenge. The world did not arise out of conflict between the gods, but as an act of creation by the one god Yahweh who declared this earth to be a good and dependable habitation provided as a gift for the sustenance of humans.

This bold revision of the prevailing cosmology, however, did not dull the perception of the early Hebrews to the realities of life, for though the source of conflict was not metaphysical, that is, was not the inevitable result of the division of reality into two diametrically opposed principles, it was nevertheless deeply rooted, and indeed its primary root was startlingly clear to Hebrew faith. That root was described by Jeremiah: 'The heart is deceitful above all things, and desperately corrupt; who can understand it?' (Jer 17.9).

The riddle of a good creation and its perversion by humans inclined to evil was not addressed by biblical faith through philosophical speculation, but rather through the careful study of history. History was interpreted as a struggle of the loving God for the hearts of the human family. The events of history were understood to be guided by this God's desire to bring this family to the life of peace and justice and harmony which God had intended for humans from the beginning. It is by studying this same history that we discover the Bible's response to the problem of conflict.

4. *Covenant Community as the Yahwistic Alternative to Conflict*

'In the beginning God created . . . and God saw everything that he had made, and behold, it was very good.' Here we read of a propitious start right in the opening verses of the Bible. Nevertheless, the first human couple defied God's will, the first human brothers strove, and the good earth was defiled with the blood of fratricide. As the stories of Genesis are told, one witnesses a world sinking deeper and deeper into the chaos of sinful conflict, threatening to bring the entire created world to ruin. In the course of this shocking development, the source of the problem becomes clear: 'The Lord saw that the wickedness of humanity was great in the earth, and that every imagination of the thoughts of the human heart was only evil continually' (Gen 6.5). Genesis 1–11 thus gives the biblical picture of the world in which humans conduct their own affairs according to their own plans, passions, and desires. It is a world that is hopelessly lost, for humans on their own are a race both self-destructive and destructive of one another, in a word, a violent and dangerous race.

The realism of the Bible is hard-hitting in evaluating the human situation. And its anthropological assessment offers slim basis for an optimistic outlook on the destiny of the human race. It is only after this grim point has been made unmistakably clear that a ray of hope enters the biblical narrative. For Genesis 12 introduces an alternative plan. Inaugurated by God, its goal is the salvation of the fallen human race: 'Now the Lord said to Abram, "Go from your country . . . to the land that I will show you. And I will make you a great nation, and I will bless you, and make your name great, so that you will be a blessing"' (Gen 12.1-2). Here we see the arena within which the Bible discerns hope for humanity: God's response to the plunge of the human race into chaos was the creation of a new community. For reasons that the Bible leaves unspecified—though doubtlessly they involve the mystery of the freedom with which God endowed humanity—the human propensity for self-destructive conflict could not merely be obliterated. What could be done, however, was this: A community could be called together, redeemed, and commissioned to provide a realm within which the roots of conflict could be addressed, reconciliation established, and the state of shalom harmonious with God's will and nature restored. The authentic human state thus was not imposed upon humans through the application of violence more overwhelming than that already threatening to destroy civilization. Responsive humans were rather drawn by a loving God into a creative process in which the kind of peace would be restored which issued forth in humans living in peace with one another and with all of reality on the basis of having made peace with God.

In the perception of early Israel, what was the nature of this redemptive process, which, while inaugurated by God, drew into it as partners members of a race so given to sin as to make conflict and chaos seem an inevitable aspect of human nature? The answer which the early Yahwistic community gave to this question was not based on abstract reasoning but on a concrete experience through which that redemptive process became a reality. That was the experience of deliverance from bondage in Egypt, recalled by Jews for all subsequent ages as the birthplace of their community. It was in that event like no other that the followers of Yahweh grasped the nature of the community through which God would actively seek to restore peace and harmony within the embattled and divided human family.

The cardinal characteristic of that community was one which established a point of reference which safeguarded against the elevation of any human entity to the level of unquestioned authority, that point of reference being the one true God. Solely from the nature of the God who came to the side of slaves as they struggled to break out of their bondage was this community to infer its self-definition and purpose. This meant that the ultimate reality which determined the nature and destiny of Israel was neither indifferent to the violence and chaos which was tearing the world apart, nor partial to a particular class or party. God, as universal Creator, Judge and Redeemer, was one actively engaged to eradicate the roots of violence and chaos, wherever they were found, pernicious roots like injustice, oppression of the poor and the weak, and systems of inequality which sustained a life of privilege for the few by exploitation of the many.

Israel's decisive encounter with her God presented the universe in rigorously moral terms, for at the center of the universe she recognized the God whose righteousness and compassion reached out to the poor, the vulnerable and the oppressed. Victims lacking a human advocate could turn to this divine Defender. And the human agents of this Defender were those who had been called as a mixed company out of the negativity of slavery into the wholeness of the community of shalom. As such they were called to be an example in the world of the only genuine alternative to conflict and death, for as a people covenanted with the God of life, they embodied in their community the righteousness and compassion which drove back all that diminished life, and which created the conditions in which all of creation could flourish in shared blessing.

Already in the earliest formulation of this notion of community in the Bible (the Book of the Covenant written around 1100 BCE and found in Exod 21–23) one finds clearly stated the conviction that only in the community embodying God's standard of righteousness and compassion could conflict be resolved and harmony prevail. The community that deviated from that standard would slip into the jungle where humans create their own norms, a situation in which inevitably the powerful unjustly exploit the poor and the weak. We shall cite a couple of laws which illustrate both how Israel's sense of community was drawn from her image of the divine Deliverer, and how the righteous quality at the center of life could be violated only at the cost of sending shock waves through the entire community:

> You shall not afflict any widow or orphan. If you do afflict them, and they cry out to me, I will surely hear their cry; and my wrath will burn, and I will kill you with the sword, and your wives shall become widows and your children fatherless. If you lend money to any of my people with you who is poor, you shall not be to him as a creditor, and you shall not exact interest from him. If you ever take your neighbor's garment in pledge, you shall restore it to him before the sun goes down; for that is his only covering, it is his mantle for his body; in what else shall he sleep? And if he cries to me, I will hear, for I am compassionate (Exod 22.21-26 [EVV 22.22-27]).

These archaic laws illustrate the indivisible bond which existed between Israel's experience of slavery, her encounter with the Deliverer God, and the laws and social structures that gave form to her community. The laws of the community did not fit the prevailing pattern of that time, namely, that of static formulations attributed to an eternal heavenly decree but in fact representing a reification of the caste system of an absolute monarchy. Instead, life in this community of freed slaves was modeled directly on the example of the God who both delivered slaves and acted as advocate for every individual who suffered from injustice or want. Order and stability at all costs did not constitute the formula for peace in early Yahwism. Its community in fact was born and developed amidst revolution and conflict. At the heart of the community, however, was a vivid sense of the righteousness and compassion derived from its sole authority, the God Yahweh. This norm alone defined right and wrong. If the people contradicted it or allowed penultimate norms to encroach upon it, the only authentic basis for communal health and harmony was destroyed and the covenant was broken. In the Book of the Covenant, this threat was portrayed very concretely: If a widow or orphan were denied protection or suffered want, Yahweh would attend personally and incisively to her or his plight. If a wealthy creditor, greedy for more gain, caused a person to shiver through a cold night by holding a mantle as security, a fundamental principle of life had been violated, and the passion of the loving God would be roused to action. The concreteness of righteousness in the early Yahwistic community could not be expressed more movingly than in the motive clause rooting obedience to the nature of God: ' . . . for that is his only covering, it is his mantle for his body, in what else shall he sleep? And if he cries to me I will hear, for I am compassionate' (Exod 22.26 [EVV 22.27]).

By locating the source of its identity in the divine example, Yahwism was able to develop special ordinances for safeguarding its members from either falling back into slavery or succumbing to the temptation of subjugating and exploiting others.

The result was a set of structures and institutions dedicated to the maintenance of the righteousness and compassion that consituted the birthright of this people. For example, the impact of economic structures on human welfare was addressed courageously by two measures, the prohibition of charging interest on loans, and the development of a unique concept of inheritance right (*naḥălâ*). According to the latter, land was not to be regarded as a commodity, regulated by the laws of the marketplace and leading inevitably to the amassing of real estate by a minority to the impoverishment of the majority. There was instead to be one sole owner of the land,

Yahweh. As a righteous Lord, Yahweh granted to each family as a trust in perpetuity a portion of land adequate for its well-being. The high idealism underlying this concept came to be expressed in the notion of the Jubilee Year, a celebration to be commemorated every fifty years in which the original economic structures of the land were to be reconstructed through the manumission of slaves and the return of property lost through indebtedness; as Leviticus 25 describes it, this was the year in which was to be proclaimed 'liberty throughout the land to all its inhabitants' (v. 10). To be sure, the dominant commercial practices of the time militated powerfully against these structures, and even in Israel they had scant chance of being officially adopted by those in power. Nevertheless, the relentless protest of the prophets against the secularization and commercialization of life proves that in the minds of those who followed in the heritage of early Yahwism, laws against usury and the concepts of the *naḥālâ* and the Jubilee Year were not idle dreams, but God-given ordinances which a people neglected at the cost of conflict and social upheaval. This stringent sense of righteousness was never banished from the Hebrew consciousness. It persisted as a leaven even in the midst of fallen structures and rampant apostasy.

Some critics would nevertheless like to dismiss these stringent social ordinances of early Yahwism as visionary notions of a generation of dreamers in the time when Israel had ceased to be a nation, that is, in the exile. The benefit of this conclusion is that it facilitates hasty dismissal of notions which stand as harsh indictments of our own institutional injustice. But in fact, all of these ordinances arose directly from the corporate identity of a people which traced its birth to a miraculous deliverance from slavery. Taken as a whole, the laws, social ordinances and institutions we have described can be understood adequately only as the moral universe growing from the perspective of those personally acquainted with the evils perpetrated by a mighty civilization which placed its own glory above either the fear of God or the enrichment of the quality of life of its citizens. Having experienced the heart of the stranger and the slave, and then encountering the one Power in the universe who identifies personally with those victimized by the powers of this world, the early Hebrews caught a glimpse of a new order for the human family. It was a glimpse which was visible only from the bottom of the social stratification of antiquity, that is, from the perspective of the *ḥupšu*, that is, the slave. This sense of origins was so basic to the experience of Israel that the ancient Semitic word for slave was not subsequently discarded as a self-designation, but was retained, with one alteration: In the Hebrew language *ḥopšî* no longer means 'slave', but, quite remarkably, 'one set *free* from slavery'.[3] Like the number tattooed on the arm of a remarkable Jewish man my family was privileged to meet on a recent visit to the Nazi concentration camp at Dachau, the memory of being slaves in Egypt was indelibly imprinted on the consciousness of the early Hebrews, preparing them for service in God's plan for the entire human family. Far from being the idle dream of unrealistic, late visionaries, the vision of a community structured after the *naḥălâ* and the Jubilee is the social program of the only ones who deserve to be called society's realists, those personally acquainted with the pedagogy of oppression. The basis for their special role is expressed in one more law which we quote from the Bible's earliest law code: 'You shall not oppress a stranger; you know the heart of a stranger, for you were strangers in the land of Egypt' (Exod 23.9).

5. *The Recrudescence of Political Conflict and Prophetic Protest*

The picture of a community grounding its stability on an even-handed administration of justice and a careful attention to the rights of the poor and the powerless does not accord well with the image most people have of life in ancient Israel. For they recall Joshua's command at the walls of Jericho, 'Shout, for the Lord has given you the city. And the city and all that is within it shall be devoted to the Lord for destruction . . . ', with the people complying: 'Then they utterly destroyed all in the city, both men and women, young and old, oxen, sheep and asses, with the edge of the sword' (Josh 6.16b-17a and 21). Or a similar 'word of the Lord' comes to mind, delivered in this case by Samuel to Saul: 'Now go up and smite Amalek, and utterly destroy all that they have; do not spare them, but kill both man and woman, infant and suckling, ox and sheep, camel and ass' (1 Sam 15.3). Or one may remember the law regulating warfare in Deuteronomy, ' . . . in the cities of the peoples that the Lord your God gives you for an inheritance, you shall save alive nothing that breathes, but you shall utterly destroy them . . . ' (Deut 20.16-17a), or the words of the Psalmist, 'Happy shall he be who takes your little ones and dashes them against the rock' (Ps 137.9). Is the God of the

Hebrew Bible after all a heavenly agent of violence and destruction? And is the message we receive from that source a rationalization of the common human inclination to meet might with superior might, and to seek to resolve differences through conflict waged under the justification of divine wrath?[4]

The bellicose imagery we have just cited from the Bible was just as much at home in the ancient Near Eastern world as was the conflict myth referred to at the beginning of this paper. Even as ancient peoples accounted for the creation of the world by referring to conflict between the gods, individual nations attributed their strength to a warrior god who led them in their battles against every foe. If she wished to conform to the worldview of antiquity, Israel was constrained to argue for her place among the nations by portraying Yahweh as a patron god capable of besting any other nation's god in conflict. The alternative community ideal which arose in early Yahwism, with its accentuation of peace, justice, compassion and protection of the foreigner, is remarkable, given the prevailing view. However, tremendous pressure was placed upon the early Yahwistic community to conform to the older mythology, for as a loosely federated association of tribes gathered around a common confession, it was sorely threatened by the powerful armies of more centralized kingdoms. The traditions of 1 Samuel portray a people that had grown ashamed of its humble background, a people wanting to forget its slave pedagogy, lured by the prospect of national greatness and glory:[5]

> Then all the elders of Israel gathered together and came to Samuel at Ramah, and said to him, 'Behold, you are old and your sons do not walk in your ways; now appoint for us a king to govern us like all the nations'.

Samuel is deeply troubled by the request, and warns them:

> 'These will be the ways of the king who will reign over you; he will take your sons and appoint them to his chariots and to be his horsemen, and to run before his chariots; and he will appoint for himself commanders of fifties, and some to plow his ground and to reap his harvest, and to make his implements of war and the equipment of his chariots. He will take your daughters to be perfumers and cooks and bakers. He will take the best of your fields and vineyards and olive orchards and give them to his servants. He will take the tenth of your grain and of your vineyards and give it to his officers and to his servants. He will take your menservants and

maidservants, and the best of your cattle and your asses, and put them to his work. He will take the tenth of your flocks, and you shall be his slaves. And in that day you will cry out because of your king, whom you have chosen for yourselves; but the Lord will not answer you in that day.' But the people refused to listen to the voice of Samuel; and they said, 'No! but we will have a king over us, that we also may be like all the nations and that our king may govern us and go out before us and fight our battles' (1 Sam 8.11-20).

There is little doubt that the bellicose imagery cited earlier is closely connected with the concerted attempt made by Israel under her kings to become like other nations, displaying a level of national power and royal splendor surpassing all rivals. In this new preoccupation a shift occurred in the source to which the nation turned for its values as a community, a shift away from the examples of the righteous, compassionate Deliverer and Protector of the oppressed in the direction of the ancient Near Eastern ideal of victorious king. While the period of tribal confederacy was not free of conflict, literary evidence and historical research suggest that the ideology of total extermination derives from the age of the monarchy, having been read back into the earlier tribal period by Israel's historical schools.

The shift to a national ideal of royal splendor exerted a powerful influence on the quality of community in Israel. Foreign conquest and international trade brought in new wealth, the beneficiaries of which were the privileged classes standing closest to the king. The rudimentary egalitarianism characterizing the relations among the earlier clans began to yield to the economic forces centralized in the royal house, and the result was an increasingly stratified society, with the lower classes often suffering impoverishment and enslavement. A significant increase in social tension and class conflict was the inevitable result of this structural change. Within this stressful environment only an abused and hunted minority led by the prophets continued to defend the alternative vision of early Yahwism. All other persons enjoying public visibility in the nation seemed dedicated to the amenities of the more sophisticated system, regardless of the cost in human suffering that this entailed. Micah serves as an example of the prophetic protest against a nation adopting the very practices under which its ancestors had suffered in Egyptian slavery:

> Woe to those who devise wickedness
> and work evil upon their beds.
> When the morning dawns, they perform it,
> because it is in the power of their hand.
> They covet fields, and seize them,
> and houses, and take them away;
> they oppress a man and his house,
> a man and his inheritance (*naḥālātô*) (Mic 2.1-2).

Micah concluded this indictment with God's warning concerning the consequences of such unrighteous action: 'Therefore you will have none to cast the line by lot in the assembly of the Lord' (Mic 2.5). This is an allusion to the *naḥălâ*, and describes the situation of social collapse when the Yahwistic community would no longer have leaders to 'cast the line by lot', that is, to reestablish a just economic and social system by returning property to its rightful owners. Land would become a commodity to be purchased by those with wealth. And a system would establish itself which would give all the advantages to the opulent elite. True to Samuel's warning, the other side of this system would be the enslavement of those losing their land and their freedom. Israel would indeed become like the other nations. As in the other nations, many of the people would become slaves of the king.

The prophets fearlessly warned king and people alike that this departure from the example of Yahweh's righteousness and compassion could only lead to tension, conflict and calamity. There was only one sure foundation for community life:

> He has showed you, O man, what is good;
> and what does the Lord require of you
> but to do justice, and to love kindness,
> and to walk humbly with your God? (Mic 6.8).

To depart from this foundation could only hasten the day of total destruction. For the durability and strength of a society was not determined by human definitions and decrees, but by conformity with a divine order manifested in the acts of the God who delivered the oppressed. Isaiah distinguished clearly between false and true sources of trust (Isa 31.1):

> Woe to those who go down to Egypt for help
> and rely on horses,
> who trust in chariots because they are many
> and in horsemen because they are very strong,

>   but do not look to the Holy One of Israel
>   or consult the Lord!

In the view of the prophets, the most advanced arsenal of weapons in the world combined with multilateral military pacts and powerful police forces would fail to shore up the wobbling structures of the nation that spurned God's order of righteous compassion. For when the widow, or orphan, or debtor, or foreigner cried for help, Yahweh would answer, and no human army could defend itself against the divine judge. Isaiah made this point in the continuation of the woe oracle cited above:

>   And yet he is wise and brings disaster,
>   he does not call back his words,
>   but will arise against the house of the evildoers,
>   and against the helpers of those who work iniquity (Isa 32.2).

The prophets had a much clearer grasp than most people do today of the all-encompassing order of which all nations are a part, and in relation to which their destiny is determined. Even people of faith waver when it comes to evaluating national and international happenings in relation to the notion of a universal order of justice. We make decisions on the basis of terms determined by worldly criteria, especially the relative military strength and economic clout of different nations in international affairs, and the 'laws' of the marketplace in domestic matters. We base our decisions on such penultimate criteria because we lack a true vision of the cosmic order of the God who directs reality toward a state of universal peace and justice by blessing righteousness and condemning injustice. In contrast, consider how comprehensive, indeed cosmic, the vision of Hosea was:

>   Hear the word of the Lord, O people of Israel;
>   for the Lord has a controversy
>   with the inhabitants of the land.
>   There is no faithfulness or kindness,
>   and no knowledge of God in the land;
>   there is swearing, lying, killing, stealing,
>   and committing adultery;
>   they break all bounds and murder follows murder.
>   Therefore the land mourns,
>   and all who dwell in it languish,
>   and also the beasts of the field,

> and also the birds of the air;
> even the fish of the sea are taken away (Hos 4.1-3).

The repudiation of God's order of righteous compassion in the land set off a destructive repercussion that extended out from its epi-center like the shockwaves of a nuclear explosion, until the entire created order was cast into the abyss of chaos: the land and its human inhabitants, the beasts of the field, the birds of the air, even the fish of the sea. According to the prophets, this world we inhabit is an intricately constructed organism. Like a fine violin, through tender handling, it is capable of producing beauty and blessing. If abused on the other hand and exploited by its human caretakers, it collapses and becomes a worthless object. This same holistic view of reality is expressed in an apocalyptic addition to the Book of Isaiah:

> The earth mourns and withers,
>   the world languishes and withers,
>   the heavens languish together with the earth.
> The earth lies polluted under its inhabitants;
> for they have transgressed the laws,
>   violated the statutes,
>   broken the everlasting covenant (Isa 24.4-5).

We see here a profound insight developing within prophetic Yahwism: The order of righteous compassion with which God has blessed God's people is not an appendage attached to an indifferent created order, but the nerve center of one organism, to which humans either add their blessing through righteous living, or condemn to destructon through their wanton disregard for God, other humans, and the world of nature.

6. *The End of the Prophetic Period: An Open Question*

By the end of the period of kingship in Israel, the prophets, in their struggle to keep alive God's order of righteous compassion, were led to a grim conclusion. They had dedicated their lives to shocking the people into recognizing the destructive nature of the unrighteous path they were treading. They did not wish for the fulfillment of the divine judgment they were describing as the wages of the people's sin. Their proclamation was motivated by the hope that the people would come to their senses, recognize where their unfaithfulness was leading them, and repent. For through repentance alone could the covenant relationship be restored which was Israel's sole source of life and health. But repeatedly the prophets witnessed a people rejecting their proclamation and repudiating the God in whose name they spoke (e.g. Hos 4.6-12). And they were forced to conclude that this was an incorrigible people, hell-bent on defining life on the basis of their own criteria of might and glory, and thus dragging nation and world to destruction. The prophets were not surprised to see this phase end in destruction of the land, of Jerusalem and of the temple by the Babylonians. For in their perception it was not ultimately the Babylonians that destroyed the nation. As the anonymous prophet of the exile explained:

> Who gave up Jacob to the spoiler,
> and Israel to the robbers?
> Was it not the Lord, against whom we have sinned,
> in whose ways they would not walk,
> and whose law they would not obey? (Isa 43.24).

At the end of the prophetic period in Israel there accordingly seemed to be little basis for hope within the Israelite nation that the perennial spiral of destructive conflict could be ended. Jeremiah described Israel as a frenzied camel in heat, and asked, 'Who can restrain her lust?' (Jer 2.24). Ezekiel portrayed the entire history of Israel as a history of apostasy under the shocking images of the lewd sisters Ohola and Oholibah (Ezek 23). And both prophets looked deeply into the hidden recesses of the human heart for the key to the enigma of a people called to be a blessing to all the earth and shattering this noble calling through self-aggrandizement, which by focussing on self instead of on God was in actuality an inexorable process of self-destruction. As they peered deeply, both concluded that only a decisive new act of God could offer hope. Jeremiah yearned for the day in which Yahweh would make a new covenant with the people, not like the old covenant, which was so badly broken by Israel. This time the difference would be that Yahweh would write the law, that is, the order of righteous compassion, upon the heart of each individual (Jer 31.31-34). Ezekiel shared this hope in the vision of a transformation of the inner person: 'A new heart I will give you', Yahweh promised, 'and a new spirit I will put within you; and I will take out of your flesh the heart of stone and give you a heart of flesh. And I will put my spirit within you, and cause you to walk in my statutes and be careful to observe my ordinances' (Ezek 36.26-27). During the same period the Priestly Writer, aware of the deep roots of sin, and witnessing the ineffectiveness of earlier measures, reinterpreted the meaning of sacrifice by portraying Yahwah providing the blood which was to be offered on Yom Kippur 'to make atonement for your souls' (Lev 17.11). And finally, Second Isaiah recognized Yahweh's new approach to save the people in the innocent suffering of the Servant, who offered himself as a sin-offering for the redemption of the people (Isa 52.13–53.12).

All four of these deep probings arising in response to the shock of the Babylonian destruction shared these common themes:
1. The recent calamity was proof of the everlasting validity of God's righteous, compassionate order.
2. The human heart was bafflingly predisposed to sin.
3. Hope for the people's return to the covenant relationship as the only context within which conflict could yield to understanding and peace rested exclusively in God's transformation of the human heart through forgiveness, cleansing and renewal. Out of these themes grew another:
4. That transformation and the resulting community of the faithful would occur as a remnant-phenomenon within the wider community.

Thus at the end of the prophetic period, we find an enormous question arising out of the smoldering ruins of Jerusalem: Would Yahweh's new initiative finally bring this people to its senses? Or would Israel prove itself to be so entrenched in the ways of conflict and sin as to repudiate God's alternative vision of a community where 'steadfast love and faithfulness will meet,' where 'righteousness and peace will kiss each other' (Ps 85.10)?

7. The Contemporary Response to the Early Yahwistic and Prophetic Assessment

Those hastening to the Bible for an answer to the contemporary problem of conflict may find little comfort in the above analysis. Does it not represent merely another example of people turning to theologians with their deep concerns, and being invited only to ponder over further unresolved problems, open-ended questions, and unfinished processes? We clearly need to press our inquiry a step further.

There is a restless, tension-filled quality in the Bible's treatment of the problem of conflict which resists simplistic answers. In Scripture lofty visions of peace are accompanied by bleak assessments of the human propensity for deceit and violence. But when one acknowledges the harm done in our world by people who force simplistic solutions upon complex problems, one may be open to the fact that this tension in biblical tradition is not without significance. Indeed, it is intimately related to God's training of a Servant people to be agents of healing in the world. By recognizing the depths of divisions and tensions in life, that people is brought to realize that shalom is not a state imposed upon a passive world, but is rather a total process of creation and redemption to which responding humans are drawn as partners with God.

If we were able to continue this study on into the New Testament, we would find this point powerfully confirmed. Granted, both Testaments have their apocalyptic chapters. Especially in times of persecution, faith was preserved with the help of dramatic visions of God's plucking the faithful out of this violent world and in an instant placing them in a state of paradisiacal harmony.[6] But in both communities prophets were present to remind the faithful of the intended function of their vision of God's righteous, compassionate order: It was not intended to lull them into complacency and inaction, but to show them the goal toward which they were being called as partners in a divine plan for all creation.

Already at the earliest stages of Yahwistic faith, the nature of that righteous, compassionate order had come to remarkably clear expression, and that by reason of being drawn inferentially from the nature of the divine Deliverer encountered in the event giving birth to the people Israel, the redemption of slaves from their bondage in Egypt. Moreover, the Yahwistic understanding of that order grew with subsequent historical experience, for in the events of history the community of faith continued to discern the unfolding of divine purpose. In her historical encounters with Yahweh both as Redeemer and as Judge, Israel was taught an unforgettable lesson about conflict and its resolution: there can be no refuge from conflict if the basic qualities of righteousness and compassion do not form the heart of the community. And Israel learned that the reason for this was not abstract, but specific and personal: injustice and repression will lead inevitably to the increase of conflict and unrest, for when the poor and afflicted cry out, a compassionate God hears and comes to their defense. Superfical attempts to resolve conflict which merely repress those cries are not merely immoral, but a reproach to the God of righteousness and compassion: 'If you do afflict them, and they cry out to me, I will surely hear their cry; and my wrath will burn, and I will kill you with the sword, and your wives shall become widows and your children fatherless' (Exod 22.23-24).

On the surface this may not seem like conflict resolution at all, and may alarm us in the same way as Jesus' word that he had not come to bring peace but the sword. But both are intended to shock us into seeing the only level upon which true peace can be established, the foundation of justice and peace for all. Peace at all costs, like cheap grace, is repudiated at all periods of biblical faith. Yahweh will fight on the side of the oppressed until the injustice that victimizes some members of a community to the benefit of others is purged. Only divine shalom can resolve conflict and bring genuine peace, and divine shalom reigns only where a community models its life on the righteousness and compassion of a God who stands on the side of the weak, the poor, and the vulnerable.

This lesson learned at such high cost by Israel serves warning to every modern nation: we can build up the most powerful military systems in the world, construct sophisticated worldwide financial networks, seek to assure domestic stability through strong law enforcement, and nevertheless witness the collapse of our whole civil edifice if—as I believe is always the case with such self-aggrandizing nationalistic schemes—we do our building to the neglect of impartial, universal justice, compassion and peace.[7]

We may wish that the Bible had a simple solution to the problem of the conflicts that tear at our lives, our communities and the nations of the world. All ages have wished that, and hence all the apocalyptic imagery, ancient and modern. If only God would just come and change everything! Why does God not answer our yearning for perfect peace and world harmony with a new act of creation, forcing a stubborn world to submit to the divine will? In answer to these questions we find early Yahwists and prophets affirming such yearning, but in a specific way: God has planted the vision of an order of righteous compassion and universal shalom in our consciousness because God intends that order for the entire human family. But it is one of the qualities of that order that it becomes a reality only among those who embrace it fully and in gratitude to the divine Deliverer. This being so, God has created the yearning in our hearts as a sure sign of God's call to us to participate in the righteous, compassionate community's becoming. For it breaks into our world not by heavenly warfare, but by humans responding to the countless struggles of those in bondage with the faith that in each of these struggles participation on the side of the oppressed is nothing less than joining sides with the God of the exodus. Clearly this is not a participation confined to acts of individual piety. It implies a broad social program and an international policy. It mandates opposition through vote and protest to every political plan that circumvents the rights of the poor and weak and endangers world peace in partisan attempts to create a buoyant economy and a powerful military. It resists every effort to exclude the world community and the realm of nature from the nation's policy decisions. And it is able to resist such forms of exclusion because it derives its motivation and its vision solely from the God of the entire created order.

I personally feel that to respond to the contemporary problem of conflict with this biblical realism is the most hopeful option available. It identifies a path which diverges neither in the direction of utopian escapism nor of worldly cynicism. It interprets conflict as a sign of the yearning of a fallen world for an authentic context within which conflict may be resolved and harmony restored. It discerns God's presence in every struggle, and makes decisions solely on the basis of the righteous compassion which locates the presence of the Deliverer God in those struggles. And with the divine Deliverer, those sharing this biblical realism take their personal stand. There they seek forgiveness for their own complicity with oppression. There they experience God's cleansing and renewal as the only adequate preparation for participation in their new vocation. There they take up the task of being peacemakers in the name of divine righteousness and compassion. And in this response of grateful humans a community grows which offers itself to the world of power and conflict and human aggression as a source of hope, for it points to an alternative to self-destruction, an alternative in which humans, by virtue of their dedication to divine will, are enabled to surrender personal privilege and nationalistic glory to the higher goal of global justice, prosperity and peace.[8]

The divine order of righteous compassion and peace for which the community of faith yearns and to which it is dedicated is described beautifully by Psalm 85.4-13:

> Restore us again, O God of our salvation,
>   and put away thy indignation toward us!
> Wilt thou be angry with us for ever?
>   Wilt thou prolong thy anger to all generations?
> Wilt thou not revive us again,

that thy people may rejoice in thee?
Show us thy steadfast love, O Lord,
    and grant us thy salvation.
Let me hear what God the Lord will speak,
    for he will speak peace to his people,
    to his saints, to those who turn to him in their heart.
Surely his salvation is at hand for those who fear him,
    that glory may dwell in our land.
Steadfast love and faithfulness will meet;
    righteousness and peace will kiss each other.
Faithfulness will spring up from the ground,
    and righteousness will look down from the sky.
Yea, the Lord will give what is good,
    and our land will yield its increase.
Righteousness will go before him,
    and make his footsteps a way.

NOTES

1. In light of Bernhard Word Anderson's profound and abiding contributions to our understanding of the significance of biblical religion for contemporary faith, and specifically in consideration of his location of the exodus confession at the heart of Israel's theology, it seems appropriate to dedicate to him an essay which seeks to move from the biblical confession in Yahweh the Deliverer to the current struggle to analyze the root causes of conflict in our world and to identify ways in which conflict can be reduced and resolved. Participating in this most deserved tribute to one of this century's truly great biblical scholars and theologians is a particular joy for one who, like myself, considers Professor Anderson to be a model of the life of commitment both to scholarship and to faith.

2. Cf. B.W. Anderson, *Creation Versus Chaos: The Reinterpretation of Mythical Symbolism in the Bible* (New York: Association, 1967).

3. Cf. W.F. Albright, 'Canaanite Ḥpši and the Hebrew Ḥofši Again', *JPOS* 6 (1926), 106-108.

4. Questions such as these are addressed specificially in the essays comprising the October 1984 issue of *Interpretation*, which bears the title *War and Peace in Scripture and Tradition*.

5. For an excellent treatment of the early traditions embedded in the narrative of 1 Samuel, see P. Kyle McCarter, *1 Samuel* (AB, 8; Garden City: Doubleday, 1980).

6. See the present writer's 'The Apocalyptic Consciousness', *Quarterly Review* 4 (1984), 23-39.

7. Needless to say, the horrible specter of nuclear holocaust presses this problem upon us with an unprecedented urgency. This is reflected not only

in films, novels and articles intended for the general public, but in scholarly writings in almost all disciplines. For example, while a political scientist like Michael Mendelbaum writes an article entitled 'The Bomb, Dread and Eternity' (*International Security* 5 [1980], 3-23), a theologian like Gordon Kaufman delivers an address with the title, 'Nuclear Eschatology and the Study of Religion' (delivered as the 1982 Presidential Address to the American Academy of Religion in New York, and reprinted in the *Harvard Divinity School Bulletin*, February/March 1983).

8. For a history of the biblical notion of community and its contemporary application, see the present writer's *The People Called: The Growth of Community in the Bible* (New York: Harper and Row, forthcoming).

11

THE OLD TESTAMENT'S UNDERSTANDING OF HISTORY IN RELATION TO THAT OF THE ENLIGHTENMENT

Claus Westermann

1. *Historie and Geschichte*

The Old Testament has no concept of history, in the sense that history is only *history* that can be documented and that follows a verifiable course governed by causal laws.[1] While the Old Testament does contain historical writing in approximately this sense, it does not recognize the sharp distinction of this kind of *history* from all unverifiable events which cannot be rationally documented in dates and facts—a distinction which grows out of Enlightenment thinking. In approaching the question of history in the Old Testament, then, one cannot proceed from an understanding of history which selects from all other events only those that are *historically* documented as authentic and which makes the contrast *historical–unhistorical* an absolute criterion equivalent to authentic–inauthentic.[2]

History in this sense, which grows out of the Enlightenment, is limited to the time and to the form of nationhood. Outside this definition remain pre-history and primitive history, in which there are no documents. This definition of *history* presupposes the invention of writing. According to this definition, pre-literate communities can have no history in the strict sense. The early stages of the later civilizations, and primitive nations as well, remain excluded from history. That is a problematic demarcation which can no longer be maintained.[3]

Just as problematic is that *history* in this sense, limited to the time and to the form of nationhood, actually makes this one form of community absolute: the subject of *history* is only the nation, or nations. All other forms are subordinated to this one. A politically constituted nation [*Volk*] is usually composed of tribes; a tribe is composed of clans (families). They are henceforth recognized only as integrated into or subordinated under the state; the tribe and the family are reduced to the categories of the 'provincial' and the 'private'. They are no longer independent subjects of history.[4]

For the Enlightenment concept of history, beginning and end are *eo ipso* excluded from history. All conceptions of the course of events which lead from a beginning to an end are thus *unhistorical* from the outset, and are relegated to the realm of philosophy or religion. But then, at the same time, the history of humankind is excluded from *history*, because the subject of the primeval and final events in myths and religions is humankind. What is said of humankind can in no case be historical. A further limitation of the Enlightenment's understanding of history follows from the reduction of events to that which is verifiable through documentary evidence. What can be authenticated from the distant past through documents are primarily events fixed in names and dates: kings and the years of their reign, battles and treaties, names of defeated foes, conquered lands and vanquished cities. What cannot be comprehended in names and dates, however, are cycles of growth and decline and, in general, the part played by natural processes in historical development. What goes on silently between documented events can often be more important than the cardinal events themselves.

Historical occurrence is bi-polar: it comes to pass in events and in fixed processes, which are given in human phenomena. Historical-critical methods cannot comprehend these processes and events in the same way. Therein lies a further limitation of the concept of history formed in the eighteenth and nineteenth centuries.

2. *History in the Old Testament*

1. *'History' (Historie) and the History of Israel*

If the Old Testament deals with the history of Israel, the term 'history' here involves several levels of meaning, only one of which is equivalent to *history* in the strict sense. The growth of the Pentateuch is toward the goal of Israel's development as a nation in a settled and politically constituted way of life. Prior to this goal, however, is a series of stages, none of which can be called strictly *history*, and whose form of linguistic expression is thus not historical writing. Let us assume that somewhere in the world discoveries were made which brought to light texts that corresponded to the patriarchal history. One would expect them to be studied not by historians but by ethnologists or sociologists. There are no *historical* texts which, despite all the energy expended on them by exegetes, would show the patriarchal history to have a *historical* 'core'. We have in the Pentateuch a work of history only in the sense that it intends to present the pre-history of the nation Israel. It is not, however, a *historical* work in the sense of the nineteenth century's understanding of history. For its fundamental linguistic unit is the narrative: the patriarchal history has grown up out of narratives. But narrative is not a form of *historical* presentation. 'Israel's history' has a broader meaning than the '*history* of Israel'.

The movement beyond the pre-*historical* into the *historical* is shown in exemplary fashion in Genesis 36, the final chapter of the patriarchal history proper. In this chapter the descendants (*tôlᵉdôt* = history) of Esau are presented in three sections, which correspond to three stages of the history of Esau (= Edom). The chapter enumerates the sons of Esau in the first section (vv. 1-14); in the second (vv. 15-19) the princes of Esau (paralleled by the sons of the Horite Seir and the princes of the Horites, the previous inhabitants, in vv. 20-30); and in the third section the kings of Edom (vv. 31-39). The history of the family, the tribe and the nation follow on one another, each in its own linguistic form. It would not be appropriate to apply to this chapter the criterion *historical–unhistorical*, according to which only the material contained in the royal chronicles would be *historical*, while the other two sections would be *unhistorical*. Both of the first two sections are considered by the author to belong as much as the third to the history of Edom. All three sections participate in reality. All three sections speak of actual events—of the three successive stages of one and the same community. It is only that these three stages are presented in different forms of speech. The understanding of history which underlies this chapter is broader than that of the nineteenth century.

In addition to the pre-political, the Old Testament also recognizes a post-political stage in Israel's history. Israel continues to exist after its political collapse. In political significance it is reduced to a province, the province of an empire, and from that point forward continues to have political significance in the strict sense only as a component of an empire. It is registered and appraised in the central offices of the empire, in the edicts of this province's administration, in the succession of its administrators, in the case of revolts, of religious conflicts, etc.

But even in these circumstances the history of Israel continues underground in the province of Judah. It perseveres in a historical consciousness which continues to know itself as Israel and which understands its present situation as a stage in the history of the nation on the basis of the nation's past, including its political catastrophe. This is demonstrated in the historical works which arose during this period, the Deuteronomistic and Chronicler's histories. It is also evident in Lamentations and in Israel's future expectation. There corresponds, then, to the pre-*historical* phase of Israel's history, a post-*historical* phase. This post-*historical* phase is made possible in that the nation preserves its identity as a nation in its religion, and in that the communal form of the family continues to uphold its function as the bearer of the religious tradition—a function which it had in the pre-political stage of Israel's history—and at the same time preserves the historical traditions as well.

The historical works of this post-political phase have a strongly '*unhistorical*' character; their *historical* worth is, in part, questionable. Nor does their significance lie in their historical-critical verifiability, but in their preservation of the identity of Israel in the post-political phase of the nation's history. This significance attaches in even greater measure to the emergence, in this late period, of the Old Testament as canon, the Bible of the nation Israel, which was nothing less than decisive for the preservation of Israel's identity. Precisely from this post-political situation it is understandable that all three phases of the history reported in the Bible belong to the historical understanding of those who formed the canon: the pre-*historical*, the *historical* and the post-*historical*. It is these three phases together that constitute the history of Israel. Thus the historical understanding of the Enlightenment is, in this respect, inadequate.

That which forms these three components of Israel's history into a coherent history in three phases is the action of God on Israel's behalf and the response of Israel to this divine action. This reciprocal relation between God and Israel is not confined to the middle phase but encompasses all three. That is possible because the action of God is not restricted to the social form of the nation but comprehends also the pre-political and post-political forms of community: the family, the tribe, the religious community and individuals as a part of humankind. This comprehensive divine action is governed by two poles. In the Old Testament God's saving and judging activity is differentiated from his acts of blessing; the one is accomplished through events, the other in the fixed processes of growth and decline, of vitality and decay. He acts not only in a history of salvation, governed by the 'mighty acts of God', which reach from the deliverance from Egypt to the judgment on Jerusalem, but also in the pre-historical period of the patriarchs, and in the post-historical as well. Moreover, both in the latter and in the former, he works through families and small groups.

2. The Relationship of Historical to Non-historical Forms of Community and Forms of Speech

Forms of community. The Old Testament's understanding of history is shown with particular clarity in the history of the succession to David's throne because in it the new form of life represented by the nation-state is a completely new discovery. It is a discovery of the political as an autonomous sphere of life, with its own laws of historical causality, in particular contrast to the histories of the patriarchs and the judges. Precisely because the political is here discovered for the first time, the struggle to understand and to master the new form on the basis of the old can be recognized in the Throne Succession Narrative. The struggle is that of trying to make the experience of reality characteristic of the old era fruitful for the new. In the case of the monarchy there is the possibility that familial experiences can be exploited for their political significance. Actually, the Throne Succession Narrative deals in large part with family conflicts, beginning with the adultery of David in 2 Samuel 12. But here, in contrast with the treatment of the same motif in the patriarchal history, the political effect is made clear. Gerhard von Rad saw in this a 'marked deficiency, in that political conflicts are anchored so exclusively in the personal and family spheres'.[5] At the basis of this critique is the assumption that familial affairs have no place in *historical*-political events, which have to do instead with the nation, not with the family.

To the contrary, the author of the Throne Succession Narrative consciously presents the succession to the throne as a complex combination of familial and political events. One encounters here the same motifs as in the patriarchal history: the childlessness of Michal; David's adultery (the temptation of the powerful to break into the family and take for himself whatever he wants; cf. Gen 6.1-4; Gen 12); the death of the favorite wife's son; Ammon's violation of Tamar; Absalom's desertion of his father's house and his return; rebellion against the father; rivalry between brothers. The only way in which the operation of the new form of government, the dynasty, can be presented is in terms of familial events.

The contrast reaches its climax in the death of Absalom and David's lament over his death. The author shows the two lines which merge in his work and which have led to this contrast when Joab, the army commander, must compel David to attend to what is politically necessary. The conclusion with Solomon's succession to the throne thus contains its dark side. Leading up to it is a broken continuity, which thus brings into the history of the monarchy a critical aspect. All that glimmers in the kingdom of Solomon is not gold.[6]

Another example of reflection aimed at reconciling two different forms of community is the Joseph narrative. It presents an encounter between the form and understanding of life characteristic of families following their herds, and that of a royal court. The monarchical form of government is sharply rejected by the brothers of Joseph at the beginning; at the conclusion it is the monarchy with its surplus economy which saves the family threatened by famine. This narrative is connected to the controversy over kingship as a form of government early in the monarchical period, during which some were friendly and others hostile toward the monarchy. The editor of the Joseph story wants to point out to its opponents the positive economic aspects of this form of government; in doing so, however, he lets its dangers and temptations appear as well. But above all he wants to show them that the essential elements of family-centered life can be taken up into the new monarchical form of government.

Both of these examples show that very serious consideration was given in Israel to the relation between the two forms of community. In both cases this consideration took place in the passage of unsettled family groups to the sedentary, national form of life in the monarchy. Since this passage signified a threatening break with tradition, it is perfectly understandable that the monarchy would be rejected precisely by the conservatives. For them acceptance of the monarchy was only possible to the extent that earlier forms of community were integrated into the new.

These two examples also make clear that it is not possible in the Old Testament understanding of history to isolate the national-political form of life from all others and to ascribe to it an absolute value.

Forms of Speech. The Old Testament understanding of history is also differentiated from that of the nineteenth century by forms of speech. The form of speech characteristic of a purely rational understanding of history in terms of causal determination is that of the report, or that of historical writing based on documents, which are themselves dependent upon reports. It is concerned with facts, with dates and with causal connections. The report form is appropriate to it; that is universally granted. The Old Testament also knows and uses this report form for the *historical* phase from the beginning of the monarchy until the exile.[7] But because the history of Israel encompasses, for the Old Testament, both a pre-political and a post-political phase, history can also be presented in narratives. The pre-political period of Israel's history has grown up out of narratives, the passage from the pre-political to the political phase is depicted in narrative, and narratives can appear in the midst of a historical report (e.g. 1 Kgs 9).[8] In addition to narrative, the primeval history and the patriarchal history contain genealogy, and the patriarchal history also contains itineraries (a narrative and enumerative form of speech).[9] While in the narratives the concern is with events and their consequences, the genealogies preserve the continuity of events in the sequence of generations. Both are pre-*historical* and pre-national forms of historical presentation which emerge from the family setting. While both were earlier seen as secondary constructions, as by Wellhausen and Gunkel, they are now recognized, particularly through ethnological studies, in terms of their own original significance. The way in which genealogy passes into royal chronology is shown in Genesis 36 (see above).

There is a whole series of other forms of speech for the transmission of pre-*historical* events. A characteristic example is provided by the tribal speeches (Gen 49; Deut 33) about the history of the tribes prior to the emergence of the nation. The etiological motifs in the narratives should also be included here, in particular the naming of a place after an event. These etiological narratives were formerly seen without exception as *unhistorical*; their original significance has since been recognized (see the discussion between M. Noth and J. Bright).

3. *The Problem of the Exclusion of Religion from 'History'*
In his essay on the throne succession of David, Gerhard von Rad refers to the judgment of the historian, Eduard Meyer, on this story. Meyer is disturbed 'that these thoroughly profane texts serve Jews and Christians as holy Scripture'. Von Rad objects to the contrary that these stories mention God in three important places (2 Sam 11.27; 12.24; 17.14).[10] In addition to this we need to reflect on the context out of which the history is transmitted to us.

It was already pointed out that the Old Testament does contain historical writing in the specific sense of the term; this is limited essentially to the four books of Samuel and Kings and to the time of the nations Israel and Judah. But the demarcation of *historical* texts in the Old Testament is possible only to a very limited extent. This is true in the first place because the texts to be recognized as *historical* in Samuel and Kings are embedded in the redaction of the Deuteronomistic History, which as a whole has a thoroughly religious orientation. Thus the distinction of the political from the religious elements is extremely difficult, if not impossible. That the author of the Deuteronomistic History wants to speak of what has happened between God and his people is shown most clearly in the early history of prophecy, which has been incorporated into his work.[11] But also the traditions which lie behind this work, such as the Throne Succession Narrative or the History of David's Rise, speak self-evidently of the action of God in history (in more places than the three listed by von Rad); the authors do not want, nor are they able, to abstract this history from its connection with God.

In addition, a delineation of those texts which are *historical* is only possible to a limited extent, because the historical books in the canon of the Old Testament belong to a totality which consists of three parts: history–word–answer.[12] Against the reproach of Eduard Meyer it must be said that Scripture is the Old Testament in its totality. To the history of Israel in all of its phases there belongs first the word of God issued into history, and in addition the answer of the people in word and deed. Corresponding to this, the history of Israel is an essential part of both the other divisions of the canon, the Prophets as well as the Psalms.

Those elements of the Prophets and the Psalms in which we can recognize the emergence of a historical consciousness in Israel show, on the other hand, that the sphere of the *historical*-political in the Old Testament is not to be dissociated from the relation of the people of Israel to God.

In the Psalms. In the laments of the people there is the motif of contrast: the people cry out of their distress, urging God to remember his earlier acts of salvation and holding up this contrast before him. Why? Past history is actualized in the prayer of the people, which demonstrates an explicit historical consciousness. In the Psalms of praise the redeemed, in their joy directed to God, narrate his saving acts as a sequence of events: their distress–their entreaty–God's attention–God's intervention. They have experienced a history with God. It can then be understood that out of this grow entire historical Psalms. Without this historical consciousness which arises in experiences with God there would never have emerged the great historical works of the Old Testament.

In the Prophets. The relation of word and history is so explicit in the prophets that one needs only to refer to a few points. The prophecy of salvation, or promise, accompanied Israel in its entire history. We should not separate the promise of the land in the patriarchal history, or the promise of deliverance from Egypt, from the events which than took place. These promises had an eminently historical significance, even if they cannot be regarded as '*historical*' according to the stringent criteria of *historical* criticism. They have set events in motion. In the tension which arose between promise and fulfillment the Israelites and their ancestors learned to understand history as a journey, as duration, as continuity. The prophets' announcements of judgment, to which the same remarks apply, have in addition the *historically* evident significance that they were able, as particularly Deutero-Isaiah demonstrates, to bridge the abyss of national collapse, which brought with it the termination of the kingdom and the end of the temple. Apart from prophecy, the emergence of the Deuteronomistic History is inconceivable. But apart from prophecy, the emergence of the historical conception in the three other phases mentioned is just as inconceivable.

The founders of the Enlightenment concept of history could draw a line of demarcation between *history* and religion in a phase of human history which began with the first movements toward enlightenment in antiquity. In these movements the separation of politics from religion was made possible by leaving to individual citizens the choice of belonging to a religious community, leaving the citizenry as a whole without a religious affiliation. But this separation cannot be applied to a phase in which being a part of the state is identical to being a part of the national religion. It makes a fundamental difference whether the religion is sustained by the nation as a whole constituted as a state, or whether it is sustained by one religious group among others with the same nation.

4. *Beginning and End, the History of Nations and the History of Humankind*

For the *historian* there is no such thing as beginning and end, because neither is *historically* verifiable. Since for the *historian* history is identical to the history of a politically constituted nation, or nations, there can be no history of humankind. One can speak of world empires, but there has never been a world empire in the sense that humankind has been united in *one* nation.[13] But this does not accord with our natural way of thinking. Rather, it would seem, if a person has a beginning and an end this would apply as well to humankind as a whole. For that reason people all over the world have been speaking for millennia of the beginning and the end, and also of the history of humankind; one has only to think of the doctrine of world epochs.

The concept of a history of humankind has been taken up in philosophy of history. A typical idealistic example is Karl Jaspers in *The Origin and Goal of History*.[14] He sees in the midst of world history what he calls the 'axial period', between 800 and 200, but especially around 500 BC. In this period the age of myth has come to an end, and the step into the universal and spiritual has been made. At the beginning it is limited to one general locale but then it is spread over the world. The axial period assimilated all others, and from it world history receives a single structure which penetrates everywhere. The axial period signifies the joining together of humankind in the action of world history.

To this could be added the example of materialism. The Marxist-Leninist understanding of history speaks of a determinism of history in five phases. First is the epoch of the primitive community, then the epochs of slavery, feudalism, capitalism and finally socialism, in its two phases of socialization and the classless society.

The Bible too has a conception of the history of humankind, but in it the world and humanity are bound inseparably together. Both are God's creation. As God's creation they have a beginning, and to the beginning there corresponds the end. Only the creator is eternal, not the world. The history of humankind in the Bible is consistently conceived in terms of beginning and end. This is shown already in the primeval history in which the creation of humankind corresponds to the judgment of annihilation in the deluge. In this the Bible is not in agreement with *history*, because the latter does not recognize the beginning or the end of humankind. The Bible does, perhaps, coincide with the natural sciences for which the human race has a beginning and is proceeding toward an end.[15]

The biblical primeval history clearly distinguishes between the beginning of humankind and the beginning of nations and states. In

Genesis 1–9 it speaks of the creation of the world and of human beings, and of the origin of all humankind. Only then, in Genesis 10 and 11, does it go on to speak of the division of humankind into nations. Things are quite different in the near eastern empires, Assyria-Babylon and Egypt, in which humankind originates together with the monarchy and the state: 'When kingship was lowered from heaven'. In this respect the historical understanding of the nineteenth century is closer to the ancient near eastern conception than it is to that of the Bible.

The distinction between the creation of humankind and the origin of the state corresponds to a fact that has not yet been properly explained: the motifs of creation and of the primeval period found all over the world are in striking agreement with one another.[16] With reference to this primeval event one can speak of a form of human culture which is decidedly prior to that of the state. Corresponding to this, in the Bible the family-oriented form of community is coordinated with creation, but not with the state.[17]

There is also a correspondence between what the Bible says about the beginning and what it says about the end, especially insofar as the subject of the final events, as of the primeval events, is humankind. Beginning and end correspond to each other in a whole series of motifs, especially in Revelation, as has often been observed.

It is particularly characteristic of biblical apocalyptic, which is indeed common to both Testaments, that what is said in it about final events is connected with the Old Testament understanding of history. With the end of history, the history of the nations and also the particular history of God's people come to an end and flow again into the history of humankind. From the perspective of history's end, the history of humankind is fitted into a sequence of periods. Thus, the great empires have a particular significance for the apocalyptic drama, particularly in the book of Daniel—the image composed of four elements in ch. 2, and the sequence of four beasts in ch. 7. It is this apocalyptic view which first makes possible a conception of world history: the history of the nations moving toward its end becomes the history of humankind. Such a conception is only possible as a product of the Old Testament understanding of history which looked on the totality of events as a whole.

It is certainly no accident that this conception of the events of the end in terms of the history of humankind has its locus in the third phase of Israel's history, when Israel was merely a province within an empire. This demonstrates again the Old Testament's comprehensive understanding of history as a totality.

NOTES

1. To my colleague, B.W. Anderson, in grateful memory of our encounters in Heidelberg, and the semester during which we taught together at Drew.
[Translator's note: The two German words, *Historie* and *Geschichte*, are both rendered by the English 'history'. In this essay when 'history' translates *Historie*, or its derivatives, it will be italicized. Otherwise, it is to be understood as a translation of *Geschichte*.]

2. The designation 'the *historical* Jesus' is problematic, because the New Testament contains no *historical* reports. Likewise problematic is the designation of a method of interpretation as *historical*-critical, if it deals with non-*historical* texts.

3. In place of the framework of *historical* dates, e.g. the dates of kings, primitive peoples have genealogies, which exercise the same function.

4. The absolute priority of the political is demonstrated also in a present tendency to broaden the concept of the political excessively.

5. Gerhard von Rad, 'Die Anfänge der Geschichtsschreibung im alten Israel', *TBü* 8 (1958) 148-88 (ET: 'The Beginnings of Historical Writing in Ancient Israel', *The Problem of the Hexateuch and Other Essays* [Edinburgh: Oliver & Boyd, 1966] 166-204).

6. I have shown this in more detail in my essay, 'Zum Geschichtsverständnis des Alten Testament', *Probleme Biblischer Theologie. Festschrift Gerhard von Rad* (ed. H.W. Wolff; Göttingen: Vandenhoeck & Ruprecht, 1971) 611-19.

7. The New Testament, on the other hand, contains no *historical* reports. This is one of the reasons why Old Testament and New Testament studies are so estranged from each other.

8. In our understanding of history that would be impossible, because we tend to feel that the historical novel (Felix Dahn, Gustav Freitag) and historical drama (Shakespeare, Schiller) must be sharply separated from a *historical* report.

9. See C. Westermann, *Genesis* (BKAT 1/1, 2; Neukirchen-Vluyn: Neukirchener Verlag, 1966-81) 1.8-23; 2.46-51.

10. 11.27, 'But the thing that David had done displeased Yahweh'. 12.24, '. . . and Yahweh loved him (Solomon)'. 17.14, 'For Yahweh had ordained to defeat the good counsel of Ahithophel'.

11. The author of this historical work understands the speech and action of the prophets, and the reaction of the kings and the people, as a component of the history of the monarchical period.

12. For a more detailed treatment, see my *Elements of Old Testament Theology* (Atlanta: John Knox, 1982).

13. To speak of 'world history' means to speak of the history of the nations of the world, but not of the history of humankind.

14. New Haven: Yale University, 1953.

15. This agreement of the Bible with the natural sciences, over against history, is of the greatest significance. The concept of 'progress' must be thought through anew from this perspective.

16. The same applies to pre-*historical* forms of speech, such as the narrative.

17. The family will exist so long as humankind exists. The same cannot be said of the state.

12

THE OTHER WOMAN
A Literary and Theological Study of the Hagar Narratives

Phyllis Trible

To honor Bernhard W. Anderson, I offer an exegesis of the Hagar narratives (Gen 16.1-16; 21.9-21).* Two considerations prompt this choice. First, as a part of Genesis, the stories belong to a book that currently occupies the scholarly attention of Professor Anderson.[1] Second, I employ the rhetorical critical methodology advocated by our mutual teacher James Muilenburg and also used by Anderson himself.[2]

Though Abraham prevails in scripture as the symbol of faith, his story pivots on two women, Sarah and Hagar, who shape and challenge faith. Their own stories diverge, however, to give Sarah the better portion. Wife of a wealthy herdsman (Gen 13.2),[3] she holds privilege and power within the confines of patriarchal structures.[4] To be sure, on two occasions Abraham betrays her, passing her off as his sister to protect himself (12.10-20; 20.1-19), but each time God comes to her rescue. Without effort, this woman along with her husband enjoys divine favor. Yet her exaltation poses major tension in Abram's story because 'Sarai is barren; she has no child' (11.30, RSV*). She is also old. Indeed, 'it has ceased to be with Sarah after the manner of women' (18.11, RSV*; cf. 17.17). Her situation would seem to thwart the divine promise of an heir for Abram.[6] Hence, Sarai plans to secure a child through her maid Hagar, who becomes thereby the other woman in Abram's life.

As one of the first females in scripture to experience use, abuse, and rejection, Hagar the Egyptian slave claims our attention. Knowledge of her has survived in bits and pieces only, from the oppressor's perspective at that, and so our task is precarious: to tell Hagar's story from the fragments that remain.

The fragments come from separate scenes in the Abrahamic saga.[7] The first (16.1-16) precedes by several chapters and the second (21.9-21) just follows the birth of the child God eventually gives to Sarah herself.[8] Similar structures and subjects order these scenes. In both, narrative introductions and conclusions surround two episodes. The first episodes, located in Canaan, highlight Sarah as she deals with Hagar and Abraham; the second ones, located in the wilderness, feature Hagar encountering the deity. Besides providing continuity, these structural and content parallels between the two scenes also highlight their differences. For Hagar in particular, the plot of the first story is circular, moving from bondage to flight to bondage, while the action of the second is linear, proceeding from bondage to expulsion to homelessness.[9]

A Circle of Bondage

Scene One: Genesis 16.1-16

A. Introduction, 16.1. The opening sentence of scene one emphasizes Sarai. Reversing the usual Hebrew word order, it places before the verb her name as subject. 'Now Sarai, wife of Abram, did not bear a child to him' (16.1). The statement of the problem leads in the second half of the sentence to an answer: 'but to her (was) an Egyptian maid whose name was Hagar'.[10] Beginning with Sarai and ending with Hagar, the narrated introduction opposes two women around the man Abram. Sarai the Hebrew is married, rich, and free; she is also old and barren. Hagar the Egyptian is single, poor, and bonded;[11] she is also young and fertile. Power belongs to Sarai, the subject of action; powerlessness marks Hagar, the object.

B. Episode One, 16.2-6. From the introduction the story moves to its first episode. At the beginning, Sarai speaks in the imperative mood.[12] Dialogic order and verb construction match content to present this woman as the commanding figure. While confirming the problem and solution that the storyteller has just reported, she makes subtle changes:

> And Sarai said to Abram,
> 'Look now, Yhwh has prevented me
> from bearing children.
> Go, then, to my maid.
> Perhaps I shall be built up from her.' (16.2a)

Unlike the narrator, Sarai speaks of building up herself through Hagar rather than of bearing a child to Abram (cf. 16.1, 15). Even in a man's world, the woman's voice sounds a different emphasis.[13] Moreover, unlike the narrator, she attributes her barren plight to Yhwh and thus seeks to counter divine action with human initiative.

What the deity has prevented, Sarai can accomplish through the maid whose name she never utters and to whom she never speaks.[14] For Sarai, Hagar is an instrument, not a person. The maid enhances the mistress.

Sarai's words effect obedience. Abram makes no attempt to halt the plan; instead, he yields so passively that the storyteller must answer for him. 'And Abram heard [obeyed] the voice of Sarai' (16.2b). Continuing to underline *his* acquiescence, the narrated discourse reports *her* action:

> Sarai, *wife* of *Abram*, took Hagar the Egyptian, her maid,
> after *Abram* had dwelt ten years in the land of Canaan,
> and gave her to *Abram* her *husband*, to him (*lô*) for a *wife*. (16.3)

Once again in the structure of a sentence, two females encircle Abram (cf. 16.1). Yet they are unequally matched. As subject of the verbs *take* and *give*, Sarai exercises power over Hagar, the object. Though her actions relate the two women, the absence of dialogue maintains distance between them. Further, repeated use of the relational language wife, maid, husband, and wife accents the growing opposition. In making Hagar Abram's wife, not concubine,[15] Sarai has unwittingly diminished her own status in relationship to this servant. But she still retains full control over Abram. As he first obeyed her voice in a narrated sentence of few words, so now he explicitly fulfills her command, 'Go (*bô'*), then, into (*'l*) my maid' (16.2): 'And he went (*bô'*) into (*'l*) Hagar' (16.4a, RSV).[16] No mighty patriarch is Abram, but rather the silent, acquiescent, and minor figure in a drama between two women.

Sarai has spoken; Abram has agreed. Sarai has acted; Abram has obeyed. But now the plot shifts to Hagar, the one through whom Sarai wishes to be built up. Making the maid subject, not object, the narrator reports, 'She conceived' (16.4b). Although this result is precisely what Sarai wants, it prompts an insight on Hagar's part that her mistress has not anticipated. 'When she [Hagar] saw that she had conceived, her mistress was slight in her eyes' (16.4c). Hagar is other than a tool; for that difference Sarai has failed to allow.

The Hebrew expression, 'her mistress was slight (or trifling) in her eyes', inspires various interpretations. Many translators alter the syntax to make Hagar the subject of the verb. They also attribute to the verb (*qll*) the legitimate, though not necessary, meaning of contempt or disdain. Accordingly, one reads, 'When she knew she was with child, she despised her mistress' (NEB); or 'when she saw that she had conceived, she looked with contempt on her mistress' (RSV).[17] Yet the verb with its correct subject also offers the less harsh reading that is present in the translation, 'Her mistress was lowered in her esteem' (NJV).

Though strife between barren and fertile wives is a typical motif in scripture,[18] in this study the typical yields to the particular. Seeing, that is, perceiving her own conception, Hagar acquires a different vision of Sarai. Hierarchical blinders disappear. The exalted mistress decreases while the lowly maid increases. Not hatred but a re-ordering of the relationship is the point. Unwittingly, Sarai has contributed to Hagar's insight. By giving Hagar to Abram for a wife, Sarai hoped to be built up. In fact, however, she has enhanced the status of the servant to become herself correspondingly lowered in the eyes of Hagar.

This unexpected twist provides an occasion for mutuality and equality between two females, but it is not to be. If Hagar has experienced new vision, Sarai remains within the old structures.[19] Still in charge, she speaks to Abram, faulting him for the outcome of her plan and appealing to Yhwh for judgment. While she uses the same vocabulary as the narrator to describe Hagar's response, the words on her lips have a pejorative meaning:[20]

> And Sarai said to Abram,
>> 'May the wrong done to me be upon you!
>
>> *I* ('*ānōkî*) gave my maid to your embrace
>> but when she saw that she had conceived,
>> then I was slight in her eyes.
>
>> May Yhwh judge between you and me!' (16.5, RSV*)

The mistress wants returned the superior status that she unwittingly relinquished in using Hagar. Further, she demands that her husband rectify the wrong, since he now holds authority over Hagar too. But Abram, speaking for the first time in this scene, chooses not to exercise power and thus remains passive:[21]

> But Abram said to Sarai,
>> 'Look, your maid is in your hand.
>> Do to her the good in your eyes.' (16.6a)

The idiom, 'the good in your eyes', plays upon the reference to Hagar's eyes: 'Her mistress was slight in her eyes'. The vision of the mistress opposes the insight of the maid. What is good for the one is suffering for the other.

If Sarai's opening speech to Abram ordered the use of Hagar (16.2), now her words to him, with his reply, lead to the abuse of the maid. Succinctly, the narrator declares, 'And Sarai afflicted her' (16.6b). Once again the two women meet unequally as subject and object, vanquisher and victim, and this time Hagar has lost her name (cf. 16.3). Moreover, the absence of dialogue continues to separate the females. Inequality, opposition, and distance breed violence: 'Sarai afflicted her'. The verb *afflict* (*'nh*) is a strong one, connoting harsh treatment. It characterizes, for example, the sufferings of the entire population in Egypt, the land of their bondage.[22] Ironically, here it depicts the torture of a lone Egyptian woman in Canaan, the land of her bondage to the Hebrews. Sarai afflicted Hagar.

In conceiving a child for her mistress, Hagar has seen a new reality that challenges the power structure. Her vision leads not to a softening but to an intensification of the system. In the hand of Sarai, with the consent of Abram, Hagar becomes the suffering servant, indeed the precursor of Israel's plight under Pharaoh. Yet no deity comes to deliver her from bondage and oppression; nor does she beseech one. Instead, this tortured female claims her own exodus. 'Sarai afflicted her, and so she fled (*brḥ*) from her'—even as Israel will later flee (*brḥ*) from Pharaoh (Exod 14.5a). Thus, episode one closes with Hagar taking command of her own life under the threat of Sarai.

C. Episode Two, 16.7-14. The opening of episode two plays upon this ending:

> And Sarai afflicted her.
> So she fled from her.
>
> But the messenger of the Lord found her. (16.6b-7a)

In the first and third sentences, Hagar is the direct object of verbs with different subjects. While the afflicting of her by Sarai is hostile treatment, the finding of her by the deity holds uncertain meaning. The divine action may either counter or confirm Sarai's action. If the finding counters the afflicting, then the flight of Hagar in the middle of the sequence signals a new direction that the deity enhances, encourages, and, in fact, empowers. But if the finding confirms the afflicting, then the flight of Hagar is a futile activity that the deity circumscribes, controls, and, in fact, cancels. The juxtaposition of the three sentences poses ambiguity in the development of the narrative. Resolution awaits further action by the messenger of the Lord.

Before continuing with the divine action, the storyteller provides a brief note about Hagar's location. Like Israel in years to come, this runaway pregnant maid has fled from the house of bondage to the wilderness. For her it is a hospitable place, symbolized by a spring on the way to Shur, a region at the Egyptian border.[23] There, with water to nourish life, Hagar is almost home. How different are her circumstances from Israel's exodus! When 'Moses led Israel onward from the Red Sea, and they went into the wilderness of Shur, they went three days in the wilderness and found no water' (Exod 15.22, RSV). Indeed, Moses had to ask the Lord for water. But Hagar does not cry out to any god, most especially not to Yhwh whose action in closing Sarai's womb has brought affliction to the maidservant. Nevertheless, like Moses, Hagar encounters deity after she has fled from her oppressor (cf. Exod 2.15b-16; 3.1-2).[24] The messenger of Yhwh finds her by the spring of water in the wilderness. This Egyptian maid is the first person in scripture whom such a messenger visits.[25]

Speech alone reveals the divine presence. 'Hagar, maid of Sarai, where have you come from and where are you going?' (16.8a, RSV). For the first time a character speaks to Hagar and uses her name. Thus the deity acknowledges what Sarai and Abram have not: the personhood of this woman. Yet the appositive, 'maid of Sarai', tempers the recognition, for Hagar remains a servant in the vocabulary of the divine. Rather than freeing her from a human bond of servitude, 'the messenger of the Lord' (16.7) addresses 'the maid of Sarai' (16.8). These relational identifications pose a striking contrast even as they harbor a parallel meaning. To be 'of Sarai' is to be 'of the Lord'.

'From where have you come and where are you going?' The questions embody origin and destiny. In answering, Hagar speaks for the first time. Exodus from oppression liberates her voice, though full personhood continues to elude her. Subtly, the narrator suggests this limitation by omitting her name throughout the entire episode, most particularly in the introductions to her speeches.[26] Only feminine verb forms or pronouns identify Hagar. She herself acknowledges this incompleteness of personhood in replying to the divine question, 'From where have you come?' Though she answers in the same syntactical order that the question was posed, she transforms the content of both the prepositional phrase and the verb. 'And she said, "From the face of Sarai, my mistress, I ('ānōkî) am fleeing"' (16.8b).

'From where have you come?' From a place she has not come; rather, from a person she is fleeing. Matching the messenger's designation, 'maid of Sarai', the phrase, 'Sarai my mistress', indicates the continuing power of the social structure. Exodus from oppression has not secured freedom for Hagar. She continues, however, to resist. 'I (*'ānōkî*)', she says emphatically, 'am fleeing'. This *I* stands over against the *I* (*'ānōkî*) of Sarai (16.5). Powerlessness defies power.

'Where are you going?' is the second question. Hagar seems not to answer. Or is departure her destiny? After all, the wilderness now signifies escape from oppression, nourishment of life, and revelation of the divine. But if for her departure is destiny, for the messenger of the Lord a different answer prevails. The appositives, 'maid of Sarai', and 'my mistress Sarai', indicate that the past invades the present to shape the future. Hence, wilderness is not destination but point of return. 'The messenger of the Lord' has found 'the maid of Sarai' in order to tell her where she is going. And the divine command merges origin and destiny: 'Return to your mistress, and suffer affliction under her hand' (16.9). Truly, to be 'of Sarai' is to be 'of the Lord'. Double imperatives underscore the severity. By itself the order, 'Return to your mistress', might mean reversion to the beginning when servitude existed apart from harsh treatment. But the second command negates such an interpretation: 'Suffer affliction under her hand'. The verb (*'nh*) is the same word used for Sarai's earlier abuse of Hagar (16.6b). Further, the phrase, *under her hand*, echoes Abram's reply to Sarai, 'Look, your maid is *in your hand*; do to her the good in your eyes' (16.6a).

Without doubt, these two imperatives, return and submit to suffering, bring a divine word of terror to an abused yet courageous woman. They also strike at the heart of Exodus faith. Inexplicably, the God who later, seeing (*r'h*) the suffering (*'nh*) of a slave people, comes down to deliver them *out of the hand* of the Egyptians (Exod 3.7f.) here identifies with the oppressor and orders a servant to return not only to bondage but also to affliction.[27] Thus, the ambiguity present at the beginning of this episode finds resolution in the approval of affliction. 'Sarai afflicted her' (16.6b) and 'the messenger of the Lord found her' (16.7a) are parallel in form and meaning. Surrounded by these sentences, Hagar's flight is futile.

To be sure, two promises attend the divine command to return and suffer affliction, but each is fraught with ambivalence.[28] The first assures Hagar of innumerable descendants: 'I will so greatly multiply

your descendants that they cannot be numbered for multitude'
(16.10, RSV). Though the patriarchs of Israel repeatedly hear such
words,[29] Hagar is the only woman ever to receive them, and yet this
promise to her lacks the covenant context that is so crucial to the
founding fathers.

From this assurance of innumerable descendants the focus narrows,
in the second promise, to the birth announcement of a child.[30]
Though Hagar knows that she is pregnant, the divine messenger
sanctions what has come through human machinations. The annunciation has three basic elements: the prediction of the birth of a male
child; the naming of the child; and the future life of the child.[31]

> Truly you are pregnant
>   and will bear a son.
>
> You will call his name Ishmael,
>   for Yhwh has paid heed to your affliction.
>
> He will be a wild ass of a man,
>   his hand against everyone and everyone's hand against him.
> And against the face of all his brothers he will dwell. (16.11-12, RSV*)

As the first to receive an annunciation, Hagar the Egyptian is the
prototype of special mothers in Israel.[32] Yet for her this unborn child
signifies not just comfort but also suffering. The name Ishmael ('God
hears') affirms these two meanings.[33] Although Hagar has never
cried out to God, the deity now pays heed to her past affliction ('*nh*,
16.6) by assuring her a future through the son.[34] This promise would
seem to negate Sarai's plan to be built up through Hagar.[35] Thus
hope prevails. On the other hand, the deity has already paid heed to
Hagar's affliction by ordering her to submit further ('*nh*, 16.9) to
Sarai in the present. Suffering, then, undercuts hope. For Hagar, the
divine promise of Ishmael means life at the boundary of consolation
and desolation.

The ending of this birth announcement turns from mother to son.
Concern for the male deflects interest from the female. Ishmael is to
be a wanderer and loner, in strife even with his own people. Two
words in the description, however, reflect Hagar's story: *hand* and
face. 'His hand [will be] against everyone and everyone's hand
against him' (16.12b). Such language recalls Abram's words to Sarai,
'Look now, your maid is in your *hand*' (16.6), as well as Yhwh's
orders to Hagar, 'Return to your mistress and suffer affliction under
her *hand*' (16.9). If Hagar lives under the hand of Sarai, the hand of

Ishmael will engage in ceaseless strife against such power. Indeed, 'against the face of all his brothers he will dwell' (16.12c). The word *face* builds upon his mother's action when she said, 'From the face of Sarai my mistress I am fleeing' (16.8). In Ishmael, Hagar's story continues.

Responding to these ambivalent promises from the heavenly messenger, Hagar 'calls the name of Yhwh who has spoken to her' (16.13a). The expression is striking because it connotes naming rather than invocation. In other words, Hagar does not call *upon* (bĕ) the name of the deity (cf. Gen 12.8; 13.4). Instead, she calls the name, a power attributed to no one else in all the Bible. 'She calls the name of Yhwh who has spoken to her, "You are a God of seeing"' (16.13b).[36] The maid who, after seeing (r'h) her own conception, had a new vision of her mistress Sarai (16.4), now, after receiving a divine announcement of the forthcoming birth, also sees (r'h) God with new vision.[37] Hagar is a theologian. Her naming unites the divine and human encounter: the God who sees and the God who is seen.[38]

To this name she attaches an explanation. It yields confusion, however, because the Hebrew is obscure. 'For she said, "Have I even here seen (r'h) after the one who sees (r'h) me?"' (16.13c).[39] Perhaps Hagar is questioning her own understanding of the revelation she has just received. The God who sees her remains yet unclear to her. Following this elusive comment, the narrator adds an aetiological note identifying her location as 'the well of the living one who sees me' (16.14a). Yet the connection between her words and her locale is also nebulous.[40] In the end, then, the meaning of Hagar's question remains uncertain. We know only that the maid who names the deity 'God of seeing' must return to the suffering that Yhwh imposes upon her, specifically to the mistress who is slight in her eyes. A circle of bondage encloses Hagar.

D. Conclusion, 16.15-16. Of her return and affliction under Sarai the storyteller says nothing. Instead, scene one concludes with a formulaic report of the birth of Ishmael that exalts Abram:[41]

> *And Hagar bore to ABRAM a son,*
>> and ABRAM called the name of his son,
>>> *whom Hagar bore, Ishmael.*
> Now ABRAM was eighty-six years old
>> *when Hagar bore Ishmael to ABRAM.* (16.15-16, RSV*)

The very first word of the story was Sarai (16.1); the last is Abram. The introduction sounded the negative note, 'did not bear a child to

him'. The conclusion responds with the positive word, 'bore Ishmael
to Abram'. Moving the story from a sad beginning to a happy ending
is Hagar. Yet throughout, her own story runs counter to this
movement.

Not surprisingly, then, the narrated ending continues to undermine
Hagar. First, though it restores her name, it silences her voice.
Second, it stresses not her motherhood but the fatherhood of
Abram,[42] whom the messenger of Yhwh never mentioned. Third, in
reporting that Abram named the son Ishmael, it strips Hagar of the
power that God gave her. Furthermore, the ending also undercuts
Sarai. The one who spoke of building up herself, not Abram, through
Hagar's child receives no mention at all. Neither Hagar nor Sarai but
Abram has a son whom he names Ishmael. Patriarchy is well in
control. This conclusion to a scene otherwise focused on women
resumes Abram's story.

The Way of Transition

Genesis 17.1–21.8. The resumption of Abram's story brings changes
to all the characters. No longer Abram and Sarai, the patriarch and
his wife become Abraham and Sarah (17.5, 15). Hagar disappears,
and yet her story remains. Ishmael becomes the object of divine
rejection precisely because she, not Sarah, is his mother (17.15-21).
Thus, Abraham's story continues to pivot on these two women, and
once again Sarah receives the better portion: the divine promise of
her very own son (18.1-15).[43] Yet the matriarch laughs to herself
about the possibility of bearing a child in her old age (18.12). Unlike
Hagar, Sarah is never the recipient of a birth announcement. In fact,
Yhwh speaks to her only once ever, and then with a curt reprimand
for disbelieving laughter (18.15).

Promise and delay, doubt and deception move finally to the advent
of Isaac whom Sarah bears to Abraham solely through the grace of
God (21.1-8).[44] Her response to this miraculous birth suggests that
she is indeed built up, not in herself, however, but in giving Abraham
a son:

> Who would have said to Abraham,
>   'Children Sarah will nurse'?
> Yet (*kî*) I have borne him a son
>   in his old age.[45] (21.7, RSV*)

What the culture expects of Sarah, what she has tried to accomplish through her maid, God has at last given her. Yet, rather than alleviating her trouble with Hagar, the presence of Isaac intensifies it. Hence, additional fragments of Hagar's story emerge in a second scene.

A Line to Exile

Scene Two: Genesis 21.9-21

Though similar in design to scene one, scene two discloses a more complicated plot. Ishmael and Isaac enlarge the cast of characters to bring other changes. In contrast to its parallel (16.2-6), the first episode (21.9-14a) portrays Sarah speaking less while accomplishing more; Abraham not speaking but resisting; God intervening directly; and Hagar suffering increasingly.

A. *Introduction and Episode One, 21.9-14a.* The narrator introduces the story by hinting at further tension between the two women. Sarah provokes it.

> Now Sarah saw the son of Hagar the Egyptian,
> whom she had borne to Abraham, playing.[46] (21.9, RSV*)

The description, 'the son of Hagar the Egyptian', highlights mother, not child. The phrase, 'whom she had borne to Abraham', recalls Sarai's role in making Hagar Abram's wife. And the verb see ($r'h$), which describes Sarah's activity, earlier reported Hagar's response to pregnancy: 'When she saw ($r'h$) that she had conceived, her mistress was slight in her eyes' (16.4c). Now Sarah sees the fruit of this conception. Thus, enmity persists between the Hebrew mistress and her Egyptian maid.

What the narrator suggests, Sarah's words confirm, indeed exacerbate. Constructing opposition on inequality, she commands Abraham:

> Cast out ($gr\check{s}$) this slave woman and her son,
> for the son of this slave woman will not inherit with my son,
> with Isaac. (21.10, RSV*)

The presence of Ishmael in Canaan plagues the future of Isaac, whose inheritance is threatened.[47] In her move to eliminate the danger, Sarah anticipates vocabulary and themes from the Exodus story, but with a disturbing twist. When plagues threatened the life of his first-born son, Pharaoh cast out ($gr\check{s}$) the Hebrew slaves from Egypt.[48] If Hagar, like Israel, once fled from the land of bondage, now Sarah, like Pharaoh, wants the slave cast out (*grš*) to protect the life of her first-born son. Exalting herself and Isaac, Sarah debases Hagar and Ishmael. The phrase, 'her son', without the name Ishmael,[49] counters 'my son Isaac'; and the description, 'this slave woman', rather than 'my maid' (cf. 16.2), increases distance between Hagar and Sarah.[50] Not only is the possessive pronoun *my* missing, but also a change in nouns connotes a change in status. From being a maid (*šipḥâ*) to Sarai in the first scene, Hagar has now become a slave ('*āmâ*), serving the master of the house as his second wife.[51] By contrast, Sarah, the first wife, enjoys greater power because she herself has borne a son. As the life of the mistress has prospered, the lot of the servant woman has worsened. Throughout it all, Hagar is the innocent victim, the obedient one who has given Sarah no cause for displeasure.[52]

According to the storyteller, Abraham disapproves of Sarah's order and so departs from his usual acquiescent role. His vision, however, encompasses only his son Ishmael. Hagar his wife he neglects altogether.

> The matter was very distressing (*r'*)
> in the eyes of Abraham
> on account of ('*al 'ôdōt*) his son. (21.11)

Yet his resistance but strengthens Sarah's power, for God sides with her. Consequently, the deity alters Abraham's vision:[53]

> Do not be distressed (*r'*) *in your eyes*
> on account of ('*al*) the lad
> and on account of ('*al*) your slave woman. (21.12a)

Though most of this speech repeats the narrated language, the changes merit attention. To minimize Abraham's relationship to Ishmael, God calls him 'the lad' rather than 'your son'. Moreover, the deity describes Hagar not as 'your wife' but as 'your slave woman', a description that tellingly emulates the vocabulary of Sarah (21.10). If Abraham neglected Hagar, God belittles her.

In a second imperative, the deity explicitly confirms Sarah's order: 'Everything that Sarah says to you, heed her voice' (21.12b; cf. 16.2).[54] A reason follows: 'For in Isaac will be named to you descendants' (21.12c). In the midst of Sarah's triumph, the word descendants (*zr'*) recalls Hagar's story. Long ago in the wilderness, the messenger of Yhwh said to her, 'I will greatly multiply your descendants' (*zr'*). That promise was made to Hagar alone, without reference to the father of her child (16.10). Juxtaposed, then, these two promises of progeny, first to Hagar through Ishmael and now to Abraham through Isaac, seem to allow Hagar the singular honor of being the female ancestor of a nation. This interpretation falters, however, in light of God's closing words to Abraham:

> Also (*gam*) the son of the slave woman
> a nation I will make,
> for your descendant (*zrʿ*) he is. (21.13)

The syntax of the sentence places object before verb, thereby highlighting the child of the slave woman. For Hagar herself, this apparent afterthought is devastating because it shifts descendants from her to Abraham. In various ways, then, Sarah, Abraham, God, and even Ishmael all diminish Hagar.[55]

To protect the life of her first-born, Sarah commands Abraham, 'Cast out this slave woman and her son...' (21.10a). Supporting Sarah, God orders Abraham to obey. Though these instructions foreshadow themes and vocabulary of the Exodus story, the differences are again terrifying. When Pharaoh cast out (*grš*) the Hebrew slaves to save the life of his first-born,[56] God was on their side to bring salvation from expulsion. By contrast, here the deity identifies not with the suffering slave but with her oppressors. Hagar knows banishment, not liberation.

Abraham obeys Sarah and God to become this time the active agent in the suffering of Hagar (cf. 16.3, 6). The husband expels his slave wife and the father his son, although, in reporting these events, the narrator omits the relational ties. Abraham himself does not speak, but he does give bread and water to the outcasts. Such provisions suggest a precarious future for mother and child:

> So Abraham rose early in the morning,[57]
> and took bread and a skin of water
> and gave it to Hagar, putting it on her shoulder,
> along with the child.[58] (21.14abc, RSV)

In using the name Hagar at the end of this episode, the storyteller matches the emphasis of the beginning (21.9). Abaham's last deed maintains the focus: 'He sent her [not them] away' (21.14d, RSV). Like the verb *cast out*, this one (*send*) also anticipates vocabulary from the Exodus story, yet with a disturbing twist. As the act of Pharaoh, the verb *send away* (*šlḥ*), connotes freedom for the Hebrew slaves; as the act of Abraham, it means banishment for an Egyptian slave.[59] All the talk about Hagar now results in action against her. On this negative note, episode one concludes.

B. *Episode Two, 21.14e-19.* Though in scene one Hagar fled from Sarai, this time she has no escape. She must do what Sarah, God, and Abraham impose upon her. Their command determines her exit. 'She departed' (21.14e) responds, then, to the statement, 'he sent her away' (21.14d).[60] Whereas in the Exodus traditions the verb *depart* (*hlk*), as the response to *send away* (*svlḥ*), describes what the Hebrews want to do,[61] in Hagar's story this corresponding action is what the slave woman must do. Identical words and similar themes tell opposing stories. Departing her land of bondage, Hagar knows not exodus but exile.

A second verb gives her destination: 'she wandered in the wilderness of Beersheba' (21.14f, RSV*). In reference to physical movement, the verb *wander* (*t'h*) connotes uncertainty, lack or loss of direction, and even destitution.[62] Since this word never describes the action of the Hebrews after the departure from Egypt, its use for Hagar indicates a wilderness experience different from theirs. Sent away from the land of bondage, 'she departed and wandered in the wilderness . . . ' Through the pronoun *she*, Hagar becomes the subject of active verbs for the first time in this scene. If banishment is not liberation, nevertheless, it moves her toward personhood. The movement begins episode two.

In contrast to its parallel in scene one, this wilderness episode comprises two sections. The first (21.14e-16) depicts Hagar alone with her child; no divine messenger finds her by a spring of water. In fact, unlike the region of Shur, the territory of Beersheba provides no water at all.[63] Furthermore, it does not border Egypt. Receiving Hagar in forced exile rather than voluntary flight, this wilderness is an arid and alien place. It supplies only a deathbed for the child.

> When the water in the skin was gone,
> she left[64] the child under one of the bushes. (21.15, RSV*)

Using 'the child' (*yld*) rather than 'her child' or 'her son', the storyteller suggests emotional distance that becomes physical distance:

> Then she went and sat down over against him
> a good way off, about the distance of a bowshot.[65] (21.16a, RSV)

Unlike the bush (*sěneh*) in the wilderness of Horeb (Exod 3.2), the shrub (*śiaḥ*) under which the boy lies discloses no messenger of the Lord in a flame of fire.[66] In despair, then, Hagar contemplates the imminent death of the child. It is more than she can manage. For the only time in this entire scene, she speaks,[67] though her utterance is perhaps interior thought.[68] Deepening the portrait of this woman, the words suggest suffering and isolation in the wilderness of exile. 'For she said, "Let me not see (*r'h*) the death of the child"' (21.16b, RSV*). Having once seen (*r'h*) her conception of the child and also having seen (*r'h*) the God who sanctioned that new life (16.4, 13), the mother now moves to block her vision of its demise. Like the narrator (21.15), she uses a vocabulary of distance. She speaks of 'the child' rather than of 'my child' or 'my son'. Directed to no one, these last words of Hagar surrender to death.

Hagar wept. Pointedly, the Hebrew text says, 'she lifted up her voice and she wept' (21.16c). From ancient times, however, translators have robbed this woman of her grief by changing the unambiguous feminine verb forms to masculine constructions.[69] Such alterations make the child lift up his voice and weep. But masculine emendations cannot silence Hagar. Indeed, a host of feminine verb forms throughout this section witness unmistakably to her tears: she departed and she wandered in the wilderness; she found a place for the child to die; she kept a vigil; and she uttered the dread phrase, 'the death of the child'. Now, as she sits at a distance from death, *she* lifts up her voice and *she* weeps. Her grief, like her speech, is sufficient unto itself; she does not cry out to another; she does not beseech God. A Madonna alone with her dying child, Hagar weeps.

Of the few fragments that disclose Hagar's story, only this section (21.14e-16) depicts her apart from all other major characters. Though the child is dying, the narrated focus remains steadily upon the mother: her actions, her thoughts, her words, her emotions. With one minor exception (21.15a), she is the subject of every verb. Yet her powerlessness is present in the absence of her name. Moreover, as subject she is also object, having been cast out into the wilderness. While the wilderness she chose in scene one was hospitable, yet fleeting, the wilderness imposed upon her in scene two is hostile, yet enduring. Thus this one symbol embodies for Hagar the polarities of life and death.

In time to come Israel will also experience these polarities as its triumphal flight to freedom becomes forty years of life in the wilderness. Unlike Hagar, Israel will complain; it will murmur and rebel; it will demand food and water.[70] Yet throughout, God will be on Israel's side. With Hagar, the reverse happens. God supports, even orders, her departure to the wilderness, not, however, to free her from bondage, but rather to protect the inheritance of her oppressors.

If in the first section of this episode (21.14e-16) Hagar receives major attention, in the second (21.17-19) she begins to recede as the child comes to the forefront. God makes the difference. Narrated phrases at the ending and the beginning of the two sections signal the change. Hagar 'lifted up her voice and wept' (21.16c) yields to 'God heard the voice of the lad' (21.17a). A change in vocabulary from 'the child' (*yld*) to 'the lad' (*n'r*) also indicates this transition.

Although the mother's weeping elicits divine silence, the lad's voice evokes divine speech. Rather than finding Hagar in the wilderness (cf. 16.7), this time the messenger of God speaks remotely 'from heaven'. As on the first occasion, the deity asks a question, addressing her by name: 'What troubles you, Hagar?' (21.17c, RSV). Unlike the parallel occurrence (16.8), Hagar, now the outcast rather than the fugitive, has no opportunity to reply. God continues to speak. Whereas in her exodus she answered the Lord, here in her exile she is silenced by a deity who is concerned primarily with her son: 'Fear not, for God has heard the voice of the lad where he is' (21.17d, RSV).[71] When speaking to Hagar about her own child, God never uses the noun *son* or the pronoun *your*. Instead, the deity follows the lead of the narrator by referring to Ishmael as 'the lad'. Subtly, the motherhood of Hagar is undercut.

'Fear not, for God has heard the voice of the lad where he is.' This divine word of assurance confirms the shift from Madonna to child that the narrator has introduced. In continuing, God exalts 'the lad' while making Hagar his support:

> Arise, lift up the lad
> and hold him by your hand,
> for I shall make him a great nation. (21.18, RSV*)

Unlike the revelation in scene one, this divine speech contains no promises to Hagar (cf. 16.10). After all, the promise that *her* descendants would be innumerable has already passed to Abraham (21.12-13), and through him it comes to rest on the son. Hagar decreases as Ishmael increases. Having lived under the hand of her mistress Sarai (16.6, 9), this woman must now lift up the hand of 'the lad'.

Theophanic speech resolves the plight of the outcasts. In reporting the aftermath, the narrator depicts the woman serving the child, as God has decreed:

> Then God opened her eyes
>> and she saw a well of water;
>> and she went and filled the skin with water
>> and she gave the lad a drink. (21.19, RSV)

Once more visual language attends Hagar. At the beginning of this episode, when the water in the skin was gone, she said, 'Let me not see (*r'h*) the death of the child' (21.16b, RSV*). Now, as God opens her eyes, she sees (*r'h*) a well of water,[72] fills the skin, and gives the lad a drink. Life overcomes death. Yet this language of sight also contrasts with the conclusion of Hagar's earlier sojourn in the wilderness. On that occasion she was the theologian who named Yhwh God of seeing (16.13). This time, however, her voice ceases and her vision changes. She sees not God but material resources to nourish her child in the wilderness of exile.[73] From bondage to expulsion to homelessness, scene two now brings Hagar's story to its conclusion.

C. Conclusion, 21.20-21. Years pass with Hagar serving Ishmael. At first, the narrator credits only the deity:

> And God was with the lad;
>> and he grew up and *lived in the wilderness*,
>> and he became an expert with the bow. (21.20, RSV*)

Ishmael prospers. For him the wilderness becomes home and provides work. To complete the picture, however, the storyteller turns from the providence of God to the activity of Hagar. For the last time she appears as a character in the Hebrew Bible,[74] and for the first time she is called mother. Yet Ishmael is still 'the lad', not her son. Continuing to serve, the mother finds him a wife:

> He lived in the wilderness of Paran;[75]
>> and his mother took for him a wife
>> from the land of Egypt. (21.21, RSV*)

The choice of a wife for Ishmael highlights tension in Hagar's story. Having at first promised her innumerable descendants (16.10), God later transferred that promise to Abraham. Now in her last act, Hagar guarantees that these descendants will be Egyptians.[76] Thus the mother suggests for herself a future that God has diminished. On this poignant note Hagar's story ends, but the reader's response does not.

Reflections on Hagar's Story

Belonging to a narrative that rejects her, Hagar is a fleeting yet haunting figure in scripture. To recover her story from the fragments that remain is a precarious task; nevertheless, it yields an abundance of hermeneutical reflections. In many and various ways, Hagar shapes and challenges faith.

Read in light of contemporary issues and images, her story depicts oppression in three familiar forms: nationality, class, and sex.[77] Hagar the Egyptian is a maid; Sarah the Hebrew is her mistress. Conflicts between these two women revolve around three males. At the center is Abraham, their common husband. To him belong Ishmael, child of Hagar, and Isaac, child of Sarah. Through their husband and his two sons these females clash. From the beginning, however, Hagar is powerless because God supports Sarah. Kept in her place, the slave woman is the innocent victim of use, abuse, and rejection.[78]

As a symbol of the oppressed, Hagar becomes many things to many people. Most especially, all sorts of rejected women find their stories in her.[79] She is the faithful maid exploited; the black woman used by the male and abused by the female of the ruling class;[80] the surrogate mother; the resident alien without legal recourse; the other woman; the runaway youth; the religious fleeing from affliction; the pregnant young woman alone; the expelled wife; the divorced mother with child; the shopping bag lady carrying bread and water; the homeless woman; the indigent relying upon hand-outs from the power structures human and divine; the welfare mother; and the self-effacing female whose own identity shrinks in service to others.

Besides symbolizing various kinds and conditions of people in contemporary society, Hagar is also a pivotal figure in biblical theology. She is the first person in scripture whom a divine messenger visits and the only person who dares to name the deity. Within the historical memories of Israel,[81] she is the first woman to bear a child. This conception and birth make her an extraordinary figure in the story of faith: the first woman to hear an annunciation; the only one to receive a divine promise of descendants; and the first to weep for her dying child. Truly, Hagar the Egyptian is the prototype of not only special mothers but all mothers in Israel.[82]

Beyond these many distinctions, Hagar foreshadows Israel's pilgrimage of faith through contrast. As a maid in bondage, she flees from suffering. Yet she experiences exodus without liberation; revelation without salvation; wilderness without covenant; wanderings without land; promise without fulfillment; and unmerited exile without return.[83] This Egyptian slave woman is stricken, smitten by God, and afflicted for the transgressions of Israel. She is bruised for the iniquities of Sarah and Abraham; upon her is the chastisement that makes them whole.

Hagar is Israel, from exodus to exile, yet with differences. And these differences yield terror. All we who are heirs of Sarah and Abraham, by flesh and spirit, must answer for the terror in Hagar's story. To neglect the theological challenge she presents is to falsify faith.[84]

NOTES

1. See, e.g., Bernhard W. Anderson, 'A Stylistic Study of the Priestly Creation Story', *Canon and Authority* (ed. George W. Coats and Burke O. Long; Philadelphia: Fortress Press, 1977) 148-62; idem, 'From Analysis to Synthesis: The Interpretation of Genesis 1–11', *JBL* 97 (1978) 23-39; cf. idem, 'The Problem and Promise of Commentary', *Int* 36 (1982) 356-71.

2. James Muilenburg, 'Form Criticism and Beyond', *JBL* 88 (1969) 1-18; Bernhard W. Anderson, 'The New Frontier of Rhetorical Criticism: A Tribute to James Muilenburg', *Rhetorical Criticism* (ed. Jared J. Jackson and Martin Kessler; Pittsburgh: The Pickwick Press, 1974) ix-xviii; Anderson, '"The Lord Has Created Something New": A Stylistic Study of Jer 31.15-22', *CBQ* 40 (1978) 463-78; idem, 'Tradition and Scripture in the Community of Faith', *JBL* 100 (1981) 12.

3. Unless identified otherwise, chapter and verse citations that appear hereafter belong to the book of Genesis.

4. A correct understanding of this sentence depends upon its context. The phrase, 'within the confines of partriarchal structures', sharply curtails the privilege and power of Sarah. Further, such a description is contingent upon the contrast with Hagar and tempered by the fact of Sarai's barrenness. See below.

5. I follow the biblical text in using two spellings for the names Sarai and Sarah; Abram and Abraham. On these variants, see the commentaries: e.g., Bruce Vawter, *On Genesis: A New Reading* (Garden City: Doubleday, 1977) 220, 223; E.A. Speiser, *Genesis* (AB, 1; Garden City: Doubleday, 1964) 127; Gerhard von Rad, *Genesis* (OTL; Philadelphia: Westminster, 1972) 199-200, 202. On the stigma of barrenness, see Phyllis Bird, 'Images of Women in the Old Testament', *Religion and Sexism* (ed. Rosemary Radford Ruether; New York: Simon and Schuster, 1974) 62-63.

6. See Gen 13.16; 15.4, 5.

7. Throughout this essay the word *saga* means *story*.

8. Scholarly disciplines offer different readings of these stories. (a) Historical criticism attends to source analysis. Gen 16.1-16 is J, with the exception of a few verses from P (16.1, 3, 15, 16), while Gen 21.9-21 is E. See, e.g., S.R. Driver, *The Book of Genesis* (New York: Edwin S. Gorham, 1904) 180-84, 209-13; Sean E. McEvenue, 'A Comparison of Narrative Styles in the Hagar Stories', *Semeia* 3 (1975) 64-80. For a revision of such analyses, see John Van Seters, *Abraham in History and Tradition* (New Haven: Yale University, 1975) 192-202; cf. also Alan W. Jenks, *The Elohist and North Israelite Traditions* (SBLMS, 22; Missoula: Scholars Press, 1977) 22, 67. (b) Form criticism attends to genre, oral traditions, settings in life, and literary parallels. See, e.g., Hermann Gunkel, *The Legends of Genesis* (New York: Schocken Books, 1964); idem, *Genesis* (Göttingen: Vandenhoeck & Ruprecht, 1964) 184-93, 226-33; Robert C. Culley, *Studies in the Structure of Hebrew Narrative* (Philadelphia: Fortress, 1976) 43-46; Hugh C. White, 'The Initiation Legend of Ishmael', *ZAW* 87 (1975) 267-305. White also comments on the tradition-history of the passage. Cf. Claus Westermann, *Genesis* (BKAT, 1/2; Neukirchen-Vluyn: Neukirchener Verlag, 1981) 281-82, 412-14. (c) As a development of form criticism, motif criticism attends to the identification and classification of plot-motifs and traditional episodes within the messenger stories; see Dorothy Irvin, *Mytharion* (Kevelaer: Butzon und Bercker; Neukirchen-Vluyn: Neukirchener Verlag, 1978) 1-17, 24-26. (d) Literary criticism attends to the type-scene as it moves between fixed conventions and flexible appropriations; see Robert Alter, *The Art of Biblical Narrative* (New York: Basic Books, 1981) 47-62. Literary criticism also attends to close readings focused on the particularities of the text in its final form; cf. Zvi Adar, *The Biblical Narrative* (Jerusalem: Department of Education and Culture of the World Zionist Organisation, 1959) 119-25. More than any other, this last approach shapes the present essay.

9. For a substantial bibliography, see the M.A. Thesis of Bernadette F. Revicky, '"Hagar, Maidservant of Sarai, From What Place Have You Come and Where Shall You Go?": A Rhetorical Critical Study of Genesis 16 and Genesis 21.8-21', Andover Newton Theological School (1980) 93-100.

10. Prepositional phrases side by side offer contrast and resolution. Although Sarai did not bear a child *to him* (*lô*), to her (*lāh*) was the Egyptian maid. The Egyptian identiy of Hagar recalls the earlier sojourn of Abram and Sarai in Egypt (Gen 12.10-20).

11. In Gen 16, Hagar is identified as *šiphâ*, a virgin, dependent maid who serves the mistress of the house, whereas in Gen 21 she is called *'āmâ*, a slave woman who serves the master as a second wife. The latter term is the more oppressive. See A. Jepsen, 'Ama[h] und Schiphcha[h]', *VT* 8 (1958) 293-97. To convey the distinction, I render *šiphâ* as maid, servant, or bondwoman and *'āmâ* as slave. See Hans Walter Wolff, 'Masters and Slaves', *Int* 27 (1973) 266-68; Westermann, *Genesis*, 283.

12. These are the first words of Sarai in the entire Abrahamic saga. On the

importance of such speech, see Alter, *The Art of Biblical Narrative*, 63-87.

13. Cf. Gen 30.1-13.

14. On the legalities of this arrangement, c.f., e.g., von Rad, *Genesis*, 191-92; Speiser, *Genesis*, 119-21; Vawter, *On Genesis*, 214-15; Matitiahu Tsevat, 'Hagar and the Birth of Ishmael', *The Meaning of the Book of Job and Other Biblical Studies* (New York: Ktav, 1980) 53-76. But also cf. John Van Seters, 'The Problem of Childlessness in Near Eastern Law and the Patriarchs of Israel', *JBL* 87 (1968) 401-408; Thomas L. Thompson, *The Historicity of the Patriarchal Narratives* (BZAW, 133; Berlin: Walter de Gruyter, 1974) 252-69. On this issue in the context of current research on the patriarchal narratives, see William G. Dever and W. Malcolm Clark, 'The Patriarchal Traditions', *Israelite and Judean History* (ed. John H. Hayes and J. Maxwell Miller; OTL; Philadelphia: Westminster, 1977) 70-148; M.J. Selman, 'Comparative Customs and the Patriarchal Age', *Essays on the Patriarchal Narratives* (ed. A.R. Millard and D.J. Wiseman; Winona Lake: Eisenbrauns, 1983) 91-139.

15. Drawing upon cognate languages and legal background, some scholars do render *'iššâ* here as *concubine* rather than *wife* (e.g. Speiser, *Genesis*, 116f.; Vawter, *Genesis*, 213f.). But cf. RSV; Westermann, *Genesis*, 277. The specific Hebrew word for concubine (*pilegeš*), does not appear in Hagar's story; cf. Judg 19.1.

16. Like Sarai, Abram never uses the name Hagar nor does he speak to her; only narration reports the direct contact between them (16.4; 21.14).

17. Cf. also von Rad, *Genesis*, 190-91; Vawter, *On Genesis*, 214-15; Westermann, *Genesis*, 286-87.

18. Cf. Rachel and Leah (Gen 30.1); Hannah and Peninnah (1 Sam 1.4-6). Of special interest also is the rivalry between Hebrew and Egyptian women during the Exodus period (Exod 1.19). In our story, the contrast between bonded and free, foreign and native women reverses and intensifies to oppose the fertile Egyptian maid to the barren Hebrew mistress. On such rivalry as a plot-motif, see Irvin, *Mytharion*, 15, 17.

19. Cf. Prov 30.21-23. Recall that Sarai, as well as Hagar, is a victim of patriarchy (see note 4). On infighting among oppressed groups, see Paulo Freire, *Pedagogy of the Oppressed* (New York: Continuum, 1983) 48. Cf. Rosemary Radford Ruether, *Sexism and God-Talk* (Boston: Beacon, 1983) 165-83.

20. Tsevat understands Sarai's words to constitute a legal form ('Hagar and the Birth of Ishmael', 55); cf. Westermann, *Genesis*, 287.

21. Cf. Vawter's gentle treatment of Abram over against his harsh judgment of Sarai (*On Genesis*, 215).

22. E.g. Exod 1.11, 12; Deut 26.6; cf. Gen 15.13. See David Daube, *The Exodus Pattern in the Bible* (London: Faber and Faber, 1963) 26-27.

23. On Shur, see Denis Baly and A.D. Tushingham, *Atlas of the Biblical World* (New York: The World Publishing Company, 1971) 104; J. Simons,

The Geographical and Topographical Texts of the Old Testament (Leiden: E.J. Brill, 1959) 217. Cf. Gen 20.1; 25.18; 1 Sam 15.7; 27.8.

24. Moses' flight from Pharaoh (Exod 2.15b) and Hagar's flight from Sarai employ the same verb (*brḥ*). After fleeing, Moses 'sat down by a well' (Exod 2.15c); Hagar was 'by a spring of water in the wilderness' (Gen 16.7).

25. See Martin Buber, *On the Bible* (New York: Schocken, 1968) 39. On the messenger of God, see Westermann, *Genesis*, esp. pp. 289-91. Whether or not Hagar immediately recognizes the divine messenger is uncertain; see Tsevat, 'Hagar and the Birth of Ishmael', 56f., 64.

26. Note that the direct speeches of all the other characters are repeatedly introduced by their proper names even when such identifications are unnecessary (16.2, 5, 6, 9, 10, 11). For other instances of the correlation betwen the presence of name and speech and the phenomenon of personhood, see Phyllis Trible, *God and the Rhetoric of Sexuality* (Philadelphia: Fortress, 1978) 166-70, 190.

27. Tsevat also notes affinities between this story and the Exodus tradition, but with a different interpretation ('Hagar and the Birth of Ishmael', 69).

28. Historical, form, and redactional critics tend to separate these promises by appeals to earlier forms of the text. Their conclusions are often contradictory. See, e.g., Vawter, *On Genesis*, 217; Van Seters, *Abraham in History and Tradition*, 194-95; Claus Westermann, *The Promises to the Fathers* (Philadelphia: Fortress, 1980) 12-13; Westermann, *Genesis*, 292-95; Robert Wilbur Neff, 'The Announcement in Old Testament Birth Stories' (Ph.D. dissertation, Yale University, 1969), 97-102; Tsevat, 'Hagar and the Birth of Ishmael', 57-60. My concern is with the coherence of the final form of the text.

29. E.g. Gen 15.5; 22.17; 26.4; 28.3. Note that the term 'your descendants' (*zr'*) refers not to the seed of Abram, even though he is the biological father, but rather to the offspring of Hagar; cf. Gen 3.15 where *zr'* again specifies the 'seed' of the woman rather than of the man.

30. *Contra* Van Seters who finds 16.10 incompatible with 16.11 (*Abraham in History and Tradition*, 194).

31. For a form critical analysis, see Neff, 'The Announcement in Old Testament Birth Stories', 55-69, 104-108; also Robert Wilbur Neff, 'The Annunciation in the Birth Narrative of Ishmael', *Biblical Research* 17 (1972) 51-60.

32. Of the six birth announcements studied by Neff (Gen 16.11-12; Gen 17.19; Judg 13.5, 7; 2 Kgs 13.2; 2 Chr 22.9-10; Isa 7.14-17), only two (Gen 16.11-12 and Judg 13.5, 7) are spoken directly to women (Hagar and Ms Manoah). Cf. also the Shunammite woman in 2 Kgs 4.16. Note that the prophet Elisha, not a divine figure, speaks to her. In the New Testament a birth announcement is spoken directly to Mary (Luke 1.26-38); cf. the announcement to Zechariah about Elizabeth (Luke 1.13ff.).

33. For discussions of the name Ishmael, see Mitchell Dahood, 'The Name yismā''ēl in Genesis 16,11', *Biblica* 49 (1968) 87-88; idem, 'Hebrew-Ugaritic Lexicography VII', *Biblica* 5 (1969) 350ff.; idem, 'Nomen-Omen in Genesis 16,11', *Biblica* 61 (1980) 89. Cf. Irvin, *Mytharion*, 15.

34. The theme of deliverance from the afflictions in Egypt echoes in the line, 'Yhwh has paid heed (*šm'*) to your afflictions (*'nh*)'; cf. Deut 26.7.

35. See Tsevat, 'Hagar and the Birth of Ishmael', 67.

36. The pointing of the Hebrew text allows two meanings for this declaration: the God who may be seen and the God who sees (me). Though the Greek Bible and the Vulgate choose the second, the ambiguity of the MT is perhaps desirable to retain. See John Skinner, *A Critical and Exegetical Commentary on Genesis* (ICC; Edinburgh: T. & T. Clark, 1930) 288; Speiser, *Genesis*, 118.

37. Note that her declaration of divine seeing, with its positive emphasis, occurs after the birth announcement, not after the divine command to submit to affliction. Cf. Hagar's plight with that of the Hebrew slaves who were delivered from their affliction because God saw (*r'h*) it (Exod 3.7).

38. On auditory versus visual speech in OT theophanies, see Samuel Terrien, *The Elusive Presence* (New York: Harper & Row, 1978) *passim*.

39. Cf. Speiser, *Genesis*, 117-19.

40. Attempting to connect Hagar's words with the aetiological note that follows them, Julius Wellhausen emended the text in several ways to have Hagar ask, 'Have I really seen God and yet remained alive?' (*Prolegomena to the History of Ancient Israel* [New York: The Meridian Library, 1958], 326). Cf. Skinner, *Genesis*, 288-89; Tsevat, 'Hagar and the Birth of Ishmael', 63, 66; Westermann, *Genesis*, 296-97. Though such a question has a theological base in the assertion that no person may see the deity and live (cf. Exod 33.20; Judg 6.23; 13.20-23) and also offers yet another foreshadowing of an Exodus motif in Hagar's story, nevertheless, the reading remains an emendation. Cf. H. Seebass, 'Zum Text von Gen. XVI 13B', *VT* 21 (1971) 254-56; Irvin, *Mytharion*, 16, and the references cited there; Neff, 'The Announcement in Old Testament Birth Stories', 93-94; Th. Booij, 'Hagar's Words in Genesis XVI 13B', *VT* 30 (1980) 1-7; A. Schoors, 'A Tiqqun Sopherim in Genesis XVI 13B?', *VT* 32 (1982) 494-95.

41. Note the use of repetitions with variations. They enclose the unit as well as mark emphases within it.

42. Note the possessive 'his son' as well as the repeated assertion that the child was born to Abram; cf. Gen 25.9, 12.

43. Cf. Robert Alter, 'How Convention Helps Us Read: The Case of the Bible's Annunciation Type-Scene', *Prooftexts* 3 (1983) 115-30, esp. pp. 120-21. In light of his proposed schema for the annunciation type-scene, Alter is unable to take account of the birth announcement to Hagar.

44. See Robert Wilbur Neff, 'The Birth and Election of Isaac in the Priestly Tradition', *BR* 15 (1970) 5-18.

45. Cf. Isaac Rabinowitz, 'Sarah's Wish (Gen. XXI 6-7)', *VT* 29 (1979) 362-63.

46. The Greek Bible says that he was 'playing with Isaac'. This reading has prompted different interpretations: e.g., that Ishmael was physically abusing Isaac; that the social equality implied between the two children was unacceptable to Sarah. When the phrase 'with Isaac' is omitted, other interpretations follow: e.g. that Ishmael was masturbating; that his joyous demeanor aroused Sarah's maternal jealousy (Jubilees 17.4). See the commentaries; e.g. Driver, *The Book of Genesis*, 155; Vawter, *On Genesis*, 248-49; von Rad, *Genesis*, 232; Westermann, *Genesis*, 414-15. Note that the verb *play* (*ṣḥq*) suggests a pun on the name Isaac (*yiṣḥāq*).

47. On the legalities involved, cf. Nahum M. Sarna, *Understanding Genesis* (New York: McGraw-Hill, 1966) 155-57; Thompson, *The Historicity of the Patriarchal Narratives*, 257-58.

48. Exod 12.39; cf. 6.1; 10.11; 11.1. See Daube, *The Exodus Pattern in the Bible*, 30-34.

49. The name Ishmael never occurs in scene two.

50. Another sign of the increased distance between Sarah and Hagar, in contrast to episode one of scene one (16.3), is the absence of any direct contact between them.

51. See note 11 above; also Westermann, *Genesis*, 415.

52. Cf. the comments above on 16.4.

53. Note the repeated use of the idiom 'in . . . eyes' by the narrator, Sarai, Abram, and the deity (16.4, 5, 6; 21.11).

54. Note that in 21.12-13 God also 'heeds the voice' of Sarah by emulating her vocabulary of 21.10: the use of the name *Isaac* (v. 12) and not the names *Hagar* and *Ishmael*; the use of *slave woman* (vv. 12, 13) and of *son* (v. 13). Von Rad calls vv. 12f. the '"tense moment" in the structure of the narrative' because the reader expects God to be on the side of Abraham, not of Sarah (*Genesis*, 233).

55. Note the similarities in form and content, as well as the divergences in meaning, between the opening sections of this episode (21.9-12) and the corresponding material in Gen 16.1-2: (a) Narrated introductions set up tension between the two women (16.1; 21.9). (b) With direct discourse, Sarai (Sarah) commands Abram (Abraham) to act upon Hagar. In the first imperative (16.2a), Sarai wants to obtain a son through Hagar; in the second (21.10), she wants that son, along with Hagar, sent away from her. (c) Different narrated responses by Abram yield different results. The first time he obeys Sarai (16.2b), and the episode continues without intervention by the deity. The second time (21.11) Abram balks, and so God enters to assure that Sarah's will be done (21.12).

56. See Exod 6.1, 10.11, 11.1, 12.39 for uses of the verb *cast out* (*grš*).

57. For the phrase 'rose early in the morning' as a formula to introduce a unit of action, see Irvin, *Mytharion*, 25.

58. On the syntactical problems of the Hebrew text, see Speiser, *Genesis*, 155; Vawter, *On Genesis*, 249.

59. On uses of *šlḥ* in the Exodus story, see Daube, *The Exodus Pattern in the Bible*, 29. He suggests that the banishment of Hagar by Abraham constitutes a divorce.

60. These geographical and pronominal changes indicate that a new section of the story begins with 21.14b, *contra* many translations (e.g. RSV, NEB, NAB, NJV).

61. On the pairing of *depart* (*šlḥ*) and *go* (*hlk*), see Daube, *The Exodus Pattern in the Bible*, 34; cf. pp. 58-59.

62. See, e.g., Gen 37.15; Ps 107.4; 119.176; Isa 53.6; Job 38.41.

63. On the 'wilderness of Beersheba', see the entry 'Desert' in Simons, *The Geographic and Topographical Texts of the Old Testament*, 21-23.

64. With the NJV, I translate the verb *šlk* as *left*, to distinguish it from the verb *grš* (*cast*) in 21.10; *contra* RSV.

65. The reference to 'bowshot' foreshadows the description of Ishmael as an 'expert with the bow' (21.20).

66. *Contra* Gunkel, the shrub is not a holy place (*Genesis*, 230-31). The deity speaks to Hagar explicitly 'from heaven' (21.17).

67. In both scenes Hagar speaks in the wilderness and not in the house of Abraham and Sarah.

68. On interior thought, see Alter, *The Art of Biblical Narrative*, 69-70.

69. This change appears first in the Greek Bible; cf. RSV, NAB. For attempts to justify the change, see, e.g., Skinner, *Genesis*, 248f. But cf. Speiser, *Genesis*, 155f.

70. See George W. Coats, *Rebellion in the Wilderness* (Nashville: Abingdon, 1968).

71. Cf. the play on the name Ishmael. For a form critical study of this divine speech, see Westermann, *Genesis*, 419.

72. See Westermann, *Genesis*, 420.

73. Certain themes and vocabulary suggest associations between this text and Gen 22.1-9. In both stories two sons of Abraham are under threat of death; at the crucial moment the deity intervenes to spare the children. God opens the *eyes* of Hagar; she sees (*r'h*) a well of water, and gives the lad a drink (21.19). Abraham lifts up his *eyes*, sees (*r'h*) a ram that the Lord has provided (*r'h*), and sacrifices it instead of his son (22.13-14). Note also the repeated use of phrases and words, such as 'Abraham rose early in the morning' (21.14; 22.3); 'angel of God (Lord) called to . . . from heaven' (21.17; 22.11); 'fear' (*yr'*, 21.17; 22.12), 'the lad' (21.17, 18, 20; 22.5, 12); 'hand' (21.18; 22.10, 12). Cf. Alter, *The Art of Biblical Narrative*, 181-82. Similar geographical settings may also relate these stories (see Baly and Tushingham, *Atlas of the Biblical World*, 104). For a meditation, see Arthur I. Waskow, 'The Cloudy Mirror: Ishmael and Isaac', *Godwrestling* (New York: Schocken, 1978) 23-33.

74. Though reference is made to Hagar in the genealogical list of Gen 25.12, she herself does not appear as a character.

75. On Paran, see Baly and Tushingham, *Atlas of the Biblical World*, 93, 104; Simons, *The Geographical and Topographical Texts of the Old Testament*, 22.

76. Cf. the ancient Near Eastern custom of the father securing a wife for his son (Speiser, *Genesis*, 156). Note the continuing emphasis on the Egyptian theme in the genealogical introduction of Gen 25.12 as well as in the geographical reference to Shur opposite Egypt (25.18; cf. 16.7).

77. I use the word *sex* to designate people, female and male. The word *gender* I reserve for grammar. See William Safire, 'On Language: Vox of Pop Sixpack', *The New York Times Magazine* (19 December 1982) 18-19.

78. Recent studies on the interrelationships of racism, classism, and sexism are pertinent here; cf., e.g., Rosemary Radford Ruether, *New Woman/New Earth* (New York: Seabury, 1975) 115-33; Adrienne Rich, *On Lies, Secrets, and Silence: Selected Prose 1966-1978* (New York: W.W. Norton & Co., 1979) 275-310.

79. The list that follows reflects stories of contemporary women who identify with Hagar. Cf. also Margaret Laurence, *The Stone Angel* (Toronto: McClelland and Stewart, 1968).

80. While racial ties between the ancient Egyptians and black people are problematic, cultural affinities are certain. Hagar was an African woman. On this issue in general, see Robert A. Bennett, Jr, 'Africa and the Biblical Period', *HTR* 64 (1971) 483-500.

81. By historical memories, I mean to exclude Gen 1-11.

82. See Zvi Adar, *The Biblical Narrative*, 124.

83. In light of these contrasts, note the irony of Paul's equating Hagar with the Sinai covenant (Gal 4.21-31). Cf. Walter Brueggemann, *Genesis* (Atlanta: John Knox, 1982) 184.

84. The place of Hagar in Islam also deserves mention. She does not appear in the *Qur'ān* but in the Hadiths; see Arendt Jan Wensinck, *A Handbook of Early Muhammedan Tradition* (Leiden: E.J. Brill, 1960) 90.

* * *

Throughout this essay, biblical quotations identified by RSV come from the Revised Standard Version. Alterations of this translation are indicated by an asterisk after RSV (RSV). My own translation, designed to convey Hebrew style, vocabulary, and syntax rather than felicitous English, are left unmarked.

This article is adapted from Phyllis Trible, *Text of Terror: Literary-Feminist Readings of Biblical Narratives* (Philadelphia: Fortress Press, © 1984). Used by permission.

13

THE 'LAND' IN THE PRE-EXILIC AND EARLY POST-EXILIC PROPHETS

Walther Zimmerli

The classical prophets of the pre-exilic period were the great disturbers of the peace within the world of Old Testament Israel. This was not because of any particular individual characteristics which could be attributed to them, but because they had been encountered by the reality of Israel's God. 'The lion has roared; who will not fear? The Lord Yahweh has spoken; who can but prophesy?' (Amos 3.8).[1] Thus, everything that they say is bound up either expressly or implicitly with this address of Israel's God. That applies also to their speech about the land, to which particular attention will be paid in this essay.[2]

Already the earliest of the writing prophets, Amos, makes clear that Israel recognizes that it is not indigenous to its land. The land was first given to Israel in the brightness of its early history by Israel's God. As it is expressed in the words of God, 'Yet I destroyed the Amorites before them, whose height was like the height of the cedars, and who was as strong as the oaks; I destroyed his fruit above, and his roots beneath' (2.9). Where Israel is guilty of self-confidently presuming itself to be secure behind this knowledge as a barracade of religious insurance, even though it refers to God who brought it out of the land of Egypt, there is to be heard in the mouth of God whose sovereignty extends in the same way to the nations the biting formulation: 'Are you not like the Ethiopians to me, O people of Israel . . . ? Did I not bring up Israel from the land of Egypt, and the Philistines from Caphtor and the Syrians from Kir?' (9.7).

At the same time, Amos knows of his God's close relationship with Israel: 'You only have I known of all the families of the earth'. But precisely because of this he draws the terrible consequence: 'Therefore I will punish you for all your iniquities' (3.2). This consequence has also to do with the land. The message of Amos entails that Israel will again be removed from the land. Because of this message he is denounced and expelled from the land by the high priest of the royal shrine at Bethel, with the observation: 'the land is not able to bear all his words' (7.10). While the pre-classical prophets occasionally threatened kings and their courts with divine judgment, in the case of Amos the threat is expanded with radical intensity to the entire people: Jereboam will die by the sword and Israel will be led into exile, 'away from its land' (7.17). Addressing himself directly to the priest who wants to prohibit his speaking, Amos says, 'You yourself shall die in an unclean land'. As von Rad has shown,[3] accompanying the historical component of the gift of the land, there is the cultic assessment: the land is 'Yahweh's land'. Life outside the land given to Israel is life away from the 'pure' land, i.e. the only land in which the priestly conduct of worship can be performed. Only those who are in the land are near to Yahweh, or in the realm of 'life'.[4]

The proclamation of Amos is based on knowledge of the legal demands of Israel's God. The debate about whether Amos has before him an already codified law, ultimately of amphictyonic origin, or whether he possesses a legal consciousness rooted in the clan, or whether he independently articulates a general moral knowledge of God's desire for justice, need not be taken up here. I am still inclined as before to believe that he was acquainted with a specific understanding of Israel's more ancient divine law.[5] In addition to general references to legal violations against the poor, he also offers concrete formulations: 'They lay themselves down . . . upon garments taken in pledge . . .; they drink the wine of those who have been fined'. These are intended to call to mind the older stipulations of the covenant code:

> If you lend money to any of my people with you who is poor, you shall not be to him as a creditor, and you shall not exact interest from him. If ever you take your neighbor's garment in pledge, you shall restore it to him before the sun goes down; for that is his only covering, it is his mantle for his body; in what else shall he sleep? And if he cries to me, I will hear, for I am compassionate (Exod 22.25-27).

To practice justice and righteousness is, in sum, the legal demand of God who brought Israel into its land. That is what is to be done in Israel. The most zealous worship at the holy place in the pure land is no substitute for it: 'I hate, I despise your feasts, and I take no delight in your solemn assemblies . . . Let justice roll down like waters, and righteousness like an ever-flowing stream' (5.21, 24).

His younger contemporary, Isaiah, is strongly reminiscent of Amos in his early proclamation—his attack on the cult, the wanton feasts, the women of the capital city, the violation of the rights of the underprivileged. His demand to 'Seek justice, correct oppression; defend the fatherless, plead for the widow' (1.17) is addressed to the zealous activity of the cult in Jerusalem.

However, Isaiah's talk of the land is perceptibly different from that of Amos. In the authentic words of this prophet, who speaks of the 'Holy One of Israel', one hears nothing of the exodus from Egypt or the destruction of the Amorites.[6] There is no hint of the consciousness of not being indigenous to the land. His conception of the land is shaped by his familiarity with Zion as the site of God's presence. If the formerly 'faithful city . . . full of justice' could be described in retrospect with the words, 'righteousness lodged in her' (Isa 1.21), it may be that behind the possible memory of the prosperous time of David there still echoes the pre-Israelite memory of a divinity *Ṣedeq*, whose name is preserved in the names of the pre-Israelite kings Melchizedek and Adonizedek.[7] For Isaiah, it is the early period of the righteous city, the city of *Ṣedeq*, that stands at the beginning, not the wilderness period nor the entry into the land.

Thus in the portrayal of judgment, which Isaiah proclaims no less than Amos, the destruction of the city and its surrounding territory is much more in view than the loss of land brought about by the deportation of the population. This can be seen clearly in the prophecy against Ariel, 'the city where David encamped' (29.1-8). In 5.13 there is a reference to the removal of the people, which has in view, according to the details that follow, not the loss of the land but the perishing of the noble and the humble because of hunger and thirst in the process of deportation. At the center of the call narrative stands the threat of the devastation of the land.[8]

To this corresponds what Isaiah says of salvation. In passages which differ from similar passages in other pre-exilic prophets, the view can shift unexpectedly in the middle of a judgment speech to the possibility of deliverance. Beyond refining by fire, the 'city of righteousness' stands once more, according to 1.26. He announces to the Philistine ambassadors, whose land rejoices in the hope of freedom at the death of the Assyrian king, a new invasion of destructive power from the North, but adds: 'What will one answer the messengers of the nation? "The Lord has founded Zion, and in her the afflicted of his people find refuge"' (14.32).[9] The enigmatic prophecy of salvation in 28.16-17 points in the same direction. In the midst of a threat against those in Jerusalem who consider themselves secure in their policy of alliance it states: 'See! I am placing on Zion a foundation stone, a *bōḥan* stone, a precious foundation-cornerstone. One who believes must not run in fear.'[10] This is the reconstruction of Zion. But it is true of this new structure that 'I will make justice the line, and righteousness the plummet'.[11] In Ezekiel as in Deutero-Isaiah this expectation of a new Zion as the site of God's presence is combined in a new synthesis with the expectation of a new exodus (Ezek 20.32ff.; Isa 52.7-10). Here we must mention again the Ariel prophecy where, after Ariel is lowered into the deepest dust, there is a sudden divine turn toward precisely this place, and the multitude of the enemy is scattered like chaff.[12]

'Justice and righteousness'—that was also the norm on which Amos saw his people run aground. In the case of Isaiah it can now be seen how this norm was immediately related to ownership of land. In Isaiah 5.8 he says, 'Woe to those who join house to house, who add field to field, until there is no more room, and you are made to dwell alone in the midst of the land'. Behind this cry stands a distinctive knowledge of the property laws at work in Israel. Every Israelite is entitled to his particular share of the land. In the jubilee legislation of Leviticus 25, which is probably later, the attempt is made in the 'year of release' to reinstate the arrangement which was distorted in the intervening years. In Isaiah's day this distribution of the land in accordance with the will of God was being grossly violated by the accumulation of landed estates (however the development of this state of affairs should be explained historically).[13]

It is remarkable that Isaiah's contemporary, Micah, coming from Moresheth in the territory of Judah, attacks in his prophecy precisely the same distortion in land distribution:

> Woe to those who devise wickedness and work evil upon their beds!
> When the morning dawns, they perform it, because it is in the
> power of their hand. They covet fields and seize them; and houses,
> and take them away; they oppress a man and his house, a man and
> his inheritance (Mic 2.1-2).

The key word *nḥlh*, which also appears with striking frequency in the deuteronomic sphere, shows in what the problem consists: destruction of the beneficial divine distribution of the land, attention to which is paid by Naboth, who refuses to sell the portion that belongs to his family. 'The Lord forbid that I should give you the inheritance of my fathers' (1 Kgs 21.3).

Isaiah and Micah attack unjust dealings in property. It is then instructive to note how differently the two of them speak of the divine response of punishment. In Isaiah 5.9-10 there is first the destruction of the houses of the great landowners who perpetrated the injustice. Next appears the refusal of the land to provide an adequate harvest. In the case of Micah the allusion to the division of the land within the *qhl Yhwh* is more concrete. Unfortunately, the text in 2.4-5 is not intact. Alt finds here a new *anadasmos gēs*, in which the landownders no longer have anyone who can cast the measuring line to determine an allotment for them, while the oppressed will again receive their lost portion.[14] Wolff, on the other hand, understands the statement more generally to mean that 'a sacral distribution of the lost property for the benefit of the dispossessed is no longer to be expected'.[15] The present text, which he regards as containing secondary expansions, refers in any case to the exile which deprives the entire people of the land.

If with Isaiah the emphasis falls on Jerusalem and the complete absence in Israel's history of a basis for possession of the land, then Hosea, the only prophet actually from the northern kingdom, stands most clearly in opposition to this view. In his prophecy there is no mention of Jerusalem-Zion. None of the sanctuaries of the northern kingdom mentioned by him has a central status corresponding to that of Jerusalem for Isaiah. Instead, the traditions of Egyptian origin, wandering in the wilderness and Israel's conquest emerge as the most important. Knowledge of the land as God's gift receives from Hosea a fundamentally critical significance. Admittedly one does not recognize in his words the social demand for just property laws observed in Isaiah and Micah. The social component of prophetic criticism is not completely lacking in Hosea, but it does recede perceptibly. On the other hand, emphasis falls on the polemic against the common belief that the gifts of the land—grain, wine and oil—are from the local baals, or at least from Yahweh worshipped in a baalized form. For that reason Hosea offers a passionate indictment of the priests in ch. 4. They were supposed to be the guardians of genuine knowledge of Israel's God. To the contrary, they had led the nation into vegetation worship with its form of cultic prostitution. 'The men themselves go aside with harlots, and sacrifice with cult prostitutes, and a people without understanding shall come to ruin' (4.14).

The significance of the land comes to light not only in this critique, however. It leads to the formulation of a specific theology of history, encompassing the past and the future, which had its effect on Jeremiah and was radically expanded by Ezekiel. Thus Hosea speaks of the call of Israel out of Egypt, the bright period of wandering through the arid wilderness, and the fall into sin, which occurred in the entry into the rich and fertile land.

> Like grapes in the wilderness, I found Israel. Like the first fruit on the fig tree . . . I saw your fathers. But they came to Baal-peor and consecrated themselves to Baal, and became detestable like the thing they loved [as their lover?] (9.10).

> It was I who knew you in the wilderness, in the land of drought; but when they had fed to the full, they were filled, and their heart was lifted up; therefore they forgot me (13.5-6).

Corresponding to this early history rooted in Egypt is the history of judgment into which God will lead his people. He brings them back precisely to the beginning: 'they shall return to Egypt' (8.13; 9.3). Considering the immediate threat of Assyria, which already in Hosea's day had broken into Israel's neighboring territory, the Assyrians are suited to this purpose. 'They shall not remain in the land of Yahweh; but Ephraim shall return to Egypt, and they shall eat unclean food in Assyria' (9.4) [literally: those who eat shall make themselves unclean; cf. Amos 7.17]. Assyria can be seen as the climax of the threat. If the division of the text in 9.6 is correct, it reads: 'For behold, they are going to Assyria; Egypt shall gather them, Memphis shall bury them' (see also ch. 11). But then Hosea can also simply speak of God's judgment forcing his people back into the wilderness period: 'I, Yahweh, am your God from the land of Egypt; I will again make you dwell in tents, as in the days of the feast [of tabernacles?] (12.9 [MT 12.10]).[16] But God's intention to judge is most completely interwoven with his intention to be gracious in 2.14-15a (MT 2.16-17a): 'Therefore, behold, I will allure her, and bring her into the wilderness, and speak tenderly to her. And there I will give her her vineyards, and make the valley of Achor a door of hope.' The land with its precious produce will again be given to a people returned to its God. Thus the return of the land is also part of the expectation of salvation by the prophet who himself may have experienced the terrible catastrophe of Israel/Ephraim under the attack of Assyria.

Jeremiah and Ezekiel, whose reference to the land will be examined further, belong to the period of the late seventh and early sixth centuries. In the East the Babylonians had displaced the Assyrians.

Of the 'two houses of Israel' of which Isaiah spoke (8.14) the smaller—Judah, which now applied the designation of God's people, Israel, to itself—still existed and preserved the treasures of the Jerusalem temple and the Davidic dynasty.[17] As a result of the politics of the reform-minded king Josiah, who took over the political vacuum left in the province of Samaria when Assyria's power was broken, the hope for reunification flamed anew. Traces of this hope can be recognized in Jeremiah and Ezekiel (Jer 3.6ff.; 30–31; Ezek 37.15ff.).

Jeremiah's pronouncements about the land have been more precisely investigated by P. Diepold in his Göttingen dissertation, 'Israels Land' (1972). It must be recognized that the book of Jeremiah stands firmly in the Deuteronomistic stream of tradition and has been expanded and revised by that tradition. W. Thiel, whose analysis Diepold takes over, has pursued this problem.[18] Here, where it is a matter of the prophet's stance toward the land, I can restrict myself to those pronouncements which in all likelihood stem from Jeremiah himself.

With respect to his theology of history and its bearing on his evaluation of the possession of the land, Jeremiah is dependent upon Hosea, as has already been mentioned. Though not with the emphasis of Hosea, he speaks of deliverance from Egypt (2.6) and, much more colorfully, of the divine guidance through the wilderness, 'in a land of deserts and pits, in a land of drought and deep darkness, in a land that none passes through, where no man dwells', into 'a plentiful land, to enjoy its fruits and its good things' (2.7). As in Hosea the time when 'you followed me in the wilderness, in a land not sown' is seen as the shining period of the first 'love as a bride' (2.2), which is then followed in the land by the time of unfaithfulness: 'But when you came in you defiled my land, and made my heritage an abomination' (2.7). 'My land' it is called here in the mouth of God. The land is often spoken of in precisely this personal way (Diepold). It is pictured in expressions of highest praise: a desirable land, a 'heritage most beauteous (*ṣĕbî ṣib'ôt*) of all nations', as it is expressly designated in 3.19—a designation which recurs in Ezekiel 20.6, and is used as a secret code name for the land in Daniel (8.9; 11.16, 41, 45). Yahweh designates his land as 'my heritage'. The frequent use of the designation 'my heritage' already marks it as characteristic of Jeremiah's speech. And it is in the use of this designation to refer almost indistinguishably to the land and to the people that the close connection between this, God's land, and the people called by God is recognized. In the cultic defilement of God's land Israel encroaches upon God's own possession and compels him to pass judgment on people and land.

> I have forsaken my house, I have abandoned my heritage; I have given the beloved of my soul into the hands of her enemies. My heritage has become to me like a lion in the forest, she has lifted up her voice against me; therefore I hate her ... Many shepherds have destroyed my vineyard, they have trampled down my portion ... The whole land is made desolate (12.7-11).

In his view of the future Jeremiah no longer stands in the footsteps of Hosea. In his case nothing can be seen of a new leading into the wilderness or a return to Egypt from which Israel will again come into possession of its land. The land will suffer devastation. Nebuchadnezzar, called by God 'my servant', is summoned to execute punishment. The nation is to acknowledge him, so long as God gives him power. To the deportees in Babylon Jeremiah writes that they are to build houses there and live in them, to plant gardens and eat their fruit, to take wives and bear sons and daughters, to give their sons wives and their daughters husbands, who will then themselves bear children so that they will multiply and not become fewer. They are to seek the welfare of the city (Greek: of the land) to which they have been deported, and to pray for it, 'for in its welfare you will find your welfare' (29.7). Only in a completely hidden way can the prospect of a further future in the land be recognized in that peculiar, yet unmistakably authentic episode in which Jeremiah, in the midst of the invasion of Jerusalem at the command of his God buys a field outside Anathoth which is already occupied by the enemy and carefully concludes the purchase legally with a public and private bill of sale. 'Houses and fields will again be bought in this land' (32.15). The word concerning a seventy-year period of punishment (25.11-12; 29.10) cannot convincingly be denied Jeremiah. Is the reluctance of Jeremiah to abandon the land for Egypt, together with an anxious group of those left behind following the murder of Gedaliah, also to be understood on the basis of that certainty that there would once again be life in the devastated land? According to the symbolic interpretation of the two baskets of figs in Jeremiah 24, of course, the hope for the future lies in the first instance with those who suffer judgment in exile. The great promise of the new covenant in 31.31-34, which speaks of God's gift of a new posture toward the

Torah but says nothing of the possession of the land, is probably not to be attributed to Jeremiah. To draw conclusions about Jeremiah's hope for the future after 587 on the basis of those parts of the so-called 'book of consolation for Ephraim' (or from 3.6ff.) which are currently held to be authentic is (contra Diepold) hardly advisable.

In the book of the somewhat younger priestly prophet Ezekiel, already deported in 597, it is first of all linguistically striking that alongside the infrequent designation *'ereṣ yiśrā'ēl* is found the more frequent designation *'admat yiśrā'ēl*. Both expressions refer to the remainder of Israel in Judah under the theologically important, overarching name Israel. Bernard Keller[19] has undertaken the attempt to discern a conscious differentiation in this duality.

> Erets Israel is formerly the combination of adamah, the earth; of the people and of the divine presence; the glory of YHWH. Admat Israel is simply the earth which bears the mark of the absence of the people and of the glory.

The second part of the book speaks of the return of the people and of the glory of Yahweh. 'Admat Israel gives way to the erets Israel, the reunion of earth, of the people and of the divine presence' (p. 490). However, the differentiation cannot be sustained upon closer examination.[20] No theological conclusions can be drawn from the dual formulation. The specifically Ezekielian designation is *'admat yiśrā'ēl*.

Ezekiel lived in the time of the great crisis, during which parts of the population of Judah were taken into Babylonian exile in two or, according to Jeremiah 52.28-30, three groups. Among the surrounding nations the saying dishonoring the God of Israel circulated: 'These are the people of Yahweh, and yet they had to go out of his land' (36.20). Speaking directly to the land, understood by Jeremiah in almost human terms, the enemies say, 'You devour people, and you bereave your nation of children' (36.13). This formulation is strikingly similar to the evil report which the spies brought back following their reconnaissance of the land, a report which brought punishment upon the entire nation: 'The land, through which we have gone, to spy it out, is a land that devours its inhabitants' (Num 13.32).

In his severely accusatory proclamation prior to 587, Ezekiel had attributed the cause for the punishment not to the land but to the nation Israel and to Jerusalem. In both of the historical-theological summaries in chs. 16 and 23, in which Jerusalem and then the two kingdoms of Israel are pictured as abandoned women, wanton from the beginning (according to ch. 23, already in Egypt), their histories unfolded with expansive imagery, neither the land nor the conquest of the land is mentioned. Canaanizing sexual cults (in Hosea's sense) and political alliances (in Isaiah's sense) are here the grounds for the consequent judgment in 587, which provoked ridicule from neighbors and vilification of the land from elements of the population. But in Ezekiel's words, discussion of possession of the land now commences in new ways.

From other reports we know that the neighboring Edomites participated in the destruction of Jerusalem. They were themselves perhaps forced from the East by the pressure from Nabataean groups, and thrust into the land from the South. In Ezekiel 35.10 the undisguised claim to the land in the mouth of the Edomites is reported: 'These two nations and these two countries shall be mine, and we will take possession of them', and the text adds, 'although Yahweh was there'. And in a prophecy of salvation directed to the mountains of Israel, which corresponds to a prophecy of judgment against the same addressees in ch. 6 and renders it ineffective, the prophet says: 'But you, O mountains of Israel, shall shoot forth your branches, and yield your fruit to my people Israel; for they will soon come home' (36.8). For the sake of his own honor, the God of Israel remains true to his promises. This is developed in the historical-theological speech in Ezekiel 20, which is composed without use of imagery.

> On the day when I chose Israel, I swore to the seed of the house of Jacob, making myself known to them in the land of Egypt, I swore to them, saying, I am Yahweh your God. On that day I swore to them that I would bring them out of the land of Egypt into a land that I had searched out for them, a land flowing with milk and honey, the most glorious (ṣēbî) of all lands (20.5-6).

Not to Edom, but to Israel has the land been promised. The divine message of the prophet maintains persistently, whether the stiff-necked rebelliousness of the people is portrayed for the first time in Egypt and then also in the wilderness or is told in an unprecedented redescription of history, that already in the wilderness period God had decided to scatter his people among the 'lands'. But after the catastrophe, the vision of the valley of dry bones proclaims God's message: 'Behold, I will open your graves, and raise you from your graves [as my people] in the land of Israel' (37.12).[21] The expansion in 20.32ff., coming probably after 587, and taking up in revised form

Hosea 2, shows how the nation will be led out in a new exodus from
the nations into 'the wilderness of the peoples' (20.35). In a new 'face
to face' encounter God will carry out the division. The rebels will not
be permitted to enter the land again, but the rest will bring offerings
pleasing to God 'on the mountain height of Israel' (again an
Ezekielian expression). Contrary to Hosea 2, there is no mention of
the renewed bestowal of vineyards. That is the decision of Israel's
God over against any other nation that would attempt to lay claim to
possession of the land.

However, the division in the wilderness makes clear that, with
reference to possession of the land, new divisions are announced
which cut through the midst of the nation itself. More can be seen of
this in other parts of Ezekiel. The pericope in 11.14–21 speaks to the
situation between 597 and 587, however one judges the literary-
critical problems.[22] Here something is heard from those remaining
in Jerusalem about the deportees: 'They have gone far from Yahweh;
to us this land is given for a possession' (11.14). This claim to
possession is answered with a word from God, which promises that
the deportees will return and will be given a new heart and a new
Spirit, 'that they may walk in my statutes and keep my ordinances'
(11.20).

This is formulated even more sharply against those remaining in
the land after 587: 'Son of man, the inhabitants of these waste places
in the land of Israel keep saying, "Abraham was only one man, yet he
got possession of the land; but we are many; the land is surely given
us to possess"' (33.24). In response to this apparently pious recourse
to the ancient promise of land to the patriarch Abraham, which here
appears for the first time among the writing prophets (Isa 29.22; Mic
7.20; Jer 33.26 belong to post-exilic expansions) follows the blunt
repudiation:

> Thus says the Lord Yahweh: You eat flesh with the blood, and lift
> up your eyes to your idols, and shed blood; shall you then possess
> the land? You resort to the sword, you commit abominations and
> each of you defiles his neighbor's wife; shall you then possess the
> land? (33.25-26).

Here the point is developed polemically that possession of the land
and disobedience toward God's commandment are mutually exclusive.
In the concrete unfolding of the commandment we recognize the
priest, who has the ritual prescriptions for purity before him. But
there are also reminders of Amos: the shedding of blood, social

injustice; and of Isaiah: reliance on their own strong arm, and trust in power.

Concluding the book of Ezekiel is the great vision of the new temple to be erected according to the appropriate measurements. The vision is dated in the twenty-fifth year[23] and includes a sketch of a new distribution of the land with precise geographical limits bounded by the Jordan. Following the settlement of the land comes the new distribution, according to specific allotments (47.13-14)—a new Joshua event. The text displays a remarkable mixture of archaizing elements joined to earlier traditions and the bold placement of new accents. The use of the old tribal system is archaizing. In the arrangement of tribal territories, every tribe (Joseph is spread across Manasseh and Ephraim) receives a strip of land of equal size. This arrangement takes up old geographical traditions but in places revises them radically. It is expressly prescribed that also the resident aliens (*gērîm*) shall be given the right of residence and property among the respective tribal territories (47.22-23). Approximately in the middle (the distribution of seven tribes in the North and five in the South is further reminiscent of the earlier reality of the northern tribes' greater importance) there lies a thirteenth strip of land, proportioned as the rest, which is named a *tĕrûmâ* ('lifted up'), the term used of what is offered in sacrifices. The land is lifted up as a sacrifice offered to God. At its two outer boundaries lies the land of the prince. At the center is the region containing the temple, in land reserved for the priests. North of it is the region of the Levites, and south of it is the region for the city. The divine instruction, which stands over everything as Torah, is not to be ignored: the sharp separation of the most holy, in which Yahweh dwells, from that which is less holy, and the latter from that which is profane. In addition, there is the appropriate distribution of the profane. But all of it is distinguished by that which is 'lifted up' in the midst of it, the offering through which the giver of the land is honored.

That is how the attempt is made in this utopian sketch to fashion the land of Israel obediently in relation to the concrete geographical boundaries previously set out. There is no possession of the land without attention to the just arrangement of it, which gives honor to the Lord of the land and provides to every part of the nation including the *gērîm* living in the land, its proper portion.

I may be permitted to conclude by citing the observation of Moses Hess from the last century, an observation which, using different terms, comes particularly close to the prophetic view. He says,

> The first commandment of God that he has implanted in our
> hearts as the creator of all the races, the source and basic principle
> of all the others which have fallen to the lot of our people is that we
> are ourselves to practice the law which we are commissioned to
> t^ach the other historical peoples. The greatest punishment that
> has been inflicted on us for deviating from the path traced out for
> us by divine providence, that which has always oppressed our
> people the most, is that, since we have lost the land (*la terre*), we
> can no longer serve God as a nation through institutions which
> cannot be continued and developed in our present exile, since they
> presuppose a society founded in the land of our ancestors. Yes, it is
> the land (*la terre*) that we lack, in order to practice our religion.[24]

NOTES

1   Editor's note: Unless otherwise indicated, all transactions from the
Old Testament follow the RSV.

2.   The following contribution, offered as a tribute to Professor Bernhard
W. Anderson, was first presented at a symposium between the Hebrew
University of Jerusalem and the University of Göttingen, held in Jerusalem
in September 1981. The collected essays on the topic of 'Israel's Land' are to
be published by Vandenhoeck & Ruprecht.

3.   Gerhard von Rad, 'Verheissenes Land und Jahwes Land im Hexateuch',
ZDPV 66 (1943) 191-204; reprinted in *Gesammelte Studien zum Alten
Testament* (TBü, 8; München: Chr. Kaiser, 1958) 87-100; ET, 'The Promised
Land and Yahweh's Land in the Hexateuch', *The Problem of the Hexateuch
and Other Essays* (New York: McGraw Hill, 1966) 79-93.

4.   On the relation of cult and 'life' see Gerhard von Rad, '"Gerechtigkeit"
und "Leben" in der Kultsprache der Psalmen', *Festschrift für Alfred
Bertholet* (ed. Walter Baumgartner; Tübingen: Mohr, 1950) 418-37; reprinted
in *Gesammelte Studien*, 225-37; ET, '"Righteousness" and "Life" in the
Cultic Language of the Psalms', *Problem of the Hexateuch*, 243-66.

5.   For the basis of Amos's proclamation see my 'Das Gottesrecht bei den
Propheten Amos, Hosea und Jesaja', *Werden und Wirken des Alten
Testaments: Festschrift für Claus Westermann* (ed. Rainer Albertz; Göttingen:
Vandenhoeck & Ruprecht and Neukirchen-Vluyn: Neukirchener Verlag,
1980) 216-35. Also see R. Bach, 'Gottesrecht und weltliches Recht in der
Verkündigung des Propheten Amos', *Festschrift für Günther Dehn* (ed.
Wilhelm Schneemelcher; Neukirchen: Neukirchener Verlag, 1957), 23-34.

6.   Isa 10.24, 26; 17.9 are not authentic words of Isaiah and are later in
origin.

7.   Hans H. Schmid, *Gerechtigkeit als Weltordnung* (BHT, 40; Tübingen:
Mohr, 1968) 74-77.

8. The 'and removes far away' (*wĕriḥaq*) of 6.12 belongs to a subsequent expansion and may represent a 'relecture' under the impact of the event of 587. See J. Vermeylen, *Du prophète Isaïe à l'apocalyptique I* (Paris: Gabalada, 1977) 195f. Cf. also W. Dietrich, *Jesaja und die Politik* (BEvT, 74; München: Chr. Kaiser, 1976) 178, who wants to transpose vv. 12f. before v. 11 and to see in vv. 12f. an original textual element which, under the impact of the event of 701, would have been added to vv. 9b-10 changing the original sequel of verses. That, however, is hardly convincing.

9. Dietrich, *Jesaja und die Politik*, sees as a later composition the whole of Isa 14.28-32. Vollmer, *Geschichtliche Rückblicke und Motive in der Prophetie des Amos, Hosea und Jesaja* (BZAW, 119; Berlin: de Gruyter, 1971), finds in the answer to the messengers an awkward imitation of Isa 28.16. Vermeylen, *Du prophète Isaïe à l'apocalyptique I*, 301f., concludes that a 'remaniement' of a post-exilic redactor can be recognized behind the original Isaianic text by the exclusion of the 'poor'.

10. Editor's note: The author's translation.

11. Vermeylen (*Du prophète Isaïe à l'apocalyptique I*, 392-95) finds in vv. 16aβb-17a an addition which stems from the circle of pious Jews of the second temple (a view followed in many commentaries) while Dietrich (*Jesaja und die Politik*, 164-68) wants to retain at least v. 17a as original. Cf., however, Hans Wildberger, *Jesaja* (BKAT, 10/3; Neukirchen-Vluyn: Neukirchener Verlag, 1981) 1069f., 1075-77.

12. With Wildberger (*Jesaja*) I wish to find in Isa 29.1-7 the original Isaianic text, against Vermeylen (*Du prophète Isaïe à l'apocalyptique I*, 401-403) who confines it to Isa 29.1-4 and against Dietrich (*Jesaja und die Politik*, 188) who, with the most radical *Forschungsmeinung*, confines it to Isa 29.1-4a.

13. H. Donner ('Die soziale Botschaft der Propheten im Lichte der Gesellschaftsordnung Israels', *Or Ant* 2 [1963] 229-45) thinks along the lines of A. Alt ('Der Anteil des Königtums an der sozialen Entwicklung in den Reichen Israel und Juda', *Kleine Schriften III* [München: Beck, 1959] 348-72) of a negative result of the feudal system; and H. Bardtke ('Die Latifundien in Juda während der 2. Hälfte des 8. Jahr.', *Hommage à A. Dupont-Sommer* [Montpellier: Univ. Paul-Valéry, 1971] 235-54) of a surplus *of money which fugitives from the catastrophe of the northern empire brought to Judah and invested in property.*

14. A. Alt, 'Micha 2,1-5 ΓΗΣ ΑΝΑΔΑΣΜΟΣ IN Juda', *Interpretationes ad Vetus Testamentum pertinentes Sigmundo Mowinckel septuagenario* (Oslo: Lund og Kirche, 1955) 13-23; reprinted in *Kleine Schriften III*, 373-81.

15. H.W. Wolff, *Dodekapropheton 4: Micha* (BKAT, 14/4; Neukirchen-Vluyn: Neukirchener Verlag, 1982) 50.

16. H.W. Wolff, *Dodekapropheton I: Hosea* (BKAT, 14/1, 2; Neukirchen-Vluyn: Neukirchener Verlag, 1965 [ET: *Hosea* [Hermeneia; Philadelphia: Fortress, 1974]) 207 translates 'as in the days of meeting'. H.-J. Kraus,

Gottesdienst in Israel (München: Chr. Kaiser, 1962) 156 (ET: *Worship in Israel* [Richmond: John Knox, 1966] 32) postulates a 'tent festival' which lived on in the Feast of Tabernacles.

17. L. Rost, *Israel bei den Propheten* (BWANT, 4; Stuttgart: Kohlhammer, 1937). W. Zimmerli, 'Israel im Buche Ezechiel', *VT* 8 (1958) 75-90.

18. W. Thiel, *Die deuteronomistische Redaktion von Jeremia 1–25* (WMANT, 41; Neukirchen-Vluyn: Neukirchener Verlag, 1973); and *Die deuteronomistische Redaktion von Jeremia 26–45* (WMANT, 52; Neukirchen-Vluyn: Neukirchener Verlag, 1981).

19. B. Keller, 'La terre dans le livre d'Ezekiel', *RHPR* 55 (1975) 481-90.

20. All three examples for *'ereṣ yiśrā'ēl* occur in the second half of the book. However, Ezek 27.17 is part of the context of a prosaic list of trading partners and wares, originating perhaps from a trading post of Tyre, which has been inserted only later into the song of lament in the qinah-meter of Ezekiel. Ezek 40.2 stands in a context in which the return of the glory of God is for the first time imminent. And Ezek 47.18 stands in a record of the boundary of the land to be newly apportioned, which has a remarkably close parallel in Num 34.3-12 and may on no account be interpreted apart from it if the specific theological postion of Ezekiel is to be understood. Cf. for the particulars my *Ezechiel* (BKAT, 13) 654, 997, 1216. On the other hand the seventeen examples for *'admat yiśrā'ēl* are spread freely over both parts of the book without the special connotation maintained by Keller having been brought to expression in them.

21. The use of the image of the opened graves for the interpretation of the figure of the revived bones of the dead does not justify the separation of 37.11-14 from 37.1-10 as in D. Baltzer, *Ezechiel und Deuterojesaja* (BZAW, 121; Berlin: de Gruyter, 1971) 100-18 and in P. Höffken, 'Beobachtungen zu Ez 37,1-10', *VT* 31 (1981) 305-17.

22. Against H. Brownlee who sees in Ezekiel a person who, like Jeremiah, remained chiefly in the land in 587. He maintains that 11.14ff. is contemporaneous with 33.24-26 and judges the present arrangement of the book as a result of a complicated process of redaction. See 'The Aftermath of the Fall of Judah according to Ezekiel', *JBL* 89 (1970) 393-404, and 'Ezekiel's Parable of the Watchman', *VT* 28 (1978) 393-408.

23. If my supposition that the striking predominance of the number 25 in the description of the new temple is connected with the twenty-fifth year as the mid-point of the year of release in which, according to Lev 25, not only slaves obtained their freedom but also alienated land reverted to its previous owner, then 'the land' plays an important, unnoticed role in connection with dating. See my 'Das "Gnadenjahr des Herrn"', *Archäologie und Altes Testament: zum 70. Geburtstag K. Galling* (ed. Arnulf Kuschke; Tübingen: Mohr, 1970) 321-32; reprinted in *Studien zur alttestamentlichen Theologie und Prophetie* (TBü, 51; München: Chr. Kaiser, 1974) 222-34.

24. Cited according to Martin Buber, *Israel und Palästina: Zur Geschichte einer Idee* (Zürich: Artemis-Verlag, 1950) 149-50; ET: *On Zion: The History of an Idea* (New York: Schocken, 1973) 118.

PART IV

APPROPRIATING THE WORD

14

BARTH AND BLOCH ON JOB:
A CONFLICT OF INTERPRETATIONS

Daniel L. Migliore

In his presidential address to the centennial meeting of the Society of Biblical Literature in 1980, Bernhard W. Anderson identifies a 'major debate' in current biblical interpretation. The central issue of this debate, he writes, is 'whether primary theological emphasis should be placed on the tradition *process* or on the final *result* of the process, scripture'.[1]

Anderson has no doubt that 'the final text deserves a place of theological privilege'. It is, after all, this form of the text that has functioned as norm in the community of faith, both synagogue and church, throughout the centuries to the present. Anderson rightly faults much biblical scholarship in the past as having been 'too atomistic, too analytical, and not concerned enough with the unity and totality of scriptural units or canonical books'.[2] When biblical study no longer seeks to illuminate the final text, it quickly moves into the realm of 'uncertainty and hypothesis'.

At the same time, Anderson cautions against absolutizing the final form of the process of tradition. He advances two arguments in favor of taking seriously the process of tradition as well as the final form of the text. First, the text has historical character: it 'pulses with the life of a people' and contains a pluriform rather than a uniform witness.

> It is important, therefore, to engage in ear training, by whatever methods available, so that we may hear the various theological voices that constitute the choir of the final text. These choral voices may not always be in harmony; in fact, there may be dissonance (contradiction), but all of them should be heard if we are to listen to the witness of the text.[3]

And second, while later stages of the tradition may represent an advance over earlier stages, it is also possible that the later stages could 'blur, obscure or reverse the theological perception of an earlier stage'.[4]

The debate which Anderson summarizes so clearly is by no means confined to specialists in biblical exegesis. A remarkable example of the divergent hermeneutical emphases on the process of tradition on the one hand and on the final scriptural text on the other is found in the conflicting interpretations of the Book of Job by the neo-Marxist philosopher, Ernst Bloch, and the church theologian, Karl Barth.[5] Bloch's idiosyncratic version of the history of traditions approach results in a brilliant humanistic reduction of the witness of the text. Abandoning the search for the meaning of the text in its final canonical form, Bloch's interpretation is controlled by his philosophical presuppositions, viz. that utopian hope is the motor of history and that the human aspiration for freedom and justice requires the negation and transcendence of all arbitrary and oppressive power, including and especially the power called God. By contrast, Barth insists on ascertaining the meaning of the Book of Job as scripture in its unity and totality without suppressing its real diversity and inner tension. Although the issue of freedom is as central for Barth as it is for Bloch, in Barth's view the concrete storied depiction of both the freedom of God and the freedom of Job is the key to a right understanding of the book. Barth's interpretation is both penetrating and inclusive, but the question remains whether he has allowed the diversity of voices within the canonical choir to be fully heard.

I

In *Atheism in Christianity* Ernst Bloch argues that biblical messianism is the source of dynamic, revolutionary atheism.[6] This thesis is intended to cut two ways: against a conformist bourgeois theism on the one hand and against a rationalistic, bureaucratic Marxism on the other.

Proper biblical criticism for Bloch is 'detective work', the discovery in the Bible of the voices of those who refuse to accept their suffering and bondage as necessary. He contends that while texts can be improved by later expansion and revision, they can also be reworked in such a way that disturbing elements are suppressed or falsified. 'All the more important, in that case, to dig for, and catch the sound of, the other voice underneath.'[7]

Bloch is deeply suspicious of the biblical text in its canonical form. He postulates that a theocratic revisionary process of tradition occurred during the time of Ezra and Nehemiah. This theocratic theology stood 'in opposition to all prophetic notions about exodus from Pharaoh, even in the concept of Yahweh'. In the interests of the ruling class, a pious distortion of all 'subversive passages' took place. It is the task of detective biblical criticism to expose this distortion by asking the *cui bono* question. While the question of whose interests are being served is relevant in all literary and historical criticism, this question has been largely ignored in biblical criticism. 'Biblical criticism needs the broadening that will come from continually tracking down the interestingly different, rebelliously different readings in the available text.'[8]

According to Bloch, 'the Bible has always been the church's bad conscience'.[9] That is because there is a 'murmuring' in the Bible, a protesting against injustice, poverty and oppression, a dreaming of a new form of life which overcomes national and class alienation. There is, in other words, an underground Bible which is far removed from the social conformism and repressiveness of the 'hard-baked ecclesiastical, canonical redaction'. The Bible of the poor (*Biblia pauperum*) fights against every Baal, tries to overthrow 'every state of affairs in which man appears as oppressed, despised and forgotten in his very being'.[10] Consequently, Bloch argues that the watchword of biblical criticism should be not 'de-mythologization' but 'de-theocratization'. Through biblical criticism as detective work 'it is possible to see more acutely than ever that there are in fact two Scriptures: a Scripture for the people and a Scripture against the people'.[11]

In Bloch's view, among the subversive passages of Scripture—which include the stories of the serpent of Paradise, the tower of Babel, Jacob's struggle with the angel, the exodus from Egypt, and God's becoming human—is the Book of Job. The murmuring of the children of Israel reaches a highpoint in this book. With good reason it was always considered dangerous by the guardians of orthodoxy.

Bloch's detective criticism of Job makes several claims. First, the Job of the poetic dialogue is radically different from the Job of the prose framework. In the dialogue (an innovative literary form within Israel, Bloch notes) Yahweh is openly attacked. Why does God remain silent and aloof while the wicked grow mighty in power and the poor go hungry? For Bloch Job's indictment against God represents a breakthrough in religious consciousness. While the prophets before Job had attacked injustice, now God himself is under attack. Here 'the great reversal of values begins—the discovery of utopian potency within the religious sphere: that a man can be better and behave better, than his God'.[12] As Job perseveres in his attack on God, his friends become increasingly hostile and mouth 'prescribed, unrealistic cliches'. They are enraged because the rebel Job preaches not patience but 'an end to patience'. Despite the 'bigoted babble' of the four religious hypocrites—Eliphaz, Bildad, Zophar and Elihu—Job dares to expose God as a tyrant who rules by almighty, arbitrary power. All this means, according to Bloch, that 'a man has overtaken, has enlightened his own God. That, despite the apparent submission at the end, is the abiding lesson of the Book of Job.'[13] Even more pointedly, Bloch contends that 'the elemental category of Exodus is operative in a most powerful transformation. After the exodus of Israel from Egypt and of Yahweh from Israel, Job makes his exodus from Yahweh.'[14]

Second, the speeches of Yahweh and the repentance of Job in chs. 38–41 are totally inconsistent with the logic of the poetic debate. Yahweh's speeches are theocratic rebuttals of rebellion. In them Yahweh answers Job like an 'intimidating schoolmaster'. Whereas Job's critique of the actual world is the hint of a better one, the Yahweh of the speeches merely proposes one riddle after another. This tactic only serves to cover up the injustice of the present order of the world by a cloud of mystification. Bloch sees in Yahweh's naturalistic replies to Job's moral questions a 'whiff of demonic pantheism'. Yahweh's works are no longer anthropocentric as in the Genesis story of creation. Instead, a mysterious and inhuman divinity is at work in these hymns to Behemoth and Leviathan. In Bloch's judgment, 'the whole theophany is so alien to the Bible that it is almost as if another God were there'.[15] The religion of these speeches is 'pre-prophetic, pre-Canaanite demonism'.

How then does Bloch account for the Yahweh speeches and Job's conversion at the end of the book? He dismisses the possibility of later interpolation in view of the poetic power and linguistic unity of this material with what precedes it. He proposes instead that 'it may have been added by the author so that he could safely give vent to his heresy—which he succeeds in doing'.[16] In other words, the poet cleverly added a theophany and a repentance scene to his rebellious poem, in order to please or at least confuse orthodox censors. So amended and inserted into the framework of the old folk narrative, the heretical attack on God avoided its otherwise inevitable suppression.

Third, Bloch contends that the hope of Job is utterly different from what it is assumed to be by the traditional piety of the church. Job hopes not for a heavenly redeemer but for a historical avenger.

Harmonizing interpretation tries to identify the strange figure (*gō'ēl*) of 19.25-27 with Yahweh. In this manner 'Job and his unequivocal message continue to be turned upside down . . . even after the horrors of Auschwitz'.[17]

Although Job is a 'Hebrew Prometheus' rather than a patient sufferer, the cover-up has succeeded all too well: 'the popular story has beaten the poem, the rebel has been received into the church as the epitome of long suffering'.[18] The pious words of the prologue (1.21) have succeeded in extinguishing 'the whole fiery center of the book'.[19] Despite the fact that the dogma of mechanistic reward and punishment has repeatedly been proved false by 'terrible experience', the defenders of piety and orthodoxy demand complete surrender to God and the existing state of affairs. Their God speaks not a single messianic word. Yahweh's appearance, ironically, confirms the fact that in regard to the moral order, there is no God. Bloch does not say this to give cheap comfort to 'easy-going atheists'. On the contrary, he knows that unanswered questions remain: what shall we make of the cruelty of nature, of disease, disorder, alienation, and finally, death? How can there be any hope in the face of the reality of death? Even when leave is taken of Yahweh, 'an unfeeling universe remains, one still so badly adjusted to human finality'. The struggle for justice and against inhumanity, the attempt to achieve utopia, to fulfill the potential of life, to actualize what is not yet—all this calls for 'some corresponding factor at the heart of the world'.[20] Thus Job's questions are answered only by a continuous human exodus grounded in the hope principle, viz. that there are objective possibilities in the historical process which support the utopian aspirations of humanity. 'There is always an exodus in the world, an exodus from the particular status quo. And there is always a hope, which is connected with rebellion—a hope in the concrete given possibilites for new being.'[21]

The faith of Bloch's Job is altogether different from the faith of Job in the theocratic tradition: 'Job is pious precisely because he does not believe', does not believe in a Caesar-like God, a Pharaoh in heaven. Job does not believe 'except in exodus, and in the fact that the last human word has not been said'.[22]

From the preceding account it is clear that Bloch sees Job—whom he places in the company of Moses, Jesus, Thomas Munzer and Mozart's Don Giovanni—as a model of transcending without transcendence, as a classic expression of the hope principle which motivates and informs all critical and creative historical and cultural activity. Bloch interprets the Book of Job and indeed the entire Bible in terms of his idealist-Marxist philosophy of history. This philosophy is made the criterion of the Bible; the biblical text in its canonical form is not allowed to have any positive, let alone decisive, word in the identification of God, Job and the dynamics of their common history.

Let us briefly summarize Bloch's hermeneutical principles as they appear in his interpretation of Job:

1. Interpretation is detective work whose goal is to uncover the dangerous revolutionary voices of the biblical tradition. The final text is a distortion of these all too disturbing voices.

2. For Bloch the tradition process reflects not simply conflicting ideas but social conflicts. There are two Bibles: the Bible of the rulers and the Bible of the poor. The two Bibles embody two conflicting sets of social interests. Since the underground Bible has been suppressed by theocratic revision, Bloch pursues a hermeneutics of suspicion and makes the *cui bono* question central to the task of interpretation.

3. For the narrative frame provided by the canonical text, Bloch substitutes the hope principle, i.e. his own neo-Marxist philosophy of history which traces the human struggle for freedom from all oppression. The meaning of the poetry of Job is furnished by the neo-Marxist narrative of revolutionary struggle for freedom and justice.

4. Job's daring 'exodus from Yahweh' is the expression of a new piety, the piety and hope of humanistic messianism. Qualitites once ascribed to deity are now transferred to future humanity. Suffering humanity represented by Job awaits not a redeemer God but a historical avenger (for Bloch perhaps a hint of the revolutionary vanguard) who will establish justice on the earth.

II

Barth's small commentary on the Book of Job is found in *Church Dogmatics*, IV/3, Part 1, in the context of his comprehensive doctrine of reconciliation.[23] His two earlier christological themes, 'The Lord as Servant' (IV/1) and 'The Servant as Lord' (IV/2) are now augmented by a third theme: 'The True Witness'. Barth has recourse to the story of Job for a concrete description of the relationship between the free God and a free witness of God who experiences great suffering. While Barth seldom engages in direct christological interpretation of the text, he clearly believes that Job is 'a type of

Jesus Christ, a witness to the True Witness'.[24]

Barth acknowledges the literary and historical problems of this book—the obvious differences between the folk story and the poetical speeches, the strangeness of the speeches of Yahweh, the many alterations the text has undergone in the course of its transmission, etc. He is open to the various analyses of the text into its component units and to the illumination which they might provide. Nevertheless, he insists that the book most finally be read and understood as a whole. 'At some time and by some person all this came to be seen and understood as the unity it now constitutes in the canon.'[25]

Interpreting the Book of Job with what may be called canonical sensitivity, Barth refuses to summarize its 'point' or distil its 'lesson'. Instead he compels the reader to work through the book itself and even to read it as a story which moves in an often puzzling and zigzag manner. The narrative quality of the book considered as a whole is evident not only in the folktale which provides the framework of the dialogue cycles but also in the dramatic movement from the debates between Job and his friends to the climactic appearance and speeches of Yahweh. Only by careful attention to the entire book in its present form are we able to identify the real Job and the real Yahweh of the book in distinction from what we might assume or imagine Job and Yahweh to be. Neither the identity of Yahweh nor the identity of Job is given in advance or achieved through abstract definitions. Their true identities as free God and free human witness are rendered in what Barth calls the 'drama', 'history', or 'story' of their relationship provided by the text in its unity and totality.

According to Barth, the fundamental error of the friends of Job is that they have reduced God to a non-historical, unchanging, predictable principle. For the friends God is simply the name of the law of repayment or retribution. Their God is not the living God but an abstraction. 'They preach timeless truths . . .'[26] Their abstractions are clichés and 'cut flowers'. Utterly foreign to them is the possibility of a new occurrence between God and the believer—'the whole idea of the historicity of the existence both of God and of man is . . . completely alien to them'.[27] Corresponding to their static and non-historical view of God is their theoretical and lifeless understanding of faith. Faith for the friends is rather like submission to arbitrary fate or immutable cosmic law. By contrast, faith for Job is, if anything, a free response to the living God. It is defined not by the law of *Do ut Des* but by a readiness to serve God 'for nought' (1.9).

Thus Barth no less than Bloch highlights the sharp criticism of religion contained in the text. Both interpreters expose the platitudes and abstractions of the orthodox defenders of God, and both fight against a conception of God as absolute and immobile. Not surprisingly, however, Barth's understanding of the tensions within the text is very different from Bloch's. In the first place, Barth contends that if the relationship between God and Job is open and dynamic rather than closed and static, a concrete history which must be portrayed dramatically, then the argument that the Job of the prologue/epilogue and the Job of the dialogues are mutually exclusive quickly crumbles. According to Barth, when catastrophe strikes Job, he experiences not only the losses described in the prologue but also the radical concealment of God. In his affliction Job does not recognize his God anymore; he does not recognize the features of the God who had freely chosen him as his partner and whose partner Job had freely become. 'The poet now takes up the story, and as he understands the catastrophe which has come on Job according to the saga, it has affected him not merely externally but in his innermost and total life, radically challenging and questioning him.'[28]

Barth insists that Job's complaint against God in the name of God is 'honorable'. Indeed, it is the 'appropriate' form of obedience in this moment in Job's history with God.[29] Job 'could not have been obedient if he had not raised this complaint and carried it through to the bitter end and in spite of all objections'.[30] At the same time, Barth speaks of an element of 'arrogance' and 'violent impatience' in Job's protest.[31] Here Barth identifies a theme which is systematically excluded by Bloch: the critique of self-righteousness in the pursuit of a good and righteous cause.

Second, even in the speeches of Yahweh, Barth sees evidence of a non-coercive appeal to Job rather than an expression of arbitrary and dictatorial divine power. He observes that the speeches take the form of questions to Job and thus respect his freedom. 'He is not overwhelmed nor belabored nor smitten to the ground . . . What is said to him is not enforced upon him in an authoritarian and dictatorial manner.'[32] As Barth sees it, God's surprising strategy in the speeches is to allow the creation to bear witness to its own freedom which has its source in the sheer free grace of God. He reminds Job of the wild animals who 'defy all attempts at domestication or practical use'.[33] By pointing to the gratuity, freedom and practical uselessness of the life of these animals, God questions whether Job does right to think that the cosmos is ordered anthropo-centrically, whether it must fit his ideas, wishes and purposes. In short, God asks whether Job has forgotten that the God who elected him in freedom remains the free God. And according to the story, Job responds in humility to God who speaks out of his darkness. The Book of Job does not analyze this event of personal encounter. It simply narrates the fact that 'the step forward in the history of the reciprocal co-existence of God and Job . . . is finally taken'.[34] No solution of the problem of suffering is offered here or anywhere else in the book. We are simply told that in the end God freely justifies his free servant Job and condemns the falsehood of his accusers.

Finally, and again in sharp contrast to Bloch, Barth denies that there is a cleavage in Job's thinking about God and the power that will finally vindicate him. Barth accepts the description of Job's turmoil as 'a flight from God to God', but interprets it in the sense of a flight from God in his present hiddenness to God in his future revelation. Job does not think of seeking for a better God and surely not of expecting salvation from a merely human avenger. Barth points to the eschatological dimension of Job's hope expressed in 14.13-15 and 19.25-27. These texts express confidence that a limit will be set by God to the hiddenness in which he now meets Job. This present hiddenness constitutes only a 'partial action' in the history of God and Job.

> He looks to the one and only God who 'even now' (16.19), even in the hostility of His attitude, is the same as He will be, who will set that limit in His own time and manner, who is thus his Witness, Advocate and Guarantor, who even now is for him as He is against him. In this way, and this way alone, Job is a real Israel, a witness of the truth, and as such also a witness of Jesus Christ.[35]

Barth concludes:

> When men think and speak . . . non-historically and within the framework of . . . orderly structure, there is no place in their utterances for two factors, namely the free God and the man freed by and for Him. Yahweh as the free God of the free man Job, and Job as the free man of the free God, together in their divine and human freedom enter into the crisis in which God becomes so incomprehensible to Job even though He will not let him go, and Job becomes so angry against God even though he will not let Him go.[36]

The friends do not appreciate this historicity of the covenant between

God and humanity. They 'lack all awareness or taste for either divine or human freedom'.[37]

Paralleling our earlier summary of Bloch's hermeneutics, the hermeneutical principles at work in Barth's interpretation of Job may be stated as follows:

1. Barth insists on reading biblical texts in their entirety, as wholes, and in their final redaction. He recognizes that a history of tradition precedes the final form of the text, but he refuses to grant normativity to any earlier stage of the tradition.

2. Barth is sensitive to the narrative quality of many biblical texts. After being analyzed by various literary and historical methods, biblical stories in their unity and totality should be read with what Barth calls elsewhere a 'tested and critical naivete'.[38]

3. Barth is very suspicious of abstract, a priori definitions of God or humanity. He concentrates on the distinctive understandings of the identity of God and the identity of God's covenant partner as they are depicted in the dynamic movement of biblical narrative. Specifically, the freedom of God and the freedom of God's covenant partner are to be read off the biblical narratives rather than replaced by or subsumed under some a priori conception of true freedom.

4. Barth's interpretation of the Book of Job leads not to a humanistic messianism but to a messianic humanism,[39] to a hope in God, even in acute suffering, as the Lord who is free, faithful and gracious. God's freedom, however concealed by the darkness of history and personal experience, is a freedom for humanity within the context of God's cosmic purposes.

III

Common to the interpretations of Job by Bloch and Barth are the critique of religious clichés and false conceptions of trancendence as well as the affirmation of a basis for freedom and hope in the midst of suffering. For Bloch Job's exodus from Yahweh is a breakthrough in the history of the struggle of humanity against oppression and injustice. For Barth Job in his affliction is a free witness to the undomesticatable freedom of God whose purposes, however incomprehensible, are trustworthy rather than ultimately hostile. Both Bloch and Barth speak of Job's hope, but they disagree radically about the basis and object of that hope. For Bloch Job hopes not in Yahweh but in the coming of an avenger of injustice. For Barth Job hopes in the coming of the just and faithful God whose presence he now experiences as deeply hidden.

An adequate assessment of Barth's canonical interpretation of Job would take us far beyond the limits of this essay. Many questions would have to be raised: To what extent does the particular logic of the doctrine of reconciliation in the *Church Dogmatics* shape Barth's reading of Job? Does Barth allow the dialectic of God's hiddenness and revelation to overshadow the tension between God's promise and fulfillment? Is Job's hope in eschatological justice something more than hope in God's revelation of what is now hidden? While Barth's lifelong commitment to theologically grounded social criticism is beyond dispute, does his interpretation of Job give more attention to the conflict of truth and falsehood than to the struggle between God's justice and real injustice? While these questions are important, I cannot pursue them here. There is space only for a few critical reflections on Bloch's hermeneutical method.

One clear failure of Bloch's detective work is its helplessness before the extraordinary dynamism of the faith of Job: the coincidence and tension of rebellion and prayer, protest and patience, resistance and repentance. Bloch sees these tensive elements of faith as mutually exclusive, and consequently his portrayal of Job's limitless rebellion is as distorted as the traditional picture of Job's supine patience in the face of injustice. Barth's narrative approach captures these tensions much better, although his interpretation, consistent with classical Reformation thought, tends to read the book more in terms of justification by faith alone than in terms of hope in God's promised future which 'stabs inexorably into the flesh of every unfulfilled present'.[40]

Bloch's reductionism is also evident in the choice that it demands between honest atheism on the one hand and faith in God as either utterly arbitrary or entirely predictable on the other. Excluded is the possibility that God relates to the world in both freedom and faithfulness. While there is order, stability and coherence in this relationship, the order is never static, the stability never fixed, the coherence never so absolute as to be easily predictable. In faithfulness God does new things and acts in new ways. God works through exodus *and* exile, through cross *and* resurrection. The God Bloch fights against, like the God of Job's friends, is an abstraction rather than the living God. Bloch has good reason to attack this abstract God who serves only to justify the status quo of suffering, injustice and death. But this is not the God to whom Job cries in his affliction. In outrage and despair Job calls on the living God and trusts that his justice will finally prevail.

Bloch's attempt to discredit the speaches of Yahweh as a sinister deviation from biblical anthropocentrism and a decline into nature demonism is ironical. The effects of modern industrial and military exploitation and destruction of the environment, conducted by capitalist and socialist countries alike, have increasingly exposed anthropocentrism as a dead-end. Biblical theocentrism is the humanizing alternative to both destructive anthropocentrism and nature worship. Barth's celebrated emphasis on the 'humanity of God', which constitutes the horizon of all of his biblical interpretation, points in a very different direction from both the false transcendence which Bloch criticizes and the uncritical anthropocentrism which he espouses.

The intersecting but vastly different interpretations of Job by Bloch and Barth represent in part a disagreement about whether this biblical book can and should be read as a literary whole, even as a narrative whole.[41] Robert Alter has recently offered some fresh insights on the topic of biblical narrative.[42] He contends that narrative in the Bible is an attempt to depict 'the enactment of God's purposes in historical events'. However, this enactment is always complicated by two dialectical tensions: the tension between the divine promise and its ostensible failure to be fulfilled, and the tension between God's will and human freedom. Alter argues that 'the various biblical narratives in fact may be usefully seen as forming a spectrum between the opposing extremes of disorder and design'.[43] On the disorder end of the spectrum would be books like Judges, Samuel and Kings where both narrator and narrative actors struggle 'to reconcile their knowledge of the divine promise with the awareness of what is actually happening in history'.[44] On the design end of the spectrum would be the Book of Esther which has a 'fairy-tale' quality about it—'the lovely damsel, guided by a wise godfather, is made queen and serves her people'.[45] Lacking the historical verisimilitude characteristic of most biblical narrative, the Book of Esther demonstrates God's providential care 'with a schematic neatness unlike that of earlier historicized fiction in the Bible'.[46] Alter conjectures: 'It may well be that a sense of some adequate dialectical tension betwen these antitheses of divine plan and the sundry disorders of human performance in history served as an implicit criterion for deciding which narratives were to be regarded as canonical'.[47]

Applied to the Book of Job, Alter's 'implict criterion' suggests that the prologue/epilogue, taken by itself, is no less 'heterodox' than the poetic debate read in isolation from the rest of the book. If the latter comes close to the disorder end of the biblical narrative spectrum, the former reaches the design extreme, having like Esther a 'fairytale' quality. Hence, against Bloch, it is reasonable to argue that the final redactor of Job may have been as worried about the distortion of biblical faith in the independent folk-tale of the prologue/epilogue as he was aware of the heterodoxy of the poetic debate in isolation from the whole.

These criticisms of Bloch's detective hermeneutics are not intended to belittle the value of his work. On the contrary, his reclaiming of the rebel Job and his emphasis on the *cui bono* question in biblical interpretation should serve to disturb the consciences of exegetes and theologians alike. In biblical scholarship, church history and systematic theology the question of whose interests are being served has often been neglected. This question which agitates Bloch so much should be made part of the hermeneutical and theological agendas of our time. Whether there is evidence that class interests played a role in the formation of the canonical Job is a question which the author of this essay is not competent to judge. But there can be little doubt that in the post-canonical history of the interpretation of Job up to the present the picture of a docile Job in the midst of suffering and injustice has indeed served the interests of masters and rulers. A one-sided concentration on the submission of Job has been used to support the kind of theocratic religion from which Bloch seeks exodus. Just for that reason the rebel Job, whose passion for justice Bloch makes the 'fiery center' of his distorted portrayal and whose passionate complaints Barth calls both 'honorable' and 'appropriate', is a crucially important voice in the canonical choir which must not be lost in the retrieval of the witness of the whole book for our time.

NOTES

1. Bernhard W. Anderson, 'Tradition and Scripture in the Community of Faith', *JBL* 100 (1981) 7.
2. *Ibid.*, 17.
3. *Ibid.*, 18.
4. *Ibid.*

5. For a brief but insightful comparison of these two interpreters of Job, see Helmut Gollwitzer's introduction in Karl Barth, *Hiob* (BibS[N], 49; Neukirchen: Verlag des Erziehungsvereins, 1966).

6. Ernst Bloch, *Atheism in Christianity* (New York: Herder and Herder, 1972).

7. *Ibid.*, 70.

8. *Ibid.*, 71.

9. *Ibid.*, 21.

10. *Ibid.*, 82.

11. *Ibid.*, 83

12. *Ibid.*, 108.

13. *Ibid.*, 110.

14. *Ibid.*

15. *Ibid.*, 112.

16. *Ibid.*, 113.

17. *Ibid.*, 115.

18. *Ibid.*, 116.

19. *Ibid.*

20. *Ibid.*, 121.

21. *Ibid.*, 122.

22. *Ibid.*

23. Karl Barth, *Church Dogmatics* (IV/3/1; Edinburgh: T. & T. Clark, 1961) 383-88, 398-408, 421-34, 453-61.

24. *Ibid.*, 388.

25. *Ibid.*, 384.

26. *Ibid.*, 457.

27. *Ibid.*, 458.

28. *Ibid.*, 399.

29. *Ibid.*, 405-406.

30. *Ibid.*, 406.

31. *Ibid.*, 406-407.

32. *Ibid.*, 430.

33. *Ibid.*, 431-32.

34. *Ibid.*, 433.

35. *Ibid.*, 435.

36. *Ibid.*, 460.

37. *Ibid.*

38. *Church Dogmatics* IV/2, 479.

39. For the distinction betwen 'humanistic messianism' and 'messianic humanism' I am indebted to Paul L. Lehmann, *Ideology and Incarnation* (Geneva: The John Knox Association, 1962).

40. Jürgen Moltmann, *Theology of Hope* (New York: Harper & Row, 1967), 21.

41. See the suggestive essay by Alan Cooper, 'Narrative Theory and the Book of Job', *Studies in Religion* II/1 (1982), pp. 35-44.

42. Robert Alter, *The Art of Biblical Narrative* (New York: Basic Books, 1981), 33.

43. *Ibid.*

44. *Ibid.*, 33-34.

45. *Ibid.*, 34.

46. *Ibid.*

47. *Ibid.*

15

THE WORD OF GOD AND THE PEOPLE OF ASIA

D. Preman Niles

Asian theologians are beginning to realize more and more how important it is to listen to the context in which one attemps to interpret the Word of God revealed in the Bible if it is indeed to communicate. This realization becomes apparent, for instance, in the experience of an Asian theologian, Kosuke Koyama, who once attempted to expound John 1.1f. to a colleague of his, a Buddhist monk. He began, 'In the beginning was the WORD; and the WORD was with God; and the WORD was God. All things were made by this WORD . . .' The Buddhist monk slowly raised his hand and stopped Koyama saying, 'This strikes me as a very noisy religion!' How can a noisy religion that gives rise to a noisy theology communicate to one for whom the Ultimate is Silence! To whom then were we trying to communicate? Perhaps the following humorous episode illustrates the answer. An Indian bishop visiting a foreign country went into a shop and asked for something in his own language. An Indian priest accompanying him said, 'But, Bishop, they don't understand Malayalam!' The bishop retorted, 'Even if I speak in English they won't understand. If I speak in Malayalam at least *I* will understand!' A noisy religion giving rise to a noisy theological language may at best communicate to a noisy group of theologians!

Lest all of this be understood simply as a caricature, let me present the matter of 'noisy theology' in another way. When the self-hood of Asian theology was being asserted in the early 1970s, it was articulated in terms of 'the Critical Asian Principle'. Emerito Nacpil spoke for all of us when he explained this principle in these words:

> For one thing, it is a way of saying where our area of responsibility is, namely, the varieties and dynamics of Asian realities. We are committed to understand this context both sympathetically and critically. For another thing, it is a way of saying that we will approach and interpret the Gospel in relation to the needs and issues peculiar to the Asian situations. It functions therefore as a hermeneutical principle. Third, it is a way of saying that a theology worth its salt at this time in Asia must be capable not only of

illuminating the Asian relities with the light of the Gospel, but also of helping to manage the changes now taking place along lines more consonant with the Gospel.[1]

First, the doing of theology is envisaged as a matter of relating the gospel to the situation, so that Asian realities may be illumined by the light of the gospel. Second, theology must do more than illuminate the realities in a Christian way. It must also try to manage the changes taking place in a Christian way. In brief, Christian theology should not only dictate to the context but must also attempt to manage the context. Now to many this seems to be no more than an Asianized version of missionary theology in that Asian Christians are now supposed to do, perhaps with a greater sympathy for the context, what their missionary forebears tried to do.

Despite this criticism, the articulation of the Critical Asian Principle did achieve a certain independence for Asian theologians. What M.M. Thomas says with regard to Indian theology may be said for all Asian theologies: 'Indian theology must be judged in the light of the mission of the Church in India, and need not be brought to any other bar of judgment'.[2]

In appropriating this independence, however, the experience of Asian theologians has made them question the assumption that theology is simply a matter of relating Text to Context. The questioning takes place essentially along two lines.

First. Is the Context simply a thing—a mere conglomeration of Asian realities to which the Text has to be related? Rather, is not the Context the people themselves who live amongst these realities? What does the Text have to say to them as they relate to these realities and struggle for life in the midst of these realities? Can it indeed speak to them unless it too is a living Word that listens to their word—their *story*—and speaks to them as a living story—the *story* of God's compassion for people that is concretely expressed in his relationship with Israel and in his self-disclosure in Jesus the Messiah?

Out of this questioning has arisen an important understanding of what Asian theology ought to be. Theology has to do with 'retelling the story', whether it be the story of Asian peoples understood as the *minjung*[3] or whether it be the biblical story. For biblical scholars who have been brought up on a diet of *Nacherzählung*, this may not be a strange way of doing theology. But the Asian emphasis on 'retelling the story' seems to go further and to ask questions like 'Whose story are we retelling and why?' and the more personal question, 'Who is retelling the story and why?' Implicit in these questions is the matter of ideology, for both raise the critical question, 'On whose side are you?' Underlying the stand indicated by these questions is the conviction that there can be no disinterested theology. One's theology also reveals one's identity.

Second. Is theology always a matter of relating Text to Context? Is it not also a matter of relating Context to Text so that the Context may speak to the Text? Is Asia only there to receive? Has it nothing to contribute? If it does, then theology can no longer be viewed as a monologue. It is a *dialogue.*

If theology is a dialogue, then plurality is of the very essence of theology. There can then be no *one theology*; there can only be theologies. Coming primarily out of the experience of inter-religious dialogue, this insight on the one hand relativizes all truth claims, because we are all pilgrims on the way to realizing the Truth. It demands humility. On the other hand it requires that we speak boldly about the Truth as we perceive it from our angle of vision, even though it may contradict and conflict with the Truth as it is perceived from another angle of vision. Dialogue is both listening and speaking. It is both contemplation and movement, so that it may lead to a broadening of one's angle of perceiving the Truth even though such perceiving may entail living with inner contradictions and conflicts both in the new vision and in oneself. If the theology of 'retelling the story' primarily raises the issue of ideology, the experience of dialogue primarily raises the issue of metaphysics—a broadening or even a change in one's angle of vision, so that it permits one to hear and to be heard in the context of Asia with its plurality.

These questions and the groping towards possible answers are not just academic exercises—simply a process of attempting to relate Text to Context or, for that matter, relating Context to Text. Rather, the questions and the seeking for possible answers are located in the experience of certain Asian theologians who have been trying to overcome two forms of alienation: an alienation from the masses of Asia, 85% of whom are poor, and an alienation from the religions and religious perceptions of Asian people. In other words, the two sets of questions isolated above come out of attempts to belong to and listen to the dual context of Asia, namely, its peoples and their religions, rather than out of attempts to relate to and speak to the context of Asia. In so doing, we have gained new insights on how we appropriate the Word in the context of Asia. These insights are new in the sense that they are new for us. But many of these have been a part of Asian Christian traditions that have largely gone unnoticed. Hence, the intention of this paper is not so much to isolate these insights and argue for them as to set out the processes or experiences through which these insights have been gained.

In speaking of two areas or, better, two facets of emerging Asian theology, I have suggested a distinction that is in fact arbitrary.[4] Yet, a distinction, however artificial, may be helpful in seeing how both sets of questions raise different but interrelated issues for appropriating the Word in the context of Asia. In order to do this, I shall separate the two and concentrate primarily on the work of Korean theologians to illustrate the theology of retelling the story and on the work of Indian and Sri Lankan theologians to illustrate Christian theology emerging from the context of interreligious dialogue.

Hyun Younghak seems to have had both these facets or emphases in mind when he advised his colleagues, 'When writing a paper, do not descend to mere argument. Tell your story! When doing a book review, do not behave like an examiner. Write a letter to the author and enter into a dialogue!' A descriptive essay such as this one that attempts to survey and describe a scene cannot just be my story. It is the story of many. Yet, in some ways, it is also my story in that it speaks of my own pilgrimage in the context of the many voices of Asia. And as I dialogue with these, I continue a dialogue that started many years ago with my *guru*, Professor Bernhard W. Anderson, to whom this essay is respectfully dedicated.

The Word in Minjung Theology

The Korean intellectual and poet-dramatist, Kim Chi-ha, who has been imprisoned for most of his life, has probably done the most to generate a new intellectual ethos of which the *minjung* is the center. This intellectual ethos or revolution is evident not so much in classrooms, lecture halls or even in the study rooms of professors. Rather, it is most clearly evident in the market places and sweatshops, in the various student uprisings beginning with the 1960 student uprising that threw out President Syngman Rhee, in the labor movements, in church groups of pastors and intellectuals who have been closely identified with the Korean Urban Industrial Mission, and not least of all in the prisons of Korea.[5] The *minjung-theology* (one word in Korean) movement that began to emerge in the late 1960s and early 1970s is but one part of this larger intellectual ferment.

Before moving on to a description of the *minjung-theology* movement, it will be helpful to see how Kim Chi-ha himself described the *minjung* in relation to biblical faith. When on trial at the Seoul District Court, the public prosecutor asked Kim Chi-ha to clarify what he meant by the term *minjung*. To the prosecutor and to those whom he represented, the term smacked of communism and seemed not to be very different from the term *inmin* used in North Korea for the proletariat. Kim Chi-ha replied:

> In Genesis God says to them, 'Be fruitful, multiply and fill the earth'. The *minjung* are those who have increased and occupied the ends of the earth, revolutionized the world, built societies, and advanced the course of human history. They physically make up the substance of, what we call, humanity. In other words, the *minjung* are those who eat the food produced by their own labor, who till and cultivate the soil, and protect their country and its culture not just with words but with their very lives. I think of the *minjung* in these concrete terms.
>
> The concept of the *minjung* should be contrasted with the concept of the regime or the ruling authority and differentiated from the intellectuals who take a middle position betwen the *minjung* and the rulers. Authority or power originally comes from the *minjung*. But when it is institutionalized it becomes a tool to suppress the *minjung* in whom its roots lie. Therefore, in the course of history, the *minjung* have risen up in revolts to reappropriate the power which they lost and in so doing restore social justice. In my opinion, when the ruling power or authority perverts justice and takes an anti-*minjung* stand, then justice is on the side of the *minjung* and injustice on the side of the ruling authority. Throughout the course of human history we witness the constant change from the rule of power to the rule of the *minjung*, from the history of dictatorship and oppression to that of liberation and democracy.

In answer to the question, 'Why are the urban humble (lower) people the protagonists in your works?', Kim Chi-ha replied:

> The reason is that the Christian Gospel (Jesus) came to earth first of all to save the sinners and the humble people. At the present time, the church should be filled with the exploding force of the life and toil of the humble people. The most miserable of the lower people should become the subjects and the vanguard of the work of

salvation. In my works my purpose is to point to a certain mystery in the glory of God which reveals itself in the salvation effected through those in extreme misery. Through my experience I have the strange conviction that the Messiah, whom we Christians are longing for and calling upon in our daily prayers, does not come from those who are sophisticated like ourselves, but from these people (wicked prisoners) who are suppressed by us and live in the bitterness of starvation. So, I have tried to formulate and express in my works this conviction concerning the Messiah who comes from the bottom.[6]

In the thinking of Kim Chi-ha, a fusion has already taken place between the story of the *minjung* in Korea and the story of the *minjung* in the Bible, so that in many ways the two seem interchangeable. For him, the concrete evidence of this fusion is the church which 'should be filled with the exploding force of the life and the toil of the humble people'. The intellectual, who is differentiated from the *minjung* on the one side and the rulers on the other, has a role to play. Traditionally in Korean society, as for that matter in all societies, the intellectual has tended to side with the ruler and to provide the intellectual buttressing for the ruler's thinking and ideology as a way of earning both rice and security. The challenge now to the Christian intellectual is to side with the *minjung* and tell the two stories, either separately or in the way they mesh together, so that the *minjung* are seen in their proper role as the protagonists of history—not its objects but its subjects. To side with the victim against the ruler, as is evident in the case of Kim Chi-ha and many others, is to share the lot of the victim. Basically, this is the thrust of *minjung-theology* and the way in which the Word is being appropriated, at least in some Christian circles, in Korea.

Let us now step back from this summary to look briefly at some of the ingredients that make up *minjung-theology*. Then we will draw out some of its implications for appropriating the Word in the context of Korea.

In his paper on 'Historical References for a Theology of *Minjung*',[7] Suh Nam-dong substantiates with reference to Korean history the general observation of Kim Chi-ha that throughout the course of human history there has been the constant change from the rule of power to the rule of the *minjung*. Using the method of 'socio-economic history'[8] and relying on the research of several Korean scholars, he reconstructs Korean 'history from below'[9] to show 'a progressive expansion of the social base of the ruling power'. His intention is to show how the *minjung* gradually liberated themselves from the position of being historical object to become historical subject. Suh's reconstruction provides the socioeconomic background against which the *minjung* reality should be understood. It also provides a catena of events in which the *minjung* consciousness was politically visible in history. However, as Suh himself notes, even though such research is invaluable for understanding the socio-economic background of the *minjung*, it still remains the work of scholars and does not really reveal the consciousness or inner spirit of the *minjung*. For, the *minjung* themselves do not write histories or, for that matter, narrate events. They tell or perform stories—folk-tales, folk-dramas, etc. It is these that form the social biography of the *minjung*, and express their sufferings and aspirations. In these, the *minjung* are the subjects.

While it is clear that the stories of the *minjung* should be the proper study for *minjung-religion* and *minjung-theology*, the crucial question has been how one studies and appropriates them, because simply to describe them in a scholarly and analytical way would reduce the *minjung* to an object for study. There had to be a different approach. Long periods of living with and experiencing the stories of the *minjung* has made it clear that the stories of the *minjung* express their *han*, and that this experience is the key towards understanding the 'subjectivity' of the *minjung*.

Suh Kwang-sun explains *han* in the following way. At the personal level *han* may be seen as a psychological term 'that denotes the feeling of a person which has been repressed either by that person or through the oppression of others'. It could lead to all forms of psychosomatic illnesses. At a social level, it may be seen as a sociopsychological term that denotes the experience of 'slaves in the face of their social fate experiencing the contradictions of society'. At a third level, it may be seen as a psychopolitical term. 'When people realize that they have been oppressed by foreign powers ... the feeling of *han* rises up to the level of psycho-political anger, frustration and indignation.' These three levels of *han* interpenetrate one another, so that the *han*-experience of an individual could be that of the whole community and vice versa.[10]

Although *han* as a feeling or experience may be explained in these terms, especially for the benefit of foreigners, in actuality it is not just a feeling or a mental state. Time and again, Koreans speak of it as a 'bodily experience'. Suh Nam-dong explains, '*Han* is the suppressed, amassed and condensed experience of oppression . . . that forms a kind of 'lump' in one's spirit'.[11] This explains why Kim Chi-ha on the one hand envisages unresolved *han* concretely as an all-devouring monster in his plays *Sacred Place* and *Malttuk* and, on the other hand, portrays it as the revolutionary Jesus figure, Chang Il-dam, in his play with the same name.[12] This is also the reason why gestures and bodily movements form an important part in the reenacting of the *minjung*. These are not mere accompaniments to the words but are themselves also the expression of the *han* of the *minjung*. Hence, as Hyun Younghak points out, 'Beginning to do theology in such a way [*minjung* way] is exciting, for you feel theology with your body and dance with it before you think it'.[13] In other words, a bodily participation in the *han* experience of the *minjung* seems to be a *sine qua non* for the doing of *minjung-theology*.

It would take too long to sketch in any detail the various forms of thinking and action that have emerged through participating in and listening to the context of the *minjung*. Let me, however, briefly indicate three main trends and some of the issues they raise and then expand on the third trend that seems most pertinent for seeing how the Word is being appropriated.

1. We have tended to use '*minjung-theology*' as a generic term to cover several different aspects of the reflection on and by *minjung*. The broad use of this term is now being challenged, because it tends to subsume all forms of *minjung* expression under the category of theology. As Suh Nam-dong points out, there is an unnecessary hurry to Christianize or theologize *minjung* expressions or stories without allowing them to speak on their own terms. Worse still, many of these expressions or stories are wrenched free from their own sociohistorical contexts and are simply used as vehicles for expressing Christian insights.[14] These efforts tend to blunt the challenge that the *minjung* pose both for theology and for politics. Suh Nam-dong himself is now involved in retelling the *minjung* stories taking into account the culture of the *minjung* and their social and political history; he calls these 'counter-theology'.[15] In other words, he argues against too quick a fusion between the two stories, that of the *minjung* and that of the Christian tradition, and calls for a retelling of the *minjung* story in its own terms, so that it may be seen in its own right as one of the many stories of the *minjung* of the world. Partly because of his criticism and also independently, there is now a great deal more research into *minjung* socioeconomic history and

into *minjung* culture and religions like Shamanism and *minjung* Buddhism.[16]

2. The works of *minjung* poets, dramatists and artists, like Kim Chi-ha, are probably the most important form of retelling the story of the *minjung*. These attempt to broaden the scope of the *minjung* stories so that they may take into account present realities and contradictions and keep political hope alive. These forms are not only counter-theological in the sense noted above, but also anti-rational, and evoke responses through 'symbol' and 'rumor'.

Part of the criticism against rational presentations of the *minjung* reality and experience is that they expose too much. They speak too clearly in the language known to the ruling power, so that the ruling power finds it easier both to put down the movement and to co-opt creative *minjung* categories into its own language and thus subvert the thinking of the *minjung*. Besides keeping political hope alive, retelling *minjung* stories should also serve to prevent the ideological penetration of the *minjung* by the ruling power.

The advantage of symbols is that they come out of a common reservoir of *minjung* history and experience and point beyond themselves to a new reality—the vision of a new society. As Oh Jae-shik explains,

> The symbol opens up levels of reality which otherwise are hidden and cannot be grasped in any other way. By opening up the reality it also opens up the soul . . . inviting the soul to look at what it points to. The symbol as pointer also participates in what it points to . . . A symbol is bodily language. The more remote is the reality to come, the more tangible is the bodily evidence required.[17]

The other criticism against rational discourse is that it reduces the *minjung*—their suffering and their aspirations—into neat little categories that not only turn the *minjung* into objects but also stop all movement. In contrast, 'rumor' is also a form of language that communicates, even though the source of the rumor may be squashed. Hyun Young-hak points out that in Korean there are two words for rumor. One is *somoon* which is rumor in the ordinary sense— innocent stories created on hearsay and hunches. The other is *yoo-un bi-u* which is a political rumor. To make up and spread such stories is considered a political crime; and one may be severely punished for doing this.[18] For instance, Herod heard the rumor that a new king was born. He could not stop the rumor or discover its exact source, so he killed a whole number of innocent children to stop the rumor. But the rumor went on and began to shake the very foundations of Herod's power. Like 'symbol', 'rumor' too is bodily language that quickly passes from mouth to mouth creating hope in the victim and fear in the victimizer.[19] It cannot easily be stopped, as the Pharaoh realized when Moses started the rumor that the Israelite slaves in Egypt would soon be free.

3. The area that we may properly call *minjung-theology* tries to take into account both the insights and criticisms of the two forms of *minjung* expression noted above. It then attemps to reread the Bible and the various Christian traditions in the light of the *minjung* experience and in turn reinterprets the *minjung* stories in the light of biblical traditions. A full presentation of *minjung-theology* would require one to follow the 'hermeneutical circle' through its various orbits—an exercise that would entail a much longer presentation. Instead, let us take a cross-cut, and look at the major themes.

The focal theme in *minjung-theology* is the centrality of people or the 'people as subjects of history'. Stated in this form, the term 'people', which is used as a translation for '*minjung*', is not a concept but refers to a dynamic reality. As Kim Yong-bock explains,

> '*Minjung*' is not a concept or object which can be easily explained or defined. '*Minjung*' signifies a living reality which is dynamic, changing and complex. This living reality defines its own existence and generates new acts and dramas in history; and it refuses in principle to be defined conceptually.

While a conceptual definition of *minjung* is neither desirable nor possible, the *minjung* may be understood in political terms.

> The identity and reality of the *minjung* is known . . . through their own stories—their social biographies which the *minjung* themselves create and therefore can tell best. This story of the *minjung* or their social biography is told *vis-à-vis* the power structure that rules the people; and therefore power is the antagonist in the story, while . . . the *minjung* themselves are the protagonists.

The political understanding of *minjung* when contrasted with that of the proletariat brings out its religious character.

> Philosophically speaking, the proletariat is 'confined' to socio-economic (materialistic) determination, so that it is bound to historical possibilities and the internal logic of history. The *minjung* suffers these limitations in reality; yet the *minjung* as historical subject transcends the socio-economic determination of

> history, and unfolds its story beyond mere historical possibilities to
> historical novelty—a new drama beyond the present history to a
> new and transformed history.
>
> This difference between the *minjung* and the proletariat entails
> different views of history. *Minjung* history has a strong transcen-
> dental or transcending dimension—a beyond history—which is
> often expressed in religious form . . . Its folklore or cultural elements
> play a transcending function similar to religion in the perception of
> history.[20]

In appropriating biblical traditions, there is the common assumption
or even conviction that the Bible is primarily concerned about the
minjung of Israel and that this is the correct 'pre-understanding' for
reading the Bible. This 'pre-understanding' is expressed in two
interrelated questions that operate together. First, who are the
minjung in the Bible? Second, what are the theological themes that
most appropriately express the role of the people?

In pursuing this dual thrust, some Korean scholars use the
methods of socioeconomic analysis and tradition history criticism to
identify the broad group of people designated by terms such as
'widow and orphan', 'sojourner', 'slaves', etc., who physically make
up the category known as 'the poor'. In his research on the covenant
code, Sye In-suk demonstrates the central place of this group both in
the concerns of early Israelite law and in the thinking of the
prophets.[21] Scholars who take this approach to identify the *minjung*
argue that other layers of tradition coming from other interest groups
have served to hide a basic *minjung* thrust evident in the biblical
traditions, so that one has to work back to an original, *minjung*
tradition.

Other Korean scholars have relied largely on the method of
redaction criticism to surface *minjung* perspectives in the Bible. The
work of Ahn Byung-mu has been specially influential in this area.[22]
Working with the Gospel of Mark, Ahn Byung-mu shows that the
term *ochlos* figures prominently in Mark's redactional statements to
refer to the people who formed 'the audience' of Jesus' teaching and
healing. Mark consistently uses the term *ochlos* and not *laos*. The
term *laos* is used only when referring to the historical people of Israel
and in the speech of the Pharisees. Ahn therefore argues that Mark's
preference for *ochlos*, meaning a motley crowd, over *laos*, which
designates a definable national or religious group, is deliberate and
theologically important.

He points out that in Mark the term *ochlos* refers neither to a particular economic class of people nor to a religiously or politically defined group. It is a relational term. In relation to the religious and political authorities of the time, the *ochlos* are the sinners, prostitutes and tax collectors—the social and political outcasts. In relation to Jesus, the *ochlos* are the ones who listen to his words. Jesus has compassion on them, teaches and heals them. The *ochlos* follow him; they also betray him. Although not politically powerful, the rulers are afraid of them. However, they can also be manipulated by the powerful. So, one cannot idealize the *ochlos*.[23]

Yet Jesus, who repeatedly scolded the authorities and sometimes even his disciples, does not rebuke the *ochlos*. He relates to them in compassion and makes them the center of his preachng regarding the Kingdom. As Ahn points out: 'Whereas, according to the expectation of the Jews, the Son of Man was to appear at the last judgment only as the judge of the sinners and the redeemer of the righteous, Jesus actually turned towards the sinners and the lost'. If this were just blasphemy, Jesus would have been stoned to death like Stephen. To speak of the *ochlos* as the center of the Messianic Kingdom was a political crime, so that Jesus was crucified as a 'false Messiah'.

Ahn shows that Mark's preference for the term *ochlos* to denote people was prompted by two considerations. First, in actual fact, it was the crowds—those who were on the religious and political periphery during Jesus' time and are mentioned under various names in Jesus' teaching—who formed the *Sitz im Leben* for his life and ministry. Once this fact is grasped, the real theological and political depth of Jesus' teaching, death and resurrection become evident. Mark's concern seems to have been to restore an original thrust to the Gospel of Jesus that the disciples and the early church, especially under the influence of Paul, were tending to ignore. (Once, in an oral presentation, Ahn Byung-mu quipped, 'While Mark is remarkable, Paul is appalling!') Second, Mark wrote his Gospel at a time when the Jewish War was on and probably when Jerusalem had already fallen. The Jewish people, including the Jewish Christians, were being driven out from their land, and were on the way to exile like lost sheep without a shepherd. It was probably Mark's intention to recover for this *minjung* or *ochlos* the gospel of Jesus the Messiah who had presented to the *minjung* of his time an alternative in terms of the Kingdom of God that he had come to proclaim and inaugurate.

Ahn's work has been influential in two ways. First, it has helped scholars to look more closely at the theological perspectives coming out of the exilic period in Israel's history—particularly the theological perspectives of the Priestly Redactor and Second Isaiah, both of whom democratize royal traditions and emphasize the central role of the people (cf. Gen 1.26-28 and Isa 55.1-5).[24] Second, Ahn draws attention to the fact that Jesus' proclamation to 'the poor' was more than a promise of release (cf. Luke 3.4-6). Jesus says, 'Blessed are the poor for theirs is the Kingdom of God'. They are affirmed as the subjects of the Kingdom and co-rulers with the Messiah, and are not just the objects of a process of liberation. A recognition of this emphasis has led to the development of what may be broadly called 'a theology of the victim'. When Jesus interpreted his own ministry in terms of the Suffering Servant, he was reflecting the experience of the victim and forging an understanding of 'the rule of the *minjung*' that would be qualitatively different from the rule of the king. Similarly, when the early church depicted Jesus' rule as that of the Lamb that is slain but regnant (Rev 5.6), it was also speaking of a rule that would be qualitatively different from that of a king. Underlying this eschatological understanding of the rule of the *minjung* seems to be the conviction that those who have suffered the most have the capacity to care the most, so that it is out of the *minjung* that one may reasonably expect a politics of compassion as a real alternative to the politics of power.[25]

This brief presentation of the concerns of *minjung-theology* does not pretend to have done justice to its rich variety. Anyway, this has not been the main purpose of this survey. Rather, it has been to highlight the issues that *minjung-theology* raises with regard to appropriating the Word in the context of Asia, using Korea as a particular example of a larger phenomenon. We may now restate these issues with a few further explanations.

1. *Minjung-theology* sharply raises the problem of 'the two stories'.[26] It refuses to accept the premise that the God revealed in the Bible is unknown outside that history and the subsequent history it generated through the early church and the Christian missionary movements. Hyun Young-hak states this point forcefully: 'I refuse to believe in an invalid God who was carried piggy-back to Korea by some missionary. He was active in our history long before the missionaries came.'[27] The issue, therefore, is to identify the character of both stories and to work out their interrelationships. In doing this, however, there has been a strong protest against too quick a fusion between the two.

Rather, they are seen as interacting partners flowing towards the Messianic Kingdom.

2. *Minjung-theology* also raises the issue of the community that does theology. A theologian does not theologize in a vacuum, but in the context of a community, 'the people of God'. Its main contention has been that this community has been defined too narrowly and exlusively. Looking back at Korean church history, scholars have drawn attention to the fact that Korean Christianity was a *minjung* movement that time and again coalesced with popular *minjung* movements in struggles against various forms of oppression and in projecting new visions for a democratic society in which justice, *shalom* and *koinonia* will be realized. In spite of the strenuous efforts of missionaries to keep Korean Christianity apolitical, Korean Christians read the biblical stories as referring to the whole of Korea and not just to the Korean church.[28] In reactualizing this past, theologians and all those who are with the *minjung* call for an inclusive open community. Contrary to current notions critical of *minjung-theology*, the community of God's people that it envisages is inclusive, not exclusive, for it is primarily made up of all those who have been excluded and marginalized for one reason or another. As Suh Kwang-sun points out:

> *Minjung-theology* identifies itself with *minjung* in the reality of history, and it meets *minjung* in this history and hopes with *minjung* for the messianic kingdom of Jesus. *Minjung-theology* does not take sides with those people in the church who claim the kingdom for the righteous, the powerful and rich, not only here on earth to dominate *minjung* and alienate sinners and powerless but also in heaven and for eternity. *Minjung-theology* searches for an alternative community in the world in the prophetic imagination of Jesus himself and in his messianic politics.[29]

3. The strong interest in history as the movement of the people makes it possible for Korean scholars to use historical critical methods that have been sharpened elsewhere. However, the focus on *people* as the subjects of history provides a critical bias in the appropriation of biblical traditions and in turn questions the hidden bias of many Western theologians who claim that their methods are scientific and ideologically neutral. All theology is biased theology. Therefore the question is who does theology and whom does it serve?

The emphasis on the centrality of people in the doing of theology is found not only in the work of Korean theologians. Other Asian theologians also are making the same point. For instance, Aloysius Pieris states,

> Since, however, there is no people unless summoned by God, and no God worth talking about unless that God speaks through a people, all theology is about a people's God, that is to say, about God's people. The major focus of all 'God-talk' or theology, then, must be the third world's irruption as a new peoplehood announcing the liberating presence of a God who claims to humanize this cruel world.[30]

It seems strange that the issue of 'the middle' (*die Mitte*) or the center of theology, which has become *passé* in Western discussions on the Old Testament, should figure so prominently in Asian theological discussions. There are, however, certain fundamental differences between the two which we have indicated earlier and may now state in summary form. In Asian theology or theologies, the center is seen neither as an overriding concept that could theologically unlock the biblical material nor as a transcendental figure like God or Jesus Christ around whom the biblical materials cohere. Rather, the center is a people or a community through whom the Word speaks. In saying that this center is a people (*minjung*) or the poor masses of the third world, there is the further implication that the Word speaks as a living and liberating word only through certain identifiable communities. Yet, such speaking or 'God-talk' concerns not only these communities, but is addressed to all as a renewed message of salvation and redemption.

The Word and Asian Religious Traditions

The primary, though by no means only, contribution of *minjung-theology* towards articulating the problem of the two stories is to draw attention to the fact that the second story is an authentic repository of God's dealings with Asian people and that it expresses the sufferings and aspirations of Asian people. The essentially teleological nature of the biblical story and the *minjung* story, both of which view the people as the subjects of history and look forward to the time of the Messianic Kingdom, made it possible for us to see the two as parallel and yet interacting partners, so that we did not have occasion to examine more carefully the *tensions* that exist between the two. The tensions between the two stories become more apparent when we take into account, for want of a better word, 'the religious character' of the second story. We will now turn to this aspect of the problem.

The study of hermeneutics has made us aware of the fact that we approach the text with certain presuppositions, whether these be overt or covert, which address questions to the text and in turn are addressed by the text itself—a continuing process that has been identified as 'the hermeneutical circle'.[31] The problem of the two stories goes further and raises another issue. As Asian Christians we inherit two stories or traditions: one coming from the history generated by the biblical tradition and the other from one or more of our Asian religious traditions. The problem is that these two do not easily dovetail into each other. In fact, the two are quite often antagonistic because they begin with different focal images of the Truth and with different ways of perceiving reality. For example, in Christianity God is thought of as personal whereas in Hinduism and Buddhism the Ultimate is transpersonal; in Christianity reality is perceived largely in historical and anthropocentric terms while in Hinduism and Buddhism the perceptions are holistic and cosmic.[32]

Our usual response to this problem has been either to deny the validity of the second story and supress it as a perversion of the truth and worthless superstition or to fall into the trap of saying 'all paths lead to the same goal', thus explaining away rather than dealing with the problem. However, through a long process of listening to and conversing with the context of Asian religiosity, for which the word 'dialogue' is used as a technical term, we have come to realize that we have to listen to the second story in its *own* terms. As Francis D'Sa points out, there is a world of difference between knowing about the Dhamma and knowing ·the Dhamma. We can know about the Dhamma indirectly through reading or discussion and understand it in our terms. But to know the Dhamma we need the Buddha.[33] Hence the basic challenge of the second story is that it suspects the very presuppositions with which we start appropriating the Word in the context of Asia, because these presuppositions either come out of experiences and perceptions that are foreign to the second story or have arisen from a Christian reading of the second story and are still alien to the second story itself.

Since the basic challenge to doing theology in Asia comes from the second story, one could easily assume that the problem of the two stories poses a 'hermeneutics of suspicion' which can be reduced to

Asian religions versus Christianity. The challenge, however, is at a much deeper level. At an earlier stage of the debate on the hermeneutical circle, the Latin American liberation theologians raised the social and therefore ideological factor in hermeneutics.[34] (So, too, Black theologians have raised the issue of racism and Feminist theologians the issue of sexism.) But both Western and Latin American exegetes have largely ignored and even suppressed the religious dimension in this discussion because, or so it seems, Karl Barth and Karl Marx have a negative view of religion. In other words, both Western Christian theology and Marxism as purveyors of salvation and liberation tend to down-play or negate the identity of *homo religiosus*, and thus deny in particular the claim of the great non-Christian soteriological religions to mediate salvation and liberation. All the soteriological religions, including Christianity, were born in Asia; and they continue to have their home in Asia, except for Christianity which left at an early stage and later returned as a foreigner.[35] Hence the Asian contribution towards widening the hermeneutics of suspicion and thus expanding the larger discussion on the hermeneutical circle will be to raise the issue of religion itself. In so doing, we will not be raising an issue different from that raised by *minjung-theology* but will be dealing with the same issue in greater depth. To do this, we will look at the attempts of some Indian and Sri Lankan theologians who have had to face far more acutely than the Korean theologians the challenge of religion in appropriating the Word in the context of Asia.

A straightforward empirical fact presents both the challenge of Asian religions and the need for a theological reappraisal of the term 'religion'. In nearly four centuries, Christian mission in Asia, often with the support of Western colonial powers, has managed to convert only around two per cent of the Asian population to Christianity. The great religions of Asia, by and large, have resisted the Christian penetration of Asia, and in fact have staged a remarkable resurgence in the face of this onslaught.

While Christian missionaries and theologians have been beating their heads against a brick wall, students of religion have been able to explain this phenomenon. They have shown that none of the soteriological religions has made much headway against any other, and conversions from one soteriology to another have been few and far between. Usually such movements have been the result of

political pressure or have been brought about through other induce-
ments. However, massive conversions have taken place among
adherents of a cosmic or animistic religion turning to a soteriological
or metacosmic religion. Also, there have been movements from one
religion to another, particularly to Islam and Christianity, from
among the marginal caste groups or tribal people.[36] This fact leaves
us with the conclusion that the basic yearning for salvation among
Asian people has already been answered in these religions.

In his own inimitable way, T.K. Thomas drew out the implication
of this fact in a lecture on Christian mission. When one offers
something to another and the other declines the offer, there could be
three possible reasons. One reason could be that the person does not
want it. This is rejection. The second could be that the person may
not have understood what is being offered. Then, we repeat and
explain again. The third could be that the person already has what
we are offering. In Christian mission, we only think of the first two
possibilities. The third is theologically too horrendous to contemplate!
However, the fact of the matter is that it is this third possibility that
poses the basic challenge of Asian religions.

For a long time Christian theology has managed to skirt the issue
by separating the religion from its adherents and isolating a system of
beliefs and practics with which one may deal. This approach is
neither new nor endemic to Asia. Clement of Alexandria, for
instance, separated Greek religion from its adherents and mystery
cults and extracted from it its philosophy or gnosis, which he
regarded as excellent, and he baptized it into Christianity. Views
similar to that of Clement have also been in vogue in Asia among
those who speak of Asian religions as a *preparatio evangelica* and
consider these religions as finding their fulfillment in Jesus Christ.[37]
Although this approach does not deal fully with the issue itself, it
does take a positive attitude to other religions—an attitude that
permits a discriminating borrowing of symbols, ideas and even rites
in the forming of an Asian Christianity. Lakshman Wickremesinghe
calls this process 'adaptation or naturalization' in which 'Christians
began to relate the insights and values of other religions to their
Christ-centred vision'.[38] A less complimentary attitude to religion is
evident in the approach of Christian 'developmentalists' and 'libera-
tionists', who, according to Aloysius Pieris, see all non-Christian
religions as the basic cause of 'material poverty' and 'structural
poverty', and therefore feel that religion itself ought to be negated.[39]

Both these views of religion assume that a separation is possible between a religion and its adherents, so that the term 'religion' signifies religion in this abstracted form from which further abstractions can be made such as a philosophy that has supposedly been purged of its religious superstitions. The continuing difficulty with these views is that they do not take into cognizance religion as an indivisible whole of believer and belief as well as of belief and practice. Aloysius Pieris rightly protests that 'in our context, religion is life itself rather than a function of it, being the all-pervasive ethos of human existence'.[40]

Only a holistic understanding of religion will do justice to the nature of Asian religiosity, because it will not separate the truth from its practice or the religion from its adherents. As Aloysius Pieris states, 'To Know Jesus the Truth is to follow Jesus the Way'. Then with particular reference to Hinduism and Buddhism he states:

> In all the non-biblical soteriologies of Asia, *religion* and *philosophy* are inseparably interfused. Philosophy is a religious vision; and religion is a philosophy lived. Every meta-cosmic soteriology is at once a *darsana* and a *pratipada*, to use Indian terms; i.e. an interpenetration of a 'view' of life and a 'way' of life . . . The *goal* of life, in Buddhism, is the *art* of living it. The perfection to be achieved is the style of achieving it![41]

In such a holistic view of religion, the focus of attention is not on the belief system *per se* but on the believer, the *homo religiosus*, through whom and with whom one understands the particular framework of meaning and sacredness through which the believer relates to nature and society and to his or her Ultimate Destiny.[42] Among other things, the advantage of this approach is not only that one converses with and understands the framework of meaning and sacredness through the believer but also converses with the focal images (e.g. the Cosmic Christ), symbols (e.g. the Cross) and rites (e.g. the Eucharist), 'the points of semiotic density', of the believer.[43] These are the points at which all meanings cohere and new meanings are created. For example, in Sri Lanka a Christian lay workers' movement (the Christian Workers' Fellowship) celebrates a Workers' Mass usually on May Day (Labor Day). Many non-Christians not only participate in this Eucharist but also receive the sacrament. In the discussion that followed among the Christians, it was decided that these people should be allowed to participate fully for the focal event being celebrated and re-enacted was understood to be not only the 'Last Supper', at which only the Twelve were present, but also the table fellowship that Jesus had with people of all walks of life. Hence, the Mass was also seen as a precursor of the Messianic Banquet to which many from the East and the West would come. Through this interaction a new meaning had been created in the focal rite.

We may now state in summary form the actual challenge of religion to the doing of theology. First, it questions the separation of belief systems from its adherents as well as the separation of belief from practice. One has to take account of a whole—the people who live by a particular framework of meaning and sacredness. Second, it requires that we accept the fact that the basic yearning of Asian people for salvation and liberation has already been met in their religions, and that we work out a different theological framework which recognizes this fact. Third, a corollary of the first and second points, it affirms that differences need not lead to separations or 'religious ghettoism', but can lead to mutual enrichment. Therefore, the emphasis should be, rather than on the parts, on the whole, within which differences and contradictions can be held.

In essence, these are the concerns of *dialogue* which is not an abstraction from life, but a way of life in which people of several faiths live and work together. As Lakshman Wickremesinghe explains,

> They accept and appreciate the fact that their respective visions, which they affirm as uniquely central and normative for all, are irreconcilable. But it is in this very context of the mutual acceptance of irreconcilability that a deeper sharing of life, devotion and insight has to evolve between them.[44]

Such 'deeper sharing' takes place at three interrelated levels. In the words of Lynn de Silva, these are

> 1. *Intellectual*, where conceptual clarification and understanding of the teaching of the different religions is sought; 2. *experiential*, where we seek to share one another's spiritual experience for mutual enrichment, and 3. *socio-political*, where in developing nations there is a common search for community, for a just and stable society and for peace, justice and development.[45]

It will not be possible in this brief paper to describe more fully the rich and variegated process of *dialogue*, which for some at least is the more mature way of dealing with the problem of the two stories and from communicating the Gospel in a plural situation.[46] We will now move on to examine some of the consequences of the impact of dialogue and a more holistic understanding of religion on appropriating the Word in the context of Asia.

1. The first consequence of *dialogue* with persons of other faiths for doing theology has been to work out a broader framework of meaning within which several religious perspectives can be accommodated. Then, the tensions and disagreements engendered by the interplay of these perspectives need not lead to polarizations but to a deeper searching for the Truth.

An episode in the Bhagavad Gita[47] illustrates the need for such a broader framework of meaning, and may help in understanding its nature. The warrior prince Arjuna finds himself in the unenviable position of having to engage in battle against his cousins. In his debate with Lord Krishna, he expresses his reservations about the ethics of war in general and doubts about his personal duty in the given situation. Krishna, however, urges on him the need to do his duty in this situation both as a matter of practical policy and as a principle of human destiny. What in effect Krishna seems to tell Arjuna is that in discharging his human responsibility, which is his *karma*, he also fulfills his appointed destiny, which is his *dharma*.

In the face of this contradiction, having listened to the arguments of Krishna, Arjuna still longs for the confirmation of a total vision. He beseeches Krishna:

> As Thou hast declared Thyself to be, O Supreme Lord,
>   even so it is.
> But I desire to see Thy divine form, O Supreme Person.

Krishna responds:

> But thou canst not behold Me with this [human] eye of yours;
> I will bestow on thee the supernatural eye.
> Behold my divine power.
> Having thus spoken . . . the great lord of yoga then revealed to
>   Partha [Arjuna] His Supreme and Divine Form . . .
> There the Pandava [Arjuna] beheld the whole universe,
>   with its manifold divisions gathered together in one, in the
>   body of the God of gods.

No human eye can behold the divine form. Krishna bestows on Arjuna the capacity to see the transcendental vision. In it he sees all the contradicitons and paradoxes of the universe held together as one undivided whole. Through it he also receives the assurance that his particular obedience, in spite of its contradictions, will find its ultimate meaning in the Divine One who urges him to discharge his appointed task now.

The episode may be seen as paradigmatic of both the conflictual and complementary relationship between the Christian and Hindu world views. From a Christian perspective that places a primary emphasis on history, the occurrence would have meaning as an event in terms of a final historical purpose. It must lead somewhere—to the liberation of a people from oppressive forces. From a Hindu perspective that places a primary emphasis on the cosmic dimension, it would be an occurrence that has no significance apart from *how* it impacts on the whole. From a Christian perspective, Arjuna's action would be evaluated in terms of what it accomplishes. It is the actual deed that is of significance. From a Hindu perspective, Arjuna's action would be evaluated essentially in terms of his inner intention for doing it. It is the interior motive—whether it was a selfish or selfless act—that matters. Consequently, in this episode it is the interiorized vision of the cosmic Krishna that gives his action both its meaning and its authenticity.

To be sure, we have drawn the lines rather simply and sharply. But we have done this to show a basic difference in perspectives, both of which are important. On the one hand, the Christian perspective is a necessary corrective to the Hindu perspective which envisages the cosmos as a series of evolutions and devolutions so that there is no real historical goal to be reached. On the other hand, the Hindu perspective is a necessary corrective to the Christian perspective that can so easily preclude larger relationships to the whole cosmic order, including nature, in the interest of liberation and development. Therefore, in evaluating an event or a deed a 'spirituality for combat' must be necessarily complemented with a 'spirituality in combat'.

As Francis D'Sa argues, both are perspectives of the same mountain of Ultimate Meaning:

> In such a context we cannot meaningfully employ the principle of 'either-or' but that of 'both and', since for a comprehensive understanding of the mountain all possible perspectives have to be taken into consideration. If one keeps this in mind, then one will seek an organic and harmonious integration of all the complementary perspectives; one will want to find out too the interrelationship between them and the reasons for their differences. Certain aspects will be enhanced by one perspective but certain others

pushed into the background. Perhaps this enhanced aspect will challenge the other perspectives to search for less prominent details which have been totally overlooked or neglected.[48]

The plea is for an inclusive world view—a broader angle of vision—within which one might view the interrelationship between the two stories. It is not enough for Christian theology to work with a Mediterranean world view, reflected in the biblical world view, coupled with a modern western scientific world view. Other religious world views and their symbol systems also have to be taken into account. In essence, this is a matter of metaphysics. As Lakshman Wickremesinghe states, 'Theology is colored by metaphysics as much as by ideology'.[49]

2. The second consequence for theology follows from the first consequence, and raises two issues. First, it cannot be assumed that a basically Hindu-Christian framework of meaning, or world view, would serve in all contexts. Every contextual theology, the incarnated word, would work with its own set of references, so that one cannot speak of *a* theology but of theologies. We must recognize the fact that each theology is unique and particular, and therefore partial. It needs other theological partners to be in dialogue with it, so that uniqueness in diversity presumes receptive plurality. In other words, if any one perception of the Truth denies the validity of other preceptions, it is no longer a truth-claim but a prejudice. This is why Asian theology on the whole abhors exclusivistic claims, and calls for dialogue at all levels as a demand inherent in the inclusive Word of God. Second, this recognition of plurality both at the religious and theological levels questions our traditional, one might even say 'dogmatic', understanding of Christian revelation as normative. Asian theologians find that the doctrine of *Sola Scriptura* tends to be interpreted far too exlusively. Partners in *dialogue*, as Lakshman Wickremesinghe observes, 'accept their own vision, their respective founder and scriptures, as uniquely central and normative for all, but not necessarily as complete or totally exclusive'. They take seriously the promise of Our Lord that there are yet more aspects of the Truth to be revealed into which the Holy Spirit will guide us (John 16.13). Such an attitude not only permits one to see aspects of the Truth in other regions, or for that matter in other theologies, but also to search one's own tradition for the same aspects of the Truth that may be hidden in it. It is to this process that D'Sa refers when he speaks of an enhanced perspective serving to unearth less prominent details in the

other perspective that have been totally overlooked or neglected. We may take together both these related issues, and speak of the second consequence as the need for a 'receptive theology'.

In his paper, 'Christianity moving Eastwards',[50] Lakshman Wickremesinghe provides a good example of the process of receptive theology. He shows that the 'dominant symbol' of God as Father serves to communicate *inter alia* the following themes or ideas: 1. The insight of an initiating creative energy that is motivated by love and personal care. 2. A complex of images suggesting 'purpose, rationality and aestheticism' to convey the idea of a creative purpose operative in history and nature. 3. The idea that what is created, including intelligent beings, is finite and separate from the Creator even though the Father shares something of his plenitude with what he creates. 4. The insight of contingency: that all creatures are totally dependent for their existence on the gracious will of the Creator. 5. The theme of 'cross-bearing'—the voluntary bearing of the suffering resulting from sin and evil in order to release creatures from the grip of sin and evil.

Feminist exegetes have helped to deepen these insights by drawing attention to the biblical image of God as Mother. They have shown that the symbol of the maternal womb is more suitable for expressing the creating, bearing and saving activity of God and that it serves to underline the intimate connection between God and Israel (cf. Num 11.11f.; Deut 32.18; Ps 22.9f.; Isa. 42.14; 46.3f.; 49.15; 63.15f.; Jer 31.20; Hos 2.21; etc.). The imagery of the maternal womb seems to be implied also in the New Testament (e.g. Rom 8.22f.; Col 1.16). Therefore, while the paternal image of God is dominant in the Bible, the maternal image is also a significant and pervasive strand.

Wickremesinghe then shows that though the biblical image of the motherhood of God is more appropriate for evoking the 'cross-bearing' compassion of God, it does not go far enough to deal with another problem raised by the paternal image, namely, the tension or conflict between the wrath of God and the compassion of God which is located in the separation between the Creator and his creation. As Father, the Creator brings his creation into being out of a quiescent primordial chaos or, as later theology would have it, 'out of nothing'. The image of 'externality or production outside of God' is a by-product of the symbol of God as Father. Although this subsidiary image emphasizes the total dependence of the creatures on the Father's love and care, it also leaves open the possibility for an independent stratum of evil to exist outside God, so that intelligent creatures are brought into a situation which they did not originally choose. There is a tragic dimension to this image in that evil exists as an inherent possibility outside of God even before humanity freely chooses it, becomes sinful and is separated from God. In other words, the image of 'externality' has two themes: (a) the dependence of the creatures on God's sustaining love and (b) God's separation from human sin and evil to which he relates in wrath. There is a duality implied in this image which is not fully resolved in the Bible, so that those within the heavenly city are finally separated from those in the lake of fire (Rev 21.8); and God's gracious love is not reconciled with his wrath. Hence, the dominant biblical symbol of God's relation to creation is beset with inner tensions which cannot be held together.

Therefore, Wickremesinghe looks for another complex of images which would serve to avoid such an implicit dualism. This he finds in a Hindu tradition which uses the root symbol of *Sakti* to describe God's relation to creation. *Sakti* refers to the overflowing abundance of creative energy that results in creation. *Sakti* is feminine and is the divine principle that underlies the various female manifestations of the Divine such as Durga, Lakshmi and Saraswathy.

One of the important images associated with *Sakti* is that of the *Sakti-uma* in which creation is viewed as emerging from the womb of God. Wickremesinghe adduces two passages from the Vedas to illustrate this image or metaphor. In the myth of the 'Golden Germ' (*Hiranyagarbha*) it is said,

> This One, who in might surveyed the waters pregnant with vital forces, producing sacrifice is the God of gods and there is none other.

In the Prajapati myth, it is said,

> It thought, 'Would that I be many' . . .
> No one but thou, Prajapati, none besides thee,
> pervading, gave to all these forms their being.

The symbol of the divine womb views creation as an emerging from within, leading to a giving out or sacrifice. On the one hand, the theme of sacrifice, or of giving out of oneself for others, implies risk-taking and vulnerability on the part of the Creator. On the other, the creatures 'shine-forth' (*abhasa*) from the womb-like Source, and make transparent rather than merely reflect 'the immanent plenitude . . . of the transcendent God'.

Wickremesinghe goes on to argue that the image of creation as *ab divino* has advantages over the image of creation as *ex nihilo*. First, it evokes more naturally the idea of a loving Creator who is personally and intimately related to his creatures. Second, the image of the Source-Womb evokes a sense of the all-compassing One in whom we live and move and have our being (cf. Acts 17.28). In it the conflicts and barriers that sin engenders are contained within the inexhaustible and pervasive compassion of God (cf. Isa 49.15). Even evil as an inherent possibility, before human sin freely chooses it, is encompassed within the inexhaustible creative energy emerging from God. Third, the idea of sacrifice or risk-taking is evoked in the image of the Mother who overcomes her horror at the sin of her offspring, which separates the offspring from her, and makes her reach out in suffering love to win back the errant to her.

The symbol of the Source-Womb, replete with archetypal maternity, is reflected in the spirituality of Indian Christian poets who envisage God both as Father and Mother. For instance, Narayan Vaman Tilak sang on his deathbed:

> Lay me within Thy lap to rest
> Around my head Thine arm entwine
> Let me gaze up into Thy face
> O Father-Mother mine.

Krishnapillai sings to Jesus:

> Tenderest Mother-Guru mine,
> Saviour, where is love like Thine?

The Indian Christian contribution to the understanding of God as Mother is not just an arid academic theological argument. It wells out of a deep spiritual experience of the inexhaustible, all-compassing, suffering compassion of God. Hence, Wickremesinghe closes his argument with this request:

> In the Book of Revelation, we find that Semitic imagery envisages the slaughtered but regnant Lamb on the cosmic throne; and Hellenic imagery places the Alpha and Omega on the same throne. The time has come for the Indian imagery . . . of the tender Divine Mother to be on the same throne. It will make explicit what is implicit in the Scriptures.

3. A third consequence of *dialogue* for appropriating the Word in the context of Asia is to reevaluate the role of the nations (*ethnē*) in

the biblical documents. Principally under the influence of the prophetic oracles against the nations, Christian theology has tended to see the nations with their religions and cultures as somehow outside God and against his people, the *laos*. Hence, according to this viewpoint the nations must either be converted or damned.

It is true that the dominant view in the Bible is that the histories of the nations are to be drawn into the history of Israel or the Church. But there are other passages which recognize and even affirm the autonomy of the nations in the providence of God (e.g. Isa 19.19-25; Amos 9.7; Matt 2.1-12; John 4.20-23; Acts 10.30-35). This strand of tradition culminates in the Book of Revelation, chs. 21-22, where the nations come into the heavenly city without the prior intervention of Israel or the Church in their histories. As Lakshman Wickremesinghe states,

> The riches of other streams of salvation will be drawn into that realm [the New Jerusalem] by the Divine Light that illuminates and attracts. What is now hidden will then be revealed. Until then, we follow the path opened for us in this era, and seek to have a foretaste of what humankind in its fullness can be. Then, together-ness will enrich uniqueness, and uniqueness will illuminate together-ness. To that final dawn, may the Author of all lead us.[51]

The New City is open to the traffic of life, so that the nations with their treasures can come into it. This eschatological picture of the New Jerusalem demands a reappraisal of the role of the nations not only in terms of their own histories, the issue we have looked at earlier, but also in the biblical traditions. In order to do this, we should look again not simply at individual passages of Scripture but at the whole framework of the canon of Scripture.

Professor Bernhard W. Anderson himself has made an important contribution in this area. He has cogently and convincingly argued that the episode of the Tower of Babel (Gen 11) does not speak about a curse and that a multiplicity of languages and nations is not to be understood as punishment for sin. Rather, plurality is God's way of ensuring that the blessing given to humanity to multiply and fill the earth does not stagnate in one place, but is carried forward.[52] The Bible recognizes such plurality as within the providence of God (cf. Gen 10) and views the specific covenant with Israel as theologically within the larger covenant with Noah (Gen 9.1-17). From this perspective, Gen 12 begins to speak of one story, the story of Israel, among many stories; and the story of Abraham and his descendants has as its wider reference the nations to whom he is called to be a blessing (Gen 12.1-3). To be sure, the continuing relationship of Israel with the nations is beset with tensions, and the course is never smooth. Sometimes the nations are seen as seducing Israel into sin (e.g. Exod 32) and at other times as an example for Israel to follow (e.g. Jonah 3; cf. Matt 12.41f.). Sometimes the nations are viewed as Yahweh's instrument for punishing Israel (e.g. Isa 10.5) and at other times as the preservers of Israel (e.g. Jer 29.4-15) and the liberators of Israel (e.g. Isa 45.4). In other words, a simplistic monochrome view of the role of the nations has prevented us from seing the rich diversity of the *ethnē* to which the Bible bears witness. To recognize and amplify this fact is an important task especially for Asian theology, for, as Aloysius Pieris reminds us, the irruption of the third world as a new peoplehood is also in large measure the irruption of the non-Christian world. To recognize this fact is also to celebrate proleptically the coming of the nations into the New Jerusalem.

We may now restate in summary form the issues that *religion* raises for appropriating the Word in the context of Asia. In looking at the impact of religion we have argued not so much for a method as for different 'presuppositions'—for a broader framework of meaning that is more inclusive so that tensions may not lead to polarizations but to a deeper searching for the truth; and for new images or symbols that will help us to bring out what is hidden. Although in terms of doing theology we may call these the presuppositions with which we do theology, in actual fact these are more than mere presuppositions. They are themselves perceptions of the Truth received in and through a contemplation of the Divine, so that in this sense they are deeply theological or, may we say, spiritual. For, in the context of Asia, mere God-talk is nonsense, for all words have Silence as their Source and destiny. Therefore, to echo the words of a group of Indian theologians, all theo-praxis and theo-logy must come to rest in the Silence from which it originally sprang. And the struggle which then mothered that Silence will have become Shanti—Peace in the palm of God's hand. And the earth will have become the new Earth that is filled with the knowledge of the Lord as the waters cover the sea. And the wolf shall be a guest of the lamb and the leopard shall sit side by side with the kid. For they shall all know me, says the Lord, from the least to the greatest.[53]

Each in its own way, both *minjung-theology* and the theology arising from dialogue, raise the central issue of *people*. Both are Kingdom-oriented and work with different and yet related eschatological visions. The one views the people as the *minjung (ochlos)*, who are the subjects of history and co-rulers with the Messiah at the Messianic Banquet (Isa 55.1-5; Luke 13.29). The other views the people as the *nations (ethnē)* who will come with their treasures into the New Jersualem to the Divine Light that both illuminates and attracts (Matt 2.1ff.; Rev 21.22-24). In so doing, both seem in large measure to leave out of account the *laos*—those traditionally known as 'the People of God'. This is not the case, for the challenge of the *ochlos* and *ethnos* is addressed to the *laos*—the community that does theology. To accept this challenge is to recognize the fact that no *laos* can either be defined in and of itself or unilaterally in its relation to God. Underlying both streams of thelogy is the conviction that the *laos* can only be known theologically in its relationship both to the *ochlos* and the *ethnos*, rather than the *ochlos* and the *ethnos* being known in their relationship to the *laos*. Aloysius Pieris illustrates this point with the example of Jesus. Jesus himself did not baptize but was baptized in the Jordan of Israel's religiosity as represented by John (not that of the Pharisees or of the Sadducees). This was his first baptism. His second baptism was on the Cross of the people's rejection, suffering and humiliation.[54] As the *laos* in Asia, we too are called to this dual baptism, so that in dying to our old selves we might find new life. Therefore, the Word which we attempt to appropriate comes to us both as a Word of judgment on our complacency and exclusiveness and as a Word of hope and illumination in the midst of our struggles as we attempt with others to realize the Kingdom of God on earth.

NOTES

1. Emerito P. Nacpil, 'The Question of Excellence in Theological Education', *South East Asia Journal of Theology* 16 (1975) 55-58. See also Emerito P. Nacpil, 'The Critical Asian Principle', *What Asian Christians are Thinking* (ed. Douglas J. Elwood; Manila, Philippines: New Day, 1976) 3-6.

2. M.M. Thomas, 'Foreword', to Robin Boyd, *An Introduction to Indian Christian Theology* (Madras: Christian Literature Society, 1969) vi.

3. The term *minjung* is easier to describe than to define. According to Han Wan-sang, a Korean sociologist, the *minjung* are those who are oppressed politically, exploited economically, alienated sociologically and kept out of cultural and intellectual matters. Although this description

suffices to explain the condition of the *minjung* it does not do justice to the *minjung* as a socio-political category—a meaning that the phrase, 'the *minjung* are the subjects of history', attempts to express.

4. Aloysius Pieris, S.J., 'The Place of Non-Christian Religions and Cultures in the Evolution of a Third-World Theology', *CTC Bulletin* (1982) 43-61, argues that no Asian theology can afford to neglect the twin realities of 'Asian *poverty* and *religiosity*'. Although Pieris refers to the two facets of Asian theology with which I am dealing in this paper, I have avoided the use of the first term since it could be misleading with reference to *minjung-theology*, and have explained the second term in the section on 'the Word and Asian Religious Traditions'. Pieris himself gives these two terms a positive content.

5. Suh Kwang-sun, 'Korean Theological Development in the 1970s', *Minjung Theology: People as the Subjects of History* (ed. Commission on Theological Concerns of the Christian Conference of Asia [CTC-CCA]; London, New York, Singapore: Zed, Orbis, CCA, 1983) 38-43.

6. Excerpts from the Court Trial of Kim Chi-ha. See Kim Chi-ha, *The Gold-Crowned Jesus and Other Writings* (ed. Kim Chong-sun and Shelley Killen; New York: Orbis, 1978).

7. Suh Nam-dong, 'Historical References for a Theology of Minjung', *Minjung Theology*, 155-82.

8. Suh Nam-dong explains, 'The method of socio-economic history comprises a broad spectrum of social scientific methods'. He cites with approval the method used by Norman Gottwald in *The Tribes of Yahweh* (New York: Orbis, 1980) as similar to the work of Korean social scientists.

9. Attempts to read 'history from below' are not confined to Korean scholars. See, for instance, Reynaldo C. Ileto, *Pasyon and Revolution: Popular Movements in the Philippines* (Manila: Ateneo de Manila, 1979).

10. Suh Kwang-sun, 'A Biographical Sketch of An Asian Theology Consultation', *Minjung Theology*, 24f.

11. Suh Nam-dong, 'Towards a Theology of Han', *Minjung Theology*, 68.

12. See Suh Nam-dong, 'Towards a Theology of *Han*', *Minjung Theology*, 64-68.

13. Hyun Young-hak, 'A Theological Look at the Mask Dance in Korea', *Minjung Theology*, 54.

14. Suh Nam-dong, 'Cultural Theology, Political Theology and Minjung Theology'. *CTC Bulletin* (1985) 12-15.

15. Suh Nam-dong, 'Theology of Story-telling: A Counter-theology'.*CTC Bulletin* (1985) 4-11.

16. See, for instance, Suh Kwang-sun, 'Minjung and Buddhism in Korea', Chapter IV in his book on *Minjung-Theology* to be published by Orbis Press, New York. Suh Kwang-sun, *Theology, Ideology and Culture* (Hong Kong: WSCF Asia/Pacific 1983), ch. 2. Ryu Dong-shik, 'Shamanism: The Dominant

Folk Religion in Korea', A paper presented at the Inter-religious Conference, Tao Fong Shan, Hong Kong, 1983.

17. Oh Jae-shik, 'Social Movement and the Role of Symbol', *CTC Bulletin* (1985) 49-56.

18. Hyun Young-hak, 'Theology as Rumor-mongering'. *CTC Bulletin* (1985) 40-48.

19. For a good example of 'rumor' as bodily political language, see Kim Chi-ha's poem, 'Groundless Rumors', *Cry of the People and Other Poems* (Kanagawa-ken, Japan: Autumn Press, 1974) 60-88.

20. Kim Yong-bock, 'Messiah and Minjung: Discerning Messianic Politics over against Political Messianism', *Minjung Theology*, 183ff.

21. Sye In-suk, S.J., 'Law is the Rights of the Poor', *Minjung and Korean Theology* (ed. Theological Commission of National Council of Churches in Korea; Seoul: Korean Theological Study Institute, 1982) 58-85 (in Korean).

22. Ahn Byung-mu's *magnum opus* on the Synoptic Gospels is available in Korean. References in this article are to 'Jesus and the Minjung in the Gospel of Mark', *Minjung Theology*, 138-52.

23. Suh Nam-dong, while following Ahn Byung-mu, recognizes the limitations of the semantic range of the term *ochlos* for interpreting *minjung-theology* from a biblical perspective. For him, the term *ochlos* lacks clear political content. Following the Japanese scholar Tagawa, Suh Nam-dong argues that ' ... the term *minjung* in Korean and Japanese has its place and technical meaning in the area of political theology. It should be differentiated from the term *ochlos* ... It (*minjung*) must not and in fact cannot be translated into English, but must be written *Minjung* as a special word for a political theological concept.' Suh declares that Mark needed a word for *minjung*, but not knowing Korean had to be satisfied with *ochlos*! (*Minjung Theology*, 159f.).

24. For a discussion of the Priestly Creation Theology from this perspective, see Bernhard W. Anderson, 'Human Dominion over Nature', *Biblical Studies in Contemporary Thought* (ed. Miriam Ward; Somerville, Mass.: Greeno, Hadden Co., 1975) 27-45. For a discussion of Isaiah 55.1-5, see Edgar W. Conrad, *Patriarchal Traditions in Second Isaiah* (Unpublished Ph.D. dissertation, Princeton Theological Seminary, 1974), 154-65. Korean scholars would want to go further and show the differences in character between the rule of the king and the rule of the people.

25. For examples of 'a theology of the victim', see Hyun Young-hak, '*Minjung*, The Suffering Servant and Hope', A lecture delivered at James Memorial Chapel, Union Theological Seminary, New York, April 13, 1982, and D. Preman Niles, 'A Suffering People Called to be the Suffering Servant—The Political Vision of Second Isaiah', *Towards the Sovereignty of the People* (ed. CTC-CCA; Singapore: Commission on Theological Concerns, Christian Conference of Asia, 1983) 43-88.

26. For a discussion of 'the problem of the two stories' in Asian Theology, see D. Preman Niles, 'Some Emerging Theological Trends in Asia', *CTC Bulletin* (1981) 10f.

27. Hyun Young-hak, 'Do you love me?', *CTC Bulletin* (1982) 4.

28. Kim Yong-bock, 'Korean Christianity as a Messianic Movement of the People', *Minjung Theology*, 80-119, especially pp. 104-108.

29. Suh Kwang-sun, *Theology, Ideology and Culture*, 56.

30. Aloysius Pieris, S.J., 'The Place of Non-Christian Religions', 43.

31. Cf. R. Lapointe, *Les trois dimensions de l'herméneutique*, (Paris: Gabalda, 1967), 64f.

32. Francis X. D'Sa, S.J., 'The Challenge of the Indian Christian Tradition', to be published in *The Lotus and the Sun: A Theological Response to the Reality of India* (ed. CTC-CCA; Singapore: Commission on Theological Concerns, Christian Conference of Asia, 1985).

33. *Ibid.*

34. Juan Luis Segundo, *The Liberation of Theology* (New York: Orbis: 1976), 7-38, especially p. 9. See also James Cone, 'The Social Context of Theology', *God of the Oppressed* (New York: Seabury, 1975) 39-61.

35. Aloysius Pieris, S.J., 'The Place of Non-Christian Religions,' 44-49.

36. *Ibid.*, 52.

37. For convenient summaries of this view, see Robin Boyd, *An Introduction to Indian Christian Theology*, 54-57, 138, 158-59, 212, 247, 253.

38. Lakshman Wickremesinghe, 'Christianity in a Context of Other Faiths', *Asia's Struggle for Full Humanity* (New York: Orbis, 1980) 29.

39. Aloysius Pieris, S.J., 'The Place of Non-Christian Religions', 47.

40. *Ibid.*, 45.

41. Aloysius Pieris, S.J., 'Towards an Asian Theology of Liberation: Religio-Cultural Guidelines', *Varieties of Witness* (ed. D. Preman Niles and T.K. Thomas; Singapore: Christian Conference of Asia, 1979), 39.

42. For an excellent example of this approach, se A.M. Abraham Ayrookuzhiel, *The Sacred in Popular Hinduism* (Madras: Christian Literature Society, 1981).

43. Aloysius Pieris, S.J., 'Buddhist Political Visioning in Sri Lanka', *Towards the Sovereignty of the People*, 144. See also the 'Introduction', pp. 9f.

44. Lakshman Wickremesinghe, 'Togetherness and Uniqueness: Living Faiths in Inter-Relation' (The Second Lambeth Interfaith Lecture), *Crucible* (Oct.-Dec. 1979) 5. Reprinted in *CTC Bulletin* (1984).

45. Lynn de Silva, 'The Understanding and Practice of Dialogue: Its Nature, Purpose and Variations', *Dialogue 4* (1977) 3f.

46. For a good introduction to the concerns of *dialogue*, besides the works cited above, see S.J. Samartha, *Courage for Dialogue: Ecumenical Issues in Inter-Religious Relationships* (Geneva: World Council of Churches, 1981).

47. *The Bhagavadgita* (Translation and Notes by S. Radhakrishnan; London: George Allen and Unwin, 1958), ch. 11.

48. Francis D'Sa, 'The Challenge of the Indian Christian Tradition'.

49. Lakshman Wickremesinghe, 'Living in Christ With People', *'A Call to Vulnerable Discipleship* (Singapore: Christian Conference of Asia, 1982) 37. Reprinted in *CTC Bulletin* (1984).

50. Lakshman Wickremesinghe, 'Christianity Moving Eastwards'. A paper presented at the House of Saints Macrina and Gregory, Oxford, 1983. Printed in *CTC Bulletin* (1984).

51. Lakshman Wickremesinghe, 'Togetherness and Uniqueness: Living Faiths in Inter-Relation', 19.

52. Bernhard W. Anderson, 'Unity and Diversity in God's Creation: A Study of the Babel Story', *CurTM* 5 (1978) 69-81. Independently, C.S. Song also has argued for an interpretation similar to that of Bernhard W. Anderson. See his *The Compassionate God* (New York: Orbis, 1982) 22ff.

53. 'The Lotus and the Sun', Group Report of Indian Theological Dialogue, to be published in *The Lotus and the Sun*. See note 32.

54. Aloysius Pieris, S.J., 'Mission of the Local Church in Relation to Other Major Religious Tradions', *CTC Bulletin* (1983) 38-42.

16

ROMANS AND GALATIANS: COMPARISON AND CONTRAST

J. Paul Sampley

It is easy to see why Romans and Galatians have been considered companion letters. They cover many of the same topics and even make many similar points about those topics. Of all the indubitably Pauline letters[1] they share more with one another than any other two. Further, they have more in common than either one of them has with any of the others. This close affinity has caused them to be read together. Discussion of a topic in one leads regularly to a discussion of the other. For the purpose of this study, it may prove helpful to catalog here the major points where Romans and Galatians converge or appear on a glance to do so.

I

1. *Justification by faith.* Surely since the Reformation the most noticeable common point between Romans and Galatians is their shared insistence on justification by faith. The prominence of that theme in these two letters has had the further consequence of placing these two documents at the center of post-Reformation interpretation of Paul.[2] Both Romans and Galatians emphasize the special relationship between justification and faith. Both claim that faith, the total trusting dependence upon God and right relationship with God, is the only basis on which God reckons or confers righteousness (Rom 3.26; 5.1; Gal 3.11, 24). Justification terminology is primarily concentrated in Galatians and Romans;[3] the other letters generally lack references to justification.[4] Some recent studies, more cognizant of the restricted appearance of the justification terminology, have tried nevertheless to assess the impact of 'justification by faith' even where the phrase is not present.[5]

Paul condemns any attempt at justification by works, and more specifically by works of the law. Romans and Galatians both reject as impossible justification by any means other than faith. The law as an avenue to justification is explicitly ruled out (Rom 10.1-4; cf. 3.20; Gal 2.16, 21; 3.21 and 5.4). Both letters even use the same metaphor to describe the end of any Christian effort to achieve righteousness by means of the law; the Christian has 'died to the law' (Rom 7.4 and Gal 2.19).

2. *The place of the law.* Closely related to Paul's treatment of justification by faith is his understanding of the place or function of the law. Romans and Galatians both address the question of the law's place and both agree that the law is subordinated to faith. In all the Pauline letters, wherever the construction 'to be "under the law"' appears, it is tantamount to a technical phrase that means to have the law as the center of one's life, to be under the law's control, to be in subservience to it. And everywhere it is viewed as inappropriate (e.g. Gal 4.5, 21; Rom 6.14). As Paul puts the antinomy in other terms, the promise of God is made good through faith, not through law (Rom 4.13).

Of the entire Pauline correspondence, only Romans and Galatians reflect the dominical and rabbinic focus of the entire law on Lev 19.18: 'You shall love your neighbor as yourself'. In Galatians Paul warns about letting one's freedom become license and declares: 'For the whole law is fulfilled in one word, "You shall love your neighbor as yourself"' (5.14). In Romans the elaboration is greater but the point is identical: 'Owe no one anything, except to love one another; for he who loves his neighbor has fulfilled the law. The commandments . . . and any other commandment, are summed up in this sentence, "You shall love your neighbor as yourself". Love does no wrong to a neighbor; therefore love is the fulfilling of the law' (13.8-10).

So Romans and Galatians reject the law as a means of justification. They also sum up the whole law by reference to Lev 19.18. One other common feature of the two letters links them to questions of the law: both Romans and Galatians concern themselves with the significance of circumcision, one of the requirements of the law (see below).

3. *Role of the Spirit.* Only in Romans and Galatians does Paul claim that the Spirit helps believers actualize their new status as children of God. The Spirit joins with their spirit and enables them to declare their sonship: 'When we cry, "Abba! Father!", it is the Spirit itself bearing witness with our spirit that we are the children of God . . .' (Rom 8.15f.). 'And because you are sons, God has sent the Spirit of his Son into our hearts, crying, "Abba! Father!"' (Gal 4.6).

The impression of a solid connection between the two letters is even further reinforced by the antithesis of Spirit versus flesh (cf.

Rom 8.4ff. and Gal 3.3). Although the contrast of Spirit and flesh is found in other Pauline letters (e.g. Phil 3.3), it is nowhere else as prominent as in Galatians and Romans.

4. *Abraham*. Among the Pauline letters, Abraham is a major figure only in Romans and Galatians. In Romans, an entire chapter is devoted to him at a crucial point in the argument of the letter (Rom 4; cf. also 9.7 and 11.1). In Galatians, Abraham dominates the reflection of ch. 3. In Romans 4 and in Galatians 3 Paul makes the following common points concerning Abraham: (a) Abraham is linked with promise; (b) Abraham believed God (Gen 15.6); and (c) Abraham's faith preceded circumcision (Rom 4.10-11) and the giving of the law (Gal 3.17).

5. *Adoption and inheritance*. In both Galatians and Romans Paul employs a chain of images to help gentiles understand their new place in God's purpose. They who were 'slaves' have been adopted as 'sons' and are therefore entitled to an 'inheritance'. By the chain (slave to son to heir) Paul reminds the readers: 'For you did not receive the spirit of slavery to fall back into fear, but you have received the spirit of sonship . . . we are children of God, and if children, then heirs, heirs of God and fellow heirs with Christ' (Rom 8.15-17); 'so through God you are no longer a slave but a son, and if a son then an heir' (Gal 4.7). Both Romans 8 and Galatians 4 express this chain in terms of the adoption practices of Paul's time and thereby further reinforce the sense of a special connection between the two letters.

This wide range of topics and matters held in common between Romans and Galatians has rightly caused scholars to study the two letters together and to link the interpretation of them.[6] These common features have also led people to read the interpretation of one letter into the other, to interpret as if a given topic is treated the same in both letters. In such instances, the distinctive features and stresses or emphases of each document have sometimes been lost.

Closer examination of Romans and Galatians, however, reveals not only similarities such as the ones just noted,[7] but also significant differences. In fact, the differences even bear on certain of the topics noted above. For example, beyond the common points made concerning Abraham there are distinctive claims made about Abraham in Romans and in Galatians. Also, though both Galatians and Romans comment about circumcision, they do not make the same comments.

In the next section, we will examine a series of topics in Romans and Galatians where the subject matter is the same but where the claims made about them are quite distinctive.

In fact, we will argue that distinctly different situations have allowed Paul's letters to the Romans and to the Galatians to touch upon common topics, but to differ in significant ways from each other. The final section of this essay will ask what we should make of such striking differences. Specifically in the upcoming section of the essay we will argue that Galatians is written to people who have experienced a noteworthy change in their own lives, but who are being told by Paul's opponents that their change is not sufficient, that faith must be supplemented by a keeping of the law, that is by undertaking circumcision. Paul's response repeatedly stresses the *discontinuity* of the Galatians' present life with the idolatrous life they lived before faith; at the same time Paul insists that the change the Galatians have experienced is full and sufficient.[8] So, at the heart of Galatians is a stress on discontinuity, change, newness, completeness.[9]

Romans, on the other hand, does not focus on the question of the change that has taken place in people's lives; neither does it deal with a question of the sufficiency of the believers' faith. Instead, Romans— seeking as it does to gain support of the Romans for Paul's evangelization efforts further west, and written to a church that knows about Paul only indirectly and by hearsay or rumor—stresses *continuity* in God's purposes. In many ways, Paul tells the Romans that what has happened in Christ—as new and startling as that is in some respects—is not unexpected, not surprising. At the risk of over-simiplification we may say: Galatians stresses discontinuity and change; Romans emphasizes continuity.[10]

These different emphases are understandable, given what we can deduce about the occasion or purpose of each letter.[11] At issue between Paul and his Galatian opponents is the adequacy of faith, of Christ. In face of the claims of others that the (mostly) gentile converts in Galatia need to add to their faith the keeping of the law, the doing of circumcision, Paul vigorously defends the current change in their lives as sufficient and adequate. Nothing additional is needed. The Galatians simply need to live out the life of the Spirit that they have already received.

Paul's situation vis-à-vis the Romans is not as directly contentious. In Romans he offers an explanation of the way God's grace has been

working in this new movement among the gentiles and an account of
how this new working of the gospel fits in with the old, with the
promises of God, with the status of the Jews, and with the place of
the law.

In the items that follow, we will examine a series of concerns
appearing in Romans and Galatians. Though they may be similar in
some details, we will show that in many profound ways different
claims are being made in these two letters.[12] In a final section, we
will ask what is to be made of these substantial differences between
these two letters that have tended to be read together.

II

1. *The law*. The place and function of the law are central issues in
both Romans and Galatians. The treatment of the law in these two
letters illustrates one aspect of the difference to which we are
pointing. Galatians contains Paul's most negative assertions about
the law.[13] As surely as Paul's opponents elevated the importance of
the law for the life of the believer, Paul undercuts it. In the extant
correspondence, nowhere but in Galatians does Paul say the following:
(a) the law was ordained by angels (3.19); (b) it was given through an
intermediary, that is, by implication, not directly from God (3.19);
and (c) the law has a curse (3.13) from which Christ has secured
redemption for believers. Also negative or at least minimalistic is
Paul's statement that the law functioned before Christ as a pedagogue,
the one designated to keep the children in line (3.24). In fact, as the
letter unfolds, law and promise begin to be set over against one
another: 'For if the inheritance is by the law, it is no longer by the
promise' (3.18). Such a polemic finally moves Paul to a clarification
that stops short of opposing law and promise: 'Is the law then against
the promises of God? Certainly not' (3.21).

Paul is a polemicist. In his effort to bring the Galatians to clarity
concerning the law, Paul undercuts the status and importance of the
law to such a degree that he nearly sets law and promise in contrast
to one another. Paul risks rhetorical and theological overkill in his
effort to bring the Galatians back to a more balanced understanding.[14]

Romans, in contrast with Galatians, holds the law in high regard.
The law is 'spiritual' (7.14) and 'holy' (7.21); the 'commandment is
holy and just and good' (7.12). Is the law sin? No, surely not (7.7).
Did the law give rise to sin? No, certainly not (5.13). To be sure, sin

aggressively found 'opportunity in the commandment' but Paul makes no suggestion that that is the commandment's fault.

Far from presenting a contrast between law and promise as in Galatians, Romans offers several declarations of *continuity* between law and promise. The gospel was 'promised beforehand through his [God's] prophets in the holy scriptures' (1.2); a quotation from scripture (Hab 2.4) shows how the gospel works (1.17). God's righteousness, at the heart of the gospel, has now been manifested in Christ 'apart from law' but the continuity of the new manifestation with the old is immediately affirmed by the words 'although the law and the prophets bear witness to it' (3.21).

God's righteousness, whether manifested through the scriptures or through Christ, calls for faith as a proper response. To the reader's reflection whether this faith is in opposition to the law, Paul declares: 'Do we then overthrow the law by this faith? By no means! On the contrary, we uphold[15] the law' (3.31). So, according to Romans, faith and the law coordinate with one another. God's righteousness, and the gospel of which it is the centerpiece, was manifested through the law and the prophets and now is also manifested through Jesus Christ.

In other ways, Romans also stresses continuity of God's purposes in older times and in Christ. Christ's mission confirms 'the promises given to the patriarchs' (15.8). Likewise, when Paul wants to illustrate what faith in God has always involved and still entails, he constructs the typology of Abraham as the believing one (Rom 4; more on this below). Abraham is the progenitor of all who subsequently believe as Abraham did. The law and prophets and the good news about Jesus Christ are congruent with one another: Abraham's faith and the faith of Paul's readers are in harmony.

Paul's fight with his Galatian opponents regarding their overvaluation of the necessity of the law for Christians led him to downgrade the law's origin and importance for Christians. Romans, however, does not fight that same battle. The result is that the letter to the Romans comes forward with a very lofty view of the law and the prophets, of the law's function in God's ongoing purposes and of the law's place in the life of the believers. In Romans, the gospel is in continuity with the law; in Galatians, the law and the gospel stand more in contrast.

2. *Circumcision*. Circumcision, as the external ritual act confirming participation in the covenant community, also illustrates the contrast

between Romans and Galatians. Again, in Galatians, because the law has been pushed by Paul's opponents as a necessary addition to the faith these gentile converts already had, Paul rejects the notion that circumcision is necessary or proper.

Paul warns the Galatians against being seduced by those who suggest that faith and receiving the Spirit are not sufficient signs of the new life in Christ. Although Paul inpugns the motives of his opponents (they do not even keep the law themselves; they just want to have the Galatians circumcised so they can boast [6.13]), he sees that the issue focuses on a move to value the law and its circumcision requirement too highly. Paul sees this demand for more, for the keeping of the law and circumcision, as a turning back, a giving ground, a reverting to slavery.

As a result, Paul declares to the Galatians that there is no value in circumcision, or for that matter in the lack of it. This issue is neutralized. Twice in Galatians Paul rejects any claims made on the basis of circumcision or uncircumcision; neither is anything (5.6 and 6.15). What matters instead is described as 'faith working through love' (5.6) or a 'new creation' (6.15). In light of Paul's struggle with the Galatians, it is apparent why Paul proudly points out that Titus, a Greek, was not required to be circumcised (2.3).

The battle is engaged on another front as well. Paul reminds his Galatian readers, most of whom were gentiles, of the burdensome obligations that circumcision entails: 'I testify again to every man who receives circumcision that he is bound to keep the whole law' (5.3).

Galatians, written in opposition to those who insist upon adding circumcision onto already established faith, never makes a positive reference to circumcision. Paul regularly rejects circumcision as having any place—whether actual or symbolic—in the lives of the Galatian believers.

Romans, unlike Galatians, makes very positive assertions about circumcision. Circumcision is of value if one obeys the law (2.25; cf. Gal 5.3). In fact, circumcision, understood in an internalized, metaphorical way, can even describe true faith: 'He is not a real Jew who is one outwardly, nor is true circumcision something external and physical. He is a Jew who is one inwardly, and real circumcision is a matter of the heart,[16] spiritual and not literal. His praise is not from men but from God' (2.28-29). That claim prompts Paul to ask 'what is the value of circumcision?' (3.1). He answers sweepingly 'much in every way' (3.2).

At one point Paul even reflects whether a gentile who 'keeps the precepts of the law' will not be regarded as circumcised (2.26). This is consistent with the mention of gentiles in 9.30 who, though they did not pursue righteousness, have in fact attained it through the only way it is attainable, namely faith. Abraham is associated positively with circumcision, though Paul is very careful to insist on the primacy of faith. Circumcision was for Abraham a 'sign or seal of the righteousness which he had by faith while he was still uncircumcised' (4.11).

Both Galatians and Romans insist on the priority of faith. Galatians, however, never has a positive comment about circumcision—and understandably so because that practice was at the focus of the controversy that Paul was having with the Galatians. With the Romans, where the same question was not at issue, Paul makes very positive references to circumcision and, at one juncture, uses the term in a metaphorical way almost equivalent to faith.

3. *Theology and christology.* Not only are Galatians and Romans distinguished by emphases on discontinuity and continuity respectively, there is another significant contrast between the letters: Galatians sets many matters forward more christologically than theologically, and Romans tends to reverse that pattern. Romans centers about questions and claims concerning God; Galatians focuses on issues concerning Christ.[17] Of course both letters significantly mention both God and Christ.[18] We are here pointng to a matter of emphasis, to where the predominant stress lies. Krister Stendahl has noted the low profile of the christological claims in Romans 9-11.[19] Indeed, the same evaluation can be made for the whole of Romans. Let us survey the evidence.

Paul is 'set apart for the gospel of God' (1.1); the letter is written to 'God's beloved' (1.7). The thematic statement of the letter, containing the definition of the gospel, is cast in theological, not christological, categories. No reference to Christ appears there: the gospel is 'the power of God for salvation to everyone who has faith' (1.16). That is the very gospel that was borne witness to by the law and the prophets, before Christ (3.21). In like fashion, Abraham believed God and God reckoned it as righteousness (Gen 15.6; Rom 4.3, 9, 22).

Elsewhere in Romans Paul speaks of God's righteousness (1.17), God's wrath (1.18), God's judgment (2.2), God's kindness (2.4; 11.21), God's love (8.39), God's severity (11.21), God's gifts and call

(11.29). Paul urges the readers not only to keep the faith they have between themselves and God (14.22) but also to present themselves as living sacrifices to God (12.1).

In the same way, the questions that focus Paul's reflection are questions that center upon God: 'Is God unjust to inflict wrath on us?' (3.5); 'Has the word of God failed?' (9.6); 'Is there injustice on God's part?' (9.19); 'Has the potter no right over the clay?' (9.21); 'Has God rejected Israel?' (11.1). By contrast to all these questions concerning God and God's purposes, there is only one question about Christ in all of Romans (8.34).

Furthermore, the christological references that do appear in Romans often serve theological functions; that is, they are used by Paul to say something about God. For example, Paul says that he and the readers are 'joint heirs with Christ' because in faith they are all God's children (8.17). The 'belonging' to Christ in 7.4 has a theological purpose: 'that we may bear fruit for God'. Even the phrase 'Christ died for us', suggesting initiative by Christ, serves a *theological* claim in 5.6 and 5.8: Christ's death for us shows God's love for us.

One of Paul's favorite christological expressions, 'in Christ', appears relatively infrequently in Romans (6.11, 23; 8.1f. and 9.1; cf. 8.10). Chapter 6 does employ the image of being baptized into Christ Jesus.[20]

In a couple of passages in Romans, Paul uses 'Christ' or 'God' in the same linguistic constructions. What is identified in 1.1 as the 'gospel of God' (cf. 15.16) is later called the 'gospel of Christ' (15.19). In a similar fashion, Paul urges the readers of Romans to regard one another as those whom 'God has welcomed' (14.3); later in the same argument Paul says 'Christ has welcomed you' (15.7).

But for the most part Romans is persistently theological. The issues are set in terms of what God is doing, has done and will do. The questions are about God, not Christ. The claims, even most of the ones involving Christ, are made in terms of God's purposes. The good news—and even faith itself as the proper response to the gospel—is set forward in the first instance in non-chrisotological, theological categories.

The stance of Galatians is radically different. As surely as Romans is theologically centered, Galatians, because of its occasion, places more emphasis on christological than theological assertions. According to Paul in Galatians, Christians are sustained by Christ's grace (1.6), have responded to the 'gospel of Christ' (1.7),[21] and the churches in Judea that know Paul as persecutor are described as the 'churches of Christ in Judea' (1.22). Paul affirms that 'Christ lives in me' (2.20; cf. also 4.19), that Christ 'loved me and gave himself for me' (2.20), that 'Christ redeemed us from the curse of the law, having become a curse for us' (3.13), that Christ 'gave himself for our sins to deliver us' (1.4), and 'for freedom Christ has set us free' (5.1). These quotations from Galatians show how focused the issues are on Jesus Christ and how frequently and fundamentally Paul refers to christological initiative in soteriological matters.

Many other significant items in Galatians also have a christological center. Paul's gospel cannot be traced back to tradition but is grounded directly in a 'revelation of Jesus Christ' (1.12). In similar fashion, Christians—whether Jews or Greeks, whether slaves or free, whether male or female—are 'one in Christ Jesus' (3.28). In fact at the heart of Paul's struggle with the Galatian opponents is a christological issue of Christ's sufficiency. 'If you receive circumcision, Christ will be of no advantage to you' (5.2).

In his effort to establish the importance of what has happened to the Galatians in Christ and to show the sufficiency of Christ, Paul makes the most radical move in Galatians; he identifies the arrival of faith with the appearance of Christ. To that topic we now turn.

4. *Faith and its connection with Christ*. Of all the Pauline corpus only Galatians so directly links the appearance of faith with the arrival of Christ. 'Before faith came' (3.23) and 'until faith should be revealed' (3.23) are paralleled by the statement 'until Christ came' (3.24). Then 3.25 makes it unmistakable: 'now that faith has come'. The argument may be laid out as follows:

Formerly	Now
before faith came	Christ came
until faith should be revealed	faith came
we were confined under the law kept under restraint	(no longer under law 5.18)
the law was our pedagogue	no longer under pedagogue

As a means of undercutting the opponents' insistence on the importance of the law and circumcision, Paul turns their program around. Instead of the law coming into prominence in the life of the believer, as they would have it, Paul relegates the law to a (limited) function in the past, prior to faith. Now that faith has come with Christ, the believers are no longer under law, no longer under the care of the pedagogue. Law is set over against faith, Christ over against the law.

What really marks Galatians' distinctive contribution in this treatment of law and faith is that Paul transposes the contrast onto the historical plane.[22] Now the issue is not the law and what the Christian might reasonably make of it, that is, what place the law could have in one's life of faith. Now Paul introduces the idea of two historically sequential covenants, one inferior and leading to slavery, the other subsequent, superior and leading to freedom (4.24).[23] The former is allegorically understood as Mt Sinai bearing children for slavery (4.24), but the other, the one the Galatian Christians are expected by Paul to claim, is the heavenly Jerusalem bearing children for freedom (4.26). Abraham's two sons, the one by his wife's slave, the other by Sarah, come to stand for two people, for two *rival* ways of understanding life.

In a polemical counterattack, Paul has relegated the law to an inferior past and has confirmed the appearance of faith as linked directly with the coming of Christ. Before Christ, faith had not been revealed; it had not come into being.

Whereas almost every detail in Galatians is set up to drive a wedge between law and faith, between the old and the new, in Romans there is a considerable effort to stresss the continuity of God's purposes and procedures in the past and present. In Romans, when Paul wants to illustrate the faith that is necessary for the reception of the gospel, he turns to Abraham. On the basis of a reflection built on Genesis 15.6—'Abraham believed God, and it was reckoned to him as righteousness' (4.3, 9, 22, 24)—Paul shows Abraham as a type of the faithful person. Abraham is ideal for this because of his helplessness to fulfill the promise of God and because he trusts that God can and will do what God promises, even if the promise seems to be beyond the realm of possibility.

Although faith and Christ are indissolubly linked in Galatians, nowhere in Romans' depiction of Abraham as believer does Paul specify that Christ is involved. It is consistently reported in Romans 4 that Abraham believed God. But there can be little surprise in that claim because Genesis 15.6 had said it very clearly. There is not a single hint that Abraham's faith was inadequate or lacking in any way. Neither is there a suggestion that Abraham's faith was proleptic or in any fashion merely anticipatory faith. Abraham is presented as the type of the faithful person for all time, whether pre- or post-Christ.

At the conclusion of the portrait of Abraham as the paradigmatic believer, Paul once more cites Genesis 15.6 and tells the readers that those words 'were not written for his [Abraham's] sake alone' (4.23). That is the way God works; God reckons believers righteous. God did so with Abraham, and God does so with the readers of the letter to the Romans. The God of Abraham, who brings life out of death and who brings into being the things that are not, is also the God who 'raised from the dead Jesus our Lord' (4.24). If people in Paul's time believe God as Abraham did, then their faith will be reckoned to them as righteousness just as Abraham's faith was to him. Paul and his readers have come to their faith in God through the preaching concerning Jesus Christ, but it is not a different faith from what Abraham had, nor has God just begun reckoning believers righteous since Christ appeared on the scene.[24] Paul's scriptures make it clear that, from Abraham forward, God has reckoned believers righteous. It was true for Abraham, and it is true for Paul and his readers. It is the same God, faith is the same, and the righteousness is the same.

So, in this matter of faith and its relation to Christ, we observe a confluence of the two matters discussed thus far in this study. On the one side, we see Galatians stressing discontinuity and change and Romans emphasizing continuity of present with the past. On the other side, we note the christological focus of Galatians and the more theological centrum of Romans.

This reading of the Abraham portrait comports well with the *theological* definition of the gospel with which Romans opens: 'For I am not ashamed of the gospel; it is the power of God for salvation to every one who has faith . . . ' (1.16). Likewise, the *christological* elaboration (3.21ff.) of that thematic statement coordinates well with the theological thrust of the thematic statement. Just so, most of ch. 4 treats faith in its theological connections, but there is no change of mind or shift when the chapter concludes with a christological reference (4.24-25) that ties the excursus on faith back into the flow of the letter's argument.

5. *The offspring of Abraham.* In Galatians, Christ is the offspring of Abraham (3.16; reaffirmed in 3.19), and the way for one to become Abraham's offspring is to belong to Christ (3.29). Through Christ one can become child or son of God (3.26). In fact, Galatians even

ties the blessing of Abraham directly to the gift of the Spirit and makes them both present to those who are in Christ Jesus: 'that in Christ Jesus the blessing of Abraham might come upon the Gentiles, that we might receive the promise of the Spirit through faith' (3.14).

Once again, Romans presents a different, less christocentric, picture. In Romans, all who believe as Abraham did become Abraham's children directly, not through Christ. According to Romans 4, God's purpose was to make Abraham the father of all who believe without respect to whether they are Jews or gentiles. 'The purpose was to make him the father of all who believe without being circumcised and who thus have righteousness reckoned to them, and likewise the father of the circumcised who are not merely circumcised but also follow the example of the faith which our father Abraham had before he was circumcised' (4.12). God's promise to Abraham, that he would be the father of 'many nations', is hereby fulfilled (4.18).

In both Romans and Galatians, people become Abraham's children by faith. The difference is that Galatians makes that new status and that faith itself dependent upon Christ. Romans does not.

6. *Jews and gentiles*. The probably pre-Pauline, baptismal formula in 3.28 captures Galatians' picture of the relations of Jews and gentiles: 'In Christ, there is neither Jew nor Greek, neither male nor female, neither slave nor free'. The normal social structures and distinctions that have separated people from one another are overcome in Christ. In Christ, the distinctions that pertain in the world are transcended. Quoting the traditional formulation, Paul shows that his gospel is neither innovative nor inadequate. As Paul has preached the gospel to the Galatians, most of whom were formerly 'in bondage to beings that by nature are no gods' (4.8), they have received the Spirit on the basis of faith alone. No circumcision was required. And they are not required to take up Judaism via the law and circumcision now. In face of subsequent criticism that his gospel was not complete because it did not require circumcision, Paul resorts to a defense that, though it is presented in a variety of forms, ultimately may be reduced to one assertion: 'In Christ Jesus you are all sons of God, through faith' (3.26) whether Jew or gentile.

Faith is the touchstone for Jews and gentiles. Faith relativizes the question whether one is circumcised or not, whether one is a Jew or not, whether one is a gentile or not. Decision has become the criterion of admission, not ancestry, and not the keeping of certain ritual performance. 'In Christ Jesus neither circumcision nor uncircumcision is of any avail, but faith working through love' (5.6; cf. 6.15 and 1 Cor 7.19).

In Galatians, Paul's refusal to distinguish between Jews and gentiles carries over into other depictions of the two groups as well. Jews and gentiles, for example, are both understood to be under the power of sin. Scripture tells Paul that is how things were expected to be: 'The scripture consigned all things to sin, that what was promised to faith in Jesus Christ might be given to those who believe' (3.22).

Likewise, the mission of preaching the gospel is depicted by Paul in such a way as to place the gentile and Jewish missions on equal footing. Paul writes that 'the one who worked through Peter for the mission to the circumcised worked through me also for the Gentiles' (2.8). The two missions are described in this way to clarify that Paul and Cephas are on par in their calling and work, but this description has the indirect effect of equating the importance of the missions as well.

So, Galatians consistently portrays Jews and gentiles as having equal standing whether with regard to sin or the primacy of faith. Neither circumcision nor uncircumcision is of any significance: faith is of ultimate importance. Paul reminds the Galatians that they came to faith as a result of his preaching (4.13ff.). They received the Spirit on the basis of faith (3.2). In Christ all are one, whether they are Jews or gentiles. We need now to see how this same theme is handled in Romans.

In Romans, the theme of equality among Jews and gentiles is affirmed at significant junctures. There is no distinction between Jews and gentiles with respect to sin; they are equally subject to it (3.9). Scripture confirms that (3.10ff.; cf. Gal 3.22). Jews and gentiles are alike in need of grace (5.18ff.; 11.32). Jews and gentiles have the same access to faith and when they do believe, they equally share Abraham's fatherhood (4.11, 12; cf. 9.8). The 'whole world' will be 'held accountable to God' (3.19). Just so, gentiles and Jews are liable to judgment (2.6, 9). Later in the letter, the same theme returns and is elaborated: 'there is no distinction between Jew and Greek; the same Lord is Lord of all and bestows his riches upon all who call upon him' (10.12).

Galatians and Romans, therefore, agree that in many respects Jews and gentiles stand on equal footing. Galatians, because of its struggle with opponents who insist on the importance of the law and circumcision for the gentile converts, seeks on the one hand to minimize the importance of the law and on the other hand to neutralize the significance of whether one is circumcised or not. In both lines of argument, Galatians insists that Jew and gentile stand on par with one another. Perhaps because of its controversy, Galatians can go no further.

Romans can and does go further. Indeed, it insists that the Jews have a certain priority or firstness. The advantage of the Jews is first signaled in the thematic statement of the letter: 'For I am not ashamed of the gospel: it is the power of God for salvation to everyone who has faith, to the Jew first and also to the Greek' (1.16). The priority of the Jews not only pertains in faith, but also in the judgment, whether the judgment be favorable or not: 'There will be tribulation and distress for every human being who does evil, the Jew first and also the Greek, but glory and honor and peace for everyone who does good, the Jew first and also the Greek' (2.9-10).

The slogan, 'the Jew first and also the Greek', used only these three times (Rom 1.16; 2.9-10) in the Pauline corpus, has received various interpretations, chief among which are that it is

(1)　a rhetorically inclusive way of saying 'everybody';
(2)　a reflection of the growth of early Christianity, beginning as a sectarian movement within Judaism and among Jews, and then becoming predominantly non-Jewish ('the Jew first, and then the Greek');
(3)　a claim of some significant priority of the Jews over gentiles.

The first interpretation, that the phrase includes everyone by specifying Jews and Greeks, fits well enough with the Romans theme that we just developed, namely that there is no distinction between Jews and gentiles. But the interpretation flounders on other evidence from Romans where Paul unequivocally affirms several advantages granted to the Jews. (See below.)

The second interpretation is that the phrase reflects the historical movement of Christianity from within Jewish circles out to an engagement with the whole world, symbolized by 'the Greeks'. Other evidence within the letter can be read as supporting this interpretation. The 'olive tree' metaphor of 11.17ff. can be understood in such an historical way. First there was the tree. Later some branches were broken off, and wild (i.e. gentile) branches were grafted into their place. Paul's own interpretation seems to confirm this as Paul discloses 'this mystery', namely that a 'hardening has come upon part of Israel, until the full number of the Gentiles come in' (11.25).

But this second interpretation will not hold up under closer scrutiny. Part of the scene is treated as if it were the whole picture. The inclusion of the gentiles is not a shift away from the Jews. Indeed, it is very much the opposite. It is a way of causing the Jews to 'come around'. Perhaps naively, Paul hoped that his mission to the gentiles, his full exercise of his calling from God, would make his fellow Jews jealous and thus cause them to return (11.11-12). It is the best of all possible scenarios. God cares for the chosen people and in the process incorporates the gentiles into the picture, fulfilling what scripture promised so long ago. And the inclusion of the gentiles becomes the occasion for the return of Israel: 'and so all Israel will be saved' (11.26).

Those who advance the second, historically sequenced interpretation overlook significant clues in the context, particularly that the olive tree is introduced as a way of helping *gentiles* (11.13a) understand the terms on which they are included ('only through faith', 11.20), that they are not the whole tree, and that they continue in their 'contrary to nature' (11.24) standing 'provided' they remain in God's kindness to them (11.22). So gentiles in no way become the new tree; they just become a dependent (11.18) part of the old tree. It is not supplantation of all Jews by gentiles (as the translation 'the Jews first, and then the gentiles' might suggest); rather, it is the inclusion of the gentiles into the ongoing purposes of God with the Jews.

Other reasons for questioning this second interpretation may be found in the broader context of the olive tree metaphor. Prior to it, Paul has insisted that God has not rejected the chosen people (11.1; restated in 11.2) but has always kept a 'remnant, chosen by grace' (11.5). Chapter 11 concludes with Paul's fundamental affirmation that Israel continues 'beloved for the sake of their forefathers' (11.28). For Paul, the basic point is that 'the gifts and the call of God are irrevocable' (11.29). God stands good for the people established by God's call. Paul has already laid the ground for that claim in ch. 3 where he ponders the question whether Israel's faithlessness may have voided the people's special status before God. 'Does their faithlessness nullify the faithfulness of God?' (3.3). To this Paul responds forcefully: 'Of course not! Let God be true though everyone be false' (3.4).

Thus we have exposed not only the weakness of the second interpretation but also the basis for seeing what is truly at stake for Paul in the question of the fate of Israel. Israel is God's special, chosen people. It has been so in the past; it is so now and must be so for all time. At stake is nothing less than the faithfulness, the dependability of God. At issue is whether God's promises can be trusted. Paul affirms that the promises of God do not depend on human performance. God's promises are warranted by God and remain in effect no matter how faithless God's people are. For that reason, because God's faithfulness is lost otherwise, the Jews are and remain first, first in faith, first in judgment, first as God's people. The gentiles, by God's grace and on the basis of faith, are included in the promises and among God's special people, even though it is 'contrary to nature'.

The third interpretation must be upheld: 'the Jew first, and also the Greek' affirms some special priority of the Jews over the gentiles. At stake is not a valuation of peoples, an ethnic judgment. At issue is the faithfulness of God, God's promises to the special people of God. And Paul has already made that clear in 9.24 where he insists that the creative call of God has transformed 'not my people' into 'my people' (Hosea as reaffirmed by Paul in 9.25). The people of God are 'not from the Jews only but also from the Gentiles' (9.24). So, gentiles are included, but not in such a way as to jeopardize or qualify God's commitments to Israel. God's creative freedom has worked alongside God's faithfulness to include the gentiles and to honor the promises to Israel.

Accordingly, Paul can answer the questions 'What is the advantage of the Jew? Or what is the value of circumcision?' (3.1) with the broad assertion 'Much in every way' (3.2). Although in ch. 3 Paul starts out on what seems to promise a considerable list ('To begin with, the Jews were entrusted with the oracles of God', 3.2), he pursues the argument in another direction and only returns to a development of the list and the advantages of the Jews in 9.4-5: 'They are Israelites, and to them belong the sonship, the glory, the covenants, the giving of the law, the worship, and the promises; to them belong the patriarchs, and of their race, according to the flesh, is the Christ. God who is over all be blessed forever. Amen.'

So, in Galatians, because of the controversy that is the occasion for that letter, Paul only develops one side of the larger picture. There he only shows the ways in which Jews and Gentiles stand on equal footing before God; nothing is special about either Jews or gentiles. And Romans is also careful to set forward that position. But Romans does not stop there; Romans also declares a special status for the Jews.

III

What do we make of these differences? The predominant scholarly tendency in the study of Paul has been to ignore or minimize the differences, to read the position of one letter on a particular topic into the other letter. The interpretation of one letter is assimilated to the other.[25]

A second line of interpretation has surfaced occasionally and is enjoying a current revival. This line of interpretation recognizes that Paul does in fact say different things in different letters, and it accounts for the differences as development or change of thought.[26] To describe Paul's thought as 'development' or 'maturing' is at least complimentary.[27] The Corinthians were not as positive in their evaluation of Paul; they simply accused him of being wishy-washy, of vacillating. The charge appears as Paul tries to account for his on-again off-again plans to visit the Corinthians:

> I wanted to come to you first, so that you might have a double pleasure; I wanted to visit you on my way to Macedonia, and to come back to you from Macedonia and have you send me on my way to Judea. Was I vacillating when I wanted to do this? Do I make my plans like a worldly man, ready to say Yes and No at once? As surely as God is faithful, our word to you has not been Yes or No (2 Cor 1.15-18).

Paul has made it easier for the Corinthians to view him as a chameleon-like individual who adapts to the situation at hand. It is to those same people that Paul wrote:

> For though I am free from all men, I have made myself a slave to all, that I might win the more. To the Jews I became as a Jew, in order to win Jews; to those under the law I became as one under the law—though not being myself under the law—that I might win those under the law. To those outside the law I became as one outside the law—not being without law toward God but under the law of Christ—that I might win those outside the law. To the weak I became weak, that I might win the weak. I have become all things to all men, that I might by all means save some. I do it all for the sake of the gospel, that I may share in its blessings (1 Cor 9.19-23).

The Corinthians as well as some modern interpreters of Paul viewed him as an opportunist, a skillful tactician who craftily seized the moment as it suited him best, for his own self-interest. Without getting into the details of the interpretation of 1 Corinthians 9.19ff., it is possible to recognize that Paul in that passage does reveal two fundamental truths about himself. First, his life is in subservience to the gospel (9.23); and second, he does flexibly try to encounter people on their own grounds. That should be fair warning to the interpreter. Issues will be nuanced in accord with Paul's understanding of the situation. Nothing is discussed in and for itself. The balanced perspective towards which Paul aims is often not in the text itself, but lies somewhere between what Paul perceives to be the position the letter engages and the polemic that Paul directs against it.

Whatever else one may say, the situations or occasions of Romans and Galatians have a tremendous effect on the content of the letters. In fact, many of the differences in these letters can be traced directly to Paul's efforts to deal with what he perceives to be the problem. The situation or occasion of Galatians is somewhat easier to deduce than for Romans, but even there one can gain a fair picture. With Galatians, we have had several times to explain Paul's polemic or his particular position on one of the issues by noting what the opponents seem to be suggesting. They have said that Paul's gospel is inadequate, that it has to be supplemented by observing the law and by circumcision. Paul counters by declaring that the Galatians' new faith and its associated gift of the Spirit are sufficient witness to its adequacy. This would account for the christological focus of much of Galatians as well as the emphasis on change.

We must remember that Romans is an unusual Pauline letter on several counts.[28] Its length is extraordinary. It is written to persons most of whom do not know Paul directly and who came into the faith as a result of someone else's preaching. Unlike Philemon, they do not owe Paul anything (Phlm 19). They have surely heard stories and rumors—and some of them no doubt not altogether complimentary—about Paul, his gospel and the way he operates. He wants their encouragement for the evangelizing effort that he expects to pursue to the west of Rome (15.24) and that may even involve financial support.

Furthermore, one can deduce from the contents of Romans that Paul understands the Roman church to be composed of Jews and gentiles whereas the Galatian churches are made up of gentiles for the most part. What are Jews to make of a gospel that admits gentiles to fellowship without requiring them to keep the law, to do circumcision and to keep food laws? Not just the Galatians would have heard that about Paul; the Romans would have heard it also. As a result, Paul's letter to the Romans is an accounting for his gospel and how it fits into God's ancient and ongoing purposes. This would account for the emphasis on continuity that we have seen characterizes Romans; it would also help explain the theological focus of the letter.

But even if we claim that the differences that we have noted between Romans and Galatians were due to Paul's flexible adaptation to very different situations, such an assertion does not answer the question where Paul's real center is. Are we not left with discrepancies? Are we not forced to ask at some point which is Paul's true position on the matters at hand? Must we not ask in terms of the issues we have noted in this essay: Is the 'real' Paul more theological or more christological? Should Romans or Galatians be given more weight in our interpretation of Paul in these matters?[29] Is Paul more genuinely committed to talk of change and disjunction, or of continuity?

To pursue such questions is to oversimplify the hermeneutical task and to trivialize Paul's gospel. One of the problems that Paul's interpreters—from the very first of them to the latest—have always encountered is that Paul's gospel is cast in what we might call delicate balances. Paul's letters ought to be understood in part as efforts to retrieve the proper balance. For example, when some of the Corinthians determine that they already have the fullness of the eschatological new life in Christ, Paul emphasized the 'not yet'. Or, when the Corinthians express their new freedom in Christ, Paul warns them 'lest this liberty of yours somehow become a stumbling-block to the weak' (1 Cor 8.9).

When we see striking differences within the Pauline correspondence, we may be tempted to choose between the differences, to opt for the 'right' position. Indeed, the history of Pauline interpretation in more recent times suggests that in the issues treated in this essay the Galatians side of the discussion has in fact predominated. Sometimes distinctions have been ignored. At other times, Romans has been read in light of Galatians.

But before we take the easier route of picking and choosing between the differences that we note among the Pauline letters, we ought instead to weigh carefully an approach that asks whether in some more profound sense both claims, both sides of the argument may not require to be held together in a creative tension.[30] In the case of the the issues discussed in this essay, let us see what it might look like to hold them together rather than to choose between them.

How can continuity and change be held together? God's faithfulness, God's dependability to bring about what has been promised, requires continuity of past into present. The Jews must continue to be God's chosen people. The gospel, God's power that bears on faith and reckons believers righteous, must be operative from Abraham, the father of all subsequent believers, through to the most recent believer. The law and the prophets have preached the gospel beforehand; that same gospel upholds, establishes the law.

God's freedom to do new things, to choose the ways in which the promises of the past are brought into fulfillment, brings about change. Gentiles who were not originally part of God's people have been grafted in even though it is 'contrary to nature'. By the free gift of God's grace, the gospel has moved powerfully among the gentiles, bringing them from idolatry to full faith in God. Those who were powerless, who were in slavery, have now experienced a radical change in their lives as they have been empowered by the Holy Spirit and called into a new life of freedom in Christ. Faith has come to them with the preaching of Christ.

Accordingly, with Paul's gospel one cannot properly decide either for the Romans' stress on continuity or for the Galatians' emphasis on change. For the whole picture, both must be included. The same is true on the question of christology and theology. For Paul, Christ anchors the purposes of God firmly within history.

What is being done now through Christ is in continuity with the way that God has always worked. God's new work in and among the gentiles is not some startling departure from God's purposes and promises in the past, but in fact is precisely the fulfilling of them.

Recent interpretaton has—whether wittingly or not—stressed too much the Galatians side of the matters treated in this essay. The results have had a subtle but significant effect of separating Christians from their roots within Israel's traditions. Such an interpretation has made it more difficult and less likely that there will be a proper reading and role of the Old Testament in the life of faith. It can even lend itself to a gentile Christian imperialism and arrogance vis-à-vis the Jews. Indeed this deracination, this emphasis on change, has tended to cut Christians loose from the richness of the scriptures and in private piety, at least, has sometimes functioned to narrow the notion of scripture to the New Testament.

On the matters treated in this essay modern interpreters have heard Galatians better than they have heard Romans. So it was with Marcion, and so it seems to be in our time. Disjunction, separation and change have been stressed more than continuity of present with past. It is appropriate to recognize, as Paul did with the Galatians, that the power of the gospel had brought change and continues to do so in those who meet it with faith. But we must not be quite so ready to stop there. With Romans we should affirm that this gospel that now comes to us is grounded in the promises made to Abraham, and that the faith we now enjoy is directly in line with Abraham's faith and that we are thus Abraham's offspring.

The modern interpreters of Paul should not be placed in a position of having to choose between continuity and discontinuity, between christology and theology. In Paul's gospel, each requires the other for a full and proper expression.

NOTES

1. Romans, 1 and 2 Corinthians, Galatians, Philippians, 1 Thessalonians, and Philemon.

2. We cannot here assay the interpretive consequences for the resulting modern pictures and understandings of Paul.

3. For example, the verb *dikaioō* appears in only three of the Pauline letters: Romans (14 times), Galatians (8 times), and 1 Corintians (only twice, 1 Cor 4.4 and 6.11).

4. Krister Stendahl's observation is well-founded: 'Paul's idea of justification does not permeate his writings—and hence is ill suited to be a key to his theology' (*Paul Among Jews and Gentiles* [Philadelphia: Fortress, 1976] 130-31).

5. Cf. J.A. Ziesler, *The Meaning of Righteousness in Paul* (Cambridge: Cambridge University, 1972).

6. J. Christiaan Beker attempts an evalution of the similarities and differences between Rom 4 and Gal 3 (*Paul the Apostle* [Philadelphia: Fortress, 1980] 95-100).

7. Beyond the shared features already noted in these pages, other, minor matters also link the two letters. They both mention the aid for the saints in Jerusalem, the collection that was part of the agreement that Paul and Barnabas reached with some of the Jerusalem apostles (Rom 15.25ff.; Gal 2.1-10). Indirectly, items such as vice lists (Rom 1.29-32; cf. 13.13 and Gal 5.16-21) in both letters (but note similar lists in 1 Cor 6.9ff. and 2 Cor 12.19ff.) may add to the sense of further linkage.

8. 'Paul separates what Judaism joined together: possession of the Spirit and observance of the Torah... Instead of making the gift of the Spirit

complete and perfect by the acceptance of circumcision and Torah, as the opponents most likely wanted to have it, Paul contends that the former is destroyed by the latter' (Hans Dieter Betz, *Galatians* [Hermeneia; Philadelphia: Fortress, 1979] 31).

9. 'This realized aspect of Paul's eschatology is underlined by the double use of the present tense (*estin*)—the heavenly Jerusalem *is* free, she *is* our mother . . . The emphasis on realized eschatology comes in a setting where Paul has to stress in the face of Judaizing opposition that his readers' salvation is already complete . . . The enticement of a fuller gospel . . . could add nothing to such a status' (emphasis in text) (A.T. Lincoln, *Paradise Now and Not Yet* [Cambridge: Cambridge University, 1981] 22).

10. In Romans 'the focus is more on the continuity of salvation-history and on the abiding nature of faith in pre-Christian and Christian reality, that is, on the inherent quality of faith as trust and obedience rather than on Christ as the sole object and possibility of faith' (Beker, *Paul the Apostle*, 97).

11. *Ibid.*, 102.

12. Betz has rightly warned: 'we must be very careful not to simply harmonize Galatians with Romans' (*Galatians*, 176). And I would add that we should be just as wary of a harmonization that runs the other direction.

13. Halvor Moxnes, *Theology in Conflict* (NovTSup, 53; Leiden: E.J. Brill, 1980) 265: 'Paul's view of the law in Galatians is much more negative than in most parts of Romans'. Betz (*Galatians*, 176) notes Galatians' 'very negative interpretation' of the Torah.

14. It is true that, as the letter progresses, Paul rehabilitates the law and reintroduces it more positively into the discussion; cf. 5.14, 22 and 6.2. Paul cannot finally abide the disjunction of promise or gospel and law, even in Galatians. So, in 3.8 he writes: 'And the scripture, foreseeing that God would justify the Gentiles by faith, preached the gospel beforehand to Abraham . . . ' Because of his struggle with the Galatian opponents, Paul could not declare that the *law* preached the gospel beforehand to Abraham. He craftily evades that problem by referring instead to 'scripture'.

15. Or 'establish, confirm, make or consider valid' (William F. Arndt and F. Wilbur Gingrich, *A Greek-English Lexicon of the New Testament* [Chicago: University Press, 1957] 382). Cf. C. Thomas Rhyne, *Faith Establishes the Law* (SBLDS, 55; Chico: Scholars, 1981).

16. Cf. Deut 10.16; Jer 4.4; 9.26; Ezek 44.9.

17. Beker, *Paul the Apostle*, 97: 'Galatians 3 is Christocentric [sic] . . . ' So is the rest of the letter.

18. Admittedly, frequencies of occurrence do not of themselves demonstrate much, but they, along with other observations, may confirm a general picture. The following chart for Romans and Galatians shows total occurrences of each title (in parentheses) and per chapter:

	God	Christ
Romans	(143) 8.9 per chapter	(56) 3.5 per chapter
Galatians	(28) 4.6 per chapter	(37) 6.16 per chapter

A glance reveals that 'God' occurs over twice as frequently in Romans as 'Christ'. In Galatians, 'Christ' appears over a third more frequently than 'God'. Moxnes, *Theology in Conflict*, 16, has a different purpose in view, but notes that only Philippians and Galatians have more references to Christ per page than to God.

19. Krister Stendahl, 'Notes for Three Bible Studies', *Christ's Lordship and Religious Pluralism* (ed. G.H. Anderson and T.F. Stransky; Maryknoll: Orbis, 1981) 18.

20. In a related matter, recent studies increasingly—and rightly so, it seems to me—suggest that Paul's phrase *pistis Christou* that is so regularly understood as 'faith in Christ' may better be understood as Christ's faith or faith like that which Christ had. Cf. A.T. Hanson, *Studies in Paul's Technique and Theology* (London: SPCK, 1974) 69; Luke T. Johnson, 'Romans 3.21-26 and the Faith of Jesus', *CBQ* 44 (1982) 77-90; George Howard, *Paul: Crisis in Galatia* (Cambridge: Cambridge University, 1979) 64-65 (cf. his article in *ExpT* 85 [1974] 212-15). Beker, *Paul the Apostle*, 269, perhaps resolves the matter too quickly but sound judgment emerges: 'it is implicitly or explicitly always "faith *in* Jesus Christ" (except for 1 Thess 1.8). However, this does not mean that faith has a Christomonistic focus. "Faith in [Jesus] Christ" is an abbreviation for "faith in the God, who in Christ's death and resurrection has redeemed us from the bondage of sin, and has transferred us to the dominion of his righteousness"' (emphasis his).

21. 'Gospel of God' is not used in Galatians.

22. Beker, *Paul the Apostle*, 97: 'the discontinuity in salvation-history is much more apparent in Galatians than in Romans . . . '

23. Betz, *Galatians*, 175-76: 'It is clear, however, that two mythico-historical periods are to be distinguished: the period of the Law and the period of the faith. The former ends and the latter begins with the coming of Christ (v. 24) and the revelation of faith.'

24. Nor is Abraham 'christianized'. Beker, *Paul the Apostle*, 103: 'Paul clearly "Christianizes" Abraham . . . ' Beker operates out of mistaken categories when he asks 'how can Abraham be both a Jew and a "Christian"'?

25. When, for example, Beker, *Paul the Apostle*, 250, writes of the 'rupture between the Torah and Christ' in Galatians, he soon finds himself treating Romans as if Romans protrayed such a 'rupture' as clearly as Galatians.

26. Günther Bornkamm, *Paul* (New York: Harper & Row, 1971) 95, characterizes Romans as follows: 'What Paul had previously said is now not only set down systematically, but also oriented to the worldwide horizons of his gospel and mission, and gives, for the first time, his mature and considered thought'.

27. Betz, *Galatians*, 11: 'Developments of thought can be shown to have taken place between Galatians and Romans, but not between Galatians and other Pauline Letters'.

28. Moxnes, *Theology in Conflict*, 16: 'Romans occupies a special position among Paul's letters'.

29. Contrast Betz, *Galatians*, 179, where Paul is understood to have changed: 'In the course of this discussion, Paul has apparently modified his position . . .'

30. Leander E. Keck, *Paul and His Letters* (Philadelphia: Fortress, 1979) 73: 'The other polarity which makes clear how Paul understood the sovereign freedom of God is newness and constancy; specifically the radical newness of the gospel and God's constancy. Can Paul affirm both?'

17

MESSIAH AND THE PEOPLE OF GOD

Howard Clark Kee

In the 1950s, the distinguished Jewish philosopher, Martin Buber, was lecturing in the United States. The subject of one of the lectures that he gave was the basic theme of his book, *Two Types of Faith*,[1] the major thesis of which was that Judaism is the religion of the community, while Christianity is the religion of the individual. I had the privilege of hearing this lecture twice, the second time in the Theological School at Drew, where Bernhard Anderson was the Dean. Since I was at work on a little book with the title, *Jesus and God's New People*,[2] I was perturbed to hear that Christianity was concerned strictly for individuals, not for a community. Summoning up my courage to question this diminutive patriarchal figure, I asked Buber what were the grounds on which he made his assumption about the individual mode of Christian existence. He answered quickly and graciously, 'From the work of Rudolf Bultmann'.

The only surprising feature of Buber's response was that he should have taken Bultmann's word as final on such a basic issue. At that time Bultmann's work was exerting powerful influence, not only in German theological circles, but in American liberal Protestantism as well. The popular Jesus book of Bultmann[3] had reduced the message of Jesus to a call to decision. In deciding for the will of God, one died to the world and entered a new kind of life. The traditional doctrines of atonement, parousia, eternal life, resurrection were in a flash transformed into symbolic modes for expressing inner experience. The messiahship of Jesus was subsumed under his total obedience to the will of God, in a manner which recalled the late-Victorian theological preoccupation with 'the messianic consciousness of Jesus'.[4] Although Bultmann's view was shaped in large measure by the existentialist philosophy of Martin Heidegger,[5] it struck a sympathetic note in the hearts of Protestants reared on the notion that Christian faith is a matter of private relationship between the individual and God or Jesus. This outlook is reflected in Protestant hymnody of the early part of this century, from both liberal and evangelical camps. There is little difference in outlook, for example, between 'My God and I, walk through the fields together' and 'I come to the garden alone . . . and He walks with me, and He talks with me, and He tells me I am his own'. Bultmann's view seemed to provide a more sophisticated equivalent of the celestial chumminess that has characterized so much of Protestant piety.

The important question remains: what is the biblical evidence for the view that either Jesus' messiahship or the response of faith called for by the gospel is a matter of individual relationship with God? Careful assessment of the New Testament shows that the answer to both parts of this question is negative, and the distinction Buber derived from Bultmann is utterly false. Recent studies of the relationship between nascent Christianity and the beginnings of rabbinic Judaism have helped to illuminate the situation. In spite of sharp disagreements between them, E.P. Sanders and Jacob Neusner in their respective analyses of first-century Judaism have shown that the fundamental issue for both Judaism and Christianity in this period was the definition of covenant community.[6] Jews differed widely as to the answers, but they were at one on the basic issues: Who are qualified for membership in the covenant people? And how do they maintain their covenant status? Christians disagreed (both with Jews and among themselves) about the responses to these issues, but they agreed on their centrality.

New Testament scholarship should have been alerted to these factors by such central passages as Paul's struggle in Romans 9–11 over the relationship of Israel to the church, and above all by the words of Jesus at the Last Supper, which are among the few quoted in both gospels and epistles: 'This cup is the new covenant in my blood' (1 Cor 11.25; Matt 26.28; Mark 14.24).[7] The very fact that the early church chose to designate its canonical collection of writings as 'the New Covenant' should have been a clue, as well. The evidence of these documents shows that Jesus' representation of his role is always correlated with a redefinition of the covenant people. In scrutinizing this evidence it becomes clear that the imagery of messiah and of the messianic community in the New Testament always builds on Old Testament imagery, which itself correlates the figure of the messiah with the portrayal of God's people. Most christological studies are content to set up what are perceived as distinct Old Testament messianic categories, in terms of which the question is then asked by the New Testament theologian, 'Which messianic role, or which combination of messianic roles did Jesus fulfill?'[8] The writers of the gospels do not portray Jesus as merely taking over the Old Testament messianic and community structures, however, but as transforming them. To illustrate this dynamic relationship between the images of redeemer and redeemed, both in the Old Testament and the New, we shall examine three distinctively different motifs: Son of Man, primarily drawing on Mark and the Q tradition; Son of God, primarily from Matthew; and the Vine, based on John. Clearly 'Son of Man' and 'Son of God' are not unique to Mark and Matthew respectively, but each title is employed in each gospel in a distinctive manner.

I

The earliest known occurrence of the term, Son of Man, as denoting an eschatological figure is in Daniel 7. The connotations of the expression to emphasize the limitations of human existence are, of course, familiar from the Psalms and the Prophets, especially in Psalm 8.4 and the extended theophanic scene which opens the Book of Ezekiel. The four beasts from the sea, each more bizarre than its predecessor, are specifically identified (Dan 7.17) as the successive world empires that have wrested control of the world from God and that oppress his people. The culmination of this God-opposing sequence of powers is sarcastically described as 'another horn, a little one . . . with eyes of a man and a mouth speaking great things' (Dan 7.8), a character almost universally recognized to be Antiochus IV Epiphanes. When finally the true sovereign of the universe is disclosed, 'one that was ancient of days' seated upon his throne (7.9) and millions gather before him await judgment, it is to a human being—'one like a son of man' (7.13-14)—that the universal rule is assigned. Later the 'one like a son of man' is identified with the 'saints of the Most High' (7.22, 27), who are said to receive the dominion over all the kingdoms under heaven, eternally and universally. Although the recipient of the rule is first described as 'one', the subsequent explanation makes clear that this is an image of a corporate entity: the Holy Ones, God's special people who are to be delivered from their oppressors, vindicated and rewarded.

The Similitudes of Enoch, a document which surely was written as a first-century AD midrash on Daniel's vision,[9] employs the phrase, 'Son of Man', as a title for the agent of redemption. Although he also bears the designation, the Elect One, which is not in Daniel, the basic outline of the visions of 'that Son of Man' and 'the Elect One' before God echoes the details of Daniel 7. Thus God is pictured as an old man, and the Son of Man is the one to whom dominion is assigned over the whole earth and all its inhabitants (1 Enoch 46, 48, 49, 69–71). Yet Daniel's presentation of 'one like a son of man' as the symbol of 'the saints of the Most High' is also mirrored in the Similitudes of Enoch, since the role of the Son of Man is always linked with the destiny of the righteous ones who dwell with him (chs. 50, 71). The successful warfare waged against the wicked rulers and the fallen angels culminates in the prostration of the hostile ones before the throne of the Son of Man (62.6), who turns them over to the angels of punishment (62.11). The righteous are saved 'on that day', eat with the Son of Man, and are clothed in glory (62.13-15). As the one in whom the spirit of wisdom dwells, and who has access to all the secrets of righteousness (49.1-2), it is in his light that the righteous dwell (50.1) and it is on them that he pours out his secrets of wisdom and counsel (51.4). In Enoch's final vision in this section of 1 Enoch (chs. 70–71), he beholds the Ancient of Days, before whom he prostrates himself and is transfigured. Then in behalf of the righteous is born the Son of Man, who proclaims peace of the world to come; and with him they dwell forever. Thus, though the Son of Man has become in the Similitudes of Enoch unequivocally a title, and a messianic title, it has lost nothing of the communal dimensions of the holy and elect ones that it had in Daniel 7.

In the Q tradition, we see a similar linking of the destiny of the Son of Man with that of his followers. Following Luke's version of the Q material, it is evident that in Q there is an explicit connection between the role of Jesus as Son of Man on the one hand and both the pattern of life and the future hope of his followers on the other. Both tragedy and triumph are foreseen for Jesus as well as for his disciples. Hatred, exclusion, revulsion, ostracism are to be the fate of the faithful 'on account of the Son of Man' (Luke 6.22). The break with family and the replacement of traditional family obligations by exclusive attention to the work of the coming kingdom are not only demanded of his followers, but are characteristic of Jesus' own life and experience. This is apparent in the familiar saying, 'Foxes have holes, birds of the air have nests, but the Son of Man has nowhere to lay his head' (Luke 9.58). The summons to repentance typified by the preaching of Jonah in Nineveh is the model for Jesus' ministry as Son of Man (Luke 11.30). His followers are required to acknowledge him as Son of Man, and their fate at the eschatological judgment depends on their response (Luke 12.8). Similarly, those who denounce the Son of Man will, like the wicked in 1 Enoch, never obtain divine forgiveness (Luke 12.10). The coming of that judgment is depicted in Luke as the essential climax of the activity of the Son of Man (17.24, 26), as well as his disclosure to the faithful (17.30).

The first aspect of the Son of Man in Q, radically different from both Daniel and 1 Enoch, appears in the context of the answer to the questioners sent by John. Denouncing his contemporaries—presumably, the religious leaders in particular—for their dismay with both the stringency of John's demands and his own permissiveness, Jesus asserts, 'The Son of Man has come eating and drinking; and you say, "Behold, a glutton and a drunkard, a friend of tax collectors and sinners"' (Luke 7.34). In sharpest contrast to the holy and righteous ones who constitute the community of the Elect in the older apocalyptic writings, Jesus is represented as claiming the role of the Son of Man for himself even while welcoming into the fellowship of the people of God persons whose way of life and whose occupations would have excluded them categorically by the then current standards of Jewish piety.

Mark's Son of Man sayings may be grouped into three categories: those that speak of his coming as judge and vindicator; those that announce his sufferings; those that describe the authority he exercises in the present.[10] Of these the first group clearly manifests the closest kinship with the older apocalyptic tradition. The clouds that accompany the disclosure of the Son of Man in Daniel 7.13 are echoed in Mark 13.36, where there is depicted his arrival in power and his summoning of the elect—recalling 1 Enoch. Appropriately, this prediction appears toward the end of the extended synoptic apocalypse of Mark 13. The same passage from Daniel is paraphrased in Mark 14.62, where Jesus' answer to the high priest's question as to whether he is the Messiah is given in the affirmative: 'I am, and you will see the Son of Man sitting at the right hand of power, and coming with clouds of heaven' (Mark 14.62). But a second important new element is present in this seemingly traditional prediction: it is spoken on the eve of his crucifixion—an event which has no counterpart in Daniel or Enoch. The suffering of the faithful is depicted in Daniel: the lion's den, the fiery furnace, the threats of death for acts of piety. But there is no hint of the death of the Son of Man in fulfillment of his redemptive role. In Mark, however, his death is clearly anticipated, since his being raised from the dead is explicitly predicted in Mark 9.12.

The central importance of the death of the Son of Man is asserted in both direct and indirect predictions of his being put to death. In Mark 8.31, 9.31 and 10.33 we have increasingly detailed announcements of his death at the hands of his adversaries and of his subsequent resurrection. The divine determination of this seemingly tragic death is indicated in the claim that his fate is in accordance with scripture (Mark 14.21) and that even the hour of his betrayal is predetermined (14.41). A related passage (Mark 9.12) goes beyond mere prediction of his death to explain the meaning of it. Following on a reference to the role as eschatological redeemer that Jewish tradition assigned to Elijah (cf. Mal 4.5-6), Mark proceeds with a rhetorical question, 'How is it written of the Son of Man, that he should suffer many things and be treated with contempt?' The clear implication is that Jesus' role is akin to that of Elijah as eschatological 'restorer of all things'. But it is in Mark 10.45 that the most direct interpretation of the death of the Son of Man is offered: 'For the Son of Man came not to be served but to serve, and to give his life as a ransom for many'. Although it is going beyond the evidence to conclude with Rudolf Otto that Jesus is here to be seen as combining the Son of Man with the suffering servant of Second Isaiah,[11] there is no mistaking that a decisively new element is present: the former picture of the triumphant Son of Man is modified by the inclusion of a crucial intermediate stage, in which his experiences in service, suffering and death are seen as essential features of his redemptive role as savior and vindicator of the faithful. The restoration that is promised, and the ransoming death which benefits 'many', show that the suffering is not his individual, private experience before God, but that it involves the destiny of the community of the faithful.

The defining of that community is implied forcefully in the other group of Son of Man words, in which his earthly activity as Son of Man is described. Here participation in the fellowship of his followers is based on two factors, both of which fly in the face of traditional Jewish piety, especially as we know it through the Pharisaic tradition. The first is Jesus' announcement of his authority on earth as Son of Man to forgive sins (Mark 2.10). In the older apocalyptic tradition, it is the holy ones who are to be vindicated by the Son of Man. In 1 Enoch 63, even though the kings and the mighty ultimately repent of their opposition to God and their usurpation of his authority, their penitence is unavailing, and they are crushed with shame in the presence of the Son of Man. Jesus, on the other hand, calls into his fellowship forgiven sinners.

Similarly, his disciples' violation of the Sabbath law in plucking grain and preparing it for eating by rubbing the husks (Mark 2.23-28) is not only condoned by him, but he lays down as a principle that, in his role as Son of Man, he is 'Lord of the Sabbath'. This gives him the right to set aside even such a central rule for determining Jewish identity as the observance of the Sabbath. His violation and sanctioning of violation by others of dietary laws and purity of table fellowship—the central features of Pharisaic piety, as Jacob Neusner has shown[12]—show that he has radically redefined membership in the covenant community, even though the title Son of Man is not used in those connections. But those iconoclastic pronouncements are of a piece with the Son of Man sayings we have just examined. As Son of Man, therefore, the Jesus of Mark and Q resembles the figure of that designation in Daniel and Enoch: he is preparing a covenant people who are awaiting divine vindication; he will receive disclosure in triumph at the end of the present age. Meanwhile, he summons them to remain faithful in spite of suffering, to live in expectation of imminent deliverance. What characterizes the community of the Son of Man in Mark and Q, as distinguished from the community of the Son of Man in Daniel and Enoch, is not holiness but trust, not purity but penitence, not separateness but inclusiveness, not demonstration of legal conformity but acceptance of forgiveness and the ransoming death. As we have seen, it is those who acknowledge the rejected, suffering, crucified Jesus as Son of Man who are vindicated by him before God when the day of triumph comes (Mark 8.38).

II

The earliest appearance of 'son of God' as an image for Israel is in Exodus 4.22, where Moses' message to Pharaoh from Yahweh is that the latter cherishes his covenant people like a first-born son, and demands that they be released from slavery so that they can serve their God. It is this figure that is developed so poignantly by Hosea, who describes the parental love of Yahweh reaching out to the disobedient, prideful, ungrateful, arrogant son, Israel (in Hos 11–14). The final bitter metaphor of the recalcitrant child depicts Ephraim as a stubborn infant that refuses to emerge from the mother's womb

(Hos 13.13). Judgment will surely fall, although the final chapter of the book as we now have it promises restoration, healing, flourishing (Hos 14).

The image of God's son appears with a very different set of connotations in the historical tradition of the Old Testament and in the Psalms. While the destiny of Israel is still in the picture, the focus is on the leadership of the nation in the person of its king. When David indicates his intention to build Yahweh a house of cedar to replace the tent-sanctuary (2 Sam 7), Nathan is instructed to tell David that such a plan is not in accord with God's will, but that his son and successor will build a temple, 'a house for my name' (2 Sam 7.13). God will establish his rule over Israel, and 'I will be his father and he shall be my son'. That motif is dramatically developed in the Psalms, especially the so-called enthronement Psalms 2 and 110.[13] The triumph of the sovereign over all his enemies is seen as the result of his having been placed in power by God, a role which he celebrates by quoting Yahweh's direct address to him: 'I will tell of the decree of Yahweh: he said to me, "You are my son, today I have begotten you"' (Ps 2.6-7). The petition uttered in behalf of the king, asking that he may rule in justice and compassion, begins, 'Give the king thy justice, O God, and thy righteousness to the royal son!' (Ps 72.1).

The role of the king as divine son is not separated from the welfare of the covenant people, however. In Psalm 72.12-13, for example, the royal responsibility includes the deliverance of the poor and the needy, actions of compassion toward the weak and the deprived, deliverance for the oppressed and for victims of violence. Abundance of food and prosperity in the land are promised as concomitants of the son's rule (Ps 72.16). The dominant feature in the Royal Psalms as a group, and in Psalms 2 and 72 in particular, is that of the triumph of the king over his enemies, the tribute that they bring to honor him, and the worldwide fame that attaches to his name. Yet the fact that the motif of compassionate concern is to be found in these enthronement Psalms enables us to see a link between the two ostensibly disparate forms of the son imagery in the Old Testament: that of the king, and that of the nation. The two are linked by the conviction that the primary consideration is for the welfare of the covenant people, under the guidance of the prophetic leader, Moses (Exod 4.22; Hos 12.13), or under the divinely confirmed rule of Israel's king.

In the Gospel of Matthew, both aspects of the image of Son of God are represented, although the weight falls on the divine son as instrument of authority. The importance of the royal role is signaled in Matthew 1, where Jesus is identified in the first instance as 'son of David' (1.1), and the subsequent genealogy has David as its pivotal figure (1.17). Similarly, it is only in Matthew 1.23 that the prophecy of the son who is to be born of a virgin (Isa 7.14) is directly quoted, and his name is then interpreted to mean 'God with us'. But the kingly status is made explicit in the question of the magi, 'Where is he who has been born king of the Jews?' (Matt 2.2). This expectation is then confirmed by the quote from Micah 5.2 about the 'ruler who will govern my people Israel'. Then the return from Egypt, following the flight there to escape the murderous intention of Herod, is said to be in fulfillment of Hosea 11.1, 'Out of Egypt have I called my son' (Matt 2.15). Apart from the surface verbal appropriateness of this prophetic utterance, there is no link between the Exodus experience of Israel to which this prophecy of Hosea's alludes and the safe return of the holy family to Palestine after Herod's death. Nevertheless, the analogy between the divine preservation of the covenant people from bondage in Egypt and the protection of the one born to be king is evident.

The filial relationship of Jesus to God is publicly affirmed in Matthew's—and only in Matthew's—account of Jesus' baptism. Instead of the private disclosure to Jesus that is reported in Mark and Luke, 'You are my beloved son . . .' (Mark 1.11; Luke 3.22), Matthew recounts a public affirmation of Jesus' divine sonship: 'This is my beloved son' (Matt 3.17). That identification is repeated in the devil's testing of Jesus (Matt 4.3, 6), where twice the tempter declares, 'Since you are the Son of God . . .'[14] Or again, in the story of Jesus' walking on the water (Matt 14.22-33), Matthew has replaced Mark's simple statement, 'They were utterly astounded' (Mark 6.51) with the confessional utterance, 'Truly you are the Son of God' (Matt 14.33).

The most significant statement of Jesus' unique relationship to God occurs in Matthew's version of Peter's confession, where instead of the simple Markan version, 'You are the Messiah' (Mark 8.29), we find the liturgically expanded form, 'You are the Christ, the son of the living God' (Matt 16.16). The subsequent declaration—found only in Matthew (16.17)—is that this insight was revealed to Peter by God, Jesus' true father in heaven. Similarly, in Matthew's version of the passion narrative, the High Priest at Jesus' trial, the question to

Jesus about his messiahship is more explicit ('Are you the Christ, the Son of God?', Matt 26.63), and is accompanied by a solemn adjuration, 'by the living God'. While he is on the cross, Jesus is quoted by his religious mockers as having said not only that he was the King of Israel (Matt 27.42), but also that he is the Son of God (27.43). The second item appears only in Matthew. At 27.54, however, Matthew is content simply to take over from Mark 15.39 the utterance of the centurion, 'Truly this was the Son of God'.

There are implicit claims that Jesus is Son of God in such passages from Matthew as 10.32-33, where we have a basis for contrasting Matthew with both his Markan and Q sources. In the Q parallel from Luke (12.8-9), Jesus promises vindication in the presence of God by the Son of Man of all who acknowledge him. In the Markan equivalent (Mark 8.38), Jesus reports the judgment that will fall on (literally, that he 'will be ashamed of') all who deny him in this age. But in Matthew's version of this saying, Jesus speaks only in the first person singular—that is, as 'I' rather than in the third person, of the Son of Man—and the one before whom denial or acknowledgment will occur is 'My Father who is in heaven'. Thus, though the term 'son' is not used, it is everywhere implied in this section of Matthew.

In addition to the explicit or implicit appearance in Matthew of the terms 'Son of God' or 'king', Matthew heavily underscores the role of Jesus as authoritative agent. The astonishing degree to which his teaching was authoritative is noted by Matthew at the end of the Sermon on the Mount (Matt 7.28-29), but it is implied throughout the Sermon. That is especially evident in the opening third of the section, where Jesus' offering instruction from the mountain recalls the figure of Moses and the giving of the Law. Lest anyone miss that point, Matthew reports Jesus as repeatedly contrasting his interpretation of the divine will with that of Moses ('You have heard it was said of old . . . '), followed by a quotation from the Mosaic Law; 'but I say to you . . . ' in words which rest on the authority of Jesus alone (Matt 5.17-20, 21-22, 27-28, 31-32, 33-34, 38-39, 43-44. A variation which makes the same point is found in Matt 6.25, 'Therefore, I tell you . . . '). Jesus speaks on authority which inheres in his role as interpreter of the divine will.

The authority of Jesus according to Matthew is not limited to his own activity, however, but is transmitted by him to his disciples. Although this feature is present in Mark, as in the story of the commissioning of the twelve (Mark 6.7), it is dramatically heightened in Matthew 10.1, where the twelve are told that they have authority 'to heal every disease and every infirmity'.[15] Not only are they authorized to perform exorcisms and healings, but also to cleanse lepers and to raise the dead—details found only in Matthew (10.8). The commissioning address of Jesus to his followers which occupies eight verses in Mark (6.6-13) has been expanded by Matthew, partly from Q and partly from his own tradition so that it runs from 9.35 to 10.40, and constitutes one of the major discourses of Matthew's gospel. The theme throughout is authority transmitted by Jesus to his community and its leadership.

Equally striking in Matthew is his expansion of the event of Peter's confession from the succinct version in Mark 8.27-28 so that it includes not only the explicit, liturgical declaration that Jesus is the Son of the Living God, as we noted earlier, but goes on to describe the enduring nature of the new community, the authority of its leadership, and the divine confirmation of its powers. And, of course, within the entire gospel tradition the community is identified only by Matthew as 'the church'. Efforts to tone down the force of this passage in Matthew are idle, however well intentioned. It is precisely the authority operative within the church, deriving from Jesus as Son of God, which is central to the aims of Matthew in his gospel. The very fact that Peter can make this confession of Jesus as Son of God is a sign of divine revelation rather than of Peter's superior intelligence or theological instincts (Matt 16.17). Whether the rock on which the church is to be built is Peter himself in his role of apostolic authority or his confession, as Protestant interpreters have proposed,[16] the combination of christological confession and enablement of the community and its leadership is presented as the founding of the church as enduring institution (16.18). Mention in this connection of the inability of the gates, or better, powers of Hades to prevail over God's purpose recalls that it was Peter who was the prime witness of the resurrection, as even Paul acknowledges (1 Cor 15.5).

It is the bestowal of 'the keys of the kingdom of heaven', with the concomitant right of binding and loosing which is the most formidable aspect of the transmitted authority in Matthew's tradition. The kinship of this passage with Matthew 18.15-20 would be obvious, even if the latter were not also the only other pericope in the gospel tradition in which the church is specifically mentioned (18.17). Clearly more is involved than the granting or withholding of forgiveness. The question of admission to the covenant community is placed in the hands of those who control the 'keys of the kingdom'. Disagreements among members of the community are to be settled in accord with a series of adjudicative steps, beginning with the disputants and moving finally to the community as a whole. The obligations which are to be placed upon, or the liberties that are to be granted to, members of the community are pictured as having divine confirmation: 'Bound in heaven ... loosed in heaven' (18.18). Assurance of divine response to corporate prayer is offered as well, based on the presence of the Risen Christ among his own people as symbolized by their gathering in his authoritative name (16.19-20).

The climax of Matthew's development of this theme of authority, and indeed the culmination of his entire gospel, is to be found in the closing scene on the mountain in Galilee. The disciples are there because Jesus has ordered or determined that they should be there (*exetaxato*, Matt 28.16). In Matthew's narrative, the disciples had been prepared for this encounter by the divine portents that had accompanied his death and resurrection: the earthquakes that reportedly occurred in connection with the rending of the temple veil, the rolling back of the stone from the entrance to the tomb, the appearance of the angel which filled with terror the official guard at the tomb. Unlike the ending of Mark in which the appearance of Jesus is merely promised, or of Luke, where the disciples recognize Jesus only with difficulty, in Matthew's account they fall at his feet in adoration (28.9). It is to the eleven gathered in Galilee according to his instruction that he discloses the true nature of his role and of his plan for them. He is the one to whom universal authority has been given: '*All* authority in heaven and on earth' (28.28). As a consequence of his possession of this authority, they are commissioned to fulfill the world-wide mission, which is to result in the gathering of disciples from among *all* the nations of the world, and which is manifest itself in their lives according to the full range of commandments that Jesus has given to his followers to transmit to their disciples. In one of the few explicitly trinitarian formulas of the New Testament, and the only one to be found in the gospel tradition, the disciples are given the authoritative rubric in terms of which baptismal admission to the new covenant community may take place (28.19). The assurance that completes this commissioning of the community leadership is the promise of the presence of the authoritative Christ. In the trinitarian formula he is linked as the Son of God with the Father and the Holy Spirit—a presence that will continue until the consummation of the present age (28.20). From the beginning of Matthew to the end, the image of the Son of God represents the authoritative role of Jesus and the authority he has transmitted to the church until his parousia.

III

In the Gospel of John, the final climactic image of Jesus as Messiah and of the new community as his people is that of the Vine and the Branches in John 15.1-11. The figure is a familiar one, from both the Old Testament and the extra-canonical Jewish literature of the post-exilic period. The classic use of the vine as a metaphor for the people Israel is to be found in both the pre-exilic prophets and in the Psalms. In Hosea 10.1-2, Israel is pictured as a luxuriant vine. Her prosperity, symbolized by the fruitfulness, has turned her to idolatry, for which she will be visited by divine judgment. Similarly, in Isaiah's familiar parable of the vineyard (Isa 5.1-7), Israel has brought forth stinking grapes instead of the fruit intended by God, and so she is doomed to be cut down. In Jeremiah 2.21, Israel is portrayed as a vine originally planted by God, but now become wild and degenerate. She will be pruned by God for her lack of suitable fruit (Jer 6.9). By the time of Ezekiel, the image of the vine is employed to declare how utterly unfruitful Israel has become, with the consequence that she is useful only as fuel to be burned (Ezek 15.1-8; 19.10-14). She has been uprooted in the Exile, and will be consumed by fire.

The fullest development of the image in the Old Testament is in Psalm 80.8-16, where God's planting the vine is linked with the deliverance of Israel from slavery in Egypt and with the planting of the new nation in the land of Canaan, including the preparation of the land by the expulsion of the resident nations. After a period of fruitfulness, the vine is now ravaged. God is called to look once more with favor on the vine which he once planted and lovingly nurtured into prosperity and abundance.

The fruitfulness of the nation Israel is also pictured under the image of a branch (*ṣemaḥ*) in Isaiah 4.2-6, where there is a promise of the purification of the people and of the holy mountain where they worship Yahweh. Apparently this is an eschatological promise of the divine undertaking whereby Israel will be renewed and sanctified following the exile. Jerusalem will be a place of safety and renewal, under the image of 'the branch of Yahweh, beautiful and glorious'

(Isa 4.2). Another term linked to the image of the vine as a depiction of Israel is the tendril (*nĕṭîšâ*). When God's punishment falls on faithless Israel, it will be like a workman passing through the rows of the vineyard, destroying the tender shoots, though not obliterating the vineyard itself (Jer 5.10).

One of the most elaborate symbolic usages of the vine is to be found in the Syriac Apocalypse of Baruch 39.7ff., where there is a combination of imagery. Four successive kingdoms, represented by a forest, are to rise, to be destroyed, and then to be replaced by a vine and a fountain. The coming of the vine is with 'peace and great tranquility' (37.6). This is interpreted to mean 'the principate of God's Messiah' (39.7), which will 'stand forever' (40.3).

In contrast to the prophet's association of the vine with the restoration of the nation, Sirach 24.17-21 uses the metaphor to describe the role of Wisdom. Like the fragrant branches of spice trees extending their 'glorious graceful branches', and like a vine producing its first fruit, Wisdom invites all who will to share in the beauty and gratification of her gifts. Her role is reminiscent of that of Jesus in the Gospel of John as the light of the world (8.12) and the Bread of Life (6.33, 54-55), participation in which brings renewal of life.

The figure of the branch is central in the classic passage of Isaiah of Jerusalem, Isaiah 11.1. There, using the terms *ḥōṭer* and *nēṣer*, Isaiah describes the role of the one who springs from the seemingly defunct Davidic dynasty, whose work brings about the renewal of the creation, the outpouring of the divine spirit, the attainment of justice and peace, and the turning of the nations of Yahweh, drawn by 'the ensign of the peoples'. Similar links between the appearance of the messianic rule under the image of the branch and the transformed life of the covenant people and of the whole of creation are evident in Jeremiah 23.5 and 33.15, where Judah is granted to live in peace and security in the land, and in Zechariah 3.8 and 6.12, and in Micah 4.4, where the Branch, Yahweh's servant, enables Israel to enjoy security and prosperity, worshipping God in the renewed temple. Warfare is ended; the Branch has brought in the New Age in which the covenant people flourish in peace.

In the prophetic, the apocalyptic and the wisdom traditions of Israel, therefore, the twin images of vine and branches are employed to describe both the agent through whom God's purpose for his creation and his covenant people is accomplished, and the situation in the New Age when those divine goals are attained. These related symbols announce both the launching of the Messiah's work and the results of his transforming activity in behalf of God's people. It is precisely this interconnection which is central to the symbolism of John 15. The image of the vineyard to portray the judgment that is to fall on those who consider themselves to be the covenant people appears in the synoptic tradition as well (Mark 12.1-12 and parallels). There, unlike John 15, the chief features of the parable are the maltreatment of the owner's son and the shift from the vineyard to the new building (that is, to the New Covenant people) for whom Jesus is the cornerstone, in fulfillment of Psalm 118.22-23.

John transforms the imagery in yet another way, however. Instead of picturing the community as the vine and the Messiah as the Branch, John identifies Jesus as the vine and his people as the branches. The entire undertaking is under the supervision of the farmer-vinedresser who is God the Father. He it is who removes unfruitful branches, or who prunes them to increase their productivity (15.1-3). Shifting the metaphor, Jesus says that it is his word that has effected cleansing among his followers (15.3). To endure or to stand fast in this relationship with Jesus is essential if fruit is to be produced. The question is; what is the fruit (15.4-5)? To fail to remain in right relationship with the Vine is to invite judgment, with the imagery of burning drawn from Ezekiel 15 and 19 (see above). Gradually the ties between fruit-bearing and word of Jesus become clear when we are told that to bear fruit is to demonstrate that one is a disciple, and that the essence of discipleship is mutual love. The model for love among the disciples is the Father's love for the Vine, and the latter's demonstration of his love for the Father through his obedience to the Father's commandments (15.8-11).

The characteristic features of the life of mutual love emerge in this passage. Although these include joy, which Jesus provides for his own, the factor of sacrificial love—specifically laying down one's life for one's friends—is central. The sense of assurance from knowing that one is among the elect (15.19) is tempered by the certainty that the 'friends' will undergo persecution and experience hatred because of their association with the Vine (15.20-23). It is his exposure of the opponents' misdeeds and misperceptions which has aroused their hatred of him and his followers (15.24-25). The false charges which are brought against him and his friends by those who hate him and them will be countered by the Advocate who will come from the Father into their midst, the Spirit of Truth (15.26). The Spirit's testimony will be consonant with their own in his behalf.

Thus, in their destiny, their suffering, the hatred they experience, the joy, the witness to the truth, the life of Vine and branches are closely joined. The work of the Messiah-Vine has no point apart from the branches who are the beneficiaries. And the common life of the branches, as they abide in the Vine, would be inconceivable apart from the resources and values that have been provided by the Vine through his mode of life and death, as well as through the mystical union that binds him and his friends. John 16 moves on to declare how this relationship enables his fellows to withstand the pressure to abandon the community through apostasy (16.1-4), how they may live by the power of the Spirit for which he stands (16.5-15), and how they may share in the victory over the world which he has already achieved (16.33).

* * *

The examples that we have investigated show us that the messianic categories were by no means fixed with the Jewish canon or in the intertestamental literature. Rather, it should not be surprising that Jesus as portrayed in the New Testament, while drawing richly on various models and perspectives in Mosaic, prophetic and wisdom tradition, freely combines and transforms the messianic categories of ancient Israel and of post-exilic Judaism. At the same time, the messianic titles cannot be responsibly interpreted apart from the changing conceptions of covenant community, in both Judaism and early Christianity. The variety of circumstances in which the gospel was heard in the first century of the church's existence shaped the range of ways in which the early Christians understood the role of Jesus as Messiah as well as the essential nature of their own communal existence as the people of the New Covenant. When the primary emphasis of the gospel was seen to fall on God's triumph through Jesus and the impending vindication of his followers at his glorious manifestation, that dominant image in accord with which he was depicted was Son of Man, and the new community lived in expectation of the imminent coming of the New Age (Mark). When the major concern of the Christians was on God's exercise of authority over the creation and over his people through Jesus, and the community was eager to embody that authority in its common life and work as transmitted by him, then the clear preference was for

Son of God as title of Jesus, with the community depicted in terms of structure, due process, moral obligations. When the community was primarily occupied with internal relationship, even while threatened by the twin perils of persecution and apostasy, an important form of organic imagery in terms of which to portray both Jesus and his people was that of Vine and branches, drawing on the rich heritage of Israel's history, self-judgment and eschatological expectations. In this latter framework, there is no place for either predictions of the imminent end of the age nor detailed structures and processes for shaping the church along institutional lines. There is only the mutual love and support of a community of friends.

The study of christology, therefore, is inseparable from an exploration of the social settings in which the christological affirmations were made. There are no set patterns or concepts which can be precisely defined and mechanically applied. The inquiry must proceed in dialectical fashion, moving back and forth between the depiction of the new covenant community on the one hand, and on the other hand the roles and titles of the one whose life of power and obedience 'unto death' ratified that covenant. In the New Testament Jesus, as represented by these messianic titles, by no means abandons communal existence as central reality of the covenant. What he does, rather, is to renew and transform the conditions for participation in the People of God.

NOTES

1. Martin Buber, *Two Types of Faith* (London: Routledge and Kegan Paul, 1951).

2. Howard Clark Kee, *Jesus and God's New People* (Philadelphia: Westminster, 1958).

3. Rudolf Bultmann, *Jesus and the Word* (New York: Scribner, 1934).

4. For example, Vincent Taylor, *The Person of Christ* (London: Macmillan, 1958), especially chapter 13, 'The Divine Consciousness of Jesus'.

5. Martin Heidegger, *Existence and Being*. (Chicago: Regnery, 1949).

6. E.P. Sanders, *Paul and Rabbinic Judaism* (Philadelphia: Fortress, 1977); Jacob Neusner, in popular studies, such as *From Politics to Piety: The Emergence of Pharisaic Judaism* (Englewood Cliffs: Prentice-Hall, 1973), and in technical analyses, such as *The Rabbinic Traditions about the Pharisees before 70* (Leiden: E.J. Brill, 1970).

7. Although the weight of textual evidence in Luke omits the phrase, 'new covenant', Luke uses the verbal cognate to *diatheke* in 22.28-29, where Jesus promises participation in the kingdom to those for whom it has been 'covenanted by my Father'.

8. See for example, Rudolf Otto, *Kingdom of God and Son of Man* (London: Lutterworth, 1951).

9. J. Milik's inference that the Parables of Enoch are late and Christian because they are absent from the Enoch material at Qumran is wholly unwarranted. There is nothing recognizably Christian about the Parables of Enoch, and there are fundamental differences between the Son of Man there and in the New Testament, as the argument below seeks to show. A more sober and persuasive assessment of this material is that by David W. Suter, in *Tradition and Composition in the Parables of Enoch* (SBLDS, 47; Missoula: Scholars, 1979).

10. These are the groupings identified by Bultmann in his *History of the Synoptic Tradition* (New York: Harper, 1963) 108-66.

11. In *The Kingdom of God and Son of Man* (London: Lutterworth, [1938] 1951) 249-55.

12. Jacob Neusner, *Rabbinic Traditions*, passim.

13. Other Psalms that present the special divine relationship of David and the anointed kings who are his heirs include Pss 18, 20, 21, 45, 132.

14. Both propositions begin with *ei* and the indicative, rather than the contrary to fact utterance. The implicit meaning is, 'If, as in fact the case, . . .'

15. Conversely, Matthew alters Mark's statement of the inability of Jesus to perform miracles in Nazareth because of the people's unbelief (Mark 6.5) to the simple declaration that Jesus '*did not do* many mighty works there because of their unbelief' (Matt 13.58). Thereby Matthew safeguards Jesus's omnicompetence.

16. Cf. Oscar Cullmann, *Peter: Disciple, Apostle, Martyr* (Philadelphia: Westminster, 1953) 155-212. Also in his article on *ekklēsia, TDNT* 2 (1964) 518-22.

18

PAUL'S LETTER TO THE ROMANS AS MODEL FOR A BIBLICAL THEOLOGY: SOME PRELIMINARY OBSERVATIONS

J. Christiaan Beker

I

It is a joy for me to contribute to a volume of essays dedicated to Barney. And it seems appropriate to reflect in this essay on an aspect of Biblical Theology, because it was Barney who during his distinguished career at Princeton Theological Seminary incessantly stimulated and provoked his colleagues and students to ponder the quest for an authentic Biblical Theology.

Leo Baeck, the great German rabbi and scholar, once wrote: 'Gnosticism is Christianity without Judaism and, in that sense, pure Christianity. Whenever Christianity wanted to become pure in this way, it became Gnostic.'[1] However extreme this statement may be, nevertheless it warns us against any form of Biblical Theology which either assumes a radical discontinuity between the testaments or evaporates the authenticity of the religious claims of the Hebrew scriptures through spiritualization or allegorization.

If this warning has any validity, one may object to my proposal of considering Romans as a model for a Biblical Theology. Does not the Jewish charge against Paul 'the apostate of Judaism' carry sufficient weight to undermine such a proposal? How could a former rabbi, trained in the exegetical 'traditions of the fathers' (Gal 1.14), create such radical antitheses between the Torah and its *mizwoth* and between the Torah and the Messiah? Isn't it consistent with this that many early Gnostics claimed Paul as their canonical hero and that the first New Testament canon—that of Marcion—selected Paul as its main witness in support of its rejection of the Old Testament? Moreover, did not scholars like R. Reitzenstein characterize Paul 'not indeed as the first but as the greatest of all the Gnostics'?[2]

Indeed, it is arguable that Paul's theology is antithetical to the formulation of a Biblical Theology, because he seems to dismantle the two most crucial ingredients for such a theology: the continuity between the testaments, and the authentic representation of the religious claims of the Hebrew scriptures. A man whose mind is so dominated by *Kontrast-denken*,[3] by thinking in terms of black and white without opting for a middle position,[4] seems a poor model for a Biblical Theology, especially if E.P. Sanders's claim is correct that Paul destroys 'the two pillars common to all forms of Judaism: the election of Israel and faithfulness to the Mosaic law'.[5]

II

Space forbids me to offer more than some preliminary observations about the promise which Romans carries for a Biblical Theology. These observations concern the function of Habakkuk 2.4 and Genesis 15.6 in the composition and argument of the letter.

(A) E. Stauffer writes in the context of a discussion of the history-of-religions framework of the New Testament:

> Das Alte Testament ist die Bibel der Urchristenheit. Was die Männer des Neues Testaments dort lasen, wurde zum normativen Ausgangspunkt ihrer Gedankenbildung. Was das Alte Testament über Gott, Welt und Geschichte sagt, setzt das Neue Testament im allgemeinen als bekannt und anerkannt voraus. Wir haben aus dieser Tatsache die methodische Konsequenz zu ziehen: Überall da, wo die Denkvoraussetzungen der urchristlichen Theologie im Neuen Testament selbst nicht ausreichend ans Licht treten, haben wir grundsätzlich zuerst auf das Alte Testament zurückzugreifen und dort nach der Vorgeschichte unseres Problems zu fragen.[6]

This statement applies eminently to Paul's Letter to the Romans, especially when we recall that the center of his thought lies in his hermeneutic rather than in his systematic-theological endeavor. Paul's way of doing theology occurs in the context of a lively dialogue with Scripture. 'About one-third of all New Testament quotations [of the Old Testament] are cited by Paul.'[7] His citations are restricted to the four main letters (Romans, 1 and 2 Corinthians, Galatians). If we exclude Ephesians (four times) and the Pastoral Epistles (twice) along with the frequent allusions to the Old Testament in his letters, the following figures surface: Romans, 53 times; 1 Corinthians, 16 times; 2 Corinthians, 9 times; Galatians, 10 times. Thus Paul cites the Old Testament explicitly 88 times, of which 53 occur in Romans.[8]

However impressive the statistical evidence is, it does not tell us anything about the weight and function which Paul assigns to certain Old Testament passages. Let me turn now to the importance of

Habakkuk 2.4 and Genesis 15.6 for the argument of Romans.

(B) The citation of Habakkuk 2.4, 'He who through faith is righteous shall live', in Romans 1.17 constitutes according to a widespread scholarly consensus the *Leitmotif* for Romans and determines the composition of the letter as a whole. In fact, Romans 1.18–4.25 explicates Habakkuk 2.4a ('He who through faith is righteous'), whereas Romans 5.1–8.39 deals with the issue of 'life' (Hab 2.4b) as the correlation of justification. Subsequently Romans 9–11 address the question of Israel's relation to faith-righteousness and Romans 12–15 the praxis of 'life' in everyday circumstances.

What now is the relation of the *Leitmotif* Habakkuk 2.4 to the theme of the letter as expressed in Romans 1.16-17? Commentators have noticed that Paul frequently undergirds a thesis with an Old Testament witness (cf. Rom 1.2) and that this citation serves to confirm Paul's emphasis on 'faith' in Romans 1.17b ('through faith for faith'). However true that may be, we must observe that Paul interprets the prophetic text in a context which—while underscoring its meaning—also probes the condition of its validity. In other words, the anthropological focus of Habakkuk 2.4, stressing the human quality of religious faithfulness in the midst of trouble, is actually turned on its head. The condition for being a *zaddik* is not human endeavor, but rather the faithfulness or righteousness of God as revealed in the gospel (Rom 1.17). However much Paul leaves open and unexplored in Romans 1.16-17, it is clear that the Old Testament text is only valid once a prior question has been answered, i.e. the question of the condition for being a *zaddik* or 'righteous'.

And so, when we arrive at the first confirmation of the thesis of Habakkuk 2.4 in Romans 3.28 ('For we hold that a man is justified by faith apart from works of law'), we discover (1) that the particularity of the Jewish context of the *zaddik* in Habakkuk 2.4 has been universalized into *anthrōpos* ('a man'); (2) that the human agent of faith has become the passive recipient of God's righteousness ('justified'), and (3) that the *ek pisteōs* ('through faith') of Habakkuk 2.4 is sharply contrasted with the *erga nomou* ('works of law'). Moreover, when the explication of Habakkuk 2.4a ('he who through faith is righteous') is concluded at the end of Romans 4, we notice that Paul's interpretation of Habakkuk 2.4 is substantiated by a second Old Testament text, Genesis 15.6: 'Abraham believed God, and it was reckoned to him as righteousness'. Paul interprets Habakkuk 2.4a with the help of Genesis 15.6 in order to demonstrate that the possibility of being a *zaddik* or a righteous person depends, to be sure, on faith alone (and is therefore applicable to both Jew and Gentile), but that this faith has as its object the divine gift of 'reckoning' and thus excludes human achievement or 'boasting' (Rom 4.2).

What is interesting about this is that two Old Testament texts which in their own contexts celebrate faith as the condition for righteousness are interpreted by Paul in a radically different manner: they do not celebrate primarily a human quality, but God's faithfulness in Christ as the execution of his grace in Christ, which justifies the sinner (Rom 4.5, 24, 25). In other words, the anthropocentric meaning of Habakkuk 2.4 is not reinforced by Genesis 15.6. Rather, Genesis 15.6 in Romans 4 confirms the theocentric meaning of Habakkuk 2.4 in Romans 1.17. Paul accomplishes this by centering his interpretation of Genesis 15.6 on God's *logizesthai*, his 'reckoning' which dominates Romans 4.1-12 and is confirmed by Romans 4.24-25.

(C) The full impact of Habakkuk 2.4 for the argument of Romans becomes clear when we perceive the following points: (1) Paul's purpose in Romans; (2) the relation of Habakkuk 2.4 to Genesis 15.6 in Galatians and Romans, and (3) the function of the second clause of Habakkuk 2.4, 'shall live' (*zēsetai*).

(1) The characterization of Romans as 'a dialogue with Jews' pertains especially to chs. 1–4. Notwithstanding its deeply reflective character, Romans is not a dogmatic treatise but theology as praxis. Circumstances dictate Paul's preoccupation with 'the Jewish question'. A twofold conflict compels him to explicate the twin poles of his theological conviction: the equality of Jew and Greek and the basic salvation-historical priority of Israel in the gospel (Rom 1.16). Indeed, the times and circumstances call for this explication. Not only is there a conflict in the Roman church between a Gentile majority and a Jewish minority (chs. 14 and 15), but there also looms a conflict in Jerusalem which Paul is about to visit with the collection-money from his Gentile churches. So in his effort to demonstrate that the equality of Jew and Gentile in the church does not suspend Israel's priority in God's salvation-history, Paul must combat both Gentile and Jewish pride. His attack on Gentile pride highlights Israel's enduring privileges (Rom 11.13-32), whereas his attack on the Jews intends to demolish their pride in their election and their possession of the Torah (Rom 1.18–4.25). Paul then is

engaged in a debate which emphasizes both continuity and discontinuity with the Jewish tradition. Especially in Romans 1–4 Paul is engaged as 'the ambassador', attempting to persuade his Jewish dialogue-partner about the reality of his situation under the law and about the fulfillment of the Hebrew scriptures which God's action in Christ has provided.

Thus both Paul's rhetoric and his theological pitch are very different when compared with Galatians, where a similar theological topic—justification by faith—is under discussion. First in Romans 1.17 Paul allows Habakkuk 2.4 to function in an open, non-polemical setting. Contrary to the eisegesis of may commentators, the readers are placed in a situation where the Old Testament context of the theme and the argument is evident, but its full implications not drawn until they reach 3.21ff. Moreover, contrary to Galatians, Paul does not proceed with a Christological argument; he argues on Jewish Old Testament grounds with abundant Old Testament allusions and citations from 1.18 to 3.20. It is actually astonishing that with the possible exception of Romans 2.16 the name of Jesus Christ is not mentioned. Paul's basic *theo*-logical argument intends to persuade his Jewish dialogue-partner within the parameters of a common grammar and worldview. Furthermore, it manifests a theological stance which is rare in the Pauline letters. Romans 1.18–3.20 is basically an Old Testament prophetic-apocalyptic indictment of the perversion of God's created order by Jew and Gentile alike, although its special focus is on the Jew with his elitist arrogance. Indeed, the theological linchpin of the argument is God, the Creator and Judge—which suggests the 'this-worldly' character of the God of the Hebrew scriptures and the insight that whatever Christological statements are made, they must serve the redemption by the God of creation. The prominence of Paul's Old Testament exegesis—often literal, often midrashic—in this section (Gen 1 in Rom 1.22ff.; Deuteronomy in Rom 2.11, 'no partiality'; Psalms in Rom 2.1; 3.4, 10-18, 20) is as noteworthy as his emphasis on God the Creator and Judge, before whom 'none is righteous, no, not one' (Ps 14.1; Rom 3.10) so that 'the whole world may be held accountable to God' (3.19).

Thus the point of Romans 1.18–3.20 is that the stipulation of Habakkuk 2.4 in Romans 1.17 turns out to be an impossibility in the light of the apocalyptic situation of human perversion and God's wrath. To be 'righteous through faith' is impossible in the light of this theocentric Old Testament apocalyptic indictment of the world. Against this prophetic background, the righteousness of God in Christ becomes the only possibility for the fulfillment of the promise of Habakkuk 2.4.

(2) Habakkuk 2.4 and Genesis 15.6 are closely related in Paul's mind, just as they were often grouped together in the Judaism of the period. There they had to demonstrate that the faith-righteousness of the Jew (Hab 2.4) originated in Abraham's relation to God (Gen 15.6). In both Galatians and Romans it seems indeed as if the thesis of Habakkuk 2.4 needs Genesis 15.6 for its full demonstration. Nevertheless the differences between Romans and Galatians indicate the different function of these texts in these letters. In Galatians 3, Genesis 15.6 functions as the key text for the argument (3.6), whereas Habakkuk 2.4 fulfils a secondary supportive role (3.11). However in Romans, Habakkuk 2.4 is the key text (1.17) and Genesis 15.6 serves as its support (4.3ff.). The different situations to which these two letters address themselves explain the different function of the texts. The Galatian Judaizers build their case on a specific Abraham-theology which Paul must dismantle. Thus both Genesis 15.6 and Habakkuk 2.4 occur in Galatians in sharp polemical settings and within a direct Christological context. However in Romans Paul reverses the location of Genesis 15.6 and Habakkuk 2.4—a reversal which is significant both for Paul's conciliatory method and his theological argument.

Genesis 15.6 in Galatians 3 dismantles the Abraham-theology of the Judaizers in arguing the exclusiveness and priority of faith over the later 'addition' of the law (3.5-18). In the course of the argument Habakkuk 2.4 serves to undergird the antithesis between the Torah and faith and is placed in direct opposition to Leviticus 18.5, 'He who does them shall live by them' (3.12). The argument results in a structure of realized eschatology which proclaims the fulfillment in Christ of both Genesis 15.6 and Habakkuk 2.4 (3.26).

In Romans, however, Habakkuk 2.4 is allowed to function quite differently: (a) It is not contrasted with Leviticus 18.5 as in Galatians 3.11, 12. (b) It is not used as direct support for Genesis 15.6. In fact, Genesis 15.6 is removed from the opening theme of Romans, so that its polemical edge of opposing faith to works of the law is suspended until a later stage in the argument (Rom 4) when a case for its validity has been established, i.e. after Romans 1.18–3.20. (c) Genesis 15.6 is indeed used in Romans 4 as confirmation of Habakkuk 2.4.

However—contrary to Galatians 3—it is distanced from Habakkuk 2.4 in the argument and, more importantly, functions only as its partial confirmation. In other words, it confirms the first clause of Habakkuk 2.4 ('he who through faith is righteous') but not the full extent of the second clause ('shall live').

As we have seen, Paul's interpretation of Genesis 15.6 in Romans centers on God's 'reckoning' of righteousness in Christ as the fulfillment of God's promise to Abraham (Rom 4.24-25). This reckoning annuls works of the law and demonstrates the *iustificatio impii* in Abraham (Rom 4.1-15). Because Genesis 15.6 highlights— according to Paul in Romans 4—the Christological fulfillment of the Old Testament promise, it cannot serve to point to those components of God's promises to Israel which extend beyond the Christ-event. Thus in the argument of Romans, Genesis 15.6 underscores the *discontinuous* element which the Christ-event has introduced into the relation between 'the testaments'. The promise of Habakkuk 2.4 (to be righteous through faith) is confirmed by Genesis 15.6, i.e. by God's justification of Abraham as 'the godless person' (Rom. 4.5). This 'reckoning' or justification nullifies the salvific function of the Torah and means the fulfillment of God's promises in Habakkuk 2.4 and Genesis 15.6. However, if all of God's promises are fulfilled in the Christ-event, the conclusion seems inevitable that the Christ-event simply absorbs the faith and hope of Israel and that Israel becomes synonymous with the Christian church as the true people of God.

(3) (A) Because Habakkuk 2.4 in Romans 1.17 confirms the general thesis of 1.16 (that the gospel is the power of God for future eschatological salvation), and because Habakkuk 2.4 gives the thematic outline of the letter as a whole, the future tense of its second clause 'shall live' opens up the horizon of the eschatological future which dominates the discussion of chs. 5–8 and the conclusion of chs. 9–11. This meaning of this second clause of Habakkuk 2.4 in Romans 1.17 differs sharply from its meaning in Galatians 3.11. In Romans 1.17 the clause 'shall live' points to the *eschatological future*, whereas in Galatians 3.11 it can only mean a *logical future*—a meaning parallel to the 'shall live' of Leviticus 18.5 in Galatians 3.12. Thus the Christological focus of Romans 3.21-31 with its scriptural support of Genesis 15.6 in Romans 4 does not signify either the full meaning of Habakkuk 2.4 or the climax of the letter as a whole. The Christological focus of Romans 3.21-31 and 4.24-25 becomes in fact the point of

departure for a discussion of the eschatological hope, i.e. of the 'life' promised to the believer of Habakkuk 2.4 in Romans 1.17. And so chs. 5–8 raise almost for the first time in Romans the question of 'life'(*zōē*) or 'eternal life' (*zōē aiōnios*) (2.7; 5.10, 17, 18, 21; 6.4, 22, 23; 8.2, 6, 10, 38) with its concomitant concepts of 'spirit' (*pneuma*) and 'glory' (*doxa*). Indeed, Romans 5.1-11 constitutes the preface to Romans 5–8: it explicates the theme of hope in the glory of God (5.2) as the full unfolding and actualization of the promise of life according to Habakkuk 2.4.

At this point the future clause of Habakkuk 2.4b opens up profound lines of *continuity* between the Hebrew scriptures and the gospel. Notwithstanding the radical difference between Jew and Christian as to the relation of means and end, the eschatological end will ultimately determine whether the means of Torah or the means of Jesus Christ will actualize the promise of 'life'. Christian theology cannot endure in any authentic way if it bypasses the Jew's fundamental question: 'If the Messiah has come, why is the world still so evil?'[9] And so Habakkuk 2.4b completes the theme of Romans: the actualization of the promise of life will confirm God's Messianic promises to Israel.

(B) The eschatological horizon of the theme of Romans 1.16-17, with its promise of 'salvation' (1.16) and 'life' (1.17) also involves Romans 9–11, i.e. the question of Israel's place in God's salvation-history. At first sight it seems as if the thematic statement of Romans 1.16 ('to the Jew first and also to the Greek') is forgotten in Paul's universalist argument ('to everyone who has faith'), notwithstanding its brief emergence in Romans 3.2. However, Romans 9–11 show that Israel's priority in salvation-history as the recipient of God's election is confirmed and reinforced by Israel's unique eschatological destiny (Rom 11.25-27).

My point is this: Unless the promise of the eschatological future in Habakkuk 2.4b is underscored, the validation of Israel's original priority in its eschalogical destiny cannot be maintained. For— contrary to Galatians 3 and even Romans 4, where Paul's interpretation of Genesis 15.6 seems to push him into absorbing Israel into the church—the promise of future life according to Habakkuk 2.4b points indirectly as well to Israel's peculiar role in that future, when it—along with the Gentiles and the whole created order—shall 'live' in the glory of God's triumph over everything that resist His will.

III

And so the promise of Habakkuk 2.4 becomes a new quest in the framework of Paul's gospel: the quest for what it means to be 'righteous' and for what the promise of 'life' contains. And the answer of Paul is both *continuous* and *discontinuous* with the affirmation of the Hebrew scriptures through Habakkuk. It is *discontinuous* in that for Paul the possibility of human righteousness and faith rests solely in God's faithfulness and righteousness in Christ; it is *continuous* in that for Paul the promise of life will coincide with the actualization of God's Messianic promises to Israel and to his world in his coming glory. Thus the function of Habakkuk 2.4 within the theme of Romans may be a promising start for a consideration of Romans as a model for a Biblical Theology.

NOTES

1. Leo Baeck, *Judaism and Christianity* (New York: Atheneum, 1970) 250.

2. Richard Reitzenstein, *Hellenistic Mystery Religions: Their Basic Ideas and Significance* (Pittsburgh: Pickwick, 1978) 86.

3. Jost Eckert, *Die urchristliche Verkündigung im Streit zwischen Paulus und seinen Gegnern nach dem Galaterbrief* (Regensburg: F. Pustet, 1971) 25.

4. E.P. Sanders, *Paul, the Law and the Jewish People* (Philadelphia: Fortress, 1983) 70.

5. *Ibid.*, 208.

6. Ethelbert Stauffer, *Die Theologie des Neuen Testaments* (Stuttgart: Kohlhammer, 1948) 2.

7. E.E. Ellis, *Paul's Use of the Old Testament* (Edinburgh: Oliver & Boyd, 1957) 11.

8. The majority of the references in Romans are from the Pentateuch, 16 times; Isaiah, 16 times; and the Psalms, 13 times.

9. Emil Fackenheim, *God's Presence in History: Jewish Affirmations and Philosophical Reflections* (New York: Harper & Row, 1972).

WRITINGS OF BERNHARD W. ANDERSON

1. *Books*

Rediscovering the Bible (Association Press, 1950).

The Unfolding Drama of the Bible (Association Press, 1953); rev. ed. 1971; now published by New Century Press, Piscataway, N.J.).

Understanding the Old Testament (Prentice Hall: first ed., 1957; 2nd ed. 1966; 3rd ed., 1975; 4th ed. forthcoming). British title: *The Living World of the Old Testament*; Dutch, *De Wereld van het Oude Testament*.

Israel's Prophetic Heritage, coeditor and contributor (Harper Bros., 1962).

The Beginning of History (Abingdon, Lutterworth, 1963).

The Old Testament and Christian Faith, editor and contributor (Harper and Row, 1962; Herder and Herder, 1969).

Creation versus Chaos: The Reinterpretation of Mythical Symbolism in the Bible (Association Press, 1967).

Out of the Depths: Studies into the Meaning of the Book of Psalms (Board of Missions, Women's Division, United Methodist Church, 1970). New edition: *Out of the Depths: The Psalms Speak For Us Today* (Westminster, 1974; revised and expanded edition, 1984).

Martin Noth, *A History of Pentateuchal Traditions*, translator and contributor (Prentice Hall, 1971; Scholars Press, 1981).

Will Herberg, *Faith Enacted as History: Essays in Biblical Theology*, editor and contributor (Westminster, 1976).

The Eighth Century Prophets, Proclamation Commentary Series (Fortress Press, 1978).

The Living Word of the Bible (Westminster, 1979).

Creation in the Old Testament, editor and contributor (Fortress Press, 1984).

2. *Articles and Essays*

'On the Question, "What Shall I Preach?"', *Christianity and Crisis* 8/6 (1948) 45-46.

'The Temptations of a Christian', *Religion in Life* 17/2 (1948) 163-70.

'The Place of the Book of Esther in the Christian Bible', *Journal of Religion* 30 (1950) 32-43.

'A Bird's-eye View of the Bible', *The Intercollegian*, 69/4 (1951) 15-17; also in *The YWCA Magazine* 46/3 (1952) 6ff.

'Introduction to and Exegesis of the Book of Esther', *Interpreters Bible*, Vol. III (Abingdon Press, 1954).

'Education and the Christian Faith', *Drew Gateway* 42 (1954) 3-10.

'The Book of Hosea', Studia Biblica XXVI, *Interpretation* 8 (1954) 290-303.

'Changing Emphases in Biblical Scholarship', *Journal of Bible and Religion* 23 (1955) 81-88.

'A Look at Theological Education Today,' *Drew Gateway* 31 (1961) 88-97.

'The Earth is the Lord's: An Essay on the Biblical Doctrine of Creation', *Interpretation* 9 (1955), pp. 3-20. Revised edition in Roland Frye, *Is God a Creationist?* (1983), cited later.

'The Biblical Ethic of Obedience', *The Christian Scholar* 39 (1956) 66-71.

'The Place of Shechem in the Bible', *The Biblical Archaeologist* 20 (1957) 10-19, reprinted in *The Biblical Archaeologist Reader* II (Doubleday, 1964) 265-75.

'Bible', in *A Handbook of Christian Theology* (Meridian Books, 1958), pp. 35-40; reprinted in *The Pulpit*, 29/5 (1958) as 'The Bible: A Protestant View', pp. 6-8.

'The Bible', in *The Book of Knowledge* (Groliers, 1962).

Introductory articles and annotations to the books of the Pentateuch, *The Oxford Annotated Bible* (Oxford University Press: 1st ed., 1962; revised ed., 1973).

Entries in *The Interpreters Dictionary of the Bible* (Abingdon, 1962) including: 'Creation', Vol. I, pp. 725-32; revised version in *The Cry of the Environment*, cited later; 'God, Names of', Vol. II, pp. 407-30; 'God, OT View of', Vol. II, pp. 348-51; 'Signs and Wonders', Vol. IV, pp. 348-51; 'Water' of Chaos, Vol. IV, pp. 806-10.

'Exodus Typology in Second Isaiah', in *Israel's Prophetic Heritage*, Festschrift for James Muilenburg, ed. B.W. Anderson and Walter Harrelson (Harper, 1962), pp. 177-95.

'The Old Testament as a Christian Problem', introduction to *The Old Testament and Christian Faith* (Harper, 1963), pp. 1-7.

'The New Covenant and the Old', in the above cited title, pp. 225-42.

'The Problem of Old Testament History', *London Quarterly and Holborn Review* 190 (1965) 5-11.

'Drew's Continuation Theological Education Program', *Christian Century* 79 (1962) 518-20.

'The Power of the Interpreted Word: Carl Michalson's Vision', *Christian Advocate* 10 (1966) 7-8.

'The Drew–McCormick Archaeological Expedition', *The Drew Gateway* 32 (1962) 127-34.

'Ordination to the Priestly Order', *Worship* 47 (1968) 431-41.

'The Contemporaneity of the Bible', *Princeton Seminary Bulletin* 62/2 (1969), 38-50.

'Myth and the Biblical Tradition', *Theology Today* 28 (1971) 321-27.

'Trends: Old Testament', *Theological Book List*, Theological Education Fund (1971), 2-4. See also book lists of 1974 and 1978.

'Martin Noth's Traditio-historical Approach in the Context of Twentieth-century Biblical Research', introduction to the translation of *A History of Pentateuchal Traditions* (1971), xiii-xxxii.

'Confrontation with the Bible: a Tribute to Abraham J. Heschel', *Theology Today* 30 (1973) 267-71.

'The New Crisis in Biblical Theology', *Hermeneutics and the Worldliness of Faith*, Festschrift in Memory of Carl Michalson, *The Drew Gateway*, 45/1-3 (1974-75) 159-74.

'The New Frontier of Rhetorical Criticism: A Tribute to James Muilenburg', *Rhetorical Criticism*, ed. Jared J. Jackson and Martin Kessler (Pickwick Press, 1974), ix-xvii.

'Human Dominion over Nature', *Biblical Studies in Contemporary Thought*, ed. Miriam Ward, R.S.M. (Greeno, Hadden & Co., 1975) 27-45.

'Exodus and Covenant in Second Isaiah and Prophetic Tradition', *Magnalia Dei: The Mighty Acts of God*, Festschrift in Memory of G. Ernest Wright (Doubleday, 1976) 339-60.

'The Crisis in Biblical Theology', *Theology Today* 28 (1976) 321-37.

'Biblical Faith and Political Responsibility', *Theological Bulletin*, McMaster Divinity College, Hamilton, Ont., 4/2 (1976), 2-16. Reprinted in *The Living Word* (1979), chap. 4.

'The Tower of Babel: Paradigm of Human Unity and Diversity', *Concilium* 121 (1977) 89-97; translated into various languages; expanded version, 'Unity and Diversity in God's Creation: A Study of the Babel Story', *Currents in Theology and Mission* 5 (1978) 69-81.

'Will Herberg as Biblical Theologian', introduction to *Faith Enacted as History* (1976), 9-28.

'Herberg as Theologian of Christianity', *National Review* (1977) 884-85.

'A Stylistic Study of the Priestly Creation Story', *Canon and Authority* Festschrift for Walther Zimmerli (ed. George Coats and Burke Long; Fortress Press, 1977) 148-62.

'From Analysis to Synthesis: The Interpretation of Genesis 1-11', *Journal of Biblical Literature* 97 (1978) 23-29.

'The Lord Has Created Something New: A Stylistic Study of Jer. 31.15-22', *Catholic Biblical Quarterly* 40 (1978) 463-78.

'Tradition and Scripture in the Community of Faith', presidential address, centennial of the Society of Biblical Literature, *Journal of Biblical Literature* 100 (1981) 5-21. Reprinted in *A Companion to the Bible*, essays commemorating the 20th Anniversary of the Trinity College Annual Biblical Institute, ed. Miriam Ward, R.S.M. (Alba House, 1985).

'Tradition and Theology in the Old Testament', *Religious Studies Review*, 6/2 (1980), 104-10.

'The Bible in the Church Today', an editorial, *Theology Today* 37 (1980) 1-6.

'The Messiah as Son of God: Peter's Confession in Traditio-historical Perspective', *Christological Perspectives*, Festschrift for Harvey K. McArthur (ed. Robert F. Berkey and Sarah A. Edwards; Pilgrim Press, 1982) 157-169.

'The Problem and Promise of Commentary', *Interpretation* 36 (1982) 341-55; translated in *Theologie der Gegenwart* 27 (1984) 131-42.

'Will Herberg as Theologian and Philospher in a Christian Environment', Graduate School Colloquium, Drew University, Oct. 1982.

'"The Earth is the Lord's"': An Essay on the Biblical Doctrine of Creation", rev. ed., in *Is God a Creationist? The Religious Case Against Creation-Science* (ed. Roland M. Frye; Scribners, 1983) 176-96.

'Creation in the Bible', revised edition of Interpreters Dictionary of the Bible article on 'Creation' (1962), in *Cry of the Environment: Rebuilding the Christian Creation Tradition* (ed. Philip N. Joranson; Bear & Co., 1984).

'Creation and the Noachic Covenant', in *Cry of the Environment* (1984) 45-61.

'Mythopoeic and Theological Dimensions of Biblical Creation Faith', *Creation in the Old Testament* (Fortress Press, 1984) 1-24.

'Creation and Ecology', *American Journal of Theology and Philosophy* 4 (1983) 14-30. Reprinted in *Creation in the Old Testament* (Fortress Press, 1984) 152-71.

'Coexistence with God: Heschel's Exposition of Biblical Theology', in *Abraham Joshua Heschel: Exploring his life and thought* (MacMillan, 1985). Forthcoming.

'The Song of Miriam Poetically and Theologically Considered', *Essays in Biblical Hebrew Poetry* (JSOT Supplement, 1985). Forthcoming.

'Biblical Theology and Sociological Interpretation', an address to the Catholic Biblical Association, New Orleans 1984, to appear in *Theology Today* 42 (1985). Forthcoming.

'Israel's Conquest of Palestine: In-Party Dissension over the Peasant Revolution View', *Biblical Archaeology Review*, forthcoming.

3. *Book Reviews and Notices*

Charles H. Patterson, *The Philosophy of the Old Testament*, in *The Pastor* 17 (1953) 38-39.

Randolph Crump Miller, *Biblical Theology and Christian Education*, in *Religious Education* 52 (1957) 70-74.

Samuel Terrien, *Job: Poet of Existence*, in *Encounter* 19 (1958) 437-38.

Ludwig Koehler, *Old Testament Theology*, in *Interpretation* 13 (1959) 470-72.

Sigmund Mowinckel, *The Old Testament as Word of God*, in *Journal of Bible and Religion* 28 (1960) 367-68.

James Muilenburg, *The Way of Israel*, in *Religion in Life* 31 (1962) 469-71.

James A. Sanders, *The Old Testament in the Cross*, in *The Christian Century* 79 (1962) 491.

Walter Eichrodt, *Theology of the Old Testament*, Vol. I, in *The Seminary Journal*, Protestant Episcopal Theological Seminary in Virginia, 16 (1964) 60-61.

Gerhard von Rad, *Old Testament Theology*, Vol. I: *The Theology of Israel's Historical Traditions*, in *Interpretation* 19 (1965) 337-41.

James Barr, *Old and New in Interpretation: A Study of the Two Testaments*, in *The Drew Gateway* 39 (1969) 180-83.

Biblical Essays: Proceedings of the Ninth Meeting of 'Die Oud-Testamentiese Werkgemeenskap in Suid-Afrika', in *Catholic Biblical Quarterly* 30 (1968) 416-17.

Claus Westermann, *Das Alte Testament und Jesus Christus*, in *Princeton Seminary Bulletin* 62 (1969) 184-85.

Martin Buber, *The Kingdom of God*, in *The Drew Gateway* 39 (1969) 183-85.

Niek Poulssen, *König und Tempel im Glaubenzeugnis des Alten Testaments*, in *Catholic Biblical Quarterly* 31 (1969) 45-52.

Brevard S. Childs, *Biblical Theology in Crisis*, in *Religion in Life*, 39 (1970) 608-609.

George W. Coats, *Rebellion in the Wilderness: The Murmuring Motif in the Wilderness Traditions of the Old Testament*, in *Interpretation* 25 (1971) 213-15.

Claus Westermann, *Jeremia*, in *Princeton Seminary Bulletin* 64 (1971) 97-98.

Claus Westermann, *Genesis* (fascicles 1-5), in *Journal of Biblical Literature* 91 (1972) 243-45.

Ernst Haas, *The Creation* (1971), in *Theology Today* 29 (1972) 331-34.

Dennis J. McCarthy, *Old Testament Covenant: A Survey of Current Opinions*, in *Interpretation* 27 (1973) 480-82.

John Reuman, *Creation and New Creation: The Past, Present, and Future of God's Creative Activity*, in *Interpretation* 29 (1975) 79-82.

P.A.H. de Boer, *Fatherhood and Motherhood in Israelite and Judean Piety*, in *Journal of the American Academy of Religion* 44 (1976) 725-26.

Claus Westermann, *Genesis* (fascicle 6 to end of the *Urgeschichte*), in *Journal of Biblical Literature* 96 (1977)291-94.

Rolf Rendtorff, *Das Überlieferungsgeschichtliche Problem des Pentateuch*, BZAW 147, in *Catholic Biblical Quarterly* 40 (1978) 100-103.

Bruce Vawter, *On Genesis: A New Reading*, in *Interpretation* 33 (1979) 195-97.

Robert M. Polzin, *Biblical Structuralism: Method and Subjectivity in the Study of Ancient Texts*, in *Theology Today* 35 (1979) 518-19.

Walter Brueggemann and Hans Walther Wolff, *The Vitality of Old*

Testament Traditions (1975), in *Journal of the American Academy of Religion* 46 (1978) 69-70.

Menahem Haran, *Temples and Temple Services in Ancient Israel*, in *Interpretation* 35 (1981) 410-12.

Norman Gottwald, *The Tribes of Yahweh: A Sociology of the Religion of Liberated Israel, 1250-1050 B.C.E.*, in *Theology Today* 38 (1981) 107-108.

A. Graeme Auld, *Joshua, Moses and the Land: Tetrateuch–Pentateuch–Hexateuch in a Generation since 1938*, in *Catholic Biblical Quarterly* 45 (1983) 92-93.

John Bright, *The History of Israel*, third edn, in *Interpretation* 37 (1983) 77-80.

Robert Davidson, *The Courage to Doubt: Exploring an Old Testament Theme*, in *Journal for the Study of the Old Testament* 29 (1984) 116-20.

William S. LaSor, David A. Hubbard, and Frederic W. Bush, *Old Testament Survey: The Message, Form, and Background of the Old Testament*, in *Interpretation* 38 (1984) 412-15.

Claus Westermann, *Elements of Old Testament Theology*, tr. by Douglas W. Stott, in *Journal of Biblical Literature*, forthcoming.

4. Sermons and Curriculum Materials

'The Power of His Resurrection', *The New Century Leader*, Vol. 53, No. 4 (April 1952) 16ff.; reprinted in *Adult Bible Class*, April 1952.

'The Sin of Good People', in *The New Century Leader*, Vol. 3, No. 8 (Aug. 1952) 61ff.

'God's Search for Man', in *The New Century Leader* (Feb. 1952) 15-16.

'When the Bridegroom Cometh', *Crossroads*, Vol. 2, No. 3 (1952) 7.

'In Him All Things Hold Together', *Adult Bible Class*, Vol. 48, No. 8 (1953) 16-17.

'A Pageant of Triumph', *Adult Bible Class* (May 1953); reprinted in *The New Century Leader*, Vol. 54, No. 5 (May 1953) 12ff.

'The Covenant People', fourteen Bible studies for adult classes, *Crossroads* Vol. 3, No. 2 (January-March, 1953) 17-50; Vol. 3, No. 3 (April-June 1953) 16-17, 30. Articles on 'Amos Looks at History', 'Hosea Speaks of Hope', 'Jeremiah Sees Beyond His Time', and 'Ezekiel Proclaims the Grace of God' reprinted in *This Generation*, Vol. 12, No. 4 (July-Sept, 1960) 47-52, 56-60.

The People of God: Studies in the Biblical Doctrine of the Church, pamphlet published by the Interseminary Committee, New York 1953; reprinted by the Department of Missionary Stewardship Education of the Board of Education and Publication of the American Baptist Convention, ed. by Wm. J. Keech for use in connection with the Baptist Jubilee Advance, 1960-61.

Sermon, 'Adam, Where Art Thou?', *The Intercollegian*, Vol. 72, No. 5 (Jan. 1955) 3-5, reprinted in *Pulpit Preaching*, Vol. 10, No. 3 (1957) 28-31.

'The Whole Bible', *Workers with Youth* (Methodist Publishing House) (Aug. 1956) 8-11.

'The Bible: God's Search for Man', *Workers with Youth* (Methodist Publishing House) (August 1958) 8-11.

Sermon: 'The Traveller Unknown', Exposition of Genesis 32.22-32, *Australian Biblical Review*, 17 (October 1969) 21-26.

'Theology in Song: Studies in the Psalms', Bible Studies for the Laity, *Enquiry*, September-November 1977.

Sermon: 'We Have this Treasure', *Princeton Seminary Bulletin*, Vol. IV, No. 2, New Series (1983) 116-19.

Sermon: 'Faith and the Threat of Chaos', Tape library, Riverside Church (September 1984), New York City.

INDEX OF BIBLICAL CITATIONS

INDEX OF AUTHORS

CONTRIBUTORS AND EDITORS

J. Christiaan Beker is Richard J. Dearborn Professor of New Testament at Princeton Theological Seminary, Princeton, New Jersey.

Walter Brueggemann is Professor of Old Testament at Eden Theological Seminary, St Louis, Missouri.

James T. Butler is Assistant Professor of Old Testament, Fuller Theological Seminary, Pasadena, California.

George W. Coats is Professor of Old Testament at Lexington Theological Seminary, Lexington, Kentucky.

Edgar W. Conrad is Senior Lecturer in the Department of Studies in Religion of the University of Queensland, St. Lucia, Queensland, Australia.

Paul D. Hanson is Bussey Professor of Divinity at the Divinity School of Harvard University, Cambridge, Massachusetts.

Howard C. Kee is William Goodwin Aurelio Professor of Biblical Studies at Boston University, Boston, Massachusetts.

Daniel L. Migliore is Arthur M. Adams Professor of Systematic Theology at Princeton Theological Seminary, Princeton, New Jersey.

Roland E. Murphy is George Washington Ivey Professor of Biblical Studies at Duke University, Durham, North Carolina.

Murray L. Newman is Professor of Old Testament at the Protestant Episcopal Theological Seminary, Alexandria, Virginia.

D. Preman Niles is the Associate General Secretary of the Christian Conference of Asia, Singapore.

Ben C. Ollenburger is Assistant Professor of Old Testament at Princeton Theological Seminary, Princeton, New Jersey.

J.J.M. Roberts is William Henry Green Professor of Old Testament Literature at Princeton Theological Seminary, Princeton, New Jersey.

Katharine Doob Sakenfeld is Associate Professor of Old Testament at Princeton Theological Seminary, Princeton, New Jersey.

J. Paul Sampley is Professor of New Testament at Boston University, Boston, Massachusetts.

Phyllis Trible is Baldwin Professor of Sacred Literature, Union Theological Seminary, New York.

Claus Westermann is Professor of Old Testament, University of Heidelberg.

Hugh C. White is Associate Professor of Religion at the Camden College of Arts and Sciences of Rutgers University, Camden, New Jersey.

† Walther Zimmerli was Professor of Old Testament at the University of Göttingen in West Germany. The editors note with regret that Professor Zimmerli died on December 4, 1983.

JOURNAL FOR THE STUDY OF THE OLD TESTAMENT

Supplement Series